The CHILDES Project

Tools for Analyzing Talk, Third Edition
Volume I: Transcription Format and Programs

The CHILDES Project

Tools for Analyzing Talk, Third Edition
Volume I: Transcription Format and Programs

Brian MacWhinney
Carnegie Mellon University

LEA LAWRENCE ERLBAUM ASSOCIATES, PUBLISHERS
2000 Mahwah, New Jersey   London

Lawrence Erlbaum Associates, Inc., Publishers
10 Industrial Avenue
Mahwah, New Jersey 07430-2262

Library of Congress Cataloging-in-Publication Data

MacWhinney, Brian
The CHILDES project : tools for analyzing talk / Brian MacWhinney.—3rd ed.
p. cm.
Includes bibliographical references and index.
Contents: v. 1. Transcription format and programs — v. 2. The database.
ISBN 0-8058-2995-4 (v. 1 : alk. paper) — 0-8058-3572-5 (v. 2 : alk. paper)
1. Children—Language—Data processing. 2. Language acquisition—Research—Data processing. I. Title: Child Language Data Exchange System project. II. Title.
LB1139.L3 M24 2000
155.4'136'0285—dc21

00-024971

Books published by Lawrence Erlbaum Associates are printed on acid-free paper, and their bindings are chosen for strength and durability

Printed in the United States of America
10 9 8 7 6 5 4 3 2 1

Part 1: Transcription Format

Contents of Part 1

1: Introduction

Language acquisition research thrives on data collected from spontaneous interactions in naturally occurring situations. You can turn on a tape recorder or videotape, and, before you know it, you will have accumulated a library of dozens or even hundreds of hours of naturalistic interactions. But simply collecting data is only the beginning of a much larger task, because the process of transcribing and analyzing naturalistic samples is extremely time-consuming and often unreliable. In this first volume, we will present a set of computational tools designed to increase the reliability of transcriptions, automate the process of data analysis, and facilitate the sharing of transcript data. These new computational tools have brought about revolutionary changes in the way that research is conducted in the child language field. In addition, they have equally revolutionary potential for the study of second-language learning, adult conversational interactions, sociological content analyses, and language recovery in aphasia. Although the tools are of wide applicability, this volume concentrates on their use in the child language field, in the hope that researchers from other areas can make the necessary analogies to their own topics.

Before turning to a detailed examination of the current system, it may be helpful to take a brief historical tour over some of the major highlights of earlier approaches to the collection of data on language acquisition. These earlier approaches can be grouped into five major historical periods.

1.1   Impressionistic Observation

The first attempt to understand the process of language development appears in a remarkable passage from *The Confessions of St. Augustine* (1952). In this passage, Augustine claims that he remembered how he had learned language:

> This I remember; and have since observed how I learned to speak. It was not that my elders taught me words (as, soon after, other learning) in any set method; but I, longing by cries and broken accents and various motions of my limbs to express my thoughts, that so I might have my will, and yet unable to express all I willed or to whom I willed, did myself, by the understanding which Thou, my God, gavest me, practise the sounds in my memory. When they named anything, and as they spoke turned towards it, I saw and remembered that they called what they would point out by the name they uttered. And that they meant this thing, and no other, was plain from the motion of their body, the natural language, as it were, of all nations, expressed by the countenance, glances of the eye, gestures of the limbs, and tones of the voice, indicating the affections of the mind as it pursues, possesses, rejects, or shuns. And thus by constantly hearing words, as they occurred in various sentences, I collected gradually for what they stood; and, having broken in my mouth to these signs, I thereby gave utterance to my will. Thus I exchanged with those about me these current signs of our wills, and so launched deeper into the stormy intercourse of human life, yet depending on parental authority and the beck of elders.

Augustine's fanciful recollection of his own language acquisition remained the high water mark for child language studies through the Middle Ages and even the Enlightenment. However, Augustine's recollection technique is no longer of much interest to us, as few of us believe in the accuracy of recollections from infancy, even if they come from saints.

1.2   Baby Biographies

The second major technique for the study of language production was pioneered by Charles Darwin. Using note cards and field books to track the distribution of hundreds of species and subspecies in places like the Galapagos and Indonesia, Darwin was able to collect an impressive body of naturalistic data in support of his views on natural selection and evolution. In his study of gestural development in his son, Darwin (1877) showed how these same tools for naturalistic observation could be adopted to the study of human development. By taking detailed daily notes, Darwin showed how researchers could build diaries that could then be converted into biographies documenting virtually any aspect of human development. Following Darwin's lead, scholars such as Ament (1899), Preyer (1882), Gvozdev (1949), Szuman (1955), Stern and Stern (1907), Kenyeres (1926), and Leopold (1939; 1947; 1949a; 1949b) created monumental biographies detailing the language development of their own children.

Darwin's biographical technique also had its effects on the study of adult aphasia. Following in this tradition, studies of the language of particular patients have been presented by Low (1931), Pick (1913), Wernicke (1874), and many others.

1.3   Transcripts

The limits of the diary technique were always quite apparent. Even the most highly trained observer could not keep pace with the rapid flow of normal speech production. Anyone who has attempted to follow a child about with a pen and a notebook soon realizes how much detail is missed and how the note-taking process interferes with the ongoing interactions.

The introduction of the tape recorder in the late 1950s provided a way around these limitations and ushered in the third period of observational studies. The effect of the tape recorder on the field of language acquisition was very much like its effect on ethnomusicology, where researchers such as Alan Lomax (Parrish, 1996) were suddenly able to produce high quality field recordings using this new technology. This period was characterized by projects in which groups of investigators collected large data sets of tape recordings from several subjects across a period of 2 or 3 years. Much of the excitement in the 1960s regarding new directions in child language research was fueled directly by the great increase in raw data that was possible through use of tape recordings and typed transcripts.

This increase in the amount of raw data had an additional, seldom discussed consequence. In the period of the baby biography, the final published accounts closely resembled the original database of note cards. In this sense, there was no major gap between the observational database and the published database. In the period of typed transcripts, a wider gap emerged. The size of the transcripts produced in the 60s and 70s made it impossible to publish the full unanalyzed corpora. Instead, researchers were forced to publish only high-level analyses based on data that were not available to others. This led to a situation in which the raw empirical database for the field was kept only in private stocks, unavailable for general public examination. Comments and tallies were written into the margins of ditto master copies and new, even less legible copies were then made by thermal production of new ditto masters. Each investigator devised a project-specific system of transcription and project-specific codes. As we began to compare hand-written and typewritten transcripts, problems in transcription methodology, coding schemes, and cross-investigator reliability became more apparent.

Recognizing this problem, Roger Brown took the lead in attempting to share his transcripts from Adam, Eve, and Sarah (Brown, 1973) with other researchers. These transcripts were typed onto stencils and mimeographed in multiple copies. The extra copies were lent to and analyzed by a wide variety of researchers. In this model, researchers took their copy of the transcript home, developed their own coding scheme, applied it (usually by making pencil markings directly on the transcript), wrote a paper about the results and, if very polite, sent a copy to Roger. Some of these reports (Moerk, 1983) even attempted to disprove the conclusions drawn from those data by Brown himself! The original database remained untouched. The nature of each individual's coding scheme and the relation among any set of different coding schemes could never be fully plumbed.

1.4   Computers

Just as these data analysis problems were coming to light, a major technological opportunity was emerging in the shape of the powerful, affordable microcomputer. Microcomputer word-processing systems and database programs allowed researchers to enter transcript data into computer files which could then be easily duplicated, edited, and analyzed by standard data-processing techniques. In 1981, when the CHILDES Project was first conceived, researchers basically thought of computer systems as large notepads. Although researchers were aware of the ways in which databases could be searched and tabulated, the full analytic and comparative power of the computer systems themselves was not yet fully understood.

Rather than serving only as an "archive" or historical record, a focus on a shared database can lead to advances in methodology and theory. However, to achieve these additional advances, researchers first needed to move beyond the idea of a simple data repository. At first, the possibility of utilizing shared transcription formats, shared codes, and shared analysis programs shone only as a faint glimmer on the horizon, against the fog and gloom of handwritten tallies, fuzzy dittos, and idiosyncratic coding schemes. Slowly, against this backdrop, the idea of a computerized data exchange system began to emerge. It was against this conceptual background that the Child Language Data Exchange System (CHILDES) was conceived. The origin of the system can be traced back to the summer of 1981 when

Dan Slobin, Willem Levelt, Susan Ervin-Tripp, and Brian MacWhinney discussed the possibility of creating an archive for typed, handwritten, and computerized transcripts to be located at the Max-Planck Institut für Psycholinguistik in Nijmegen. In 1983, the MacArthur Foundation funded meetings of developmental researchers in which Elizabeth Bates, Brian MacWhinney, Catherine Snow, and other child language researchers discussed the possibility of soliciting MacArthur funds to support a data exchange system. In January of 1984, the MacArthur Foundation awarded a two-year grant to Brian MacWhinney and Catherine Snow for the establishment of the Child Language Data Exchange System. These funds provided for the entry of data into the system and for the convening of a meeting of an advisory board. Twenty child language researchers met for three days in Concord, Massachusetts and agreed on a basic framework for the CHILDES system, which Catherine Snow and Brian MacWhinney would then proceed to implement.

1.5   Connectivity

Since 1984, when the CHILDES Project began in earnest, the world of computers has gone through a series of remarkable revolutions, each introducing new opportunities and challenges. The processing power of the home computer now dwarfs the power of the mainframe of the 1980s; new machines are now shipped with built-in audiovisual capabilities; and devices such as CD-ROMs and optical disks offer enormous storage capacity at reasonable prices. This new hardware has now opened up the possibility for multimedia access to digitized audio and video from links inside the written transcripts. In effect, a transcript is now the starting point for a new exploratory reality in which the whole interaction is accessible from the transcript. Although researchers have just now begun to make use of these new tools, the current shape of the CHILDES system reflects many of these new realities. In the pages that follow, you will learn about how we are using this new technology to provide rapid access to the database and to permit the linkage of transcripts to digitized audio and video records, even over the Internet. For further ideas regarding the future directions of this type of work, you may wish to connect to this site: http://www.talkbank.org.

1.6   Three Tools

The reasons for developing a computerized exchange system for language data are immediately obvious to anyone who has produced or analyzed transcripts. With such a system, we can:

1.   automate the process of data analysis,

2.   obtain better data in a consistent, fully-documented transcription system, and

3.   provide more data for more children from more ages, speaking more languages.

The CHILDES system has addressed each of these goals by developing three separate, but integrated, tools. The first tool is the CHAT transcription and coding format. The second tool is the CLAN analysis program, and the third tool is the database. These three tools are like the legs of a three-legged stool. The transcripts in the database have all been put into the CHAT transcription system. The program is designed to make full use of the CHAT format to facilitate a wide variety of searches and analyses. Many research groups are now using the CHILDES programs to enter new data sets. Eventually, these new data sets will be available to other researchers as a part of the growing CHILDES database. In this way, CHAT, CLAN, and the database function as a coarticulated set of complementary tools.

This book, the first of a two-volume set, is composed of two parts. The first part is the CHAT manual, which describes the conventions and principles of CHAT transcription. The second part of this first volume is the CLAN manual, which describes the use of the program. The second volume describes the data files in the CHILDES database.

1.7   Shaping CHAT

We received a great deal of extremely helpful input during the years between 1984 and 1988 when the CHAT system was being formulated. Some of the most detailed comments came from George Allen, Elizabeth Bates, Nan Bernstein Ratner, Giuseppe Cappelli, Annick De Houwer, Jane Desimone, Jane Edwards, Julia Evans, Judi Fenson, Paul Fletcher, Steven Gillis, Kristen Keefe, Mary MacWhinney, Jon Miller, Barbara Pan, Lucia Pfanner, Kim Plunkett, Catherine Snow, Jeff Sokolov, Leonid Spektor, Joseph Stemberger, Frank Wijnen, and Antonio Zampolli. Comments developed in Edwards (1992) were useful in shaping core aspects of CHAT. George Allen helped developed the UNIBET and PHONASCII systems (Allen, 1988). The workers in the LIPPS Group (2000) have developed extensions of CHAT to cover code-switching phenomena. Adaptations of CHAT to deal with data on disfluencies are developed in Bernstein-Ratner, Rooney, and MacWhinney (1996). Rivero, Gràcia, and Fernández-Viader (1998) suggested refinements in the transcription of data for analysis by the MLT (mean length of turn) command. Chapter 11 on sign language transcription was written and contributed by Dan Slobin, Nini Hoiting, Amy Weinberg, and colleagues of the Sign Language Work Group at the University of California at Berkeley. The exercises in Chapter 7 of Part II are based on materials originally developed by Barbara Pan for Chapter 2 of Sokolov and Snow (1994).

1.8   Building CLAN

The CLAN program is the brain child of Leonid Spektor. Ideas for particular analysis commands came from several sources. Bill Tuthill's HUM package provided ideas about concordance analyses. The SALT system of Miller and Chapman (1983) provided guidelines regarding basic practices in transcription and analysis. Clifton Pye's PAL program provided ideas for the MODREP and PHONFREQ commands.

Darius Clynes ported CLAN to the Macintosh. Jeffrey Sokolov wrote the CHIP program. Mitzi Morris designed the MOR analyzer using specifications provided by Roland Hauser of Erlangen University. Steven Gillis built an initial version of MOR rules for Dutch; Norio Naka developed a MOR rule system for Japanese; and Monica Torent helped develop the MOR system for Spanish. Julia Evans has been instrumental in providing recommendations for improving the design of both the audio and visual capabilities of the editor. Johannes Wagner, Mike Forrester, and Chris Ramsden helped show us how we could modify CLAN to permit transcription in the Conversation Analysis framework. Steven Gillis provided suggestions for aspects of MODREP. Julia Evans helped specify TIMEDUR and worked on the details of DSS. Catherine Snow designed CHAINS, KEYMAP, and STATFREQ. Nan Bernstein Ratner specified aspects of PHONFREQ and plans for additional programs for phonological analysis.

1.9   Constructing the Database

The primary reason for the success of the CHILDES database has been the generosity of the nearly 100 researchers who have contributed their corpora. Each of these corpora represents hundreds, sometimes even thousands, of hours spent in careful collection, transcription, and checking of data. All researchers in child language should be proud of the way researchers have generously shared their valuable data with the whole research community. The growing size of the database for language impairments, adult aphasia, and second-language acquisition indicates that these related areas have also begun to understand the value of data sharing.

The database has grown so much that the description of the corpora now constitutes a Volume II of this manual. In that volume, each section documents a particular corpus and lists the contributors of that corpus.

Many of the corpora contributed to the system were transcribed before the formulation of CHAT. In order to create a uniform database, we had to reformat these corpora into CHAT. Jane Desimone, Mary MacWhinney, Jane Morrison, Kim Roth, and Gergely Sikuta worked many long hours on this task. Helmut Feldweg, Susan Powers, and Heike Behrens supervised a parallel effort with the German and Dutch data sets.

Because of the continually changing shape of the programs and the database, keeping this manual up to date has been an ongoing activity. In this process, I received help from Mike Blackwell, Julia Evans, Kris Loh, Mary MacWhinney, Lucy Hewson, Kelley Sacco, and Gergely Sikuta. Barbara Pan, Jeff Sokolov, and Pam Rollins also provided a reading of the final draft of the 1995 version of the manual.

1.10   Disseminating CHILDES

Since the beginning of the project, Catherine Snow has continually played a pivotal role in shaping policy, building the database, organizing workshops, and determining the shape of CHAT and CLAN. Catherine Snow collaborated with Jeffrey Sokolov, Pam Rollins, and Barbara Pan to construct a series of tutorial exercises and demonstration analyses that appeared in Sokolov and Snow (1994). Those exercises form the basis for similar tutorial sections in the current manual. Catherine Snow has contributed six major corpora to the database and has conducted CHILDES workshops in a dozen countries.

Several other colleagues have helped disseminate the CHILDES system through workshops, visits, and Internet facilities. Hidetosi Sirai established a CHILDES file server mirror at Chukyo University in Japan and Steven Gillis established a mirror at the University of Antwerp. Steven Gillis, Kim Plunkett, and Sven Strömqvist have helped propagate the CHILDES system at universities in Northern and Central Europe. Yuriko Oshima-Takane has brought together a vital group of child language researchers using CHILDES to study the acquisition of Japanese and has supervised the translation of the current manual into Japanese. In Italy, Elena Pizzuto has organized symposia for developing the CHILDES system and has supervised the translation of the manual into Italian. Magdalena Smoczynska in Kràkow and Wolfgang Dressler in Vienna have been helping new researchers who are learning to use CHILDES for languages spoken in Eastern Europe. Miquel Serra has supported a series of CHILDES workshops in Barcelona.

1.11   Funding

From 1984 to 1988, funding for the CHILDES Project was provided by the John D. and Catherine T. MacArthur Foundation. In 1988, the National Science Foundation provided an equipment grant that allowed us to put the database on the Internet and on CD-ROMs. From 1989 to 1999, the project was supported by an ongoing grant from the National Institutes of Health (NICHHD). In 1998, the National Science Foundation Linguistics Program provided additional support to improve the programs for morphosyntactic analysis of the database and for initial work linking the CHILDES Project to the Informedia Project of the National Science Foundation Digital Libraries Initiative.

1.12   How to Use This Book

This book is Volume 1 of the two volumes that document the three CHILDES tools. Volume I is divided into two parts. The first part is the CHAT manual, which describes the conventions and principles of CHAT transcription. The second part is the CLAN manual, which describes the use of the editor, sonic CHAT, and the various analytic commands.

Volume I is designed for four types of users. Each group will want to use this manual in a slightly different way.

1.   If you are an experienced user, you will want to review each section before beginning work with a specific command or the new features of the editor. There have been major changes to the commands interface, support for non-Roman fonts, inclusion of CA format as an alternative to CHAT, many new editing features, and new facilities for linkage to digitized audio and video. Although the basic features of CHAT have not changed, the description of the use of the conventions has been clarified throughout. The chapter on PHONASCII has been dropped, because we are now supporting direct IPA transcription in the IPAPhon font. The system of UNIBET coding has now adopted the SAMPA standard. The sections on audio and video digitization techniques are also new.

2.   If you are a new user, you will want to begin by learning the system of page 16.

Next, you will want to starting reading the CLAN manual, which walks you through a basic tutorial on the use of the programs. After finishing the tutorial, try working a bit with each of the CLAN commands to get a feel for the overall scope of the system. You can then learn more about CHAT by transcribing a small sample of your data in a short test file. Try running the CHECK program at frequent intervals to verify the accuracy of your coding. Once you have finished transcribing a small segment of your data, try out the various analysis programs you plan to use, to make sure that they provide the types of results you need for your work.

3.   You may be a new user who is primarily interested in analyzing data already stored in the CHILDES archive. You will still need to learn the basics of installing and running the programs. However, you do not need to learn the CHAT transcription format in much detail and you will only need to use the editor to open and read files. You will want to use Volume 2 to understand the shape of the CHILDES database

4.   If you use the CHILDES tools to teach language analysis to students, you can use the online tutorial resources developed by Yuriko Oshima-Takane and her coworkers at McGill. These lessons provide multiple choice questions and other ways of testing you knowledge of the fundaments of CHAT. They are available at http://childes.psy.cmu.edu/CHAT.html.

5.   Teachers will also want to pay particular attention to the sections of the CLAN manual that present a tutorial introduction. Using some of the examples given there, you can construct additional materials to encourage students to explore the database to test out particular hypotheses. At the end of the CLAN manual, there are also a series of exercises that help students further consolidate their knowledge of CHAT and CLAN.

The CHILDES system was not intended to address all issues in the study of language learning, nor was it intended to be used by all students of spontaneous interactions. The CHAT system is comprehensive, but it is not ideal for all purposes. The programs are powerful, but they cannot solve all analytic problems. It is not the goal of CHILDES to provide facilities for all research endeavors or to force all research into some uniform mold. On the contrary, the programs are designed to offer support for alternative analytic frameworks. For example, the editor now supports transcription in Conversation Analysis (CA) format, as an alternative to CHAT format.

There are many researchers in the fields that study language learning who will never need to use CHILDES. Indeed, we estimate that the three CHILDES tools will never be used by at least half of the researchers in the field of child language. There are three common reasons why individual researchers may not find CHILDES useful:

1.   some researchers may have already committed themselves to use of another analytic system;

2.   some researchers may have collected so much data that they can work for many years without needing to collect more data and without comparing their own data with other researchers' data; and

3.   some researchers may not be interested in studying spontaneous speech data.

Of these three reasons for not needing to use the three CHILDES tools, the third is the most frequent. For example, researchers studying comprehension would only be interested in CHILDES data when they wish to compare findings arising from studies of comprehension with patterns occurring in spontaneous production.

1.13   Changes

The CHILDES tools have been extensively tested for ease of application, accuracy, and reliability. However, change is fundamental to the research enterprise. Researchers are constantly pursuing better ways of coding and analyzing data. It is important that the CHILDES tools keep progress with these changing requirements. For this reason, there will be revisions to CHAT, the programs, and the database as long as the CHILDES Project is active.

2:   Principles

The CHAT system provides a standardized format for producing computerized transcripts of face-to-face conversational interactions. These interactions may involve children and parents, doctors and patients, or teachers and second-language learners. Despite the differences between these interactions, there are enough common features to allow for the creation of a single general transcription system. The system described here is designed for use with both normal and disordered populations. It can be used with learners of all types, including children, second-language learners, and adults recovering from aphasic disorders. The system provides options for basic discourse transcription as well as detailed phonological and morphological analysis. The system bears the acronym "CHAT," which stands for Codes for the Human Analysis of Transcripts. CHAT is the standard transcription system for the CHILDES (Child Language Data Exchange System) Project. With the exception of a few corpora of historical interest, all of the transcripts in the CHILDES database are in CHAT format. In addition, approximately 60 groups of researchers around the world are currently actively involved in new data collection and transcription using the CHAT system. Eventually the data collected in these projects will be contributed to the database. The CHAT system is specifically designed to facilitate the subsequent automatic analysis of transcripts by CLAN.

2.1   Computerization

Public inspection of experimental data is a crucial prerequisite for serious scientific progress. Imagine how genetics would function if every experimenter had his or her own individual strain of peas or drosophila and refused to allow them to be tested by other experimenters. What would happen in geology, if every scientist kept his or her own set of rock specimens and refused to compare them with those of other researchers? In some fields the basic phenomena in question are so clearly open to public inspection that this is not a problem. The basic facts of planetary motion are open for all to see, as are the basic facts underlying Newtonian mechanics.

Unfortunately, in language studies, a free and open sharing and exchange of data has not always been the norm. In earlier decades, researchers jealously guarded their field notes from a particular language community of subject type, refusing to share them openly with the broader community. Various justifications were given for this practice. It was sometimes claimed that other researchers would not fully appreciate the nature of the data or that they might misrepresent crucial patterns. Sometimes, it was claimed that only someone who had actually participated in the community or the interaction could understand the nature of the language and the interactions. In some cases, these limitations were real and important. However, all such restrictions on the sharing of data inevitably impede the progress of the scientific study of language learning.

Within the field of language acquisition studies it is now understood that the advantages of sharing data outweigh the potential dangers. The question is no longer whether data should be shared, but rather how they can be shared in a reliable and responsible fashion.

The computerization of transcripts opens up the possibility for many types of data sharing and analysis that otherwise would have been impossible. However, the full exploitation of this opportunity requires the development of a standardized system for data transcription and analysis.

2.2   Words of Caution

Before examining the CHAT system, we need to consider some dangers involved in computerized transcriptions. These dangers arise from the need to compress a complex set of spoken and nonspoken messages into the extremely narrow channel required for the computer. In most cases, these dangers also exist when one creates a typewritten or hand-written transcript. Let us look at some of the dangers surrounding this enterprise.

2.2.1   The Dominance of the Written Word

Perhaps the greatest danger facing the transcriber is the tendency to treat spoken language as if it were written language. The decision to write out stretches of vocal material using the forms of written language involves a major theoretical commitment. As Ochs (1979) showed so clearly, these decisions inevitably turn transcription into a theoretical enterprise. The most difficult bias to overcome is the tendency to map every form spoken by a learner — be it a child, an aphasic, or a second-language learner — onto a set of standard lexical items in the adult language. Transcribers tend to assimilate nonstandard learner strings to standard forms of the adult language. For example, when a child says "put on my jamas," the transcriber may instead enter "put on my pajamas," reasoning unconsciously that "jamas" is simply a childish form of "pajamas." This type of regularization of the child form to the adult lexical norm can lead to misunderstanding of the shape of the child's lexicon. For example, it could be the case that the child uses "jamas" and "pajamas" to refer to two very different things (Clark, 1987; MacWhinney, 1989).

There are two types of errors possible here. One involves mapping a learner's spoken form onto an adult form when, in fact, there was no real correspondence. This is the problem of overnormalization. The second type of error involves failing to map a learner's spoken form onto an adult form when, in fact, there is a correspondence. This is the problem of undernormalization. The goal of transcribers should be to avoid both the Scylla of overnormalization and the Charybdis of undernormalization. Steering a course between these two dangers is no easy matter. A transcription system can provide devices to aid in this process, but it cannot guarantee safe passage.

Transcribers also often tend to assimilate the shape of sounds spoken by the learner to the shapes that are dictated by morphosyntactic patterns. For example, Fletcher (1985) noted that both children and adults generally produce "have" as "uv" before main verbs. As a result, forms like "might have gone" assimilate to "mightuv gone." Fletcher believed that younger children have not yet learned to associate the full auxiliary "have" with the contracted form. If we write the children's forms as "might have," we then end up mischaracterizing the structure of their lexicon. To take another example, we can note that, in French, the various endings of the verb in the present tense are distinguished in spelling, whereas they are homophonous in speech. If a child says /mAnZ/ "eat," are we to transcribe it as first person singular *mange*, as second person singular *manges*, or as the imperative *mange*? If the child says /mAnZe/, should we transcribe it as the infinitive *manger*, the participle *mangé*, or the second person formal *mangez*?

CHAT deals with these problems in four ways. First, it provides a uniform way of transcribing discourse phonemically, called UNIBET. Using UNIBET, we can code "mightuv" as /maItUv/ and *mangez/manger/mangé* as /mAnZe/. Second, CHAT permits transcription in IPA fonts, using standard IPA characters and diacritics. Third, the CLAN editor allows the user to link the digitized audio record of the interaction directly to the transcript. This is the system called "sonic CHAT." With these sonic CHAT links, it is possible to double-click on a sentence and hear its sound immediately. Having the actual sound produced by the child directly available in the transcript takes some of the burden off of the transcription system. However, whenever computerized analyses are based not on the original audio signal but on transcribed orthographic forms, one must continue to understand the limits of transcription conventions.

For those who wish to avoid the work involved in UNIBET transcription, IPA characters, or sonic CHAT, CHAT also allows for the specification of nonstandard lexical forms, so that the form "might (h)ave" would be universally recognized as the spelling of the contracted form of "might have." For the French example, CHAT allows for a general neutral suffix written as *-e*. Using this, we would write *mang-e*, rather than *mang-ez*, *mang-é*, or *mang-er*. CHAT provides support for a variety of solutions of this type, which must be devised on a case-by-case basis.

2.2.2 The Misuse of Standard Punctuation

Transcribers have a tendency to write out spoken language with the punctuation conventions of written language. Written language is organized into clauses and sentences delimited by commas, periods, and other marks of punctuation. Spoken language, on the other hand, is organized into tone units clustered about a tonal nucleus and delineated by pauses and tonal contours (Crystal, 1969; Crystal, 1975; Halliday, 1966; Halliday, 1967; Halliday, 1968). Work on the discourse basis of sentence production (Chafe, 1980; Jefferson, 1984) has demonstrated a close link between tone units and ideational units. Retracings, pauses, stress, and all forms of intonational contours are crucial markers of aspects of the utterance planning process. Moreover, these features also convey important sociolinguistic information. Within special markings or conventions, there is no way to directly indicate these important aspects of interactions.

One way of dealing with punctuation bias is to supplement UNIBET phonological coding with prosodic markings that indicate tonal stress and rises and falls in intonation. For those who do not wish to construct a complete phonological transcription, CHAT makes available a set of prosodic markers that can be combined either with standard words or with a phonological transcription to code the details of tone units and contours. In addition, CHAT provides a set of conventions for marking retracings, pauses, and errors. Again, having the actual audio record available through sonic CHAT helps keep a link between the transcript and the original data.

2.2.3   Working With Video

Whatever form a transcript may take, it will never contain a fully accurate record of what went on in an interaction. A transcript of an interaction can never fully replace an audiotape, because an audio recording of the interaction will always be more accurate in terms of preserving the actual details of what transpired. By the same token, an audio recording can never preserve as much detail as a video recording with a high-quality audio track. Audio recordings record none of the nonverbal interactions that often form the backbone of a conversational interaction. Hence, they systematically exclude a source of information that is crucial for a full interpretation of the interaction. Although there are biases involved even in a video recording, it is still the most accurate record of an interaction that we have available. For those who are trying to use transcription to capture the full detailed character of an interaction, it is imperative that transcription be done from a video recording which should be repeatedly consulted during all phases of analysis.

When the CLAN editor is used to link transcripts to audio recordings, we refer to this as sonic CHAT. The section on page 186 explains how to produce digitized audio files. When the system is used to link transcripts to video recordings, we refer to this as video CHAT. The section on page 190 explains how to produce digitized video movies. The CLAN manual explains how to link digital audio and video to transcripts.

2.3   Problems With Forced Decisions

Transcription and coding systems often force the user to make difficult distinctions. For example, a system might make a distinction between grammatical ellipsis and ungrammatical omission. However, it may often be the case that the user cannot decide whether an omission is grammatical or not. In that case, it may be helpful to have some way of blurring the distinction. CHAT has certain symbols that can be used when a categorization cannot be made. It is important to remember that many of the CHAT symbols are entirely optional. Whenever you feel that you are being forced to make a distinction, check the manual to see whether the particular coding choice is actually required. If it is not required, then simply omit the code altogether.

2.4   Transcription and Coding

It is important to recognize the difference between *transcription* and *coding*. Transcription focuses on the production of a written record that can lead us to understand, albeit only vaguely, the flow of the original interaction. Transcription must be done directly off an audiotape or, preferably, a videotape. Coding, on the other hand, is the process of recognizing, analyzing, and taking note of phenomena in transcribed speech. Coding can often be done by referring only to a written transcript. For example, the coding of parts of speech can be done directly from a transcript without listening to the audiotape. For other types of coding, such as speech act coding, it is imperative that coding be done while watching the original videotape.

The CHAT system includes conventions for both transcription and coding. When first learning the system, it is best to focus on learning how to transcribe. The CHAT system offers the transcriber a large array of coding options. Although few transcribers will need to use all of the options, everyone needs to understand how basic transcription is done on the "main line." Additional coding is done principally on the secondary or "dependent" tiers. As transcribers work more with their data, they will include further options from the secondary or "dependent" tiers. However, the beginning user should focus first on learning to correctly use the conventions for the main line. The manual includes several sample transcripts to help the beginner in learning the transcription system.

2.5   Three Goals

Like other forms of communication, transcription systems are subjected to a variety of communicative pressures. The view of language structure developed by Slobin (1977) sees structure as emerging from the pressure of three conflicting charges or goals. On the one hand, language is designed to be **clear**. On the other hand, it is designed to be **processible** by the listener and quick and **easy** for the speaker. Unfortunately, ease of production often comes in conflict with clarity of marking. The competition between these three motives leads to a variety of imperfect solutions that satisfy each goal only partially. Such imperfect and unstable solutions characterize the grammar and phonology of human language (Bates & MacWhinney, 1982). Only rarely does a solution succeed in fully achieving all three goals.

Slobin's view of the pressures shaping human language can be extended to analyze the pressures shaping a transcription system. In many regards, a transcription system is much like any human language. It needs to be clear in its markings of categories, and still preserve readability and ease of transcription. However, unlike a human language, a transcription system needs to address two different audiences. One audience is the human audience of transcribers, analysts, and readers. The other audience is the digital computer and its programs. In order to successfully deal with these two audiences, a system for computerized transcription needs to achieve the following goals:

1.   **Clarity:** Every symbol used in the coding system should have some clear and definable real-world referent. The relation between the referent and the symbol should be consistent and reliable. Symbols that mark particular words should always be spelled in a consistent manner. Symbols that mark particular conversational patterns should refer to actual patterns consistently observable in the data. In practice, codes will always have to steer between the Scylla of overregularization and the Charybdis of underregularization discussed earlier. Distinctions must avoid being either too fine or too coarse. Another way of looking at clarity is through the notion of systematicity. Systematicity is a simple extension of clarity across transcripts or corpora. Codes, words, and symbols must be used in

a consistent manner across transcripts. Ideally, each code should always have a unique meaning independent of the presence of other codes or the particular transcript in which it is located. If interactions are necessary, as in hierarchical coding systems, these interactions need to be systematically described.

2. **Readability:** Just as human language needs to be easy to process, so transcripts need to be easy to read. This goal often runs directly counter to the first goal. In the CHILDES system, we have attempted to provide a variety of CHAT options that will allow a user to maximize the readability of a transcript. We have also provided CLAN tools that will allow a reader to suppress the less readable aspects in transcript when the goal of readability is more important than the goal of clarity of marking.

3. **Ease of data entry:** As distinctions proliferate within a transcription system, data entry becomes increasingly difficult and error-prone. There are two ways of dealing with this problem. One method attempts to simplify the coding scheme and its categories. The problem with this approach is that it sacrifices clarity. The second method attempts to help the transcriber by providing computational aids. The CLAN programs follow this path. They provide systems for the automatic checking of transcription accuracy, methods for the automatic analysis of morphology and syntax, and tools for the semiautomatic entry of codes. However, the basic process of transcription has not been automated and remains the major task during data entry.

3:   CHAT Outline

CHAT provides both basic and advanced formats for transcription and coding. The basic level of CHAT is called minCHAT. New users should start by learning minCHAT, which is discussed in the section on minCHAT. MinCHAT looks much like other intuitive transcription systems that are in general use in the fields of child language and discourse analysis. It makes sense for the new user to focus on the use of minCHAT and to postpone reading the rest of this manual at first. However, eventually users will find that there is something they want to be able to code that goes beyond minCHAT. At that point, they should move on to learning midCHAT, as described on page 18.

3.1   minCHAT

This section describes the minimum set of standards for a CHAT file. Files that follow these standards can use most aspects of the CLAN commands effectively. The basic requirements for minCHAT involve the form of the file, the form of utterances, the writing of documentation, and the use of ASCII symbols.

3.1.1   The Form of Files

There are several minimum standards for the form of a minCHAT file. These standards must be followed for the CLAN commands to run successfully on CHAT files:

1.   When doing normal coding in English, every character in the file must be in the basic ASCII character set (see the following section).

2.   Every line must end with a carriage return.

3.   The first line in the file must be an @Begin header line.

4.   The last line in the file must be an @End header line.

5.   There must be an @Participants header line listing three-letter codes for each participant, the participant's name, and the participant's role. This line should follow immediately after the @Begin header.

6.   Lines beginning with * indicate what was actually said. These are called "main lines." Each main line should code one and only one utterance. When a speaker produces several utterances in a row, code each with a new main line.

7.   After the asterisk on the main line comes a three-letter code in upper case letters for the participant who was the speaker of the utterance being coded. After the three-letter code comes a colon and then a tab.

8.   What was actually said is entered starting in the ninth column.

9.   Lines beginning with the % symbol can contain anything. Typically, these lines include codes and commentary on what was said. They are called "dependent tier" lines.

10. Dependent tier lines begin with the % symbol. This symbol is followed by a three-letter code in lowercase letters for the dependent tier type, such as "pho"

for phonology; a colon; and then a tab. The text of the dependent tier begins in the ninth column of the dependent tier line.

11. Continuations of main lines and dependent tier lines begin with a tab.

3.1.2 The Form of Utterances

In addition to these minimum requirements for the form of the file, there are certain minimum ways in which utterances and words should be written on the main line:

1. Utterances should end with an utterance terminator. The basic utterance terminators are the period, the exclamation mark, and the question mark.

2. Commas should be used sparingly.

3. Use upper case letters only for proper nouns and the word "I." Do not use uppercase letters for the first words of sentences. This will facilitate the identification of proper nouns. However, for languages like German that use capitalization consistently to mark certain parts of speech, this restriction can be modified so that only nouns are capitalized.

4. Unintelligible words with an unclear phonetic shape should be transcribed as **xxx**.

5. If you wish to note the phonological form of an incomplete or unintelligible phonological string, write it out with an ampersand, as in **&guga**.

6. Incomplete words can be written with the omitted material in parentheses, as in **(be)cause** and **(a)bout**.

Here is a sample that illustrates these principles. This file is syntactically correct and uses the minimum number of CHAT conventions while still maintaining compatibility with the CLAN commands.

```
@Begin
@Participants: ROS Ross Child, BRI Brian Father
*ROS:    why isn't Mommy coming?
%com:    Mother usually picks Ross up around 4 PM.
*BRI:    don't worry.
*BRI:    she'll be here soon.
*ROS:    good.
@End
```

3.2 Analyzing One Small File

For researchers who are just now beginning to use CHAT and CLAN, there is perhaps one single suggestion that can save literally hundreds of hours of possibly wasted time. The suggestion is to transcribe and analyze one single small file completely and perfectly before launching a major effort in transcription and analysis. The idea is that you should learn just enough about minCHAT and minCLAN to see your path through these four crucial steps:

1. entry of a small set of your data into a CHAT file,

2. successful running of the CHECK command inside the editor to guarantee accu-

racy in your CHAT file,

3.   development of a series of codes that will interface with the particular CLAN commands most appropriate for your analysis, and

4.   running of the relevant CLAN commands, so that you can be sure that the results you will get will properly test the hypotheses you wish to develop.

If you go through these steps first, you can guarantee in advance the successful outcome of your project. You can avoid ending up in a situation in which you have transcribed hundreds of hours of data in a way that simply does not match correctly with the input requirements for CLAN.

3.3   midCHAT

After having learned minCHAT, you are ready to learn the basics of CLAN. To do this, you will want to work through the first chapters of the CLAN manual. These chapters will take you up to the level of minCLAN, which corresponds to the minCHAT level.

Once you have learned minCHAT and minCLAN, you are ready to move on to the next levels, which are midCHAT and midCLAN. Learning midCHAT involves mastering the transcription of words and conversational features. In particular, the midCHAT learner should work through the chapters on words, utterances, and scoped symbols.

Depending on the shape of the particular project, the transcriber may not need to go beyond the level of midCHAT. However, there are five topic areas for which researchers will want to look at other chapters.

1.   **Phonological Transcription.** If your research deals with speech that diverges strongly from the standard in phonological terms, you will want to make use of some form of phonological transcription. This is often important when you are dealing with very young children, language-impaired subjects, dialect speakers, and second-language learners. If you need to do phonological transcription, first read the chapter on page 120, which describes a simple system for phonemic transcription, including codes for stress and tone contours. If this level of detail is insufficient, you will want to use the IPA font when entering your %pho tier, as discussed in the chapter on page 81.

2.   **Speech Acts.** If your research focuses on speech acts, you will wish to work out a system of the sort outlined in the chapter on page 151.

3.   **Error Analysis.** If your research deals with the analysis of phonological, morphological, syntactic, or semantic errors, you will want to read the chapter on page 142. That chapter has a number of examples given at the end. Even if you do not use this full system, you may wish to mark errors using the asterisk symbol on the main line

4.   **Timing Analyses.** If you wish to construct detailed analyses of times for pauses and spoken material, you will want to look at the use of the %tim coding line discussed in the chapter on page 81. You will also want to learn about the TIME-

DUR command, as discussed in the CLAN manual.

5. **Morphological Analysis.** If you wish to analyze the child's learning of morphological markings, you will first want to look at the main line coding of morphemes discussed in the chapter on the coding of <u>page 52</u>. However, for those who want to go beyond the simple tabulation of types of markings, it is better to learn the complete system for morphological and syntactic coding presented in the chapter on <u>page 156</u>.

Finally, there will be researchers who find that none of the CHAT conventions properly express the categories that they wish to code. In such cases, researchers can create new CHAT codes, as illustrated on <u>page 116</u>.

3.4   The Documentation File

CHAT files typically record a conversational sample collected from a particular set of speakers on a particular day. Sometimes researchers study a small set of children repeatedly over a long period of time. This is a longitudinal study. For such studies, it is best to break up CHAT files into one collection for each child. Such a collection of files constitutes a corpus. A corpus can also be composed of a group of files from different groups of speakers when the focus is on a cross-sectional sampling of larger numbers of language learners from various age groups. In either case, each corpus should be accompanied by a documentation file. This "readme" file should contain a basic set of facts that are indispensable for the proper interpretation of the data by other researchers. The minimum set of facts that should be in each readme file are:

1. **Acknowledgments.** There should be a statement that asks the user to cite some particular reference when using the corpus. For example, researchers using the Adam, Eve, and Sarah corpora from Roger Brown and his colleagues are asked to cite Brown (1973). In addition, all users can cite this current manual as the source for the CHILDES system in general.

2. **Restrictions.** If the data are being contributed to the CHILDES system, contributors can set particular restrictions on the use of their data. For example, researchers may ask that they be sent copies of articles that make use of their data. Many researchers have chosen to set no limitations at all on the use of their data.

3. **Warnings.** This documentation file should also warn other researchers about limitations on the use of the data. For example, if an investigator paid no attention to correct transcription of speech errors, this should be noted.

4. **Pseudonyms.** The readme file should also include information on whether informants gave informed consent for the use of their data and whether pseudonyms have been used to preserve informant anonymity. In general, real names should be replaced by pseudonyms. This replacement may not be desirable when the subject of the transcriptions is the researcher's own child.

5. **History.** There should be detailed information on the history of the project. How was funding obtained? What were the goals of the project? How was data collected? What was the sampling procedure? How was transcription done? What

was ignored in transcription? Were transcribers trained? Was reliability checked? Was coding done? What codes were used? Was the material computerized? How?

6.   **Codes.** If there are project-specific codes, these should be described.

7.   **Biographical data.** Where possible, extensive demographic, dialectological, and psychometric data should be provided for each informant. There should be information on topics such as age, gender, siblings, schooling, social class, occupation, previous residences, religion, interests, friends, and so forth. Information on where the parents grew up and the various residences of the family is particularly important in attempting to understand sociolinguistic issues regarding language change, regionalism, and dialect. Without detailed information about specific dialect features, it is difficult to know whether these particular markers are being used throughout the language or just in certain regions.

8.   **Table of contents.** There should be a brief index to the contents of the corpora. This could be in the form of a list of files with their dates and the age of the target children involved. If MLU data are available for the children, these should be included. Such data are often extremely helpful to other researchers in making an initial judgment regarding the utility of a data set for their particular research objectives.

9.   **Situational descriptions.** The readme file should include descriptions of the contexts of the recordings, such as the layout of the child's home and bedroom or the nature of the activities being recorded. Additional specific situational information should be included in the @Situation and @Comment fields in each file.

The various readme files for the corpora that are now in the CHILDES database were all contributed in this form. They were then edited and reformatted and combined into the database manual in Volume II.

3.4.1   Checking Syntactic Accuracy

Each CLAN command runs a very superficial check to see if a file conforms to min-CHAT. This check looks only to see that each line begins with either @, *, %, a tab or a space. This is the minimum that the CLAN commands must have to function. However, the correct functioning of many of the functions of CLAN depends on adherence to further standards for minCHAT. In order to make sure that a file matches these minimum requirements for correct analysis through CLAN, researchers should run each file through CHECK. This command can be run directly inside the editor, so that you can verify the accuracy of your transcription as you are producing it. The CHECK command will detect errors such as failure to start lines with the correct symbols, use of incorrect speaker codes, or missing @Begin and @End symbols. CHECK can also be used to find errors in CHAT coding beyond those discussed in this chapter. Using CHECK is like brushing your teeth. It may be hard at first to remember to use the command, but the more you use it the easier it becomes and the better the final results.

4:   File Headers

The three major components of a CHAT transcript are the file headers, the main tier, and the dependent tiers. In this chapter we discuss creating the first major component — the file headers. A computerized transcript in CHAT format begins with a series of "header" lines, which tells us about things such as the date of the recording, the names of the participants, the ages of the participants, the setting of the interaction, and so forth. Most of these header lines occur only at the very beginning of the file. These are what we call "constant headers," because they refer to information that is constant throughout the file. Other headers can occur along within the main body of the file. These "changeable headers" refer to information that varies during the course of the interaction.

A header is a line of text that gives information about the participants and the setting. All headers begin with the "@" sign. Some headers require nothing more than the @ sign and the header name. These are "bare" headers such as @Begin or @New Episode. However, most headers require that there be some additional material. This additional material is called an "entry." Headers that take entries must have a colon, which is then followed by one or two tabs and the required entry. By default, tabs are usually understood to be placed at eight-character intervals. The only purpose for the tabs is to improve the readability of the file header information. The material up to the colon is called the "header name." In the example following, "@Age of CHI:" and "@Date:" are both header names.

```
@Age of CHI: 2;6.14
@Date: 25-JAN-1983
```

The text that follows the header name is called the "header entry." In the example cited earlier, "2;6.14" and "25-JAN-1983" are the header entries. The header name and the header entry together are called the "header line." The header line should never have a punctuation mark at the end. In CHAT, only utterances actually spoken by the subjects receive final punctuation.

This chapter presents a set of headers that researchers have considered important. You may find this list incomplete. It that case, CHAT allows you to add to it. You may also find many of the headers unnecessary. Except for the @Begin, @Participants, @ID, and @End headers, none of the headers are required and you should feel free to use only those headers that you feel are needed for the accurate documentation of your corpus.

4.1   Obligatory Headers

CHAT uses three types of headers — obligatory, constant, and changeable. There are only four obligatory headers — @Begin, @Participants, @ID, and @End. Without these obligatory headers, the CLAN commands will not run correctly.

Begin Header —   **@Begin**

This header is placed at the beginning of the file. It is needed to guarantee that no material has been lost at the beginning of the file. This is a "bare" header that takes no entry and uses no colon.

Participants Header —   **@Participants**

This header must be included as the second line in the file. It lists all of the actors within the file. The entry for this header is XXX Name Role, XXX Name Role, ..., XXX Name Role. XXX stands for the three-letter speaker ID. Here is an example of a completed @Participants header line:

```
@Participants: SAR Sue_Day Target_Child, CAR Carol Mother
```

Participants are identified by three elements: their speaker ID, their name and their role:

1. **Speaker ID.** The speaker ID is usually composed of three letters. The code may be based either on the participant's name, as in *ROS or *BIL, or on her role, as in *CHI or *MOT. In this type of identifying system, several different children could be indicated as *CH1, *CH2, *CH3, and so on. Speaker IDs must be unique because they will be used to identify speakers both in the main body of the transcript and in other headers. In many transcripts, three letters are enough to distinguish all speakers. However, even with three letters, some ambiguities can arise. For example, suppose that the child being studied is named Mark (MAR) and his mother is named Mary (MAR). They would both have the same speaker ID and you would not be able to tell who was talking. So you must change one speaker ID. You would probably want to change it to something that would be easy to read and understand as you go through the file. A good choice is to use that speaker's role. In this example, Mary's speaker ID would be changed to MOT (Mother). You could change Mark's speaker ID to CHI, but that would be misleading if there are other children in the transcript. So a better solution would be to use MAR and MOT as shown in the following example:

    ```
    @Participants: MAR Mark Target_Child, MOT Mary Mother
    ```

    Combinations of speaker and addressee can be indicated by combining three-letter codes, as in *CHI-MOT or *CHI-FAT for the child talking to the Mother or the child talking to the Father.

2. **Name.** The speaker's name can be omitted. If CLAN finds only a three-letter ID and a role, it will assume that the name has been omitted. In order to preserve anonymity, it is often useful to include a pseudonym for the name, because the pseudonym will also be used in the body of the transcript. For CLAN to correctly parse the participants line, multiple-word name definitions such as "Sue Day" need to be joined in the form "Sue_Day."

3. **Role.** After the ID and name, you type in the role of the speaker. There are a fixed set of roles specified in the file used by CHECK and we recommend trying

to use these fixed roles whenever possible. The roles given in that file are: Target_Child, Child, Mother, Father, Brother, Sister, Sibling, Grandmother, Grandfather, Aunt, Uncle, Cousin, Family_Friend, Playmate, Visitor, Student, Teacher, Investigator, Examiner, Observer, Camera_Operator, Doctor, Nurse, Patient, Client, Subject, Unidentified, Adult, Teenager, Non_Human, OffScript, and Narrator. All of these roles are hard-wired into the depfile used by CHECK. It is impossible to list all of the roles that one might wish to use. Therefore, if one of these standard roles does not work, it would be best to use one of the generic age roles, like Adult, Child, or Teenager. Then, the exact nature of the role can be put in the place of the name, as in these examples:

```
@Participants:TBO Toll_Booth_Operator Adult,
AIR Airport_Attendant Adult, SI1 First_Sibling Sibling,
SI2 Second_Sibling Sibling, OFF MOT_to_INV OffScript,
NON Computer_Talk Non_Human
```

Identification Header —   @ID:

This header is used to key the particular file into a larger system for identifying files. The basic shape of this header is as follows:

```
@ID:    eng.ne20.chi20.0110=NIC
```

This code includes the following components:

eng	Three letters to identify the language. For example, dut would code for Dutch. If the language is English, this first code can be omitted.
ne20	The second field includes three or four letters to indicate the corpus. In this case ne20 represents the New England corpus at the 20 months sample.
chi20	This is the file name without the.cha extension. Here the file would be chi20.cha.
0110	This is a four-digit field for the target child's age in years and months. In this case, the child is 1 year and 10 months old.
=NIC	This final field gives the three-letter code for the participant.

End Header —   @End

Like the @Begin header, this header uses no colon and takes no entry. It is the only constant header that is not placed at the beginning of the file. Instead, it is placed at the end of the file. It is needed to guarantee that no material has been lost at the end of the file. Experience has shown that adding this header provides an important safeguard against the very real danger of undetected file truncation during copying.

4.2   Constant Headers

The second set of CHAT headers are the nonobligatory constant headers that contain useful information that is constant throughout the file. These headers are placed at the beginning of the file before any of the actual utterances. Constant headers indicate such basic information as the speaker's age, socioeconomic status, or date of birth — information that is unlikely to change during the course of the recording session. A given researcher may be interested in the use of personal pronouns by middle-class male 2-year-olds. Having this information readily accessible allows us to search the database more efficiently. The following list of constant headers is arranged alphabetically.

Age of XXX Header —   **@Age of XXX:**

This header specifies a speaker's age in years, months, and days. Age is typically entered for the Target Child and his or her siblings, but could be entered for any speaker. The XXX symbol stands for the three-letter speaker ID. The entry for the @Age header is given in the form years;months.days as in 2;11.17 for 2 years, 11 months, and 17 days. This syntax is different from that used to represent dates.

You can figure out a child's age, at the time of the session, if you know the date of the transcript and the child's date of birth. Suppose that John (JOH) was born on May 12, 1978 and the date of the transcript is September 20, 1984. First, you calculate the number of full years since he was born. From May of 1978 to May of 1984 (Johnny's last birthday) is 6 years. Then you calculate the number of full months since his last birthday. From May 12, 1984 to September 12, 1984 is 4 months. Then you calculate the number of days from that day. From September 12 to September 20, 1984 is 8 days. So John's age would be 6 years, 4 months, and 8 days. This same computation can also be done by the DATES command, as discussed in the CLAN manual. Here is an example of the completed header line:

```
@Age of JOH:     6;4.8
```

If you do not know the child's age in days, you can simply use years and months, as in this example:

```
@Age of JOH:     6;4.
```

If you do not know the months, you can use this form:

```
@Age of JOH:     6;
```

Birth of XXX Header —   **@Birth of XXX:**

This header gives the date of birth of the speaker. The speaker is indicated by the three-letter speaker ID in place of the XXX. The entry for this header is day-month-year. Notice that the day comes first and the month second. In this notation, January 23, 1973 is reformatted as 23-JAN-1973. In all dates, months should be uppercase, all capitals, and abbreviated as follows: JAN, FEB, MAR, APR, MAY, JUN, JUL, AUG, SEP, OCT, NOV, DEC. Here is an example of an @Birth header line:

```
@Birth of SAR:    23-JUL-1961
```

Coder Header —   **@Coder:**

This line identifies the people who transcribed and coded the file. Having this indicated is often helpful later, when questions arise. It also provides a way of acknowledging the people who have taken the time to make the data available for further study.

Coding Header —   **@Coding:**

It is no longer important to use this line. During the period between 1987 and 1995, when CHAT was still being developed, it was useful to know which version of CHAT was being used. However, CHAT is now stable. In addition, because we continually use the latest version of the CHECK program to verify the use of current CHAT conventions, there is no reason to code the version of CHAT that is being used.

Dependent Tier Header —   **@Dependent:**

This line is used to list the dependent tiers that you wish to use. It is only important if you wish to have the editor read in these names so that you have command key shortcuts for inserting strings like %spa:.

Education of XXX Header —   **@Education of XXX:**

The entry for this header is the speaker's highest grade level in school. Education is indicated by the integers from 0 to 20, where the numbers after 12 indicate years of college. The speaker is indicated by the speaker ID in place of the XXX. For example, if the speaker was in the second year of graduate school, this would be represented as "18." Here is an example of an @Education line:

```
@Education of MOT: 18
```

Filename Header —   **@Filename:**

This header gives the name of the computer file, as a safeguard against accidental file renaming. If you have an @ID tier, you do not need to add this line, because the code on the @ID tier includes the filename.

Font Header —   **@Font:**

This header is used to set the default font for the file. This line is hidden in the CLAN editor. For Macintosh, the default font is Monaco:9. For Windows, it is Win95:Courier New:-13. For files that use Asian languages, there will be default fonts such as Osaka or

Beijing in this line. Font declarations can also occur in the middle of the text. For example, they allow you to set the %pho tier in an IPA font. They are also hidden when they occur inside the file.

Group of XXX Header —   **@Group of XXX:**

This header indicates the subject's group in group studies.

Language Header —   **@Language:**

This header is used to indicate the main language of the transcript.

Language of XXX Header —   **@Language of XXX:**

This header can be used to indicate the primary language of the various participants. In order to describe the basic language of a particular interaction, it is best to use the @bg and @eg markers that work with GEM. When language switching is even more intense, it may be necessary to include a %lan: dependent tier for each utterance indicating the language of the utterance. Ideas for constructing such a tier are given on page 116.

SES of XXX Header —   **@SES of XXX:**

This header describes the socioeconomic status (SES) of the child's family. The child is indicated by the speaker ID in place of the XXX. To enter the family's socioeconomic status, use standard adjectives such as: welfare, lower, working, lower-middle, middle, upper-middle, upper. Here is an example of a completed @SES header:

```
@SES of SAR: working
```

Sex of XXX Header —   **@Sex of XXX:**

This header indicates the gender of the speaker. The speaker is indicated by the three-letter speaker ID in place of the XXX. Here is an example of a completed @Sex header line:

```
@Sex of SAR: female
```

Stimulus Header —   **@Stim:**

This header indicates stimulus for elicited production.

Transcriber Header —   **@Transcriber:**

This header gives the transcriber's name or initials.

Warning Header — @Warning:

This header is used to warn the user about certain defects or peculiarities in the collection and transcription of the data in the file. Some typical warnings are as follows:

1. These data are not useful for the analysis of overlaps, because overlapping was not accurately transcribed.

2. These data contain no information regarding the context. Therefore they will be inappropriate for many types of analysis.

3. Retracings and hesitation phenomena have not been accurately transcribed in these data.

4. These data have been transcribed, but the transcription has not yet been double-checked.

5. This file has not yet passed successfully through CHECK.

4.3   Changeable Headers

Changeable headers can occur either at the beginning of the file along with the constant headers or else in the body of the file. Changeable headers contain information that can change within the file. For example, if the file contains material that was recorded on only one day, the @Date header would occur only once at the beginning of the file. However, if the file contains some material from a later day, the @Date header would be used again later in the file to indicate the next date. These changeable headers appear, then, at the point within the file where the information changes. The list that follows is alphabetical.

Activities Header — @Activities:

This header describes the activities involved in the situation. The entry is a list of component activities in the situation. Suppose the @Situation header reads, "Getting ready to go out." The @Activities header would then list what was involved in this, such as putting on coats, gathering school books, and saying good-bye.

Beginning of Gem Header — @Bg and @Bg:

These headers are used to mark the beginning of a "gem" for analysis by GEM. If there is a colon, you must follow the colon with a tab and then one or more code words.

Background Header — @Bck:

Diary material that was not originally transcribed in the CHAT format often has explanatory or background material placed before a child's utterance. When converting this material to the CHAT format, it is sometimes impossible to decide whether this background material occurs before, during, or after the utterance. In order to avoid having to make these decisions after the fact, one can simply enter it in an @Bck header.

```
@Bck:    Rachel was fussing and pointing toward the cabinet where the
         cookies are stored.
*RAC:    cookie [/] cookie.
```

Comment Header —   @Comment:

   This header can be used as an all-purpose comment line. Any type of comment can be
entered on an @Comment line. When the comment refers to a particular utterance, use the
%com line. When the comment refers to more general material, use the @Comment header.
If the comment is intended to apply to the file as a whole, place the @Comment header
along with the constant headers before the first utterance. Instead of trying to make up a
new coding tier name such as "@Gestational Age" for a special purpose type of information, it is best to use the @Comment field, as in this example:

```
@Comment: Gestational age of MAR is 7 months
@Comment: Birthweight of MAR is 6 lbs. 4 oz.
```

Date Header —   @Date:

   This header indicates the date of the interaction. The entry for this header is given in
the form day-month-year. The date is abbreviated in the same way as in the @Birth header
entry. Here is an example of a completed @Date header line:

```
@Date: 1-JUL-1965
```

This form includes information on the century. This is needed to distinguish reliably data
collected at the beginning of this century, such as the data of Stern and Stern, from data that
will be collected in the early part of the next century.

End of Gem Header —   @Eg and @Eg:

   These headers are used to mark the end of a "gem" for analysis by the GEM command.
If there is a colon, you must follow the colon with a tab and then one or more code words.

Gem Header —   @g:

   This header is used in conjunction with the GEM program, which is described in the
CLAN manual. It marks the beginning of "gems" when no nesting or overlapping of gems
occurs. Each gem is defined as material that begins with an @g marker and ends with the
next @g marker. We refer to these markers as "lazy" gem markers, because they are easier
to use than the @bg and @eg markers. To use this feature, you need to also use the +n
switch in GEM.

Location Header —   **@Location:**

This header should include the city, state or province, and country in which the interaction took place. Here is an example of a completed header line:

    @Location: Boston, MA, USA

New Episode Header —   **@New Episode**

This header simply marks the fact that there has been a break in the recording and that a new episode has started. It is a "bare" header that is used without a colon, because it takes no entry. There is no need to mark the end of the episode because the @New Episode header indicates both the end of one episode and the beginning of another.

Room Layout Header —   **@Room Layout:**

This header outlines room configuration and positioning of furniture. This is especially useful for experimental settings. The entry should be a description of the room and its contents. Here is an example of the completed header line:

    @Room Layout: Kitchen; Table in center of room with window on west
                    wall, door to outside on north wall

Situation Header —   **@Situation:**

This changeable header describes the general setting of the interaction. It applies to all the material that follows it until a new @Situation header appears. The entry for this header is a standard description of the situation. Try to use standard situations such as: "breakfast," "outing," "bath," "working," "visiting playmates," "school," or "getting ready to go out." Here is an example of the completed header line:

    @Situation: Tim and Bill are playing with toys in the hallway.

There should be enough situational information given to allow the user to reconstruct the situation as much as possible. Who is present? What is the layout of the room or other space? What is the social role of those present? Who is usually the caregiver? What activity is in progress? Is the activity routinized and, if so, what is the nature of the routine? Is the routine occurring in its standard time, place, and personnel configuration? What objects are present that affect or assist the interaction? It will also be important to include relevant ethnographic information that would make the interaction interpretable to the user of the database. For example, if the text is parent–child interaction before an observer, what is the culture's evaluation of behaviors such as silence, talking a lot, displaying formulaic skills, defending against challenges, and so forth?

Tape Location Header —   @**Tape Location:**

This header indicates the specific tape ID, side and footage. This is very important for identifying the tape from which the transcription was made. The entry for this header should include the tape ID, side and footage. Here is an example of this header:

```
@Tape Location: tape74, side a, 104
```

Time Duration Header —   @**Time Duration:**

It is often necessary to indicate the time at which the audiotaping began and the amount of time that passed during the course of the taping, as in the following header:

```
@Time Duration: 12:30-13:30
```

This header provides the absolute time during which the taping occurred. For most projects what is important is not the absolute time, but the time of individual events relative to each other. This sort of relative timing is provided by coding on the %tim dependent tier in conjunction with the @Time Start header described next.

Time Start Header —   @**Time Start:**

If you are tracking elapsed time on the %tim tier, the @Time Start header can be used to indicate the absolute time at which the timing marks begin. If a new @Time Start header is placed in the middle of the transcript, this "restarts" the clock.

```
@Time Start: 12:30
```

5:   Words

Words are the basic building blocks of all sentential and discourse structures. By studying the development of word use, we can learn an enormous amount about the growth of syntax, discourse, morphology, and conceptual structure. However, in order to realize the full potential of computational analysis of word usage, we need to follow certain basic rules. In particular, we need to make sure that we spell words in a consistent manner. If we sometimes use the form "doughnut" and sometimes use the form "donut," we are being inconsistent in our representation of this particular word. If such inconsistencies are repeated throughout the lexicon, computerized analysis will become inaccurate and misleading. One of the major goals of CHAT analysis is to maximize systematicity and minimize inconsistency. In the Introduction, we discussed some of the problems involved in mapping the speech of language learners onto standard adult forms. This chapter spells out some rules and heuristics designed to achieve the goal of consistency for word-level transcription.

One solution to this problem would be to avoid the use of words altogether by transcribing everything in phonetic or phonemic notation. But this solution would make the transcript difficult to read and analyze. A great deal of work in language learning is based on searches for words and combinations of words. If we want to conduct these lexical analyses, we have to try to match up the child's production to actual words. Work in the analysis of syntactic development also requires that the text be analyzed in terms of lexical items. Without a clear representation of lexical items and the ways that they diverge from the adult standard, it would be impossible to conduct lexical and syntactic analyses computationally. Even for those researchers who do not plan to conduct lexical analyses, it is extremely difficult to understand the flow of a transcript if no attempt is made to relate the learner's sounds to items in the adult language.

At the same time, attempts to force adult lexical forms onto learner forms can seriously misrepresent the data. The solution to this problem is to devise ways to indicate the various types of divergences between learner forms and adult standard forms. Note that we use the term "divergences" rather than "error." Although both learners (MacWhinney & Osser, 1977) and adults (Stemberger, 1985) clearly do make errors, most of the divergences between learner forms and adult forms are due to structural aspects of the learner's system.

This chapter discusses the various tools that CHAT provides to mark some of these divergences of child forms from adult standards. The basic types of codes for divergences that we discuss are:

1.   special learner-form markers,
2.   codes for unidentifiable material,
3.   codes for incomplete words,
4.   ways of treating formulaic use of words, and
5.   conventions for standardized spellings.

Before we begin our discussion of these conventions, we will quickly review the basic form of the main line.

5.1   The Main Line

In CHAT, words are transcribed on the main speaker tier. This is the line that tells us what the participants said. Each main tier line begins with an asterisk. After the asterisk, there is a three-letter speaker ID, a colon and a tab. The transcription of what was said begins in the ninth column, after the tab, because the tab stop in the editor is set for the eighth column. The remainder of the main tier line is composed primarily of a series of words. Words are defined as a series of ASCII characters separated by spaces. In this chapter, we discuss the principles governing the transcription of words. In CLAN, all characters that are not punctuation markers are potentially parts of words. The default punctuation set includes the space and these characters:

```
    ,  .  ;  ?  !  [  ]  <  >
```

None of these characters or the space can be used within words. Other nonletter characters such as the plus sign (+) or the at sign (@) can be used within words to express special meanings. This punctuation set applies to the main lines and all coding lines with the exception of the %pho and %mod lines which use the system described on page 120. Because those systems make use of punctuation markers for special characters, only the space can be used as a delimiter on the %pho and %mod lines. As the CLAN manual explains, this default punctuation set can be changed for particular analyses.

5.2   Special Form Markers

Special form markers can be placed at the end of a word. To do this, the symbol "@" is used in conjunction with one or two additional letters. Here is an example of the use of the @ symbol:

```
    *SAR:    I got a bingbing@c.
```

Here the child has invented the form "bingbing" to refer to a toy. The word "bingbing" is not in the dictionary and must be treated as a special form. To further clarify the use of these @c forms, the transcriber should create a file called "0lexicon.cdc" that provides glosses for such forms.

The @c form illustrated in this example is only one of many possible special form markers that can be devised. The following table lists some of these markers that we have found useful. However, this categorization system is meant only to be suggestive, not exhaustive. Researchers may wish to add further distinctions or ignore some of the categories listed. The particular choice of markers and the decision to code a word with a marker form is one that is made by the transcriber, not by CHAT. The basic idea is that CLAN will treat words marked with the special learner-form markers as words and not as fragments. In addition, the MOR program will not attempt to analyze special forms for part of speech.

Table 1: Special Form Markers

Letters	Categories	Example	Meaning
@b	babbling	abame@b	-
@c	child-invented form	gumma@c	sticky
@d	dialect form	younz@d	you
@f	family-specific form	bunko@f	broken
@fp	filled pause	huh@fp	-
@i	interjection, interaction	uhhuh@i	-
@l	letter	b@l	letter b
@n	neologism	breaked@n	broke
@o	onomatopoeia	woofwoof@o	dog barking
@p	phonol. consistent form	aga@p	-
@pr	phrasal repetition	it's a, it's a@pr	for disfluency work
@s	second-language form	istenem@s	my God
@sc	schwa form	I@sc	reduced to schwa
@sl	signed language	apple@sl	apple
@sas	sign & speech	apple@sas	apple and sign
@t	test word	wug@t	small creature
@u	UNIBET transcription	binga@u	-
@x	words to be excluded	uh@x	pause
@wp	word play	goobarumba@wp	-
@g	general special form	gongga@g	-

We can define these special markers in the following ways:

1. **Babbling** can be used to mark both low-level early babbling and high-level sound play in older children. These forms have no obvious meaning and are used just to have fun with sound.

2. **Child-invented forms** are words created by the child sometimes from other words without obvious derivational morphology. Sometimes they appear to be sound variants of other words. Sometimes their origin is obscure. However, the child appears to be convinced that they have meaning and adults sometimes

come to use these forms themselves.

3. **Dialect form** is often an interesting general property of a transcript. However, the coding of phonological dialect variations on the word level should be minimized, because it often makes transcripts more difficult to read and analyze. Instead, general patterns of phonological variation can be noted in the 00readme.cdc file.

4. **Family-specific forms** are much like child-invented forms that have been taken over by the whole family. Sometimes the source of these forms are children, but they can also be older members of the family. Sometimes the forms come from variations of words in another language. An example might be the use of "undertoad" to refer to some mysterious being in the surf, although the word was simply "undertow" initially.

5. **Filled pauses** includes forms like "uh" or "mmm." Usually, there is no need to mark these forms as uh@fp. However, for detailed studies of children with disfluencies it may be useful to add this additional marking. Also, if one wants to explicitly count words such as "well" or phrase such as "you know" as filled pauses, you can transcribe them as well@fp or you+know@fp.

6. **Interjections** can be indicated in standard ways, making the use of the @i notation usually not necessary. Instead of transcribing "ahem@i," one can simply transcribe "ahem" following the conventions listed later.

7. **Letters** can either be transcribed with the @l marker or simply as single-character words.

8. **Neologisms** are meant to refer to morphological coinages, whereas monomorphemic nonce forms are either child-invented forms, family-specific forms, or test words.

9. **Onomatopoeic forms** include animal sounds and attempts to imitate natural sounds.

10. **Phonological consistent forms** are early forms that are phonologically consistent, but whose meaning is unclear to the transcriber. Usually these forms have some relation to small function words.

11. **Phrasal repetition** marking is only useful for studies that focus particularly on children with fluency problems. By using this marker, it is often easier to include and exclude phrasal repetitions in particular analyses.

12. **Second-language forms** derive from some language not usually used in the home.

13. **Schwa forms** indicate a reduction of a standard form to a mere schwa in articulation.

14. **Sign language** use can be indicated by the @s.

15. **Sign and speech** use can be indicated by @sas.

16. **Test words** are nonce forms generated by the investigators to test the productivity of the child's grammar.

17. **UNIBET transcription** can be given on the main line by using the @u marker.

However, if many such forms are being noted, it may be better to construct a @pho line.

18. **Excluded form** notation is provided as a convenience for projects that want to uniformly exclude certain words from CLAN analyses. However, this can also be done using other CLAN tools, such as "exclude" files.

19. **Word play** in older children produces forms that may sound much like the forms of babbling, but which arise from a slightly different process. It is best to use the @b for forms produced by children younger than 2;0 and @wp for older children.

20. **General special form** marking can be used when all of the above fail. However, its use should generally be avoided.

Later in this chapter we present a set of standard spellings of such words for English that make use of @d and @i largely unnecessary. However, in languages where such a list is not available, it may be necessary to use forms with @d or @i. The @b, @u, and @wp markers allow the transcriber to represent words and babbling words phonologically on the main line and have CLAN treat them as full lexical items. This should only be done when the analysis requires that the phonological string be treated as a word and it is unclear which standard morpheme corresponds to the word. If a phonological string should not be treated as a full word, it should be marked by a beginning &, and the @b, @u, or @w endings should not be used. Also, if the transcript includes a complete %pho line for each word (see page 120) and the data are intended for phonological analysis, it is better to use yy (see the next section) on the main line and then give the phonological form on the %pho line.

Family-specific forms are special words used only by the family. These are often derived from child forms that are adopted by all family members. They also include certain "caregiverese" forms that are not easily recognized by the majority of adult speakers but which may be common to some areas or some families. Family-specific forms can be used by either adults or children.

The @n marker is intended for morphological neologisms and overregularizations, whereas the @c marker is intended to mark nonce creation of stems. Of course, this distinction is somewhat arbitrary and incomplete. Whenever a child-invented form is clearly onomatopoeic, use the @o coding instead of the @c coding. A fuller characterization of neologisms can be provided by the error coding system given on page 142.

If transcribers find it difficult to distinguish between child-invented forms, onomatopoeia, and familial forms, they can use the @ symbol without any following letter. In this way, they can at least indicate the fact that the preceding word is not a standard item in the adult lexicon.

5.3 Unidentifiable Material

Sometimes it is difficult to map a sound or group of sounds onto either a conventional word or a nonconventional word. This can occur when the audio signal is so weak or garbled that you cannot even identify the sounds being used. At other times, you can recognize the sounds that the speaker is using, but cannot map the sounds onto words. Sometimes you may choose not to transcribe a passage, because it is irrelevant to the interaction. Sometimes the person makes a noise or performs an action instead of speaking, and sometimes a person breaks off before completing a recognizable word. All of these problems can be dealt with by using certain special symbols for those items that cannot be easily related to words. These symbols are typed in lower case and are preceded and followed by spaces. When standing alone on a text tier, they should be followed by a period, unless it is clear that the utterance was a question or a command.

Unintelligible Speech —   xxx / xx

Use the symbol xxx when you cannot hear or understand what the speaker is saying. If you believe you can distinguish the number of unintelligible words, you may use several xxx strings in a row. Here is an example of the use of the xxx symbol:

```
*SAR:   xxx.
*MOT:   what?
*SAR:   I want xx.
```

Sarah's first utterance is fully unintelligible. Her second utterance includes some unintelligible material along with some intelligible material.

The MLU and MLT commands will ignore the xxx symbol when computing mean length of utterance and other statistics. If you want unintelligible material included in such counts, use the symbol xx instead of xxx. If you want to have several words included, use as many occurrences of xx as you wish.

Unintelligible Material on %pho —   yyy / yy

Use the symbol yy or yyy when you cannot hear or understand what the speaker is saying and you wish to represent its phonological form on a %pho line that is being consistently used throughout the transcript. If you are not consistently creating a %pho line, you should use the @u or & notations instead. If you believe you can distinguish the number of unintelligible words, and you wish to treat each word-like string as a word, use yy rather than yyy. CLAN will count each yy form as a word. Here is an example of the use of yy:

```
*SAR:   yy yy a ball.
%pho:   ta g6 6 bal
```

The first two words cannot be matched to particular words, but their phonological form is given on the %pho line.

Untranscribed Material —   www

This symbol must be used in conjunction with an %exp tier which is discussed on page

81. This symbol is used on the main line to indicate material that a transcriber does not know how to transcribe or does not want to transcribe. For example, it could be that the material is in a language that the transcriber does not know. This symbol can also be used when a speaker says something that has no relevance to the interactions taking place and the experimenter would rather ignore it. For example, www could indicate a long conversation between adults that would be superfluous to transcribe. Here is an example of the use of this symbol:

```
*MOT:    www.
%exp:    talks to neighbor on the telephone
```

Actions Without Speech —   0

This symbol is used when the speaker performs some action that is not accompanied by speech. Notice that the symbol is the numeral zero "0," not the capital letter "O." Here is an example of the correct usage of this symbol:

```
*FAT:    where's your doll?
*DAV:    0 [=! cries].
```

If the transcriber wishes to code the phonetics of the crying, it would be better to insert yyy on the main tier. Do not use the zero, if there is any speech on the tier. The zero can also be used to provide a place to attach a dependent tier.

Phonological Fragment —   &

The & symbol can be used at the beginning of a string to indicate that the following material is being transcribed in correct phonological form in UNIBET and that CLAN should not treat it as a word. It is important not to include any of the three utterance terminators — the exclamation mark, the question mark, or the period — because CLAN will treat these as utterance terminators. This form of notation is useful when the speaker stutters or breaks off before completing a recognizable word (false starts). The utterance "t- t- c- can't you go" is transcribed as follows:

```
*MAR:    &t &t &k can't you go?
```

Note that the form &k is being used instead of &c, because the notation is in UNIBET. The ampersand can also be used for nonce and nonsense forms:

```
*DAN:    &glNk &glNk.
%com:    weird noises
```

Material following the ampersand symbol will be ignored by certain CLAN commands, such as MLU, which computes the mean length of the utterance in a transcript. If you want to have the material treated as a word, use the @u form of notation instead (see the previous section).

Unless you specifically attempt to search for strings with the ampersand, the CLAN commands will not see them at all. If you want a command such as FREQ to count all of the instances of phonological fragments, you would have to add a switch such as +s"&*".

Best Guess at a Word —   [?]

This symbol is a scoped symbol discussed in fuller detail on <u>page 70</u>. It can be used to indicate that the previous word or group of words are simply the transcriber's best guess at what was being said and there is some doubt in the transcriber's mind whether this guess is correct.

5.4   Incomplete and Omitted Words

Words may also be incomplete or even fully omitted. We can judge a word to be incomplete when enough of it is produced for us to be sure what was intended. Judging a word to be omitted is often much more difficult.

Noncompletion of a Word —   ()

When a word is incomplete, but the intended meaning seems clear, insert the missing material within parentheses. This notation can also be used to derive a consistent spelling for commonly shortened words, such as "(un)til" and "(be)cause." CLAN will treat items that are coded in this way as full words. For programs such as FREQ, the parentheses will essentially be ignored and "(be)cause" will be treated as if it were "because." The CLAN programs also provide ways of either including or excluding the material in the parentheses, depending on the goals of the analysis.

```
    *RAL:    I been sit(ting) all day.
```

Note that coding omissions in this way involves important theoretical decisions, some of which are discussed in the next section.

The inclusion or exclusion of material enclosed in parentheses is well supported by CLAN and this same notation can also be used for other purposes when necessary. For example, studies of fluency may find it convenient to code the number of times that a word is repeated directly on that word, as in this example with three repetitions of the word "dog."

```
    *JEF:    that's a dog(*3).
```

Omitted Word —   0word

The coding of word omissions is an extremely difficult and unreliable process. Many researchers will prefer not to even open up this particular can of worms. On the other hand, researchers in language disorders and aphasia often find that the coding of word omissions is crucial to particular theoretical issues. In such cases, it is important that the coding of omitted words be done in as clear a manner as possible

To code an omission, the zero symbol is placed before a word on the text tier. If what is important is not the actual word omitted, but its part of speech, then a code for the part of speech can follow the zero (see page 156). The decision to code a word as missing is, of course, one that must be based on the transcriber's judgment. Similarly, the identity of the omitted word is always a guess. The best guess is placed on the main line. This item would be counted for scoping conventions, but it would not be included in the MLU count. Here is an example of its use:

```
*EVE:    I want 0to go.
```

It is very difficult to know when a word has been omitted. However, the following criteria can be used to help make this decision for English data:

1. 0art: Unless there is a missing plural, a common noun without an article is coded as 0art.

2. 0v: Sentences with no verbs can be coded as having missing verbs. Of course, often the omission of a verb can be viewed as a grammatical use of ellipsis.

3. 0aux:In standard English, sentences like "he running" clearly have a missing auxiliary.

4. 0subj: In English, every finite verb requires a subject.

5. 0pobj: Every preposition requires an object. However, often a preposition may be functioning as an adverb. The coder must look at the verb to decide whether a word is functioning as a preposition as in "John put on 0pobj" or an adverb as in "Mary jumped up."

In English, there are seldom solid grounds for assigning codes like 0adj, 0adv, 0obj, 0prep, or 0dat.

Ungrammatical Omission — 0*word

The 0*word symbol is used when the omission is clearly ungrammatical and the transcriber wishes to code that fact. Here is an example:

```
*MIK:    where 0*is my truck?
```

Ellipsis — 00word

Often the omission of a word is licensed by the standard grammatical and discourse patterns of the language. For example, answers to questions usually involve ellipsis of the presupposed part of the question. To indicate grammatically licensed ellipsis, two zeroes are placed before the word that is ellipsed, as in 00verb.

```
*FAT:    where did you go?
```

```
*ABE:    00sub 00verb 0*prep the store.
```

Of course, the marking of ellipses raises many difficult theoretical and interpretive questions.

5.5   Standardized Spellings

There are a number of common words in the English language that cannot be found in the dictionary or whose lexical status is vague. For example, how should letters be spelled? What about numbers and titles? What is the best spelling —"doggy" or "doggie," "yeah" or "yah," and "pst" or "pss"?   If we can increase the consistency with which such forms are transcribed, we can improve the quality of automatic lexical analyses. CLAN commands such as FREQ and COMBO provide output based on searches for particular word strings. If a word is spelled in an indeterminate number of variant ways, researchers who attempt to analyze the occurrence of that word will inevitably end up with inaccurate results. For example, if a researcher wants to trace the use of the pronoun "you," it might be necessary to search not only for "you," "ya," and "yah," but also for all the assimilations of the pronouns with verbs such as "didya/dicha/didcha" or "couldya/couldcha/coucha." Without a standard set of rules for the transcription of such forms, accurate lexical searches could become impossible. On the other hand, there is no reason to avoid using these forms if a set of standards can be established for their use. Other programs rely on the use of dictionaries of words. If the spellings of words are indeterminate, the analyses produced will be equally indeterminate. For that reason, it is helpful to specify a set of standard spellings for marginal words. This section lists some of these words with their standard orthographic form.

The forms in these lists all have some conventional lexical status in standard American English. In this regard, they differ from the various nonstandard forms indicated by the special form markers @b, @c, @f, @l, @n, @o, @p, and @s. Because there is no clear limit to the number of possible babbling forms, onomatopoeic forms, or neologistic forms, there is no way to provide a list of such forms. In contrast, the words given in this section are fairly well known to most speakers of the language, and many can be found in unabridged dictionaries. The list given here is only a beginning; over time, we intend to continue to add new forms.

Some of the forms use parentheses to indicate optional material. For example, the exclamation "yeek" can also be said as "eek." When a speaker uses the full form, the transcriber types in "yeek," and when the speaker uses the reduced form the transcriber types "(y)eek." When CLAN analyzes the transcripts, the parentheses can be ignored and both "yeek" and "eek" will be retrieved as instances of the same word. Parentheses can also be used to indicate missing fragments of suffixes. Thus, both the morphemicized (see the chapter on main line page 52) form "do-in(g)" and the nonmorphemicized form "doing" are legal ways of transcribing the form "doin." The majority of the words listed can be found in the form given in *Webster's Third New International Dictionary*. Those forms that cannot be found in *Webster's Third* are indicated with an asterisk. The asterisk should not be used in actual transcription.

5.5.1   Letters

CLAN offers two ways of transcribing letters. The recommended form uses the @l symbol after the letter. For example, the letter "b" would be b@l. Some transcribers find this notational form cumbersome. They may wish to use the somewhat more ambiguous but shorter form for letters. In the short form, the names of the letters in English can be written out as single characters with the exception of the letter "a," which is needed for the article and the letter "i," which is needed for the pronoun. By writing out the letter "a" as "ay" and the letter "i" as "iy," the names of the letters in the English alphabet become: ay b c d e f g h iy j k l m n o p q r s t u v w x y z. Here is an example of the use of these conventions:

```
*MOT:    could you please spell your name?
*MAR:    it's m@l a@l r@l k@l.
```

The simpler, more ambiguous form would be:

```
*MOT:    could you please spell your name?
*MAR:    it's m ay r k.
```

If you are using the ambiguous form, you should also use the spelling "aye" for the affirmative exclamation, rather than the rarer form "ay." As noted in the dictionary, the plural for the word for the letters of the alphabet "abc" is "abcs."

5.5.2   Acronyms

Acronyms should be transcribed by using the component letters as a part of a compound form. Thus, USA can be written as "U+s+a." In this case, the first letter is capitalized in order to mark it as a proper noun. However, the acronym "p+js" for "pajamas" is not capitalized. If no confusion can occur, the compound markers can be omitted. The recommended way of transcribing the common name for television is just "tv." On the other hand, it is better to include the plus sign for acronyms of children's names, as in "C+J" for the nickname for "Charles James." The plus sign is also needed for combinations such as "m+and+ms" for the M&M candy. These forms are similar to nonacronyms such as "bye+and+bye."

Acronyms that are not actually spelled out when produced in conversation should be written as words. Thus "UNESCO" would be written as "Unesco." The capitalization of the first letter is used to indicate the fact that it is a proper noun. There must be no periods inside acronyms and titles, because these can be confused with utterance delimiters. Thus, the acronym USA can be transcribed as "u s ay," if the transcriber wants to emphasize the fact that it is being produced as a series of letters.

5.5.3   Numbers and Titles

Numbers should be written out in words. For example, the number 256 could be written as "two hundred and fifty six," "two hundred fifty six," "two five six," or "two fifty six," depending on how it was pronounced. It is best to use the form "fifty six" rather than "fifty-six," because the hyphen is used in CHAT to indicate morphemicization. If you want to emphasize the fact that a number is a single lexical item, you can treat it as a compound using the form two+hundred+and+fifty+six. Other strings with numbers are monetary amounts, percentages, times, fractions, logarithms, and so on. All should be written out in words, as in "eight thousand two hundred and twenty dollars" for $8220, "twenty nine point five percent" for 29.5%, "seven fifteen" for 7:15, "ten o'clock ay m" for 10:00 AM, and "four and three fifths" for $4\frac{3}{5}$.

Titles such as "Dr." or "Mr." should be written out in their full capitalized form as "Doctor" or "Mister," as in "Doctor Spock" and "Mister Rogers." For "Mrs." use the form "Missus."

5.5.4   Kinship Forms

The following table lists some of the most important kinship address forms in standard American English. The forms with asterisks cannot be found in *Webster's Third New International Dictionary*.

Table 2: Kinship Forms

Child	Formal	Child	Formal
Da(da)	Father	Mommy	Mother
Daddy	Father	Nan	Grandmother
Gram(s)	Grandmother	Nana	Grandmother
Grammy	Grandmother	*Nonny	Grandmother
Gramp(s)	Grandfather	Pa	Father
*Grampy	Grandfather	Pap	Father
Grandma	Grandmother	Papa	Father
Grandpa	Grandfather	Pappy	Father
Ma	Mother	Pop	Father
Mama	Mother	Poppa	Father
Momma	Mother	*Poppy	Father
Mom	Mother		

5.5.5   Shortenings

One of the biggest problems that the transcriber faces is the tendency of speakers to drop sounds out of words. For example, a speaker may leave the initial "a" off of "about," saying instead " 'bout." In CHAT, this shortened form appears as (a)bout. CLAN can easily ignore the parentheses and treat the word as "about." Alternatively, there is a CLAN option to allow the commands to treat the word as a spelling variant. Many common words have standard shortened forms. Some of the most frequent are given in the table that follows. The basic notational principle illustrated in that table can be extended to other words as needed. All of these words can be found in *Webster's Third New International Dictionary*.

More extreme types of shortenings include: "(what)s (th)at" which becomes "sat," "y(ou) are" which becomes "yar," and "d(o) you" which becomes "dyou." Representing these forms as shortenings rather than as nonstandard words facilitates standardization and the automatic analysis of transcripts.

Table 3: Shortenings

Examples of Shortenings			
(a)bout	don('t)	(h)is	(re)frigerator
an(d)	(e)nough	(h)isself	(re)member
(a)n(d)	(e)spress(o)	-in(g)	sec(ond)
(a)fraid	(e)spresso	nothin(g)	s(up)pose
(a)gain	(es)presso	(i)n	(th)e
(a)nother	(ex)cept	(in)stead	(th)em
(a)round	(ex)cuse	Jag(uar)	(th)emselves
ave(nue)	(ex)cused	lib(r)ary	(th)ere
(a)way	(e)xcuse	Mass(achusetts)	(th)ese
(be)cause	(e)xcused	micro(phone)	(th)ey
(be)fore	(h)e	(pa)jamas	(to)gether
(be)hind	(h)er	(o)k	(to)mato
b(e)long	(h)ere	o(v)er	(to)morrow
b(e)longs	(h)erself	(po)tato	(to)night
Cad(illac)	(h)im	prob(ab)ly	(un)til
doc(tor)	(h)imself	(re)corder	wan(t)

The marking of shortened forms such as (a)bout in this way greatly facilitates the later analysis of the transcript, while still preserving readability and phonological accuracy. Learning to make effective use of this form of transcription is an important part of mastering use of CHAT. Underuse of this feature is a common error made by beginning users of CHAT.

5.5.6   Assimilations

Words such as "gonna" for "going to" and "whynt cha" for "why don't you" involve complex sound changes, often with assimilations between auxiliaries and the infinitive or a pronoun. For forms of this type, CHAT allows the transcriber to place the assimilated form on the main line followed by a fuller form in square brackets, as in the form:

```
gonna [: going to]
```

CLAN allows the user to either analyze the material preceding the brackets or the material following the brackets, as described in the section of the chapter on options that discusses the +r switch. An extremely incomplete list of assimilated forms is given below. None of these forms can be found in *Webster's Third New International Dictionary*.

Table 4: Assimilations

Nonstandard	Standard	Nonstandard	Standard
coulda(ve)	could have	mighta	might have
dunno	don't know	need(t)a	need to
dyou	do you	oughta	ought to
gimme	give me	posta	supposed to
gonna	going to	shoulda(ve)	should have
gotta	got to	sorta	sort of
hadta	had to	sorta	sort of
hasta	has to	wanna	want to
hafta	have to	wassup	what's up
kinda	kind of	whaddya	what did you
lemme	let me	whyntcha	why didn't you
lotsa	lots of		

If you transcribe these forms as single morphemes, they will be counted as single morphemes and programs like MOR will recognize them as wholes. If you do not believe that they are morphemic units, you can break them up into components in two ways. First, forms involving alterations of "you" to "cha,""chu," or "ya" can be represented by having "ya,""chu," and "cha" as alternative spellings for "you". Second, you can analyze these forms using the replacement notation. Thus, transcribers can choose to either enter "could cha" or "couldcha [: could you]". If you have chosen to represent "yu" as "ya", you must remember to include "cha," "chu," and "ya" in your search lists. Another way of representing some of these forms is by noting omitted letters with parentheses as in: "gi(ve) me" for "gimme," "le(t) me" for "lemme," or "d(o) you" for "dyou." However, this method is not good, if you are convinced that these forms are monomorphemic.

5.5.7 Exclamations

Exclamations and interjections, such as "ah" and "gosh," are very frequent. However, because their phonological shape varies so much, they often have an unclear lexical status. The following table provides standard shapes for these words. For consistency, these forms should be used even when the actual phonological form diverges from the standardizing convention, as long as the variant is perceived as related to the standard. Rather than creating new forms for variations in vowel length, it is better to use forms such as "a:h" for "aah". The MOR program uses a standard set of these forms in its fillers and communicators files, that you may wish to consult. Words that are marked with an asterisk cannot be found in *Webster's Third New International Dictionary*.

Table 5: Exclamations

Exclamation	Meaning	Exclamation	Meaning
*ah	relief, joy	*pst	listen here
*ahhah	discovery	sh	silence
aw	sympathy	*tsk	shame
golly	gee whiz	tut	pity
gosh	gee whiz	ugh	disgust, effort
ha(h)	triumph	*uhoh	trouble
*haha	amusement	vroom	car noise
*heehee	amusement	whee	exuberance
*mmm	tasty, good	wow	amazement
*num	tasty	yea	a cheer
*nummy	tasty	(y)eek	fear
*numnum	tasty	y(o)ikes	mild fear
ouch	sudden pain	*yum	tasty
ow	hurt	yummy	tasty
oy	dismay	yumyum	tasty

5.5.8   Interactional Markers

Another set of interjections, such as "uhhuh" and "yep," signal agreement, disagreement, and pauses. A sampling of these forms is given below. Words that are marked with an asterisk cannot be found in *Webster's Third New International Dictionary*.

Table 6: Interactional Markers

Marker	Function	Marker	Function
ahem	ready to speak	nah	no
*emem	I don't know	uhhuh	yes
*er	pause	*uhhum	yes indeed
*hunmmm	no	*uhuh	no
*hunhunh	no	*uh	pause (any vowel)
huh	questioning	um	pause
hmm	thinking, waiting	ye(a)h	yes
hmm?	questioning	*yeahhuh	yes (contradicting)
*mmhm	yes	yep	yes
nope	no	yup	yes
*nuhuh	strong no	whoops	blunder

5.5.9   Spelling Variants

There are a number of words that are misspelled so frequently that the misspellings seem as acceptable as the standard spellings. These include "altho" for standard "although," "donut" for "doughnut," "tho" for "though," "thru" for "through," and "abc's" for "abcs." Transcribers should use the standard spellings for these words. In general, it is best to avoid the use of monomorphemic words with apostrophes. For example, it is better to use the form "mam" than the form "ma'am." However, apostrophes must be used in English for multimorphemic contractions such as "I'm" or "don't."

5.5.10   Colloquial Forms

Colloquial and slang forms are often listed in the dictionary. Examples include "telly" for television and "rad" for "radical." The following table lists some such colloquial forms with their corresponding standard forms. Words that are marked with an asterisk cannot be found in *Webster's Third New International Dictionary*.

Table 7: Colloquial Forms

Form	Meaning	Form	Meaning
doggone	problematic	okeydokey	all right
*fuddy+duddy	old-fashioned person	*telly	television
*grabby	grasping (adj)	thingumabob	thing
*hon	honey(name)	thingumajig	thing
*humongous	huge	tinker+toy	toy
looka	look	who(se)jigger	thing
lookit	look!	whatchamacallit	thing

5.5.11   Dialectal Variations

Other variant pronunciations, such as "dat" for "that," involve standard dialectal sound substitutions without deletions. Unfortunately, using these forms can make lexical retrieval very difficult. For example, a researcher interested in the word "together" will seldom remember to include "tagether" in the search string. There are four ways to deal with this problem. The first is to add each variant form to the 0lexicon.cdc file, which also contains other nonstandard forms. Because these variant forms are, in nearly all cases, nonhomographic with other words, researchers analyzing the transcript will simply need to include the variant in their search lists. An example of an exception to this is "den" for "then," because "den" is already the standard word for an animal's burrow. A second solution to this problem is to follow each variant form with the standard form, as given below using the [: replacement] notation discussed on page 70. A third solution is to create a UNIBET transcription of the whole interaction, preferably linked to a full sonic CHAT digitized audio record. In transcripts where the speakers have strong dialectal influences, this is probably the best solution. The fourth solution is to ignore the dialectal variation and simply transcribe the standard form. If this is being done, the practice must be clearly noted in the readme file. None of these forms are in *Webster's Third New International Dictionary*.

Table 8: Dialectal Variants

Variant	Standard	Variant	Standard
caint	can't	hows about	how about
da	the	nutin	nothing
dan	than	sumpin	something
dat	that	ta	to
de	the	tagether	together
dese	these	tamorrow	tomorrow
deir	their	weunz	we
deirselves	themselves	whad	what
dem	them	wif	with
demselves	themselves	ya	you
den	then	yall	you all
dere	there	yer	your
dey	they	youse	you all
dis	this	yinz	you all
dose	those	younz	you all
fer	for	ze	the
git	get	zis	this
gon	going	zat	that
hisself	himself		

5.5.12   Baby Talk

Baby talk or "caregiverese" forms include onomatopoeic words, such as "choochoo," and diminutives, such as "froggie" or "thingie." In the following table, diminutives are given in final "-ie" except for the six common forms "doggy," "kitty," "piggy," "potty," "tummy," and "dolly." Wherever possible, use the suffix "-ie" for the diminutive and the suffix "-y" for the adjectivalizer. The following table does not include the hundreds of possible diminutives with the "-ie" suffix simply attached to the stem, as in "eggie," "footie," "horsie," and so on. Nor does it attempt to list forms such as "poopy," which use the adjectivalizer "-y" attached directly to the stem. Words that are marked with an asterisk cannot be found in *Webster's Third New International Dictionary*.

Table 9: Baby Talk

Baby Talk	Standard	Baby Talk	Standard
*beddie(bye)	go to sleep	*nunu	hurt
*blankie	blanket	*night(ie)+night	good night
booboo	injury, hurt	*owie	hurt
boom	fall	pantie	underpants
byebye	good-bye	pee	urine, urinate
choochoo	train	peekaboo	looking game
*cootchykoo	tickle	*peepee	urine, urinate
*dark+time	night, evening	*peeyou	smelly
doggy	dog	poo(p)	defecation, defecate
dolly	doll	*poopoo	defecation, defecate
*doodoo	feces	potty	toilet
*dumdum	stupid	rockabye	sleep
*ew	unpleasant	scrunch	crunch
*footie+ballie	football	*smoosh	smash
gidd(y)up	get moving	(t)eensy(w)eensy	little
goody	delight	(t)eeny(w)eeny	little
guck	unpleasant	*teetee	urine, urinate
*jammie	pajamas	titty	breast
*kiki	cat	tippytoe	on tips of toes
kitty	cat	tummy	stomach, belly
lookee	look yee!	ugh	unpleasant
*moo+cow	cow	*(wh)oopsadaisy	surprise or mistake

5.5.13   Homophones in Japanese

Because Japanese Kanji script provides a direct disambiguation of homophones, Japanese readers are accustomed to having the different meanings kept clearly separate. To preserve this in CHAT, one can place the English meaning after the Japanese form as in these examples of common Japanese homophones from the Japanese CHAT manual (Oshima-Takane & MacWhinney, 1995).

Table 10: Homophones in Japanese

Word	Meaning 1	Meaning 2
e	e(picture)	e(handle)
ga	ga(moth)	-
ka	ka(mosquito)	-
kara	kara(empty)	kara(shell)
ne	ne(price)	ne(root)
ni	ni(two)	-
no	no(field)	-
o	o(tail)	-
to	to(door)	-
wa	wa(circle)	-

In these examples, forms such as "ga" or "o" in the second column are not translated, because they are grammatical particles.

5.5.14   Punctuation in French and Italian

The standard use of the apostrophe to mark truncation is preserved in French and Italian. In French, when a word begins with a vowel, this leads in some cases to the disappearance of the final vowel of the preceding word, as in "l' ami" and not "le ami." In standard spelling, the vowel e is elided and the two words are linked together by an apostrophe without a space. When transcribing these forms into CHAT, it is important to add a space after the apostrophe, in order to allow for direct searching for the elided pronouns and articles and in order to make more accurate morpheme counts and analyses. In particular, the following strings must be followed by a space: c' , d' , j' , l' , m' , n' , qu' , s' , t' , and y' .

For similar reasons, the dashes that are used in words such as "est-ce" or "qu'est-ce" should be replaced with spaces. Thus, these forms should be transcribed as "est ce" and "qu' est ce." In other cases, such as "abat-jour," the French hyphen indicates a true compound and should be replaced by the plus symbol, as in "abat+jour."

5.5.15 Abbreviations in Dutch

Dutch makes extensive use of abbreviations in which vowels are often omitted leaving single consonants, which are merged with nearby words. For consistency of morphological analysis, it is best to transcribe these shortenings using the parenthesis notation, as follows:

Table 11: Abbreviations in Dutch

Abbreviation	CHAT form	Abbreviation	CHAT form
'k	(i)k	nie	nie(t)
'm	(he)m	es	e(en)s
'r	(e)r	'n	(ee)n
z'n	z(ij)n	's	(i)s
'b	(he)b	't	(he)t
'ns	(ee)ns	wa	wa(t)
'rin	(e)rin	da	da(t)
'raf	(e)raf	'weest	(ge)weest
'ruit	(e)ruit		
'rop	(e)rop		

Some forms that should probably remain with their standard apostrophes include 'smorgens, 'sochtends, 'savonds, 'snachts, and the apostrophe-s plural form.

6:   Morphemes

Some students of language learning are interested in studying the development of morphological markings and the concepts underlying those markings. CHAT provides two ways to conduct morphological analysis. Superficial morphological analysis can be conducted by breaking words into morphemes on the main line. This type of morphemicization on the main line is intended mostly for initial morphological analysis. For deeper analysis, particularly in languages other than English, the %mor line should be used instead. In this chapter, we discuss morphological analysis on the main line. For more extensive morphological analysis, you should use the MOR command to produce a %mor line.

The goal of morphological analysis on the main line is simply to indicate the component morphemes present in words. To do this, CHAT uses the symbols -, +, #, ~, &, and 0. These same six symbols are also used for parallel purposes on the %mor line.

6.1   Codes for Morphemicization

Suffix Marker —   -

A single dash is used to indicate the attachment of a suffix to a stem:

```
*ALL:   I like-ed dog-s.
```

Prefix Marker —   #

Prefixes are followed by a number sign, as in this example:

```
*AUS:   un#tie my shoe please.
```

Some common prefixes include: un#, re#, dis#, over#, under#, pre#, post#, inter#, quasi#, non#, and pseudo#. Of course, many of these occur only rarely in the speech of young children.

Compound Marker —   +

This symbol marks pieces of compounds or rote forms:

```
*MAR:   I like Star+Wars.
*EVE:   where Santa+Claus?
```

Compounds that are usually written as one word, such as "birthday" or "rainbow," should not be segmented. By default, the MLU command does not treat the plus symbol as a morpheme delimiter. This means that a compound such as "Santa+Claus" is treated as a single morpheme. If you want compounds to be treated as composed of multiple morphemes, you can use switches in the commands to control this feature of the analysis.

You may also want to use the compound marker to handle the treatment of what you consider to be unanalyzed forms. Depending on your theoretical viewpoint, these might include anything from words such as "all+right" to combinations such as "put+on." It is probably not a good idea to treat too many of the child's productions as compounds, because this tends to decrease legibility and may block the operation of the program, which is typically oriented toward working with standard words. More generally, the decision to count multiword strings as rote forms or unanalyzed chunks presupposes an extensive analysis of the individual child's productive uses. One way to deal with this is to create a separate dependent tier in which you transcribe words using the compound-form notation. You can then use this dependent tier as the input to analyses and even contrast analyses based on this tier with analyses based on just a standard main tier.

Because the dash is used in CHAT to indicate suffixation, it is important to avoid confusion between the standard use of the dash in compounds such as "blue-green" and the use of the dash in CHAT. To do this, use the compound marker to replace the dash or hyphen, as in "blue+green" instead of "blue-green." Similarly, French "la-bas" should be written as "la+bas."

Clitic Marker —   ~

The tilde can be used on the main line to indicate clitics. This can be done with suffixed clitics as in Italian *da~me~lo* "give me it" or with preposed clitics as in Italian *me~lo~dai* "he gives me it."

Fusion Marker —   &

If the transcriber wants to morphemicize irregular forms such as "sang," it is necessary to use the ampersand & to mark the fact that the past tense marking "-ed" has fused with the stem. Using this marker, "sang" is coded as in CHAT as "sing&ed" and "doesn't" is coded as "do&es-'nt." This use of the ampersand within words is quite different from its use at the beginning of words to mark phonological fragments.

Omitted Affix —   -0affix

The decision to code a word as missing is, as noted earlier, very difficult. However, the decision to code an affix as missing can be based on somewhat more solid criteria:

1.   -0ing: If a progressive auxiliary occurs with the verb and there is no "ing" as in "John is run," one can judge that there is a missing "-ing."

2.   -0ed: If a verb stem occurs by itself and the referent appears to be past tense, then there is sufficient reason to judge that there is a missing "-0ed."

3.   -0s: Omission of the plural on nouns is indicated when:

(a) a singular noun is preceded by any plural quantifier (two, some, many) or demonstrative (these, those),

(b) when the verbal auxiliary marks plurality of the subject (dog are running, dog were running),

(c) when the referent is plural in the context and there is no reason to believe that the child has selected out a single referent. It is admittedly difficult to apply the last of these three criteria.

4.   -0's: Omission of the possessive is most easily detected when two nouns that are not a standard compound occur together with no possessive and are serving as a constituent of the verb, as in "I found Mommy sock." However, when the two nouns occur without a verb, as in "Mommy sock," it is not possible to know whether there is a missing possessive.

Incorrectly Omitted Affix —   -0*

This code is much like the one described above. However, it also marks the fact that the omission is an error.

6.2   Standard Forms for Affixes and Clitics

In order to permit morphemic coding on the main line for English, we provide a full set of CHAT affix markers. Below we list the standard CHAT forms for the inflectional suffixes for English, some common derivational suffixes and prefixes, and the contracted auxiliaries and negatives. However, if you wish to conduct a serious morphosyntactic study of a corpus, we do not recommend that you use this form of quick-and-dirty main line coding. Instead, we recommend that you code words in their standard form on the main line and rely on the MOR command to create a full morphemic analysis on the %mor line.

Table 12: Inflectional Suffixes for English

Suffix	Function	Suffix	Function
-ed	past	-'s	possessive
-en	participle	-s'	plural possessive
-es	third singular	-s	plural
-ing	progressive	-'	zero possessive

Here are some examples of the use of these main line forms:

```
*MOT:   Bob-'s truck drop-ed.
*MOT:   the boy-s' truck is broke-en.
```

We also recommend against the use of derivational suffixes, because it is difficult to make consistent use of these markers. Given these recommendations, you may ask why we include these codes at all. They are included for the benefit of those who do not wish to conduct fuller analyses on their data, but who wish to have an initial approximation for measures like MLU, as described in the CLAN Manual.

Table 13: Derivational Prefixes for English

Prefix	Meaning	Prefix	Meaning
anti#	against	pre#	before
dis#	reversal	pro#	in favor of
ex#	previous	re#	repetitive
mis#	erroneously	un#	reversal

Table 14: Derivational Suffixes for English

Suffix	Function	Suffix	Function
-able	adjectivalizer	-(i)fy	verbalizer
-al	adjectivalizer	-(i)ty	nominalizer
-ary	adjectivalizer	-ize	verbalizer
-er	comparative	-less	without
-est	superlative	-ly	adverbializer
-ful	adjectivalizer	-ment	nominalizer
-ic	adjectivalizer	-ness	nominalizer
-ie	diminutive	-(t)ion	nominalizer
		-y	adjectivalizer

6.3   Contractions

The coding of contractions in English is particularly problematic. Words like "don't" and "can't" can be entered in their standard form on the main line, because they will be unambiguously interpreted by MOR. In addition, the following suffixes can be used in their standard form, because they are unambiguous.

Table 15: Contractions for English

Contraction	Long Form	Contraction	Long Form
-'d	would, had	-'ll	will
-'does	does	-'m	am
-'has	has	-'nt	not
-'is	is	-'re	are
-'iscop	is (cop)	-'us	us (let's)
-'isaux	is (aux)	-'ve	have

These forms can be used as parts of words, as in "John'll", or as suffixes, as in John-'ll. Either form will work. However, the final contracted forms of /s/ and /d/ come from several sources, including "has," "is-auxiliary," "is-copula," "did," "had," and "could." In order to avoid this ambiguity, we recommend this form of transcription in these cases:

```
*MOT:    John (i)s going home.
*MOT:    John (ha)s gone home.
```

For those who like this form of transcription, it can be extended to include:

```
*MOT:    Bob (wi)ll have to get some milk.
*MOT:    I do n(o)t want any bananas.
*MOT:    you can n(o)t get the ball now.
```

Consistent use of this form of representation has many advantages. It allows a count such as MLU to represent the lengths of utterances in terms of conceptual words without being distorted by phonological assimilations. However, some transcribers may wish to represent contractions as a part of the word. In this case, they will need to use the following forms:

```
*MOT:    Bob-'ll have to get some milk.
*MOT:    I do-'nt want any bananas.
*MOT:    you can-'nt get the ball now.
*MOT:    John-'is going home.
*MOT:    John-'has gone home.
```

Suffixes can be combined in words such as "learn-er-s" or "un#think-able-ity." Words with special learner-form markers of the type given on page 32 can also be morphemicized. Thus, the plural of the word "bingbing@c" could be given as either "bingbings@c" or "bingbing@c-s." The letter "m" can be pluralized in the long form "m@l-s" or the short form "m-s."

7: Utterances

The basic units of CHAT transcription are the morpheme, the word, and the utterance. In addition, some transcribers may be interested in marking tone units. In the previous two chapters we examined principles for transcribing words and morphemes. In this chapter we examine ways of delimiting utterances and tone units.

7.1   One Utterance or Many?

Early child language is rich with repetitions. For example, a child may often say the same word or group of words eight times in a row without changes. The CHAT system provides mechanisms for coding these repetitions into single utterances. However, at the earliest stages, it may be misleading to try to compact these multiple attempts into a single line. Consider five alternative ways of transcribing a series of repeated words.

1.   Simple transcription of the words as several items in a single utterance:

   ```
   *CHI:   milk milk milk milk.
   ```

2.   Transcription of the words as items in a single utterance, separated by commas:

   ```
   *CHI:   milk, milk, milk, milk.
   ```

3.   Transcription of the words as items in a single utterance, but separated by prosodic delimiters (see page 61):

   ```
   *CHI:   milk -, milk -, milk -, milk.
   ```

4.   Treatment of the words as a series of attempts to repeat the single word:

   ```
   *CHI:   milk [/] milk [/] milk [/] milk.
   ```

5.   Treatment of the words as separate utterances:

   ```
   *CHI:   milk.
   *CHI:   milk.
   *CHI:   milk.
   *CHI:   milk.
   ```

These five forms of transcription will lead to markedly different analytic outcomes. Consider the ways in which the five forms will lead to different results in the MLU command. The first three forms will all be counted as having one utterance with four morphemes for an MLU of 4.0. The fourth form will be counted as having one utterance with one morpheme for an MLU of 1.0. The fifth form will be counted as having four utterances each with one morpheme for an MLU of 1.0.

Admittedly, not all analyses depend crucially on the computation of MLU, but problems with deciding how to compute MLU point to deeper issues in transcription and analysis. In order to compute MLU, one has to decide what is a word and what is an utterance and these are two of the biggest decisions that one has to make when transcribing and analyzing child language. In this sense, the computation of MLU serves as a methodological trip wire for the consideration of these two deeper issues. Other analyses, including lexical, syntactic, and discourse analyses also require that these decisions be made clearly and consistently. However, because of its conceptual simplicity, the MLU index places these problems into the sharpest focus.

The first three forms of transcription all make the basic assumption that there is a single utterance with four morphemes. Given the absence of any clear syntactic relation between the four words, it seems difficult to defend use of this form of transcription, unless the transcriber explicitly declares that the data should not be used to compute syntactic and sentential measures.

The fourth form of transcription treats the successive productions of the word "milk" as repeated attempts to produce a single word. This form of transcription makes sense if there is clear evidence that the child was having trouble saying the word. If there is no evidence that the word is really a repetition, it would seem best to use the fifth form of transcription. Studies of early child syntax have emphasized the extent to which the child is subject to constraints on utterance length (Bloom & Lahey, 1973; Bloom, Lightbown, & Hood, 1975; Gerken, 1991; Gerken, Landau, & Remez, 1990). However, if one decides to count all repetitions of single words as full productions, it would seem that one is overestimating the degree of syntactic integration being achieved by the child. On the other hand, some researchers have argued that treatment of words as separate utterances in the earliest stages of language acquisition tends to underestimate the level of syntactic control being achieved by the child (Branigan, 1979; Elbers & Wijnen, 1993).

CLAN provides a partial solution to this dilemma. In cases where the researcher wants to use separate utterances for each word, the commands will treat each utterance as having a single morpheme. If the fourth form of transcription with repetition marks is used, the commands will, by default, treat the utterance as having only one morpheme. However, there is an option that allows the user to override this default and treat each word as a separate morpheme. This then allows the researcher to compute two different MLU values. The analysis with repetitions excluded could be viewed as the one that emphasizes syntactic structure and the one with repetitions included could be viewed as the one that emphasizes productivity measures.

The example we have been discussing involves a simple case of word repetition. In other cases, researchers may want to group together nonrepeated words for which there is only partial evidence of syntactic or semantic combination. Consider the contrast between these next two examples. In the first example, the presence of the conjunction "and" motivates treatment of the words as a syntactic combination:

```
*CHI:    red, yellow, blue, and white.
```

However, without the conjunction, the words are best treated as separate utterances:

```
*CHI:    red.
*CHI:    yellow.
*CHI:    blue.
*CHI:    white.
```

As the child gets older, the solidification of intonational patterns and syntactic structures will give the transcriber more reason to group words together into utterances and to code retracings and repetitions as parts of larger utterances.

A somewhat separate but related issue is the treatment of interactional markers and other "communicators" such as "yes," "sure," "well," and "now." In general, it seems best to group these markers together with the utterances to which they are most closely bound intonationally. However, it only makes sense to do this if the utterances are contiguous in discourse. Here are some examples:

```
*CHI:    no, Mommy no go.
*CHI:    no Mommy go.
*CHI:    no # Mommy go.
```

However, in other cases, it makes sense to transcribe "no" by itself:

```
*CHI:    no
*MOT:    why not?
*CHI:    Mommy go.
```

7.2   Discourse Repetition

In the previous section, we discussed problems involved in deciding whether a group of words should be viewed as one utterance or as several. This issue moves into the background when the word repetitions are broken up by the conversational interactions or by the child's own actions. Consider this example:

```
*MOT:    what do you drink for breakfast?
*CHI:    milk.
*MOT:    and what do you drink for lunch?
*CHI:    milk.
*MOT:    how about for dinner?
*CHI:    milk.
*MOT:    and what is your favorite thing to drink at bedtime?
*CHI:    milk.
```

Or the child may use a single utterance repeatedly, but each time with a slightly different purpose. For example, when putting together a puzzle, the child may pick up a piece and ask:

```
*CHI:    where does this piece go?
```

This may happen nine times in succession. In both of these examples, it seems unfair from a discourse point of view to treat each utterance as a mere repetition. Instead, each is functioning independently as a full communication. One may want to mark the fact that the lexical material is repeated, but this should not affect other quantitative measures.

7.3   Basic Utterance Terminators

The basic CHAT utterance terminators are the period, the question mark, and the exclamation mark. CHAT requires that there be only one utterance on each main line. In order to mark this, each utterance must end with one of these three utterance terminators. However, a single main line utterance may extend for several computer lines, as in this example:

```
*CHI:   this.
*MOT:   if this is the one you want, you
        will have to take your spoon out of the other one.
```

The utterance in this main tier extends for two lines in the computer file. When it is necessary to continue an utterance on the main tier onto a second line, the second line *must begin with a tab.* CLAN is set to expect no more than 2000 characters in each main line, dependent tier, or header line.

Period —   .

A period marks the end of an unmarked (declarative) utterance. Here are some examples of unmarked utterances:

```
*SAR:   I got cold.
*SAR:   pickle.
*SAR:   no.
```

For correct functioning of CLAN, periods should be eliminated from abbreviations. Thus "Mrs." should be written as "Mrs" and "E.T." should become "E+t". Only proper nouns and the word "I" and its contractions are capitalized. Words that begin sentences are not capitalized.

Question Mark —   ?

The question mark indicates the end of a question. A question is an utterance that uses a wh-question word, subject–verb inversion, or a tag question ending. Here is an example of a question:

```
*FAT: is that a carrot?
```

The question mark can also be used after a declarative sentence when it is spoken with the rising intonation of a question.

Exclamation Point — !

An exclamation point marks the end of an imperative or emphatic utterance. Here is an example of an exclamation:

```
*MOT:   sit down!
```

If this utterance were to be conveyed with final rising contour, it would instead be:

```
*MOT:   sit down?
```

7.4   Tone Unit Marking

The terminators discussed in this section and the next are chiefly relevant to those researchers who wish to mark prosodic groupings in discourse. In spoken language, words cluster into tone units (Crystal, 1969, 1975). Each tone group has a stressed syllable as its nucleus. Additional syllables may cluster around this nucleus with a variety of intonational contours. In order to indicate the grouping of words into tone units and the shape of intonational contours, transcribers need to mark: (a) the identity of the accented syllable, (b) the identity of stressed syllables, and (c) the direction of the tone on the accented or nuclear syllable. If one is writing out sentences by hand, the nicest way of transcribing tone movements is to use arrow symbols as in Crystal (1975), Fletcher (1985), or Svartvik et al. (1980) These symbols could be supplemented by a musical notation scheme of the type used by Bolinger (1986) or Crystal (1969). However, none of these systems of notation can be inserted directly in computer files based on ASCII code. Although the system of Svartvik et al. is designed for computer use, it goes outside the boundaries of ASCII code and requires special purpose printing routines. In ASCII, one cannot place an arrow over a letter or raise a word higher on the page by turning the platen of a typewriter. Instead, we need to devise a set of codes that can represent the distinctions used by workers such as Bolinger, Crystal, Fletcher, and Svartvik et al. while still obeying the constraints of the ASCII system. In CHAT, these codes are available in two forms. In this chapter, we discuss a set of codes for main line coding of tone units and pitch movement. A parallel set of symbols exist for coding with UNIBET on the %pho line. The marking of stressed syllables is handled on page 63.

7.4.1   Terminating Tone Units

The three basic terminators can be further qualified to mark particular intonational contours. Those tone unit terminators which end with one of these three symbols are treated as utterance terminators when they occur at the end of the main line in CHAT. This means that the first four contours cited later are also treated by CLAN as utterance terminators.

Rising Contour —   -?

This symbol is used to indicate final rising contour. It is placed at the end of the tone unit, but is understood as applying to the tone group clustered about the preceding accented syllable or nucleus. This is the intonation pattern typically found in questions. CLAN treats it as an utterance terminator.

Exclamation Contour —   -!

By analogy with the previous symbol, this symbol is used to indicate final exclamation contour. CLAN treats it as an utterance terminator.

Falling Contour —   -.

This symbol is used to indicate final falling contour. This is the standard intonation pattern of declarative sentences. CLAN treats it as an utterance terminator.

Rise–Fall Contour —   -'.

This symbol is used to indicate final rise–fall contour. CLAN treats it as an utterance terminator.

Fall–Rise Contour —   -,.

This symbol is used to indicate final fall–rise contour. CLAN treats it as an utterance terminator.

7.4.2   Nonfinal Tone Markers

If the final punctuation on a tone unit does not include an utterance terminator, CLAN treats it as a terminated utterance. Thus, the following three symbols can be used to indicate tone units that do not terminate utterances.

Level Nonfinal Contour —   -,

This symbol is used to indicate nonfinal level contour. This contour often indicates nonfinality and is sometimes represented by a comma. CLAN does not treat it as an utterance terminator. If a series of phrases are joined together into a single utterance, this symbol or the previous one should be used to indicate nonfinal contour. Following Fletcher (1985), these terminal contours and stress symbols can be combined as in this example. (The use of slashes is discussed in the following section on page 63.)

```
*SON:   /you play -, /snakes and ladders -, //me -.
*FAT:   yes -, /I'll play -, /snakes and //ladders -.
*FAT:   /where -, //is it -?
*SON:   /over //there -.
```

```
*FAT:    /will you //get it -?
*SON:    and //that -. # and //that -.
*FAT:    //yes -.
```

There are no examples in this passage of words with stress or accent on the second syllable. For such words, the slashes would be placed right in the middle of the word. CLAN can be instructed to ignore the slashes and the contour markers when performing morphemic searches.

Falling Nonfinal Contour —   -_

This symbol is used to indicate a low or falling nonfinal contour. Like the previous symbol, it is not treated by CLAN as an utterance terminator.

Low Level Contour —   -

This symbol is used to indicate a low level contour. It is not treated as an utterance terminator.

Rising Nonfinal Contour —   -'

This symbol is used to indicate a rising or high nonfinal contour. Like the previous symbol, it is not treated by CLAN as an utterance terminator.

7.5   Prosody Within Words

CHAT also provides codes for marking stressing, lengthening, and pausing within words. The stressing of a particular word can be indicated in two ways. One way is to mark the stress levels of particular stressed syllables. Three levels of stress marking are available for this purpose.

Stressed Syllable —   /

A single forward slash is used to indicate the placement of stress on the following syllable. It is placed right inside the word, as in **rhi/noceros.**

Primary Stressed Syllable —   //

A double slash indicates the placement of strong nuclear accent on the following syllable. This is the nuclear accent that forms the center of a tone group. If the word "rhinoceros" is the center of a tone group, it would be marked as **rhi//noceros.**

Contrastively Stressed Syllable —   ///

A triple slash is used to indicate very strong contrastive stress, as in **rhi///noceros.**

A second way of marking stress refers not to a particular syllable but to a word or a group of words. This way of indicating stress uses the symbols [!] and [!!]. This method is discussed on page 70.

Lengthened Syllable —   :

A colon within a word indicates the lengthening or drawling of a syllable, as in this example:

```
    MOT:    baby want bana:nas?
```

Pause Between Syllables —   ::

A pause between syllables may be indicated by two colons, as in this example:

```
    MOT:    is that a rhi::noceros?
```

Be careful not to confuse a pause in the middle of a word with lengthening or drawling. There is no special CHAT symbol for a filled pause. Instead words like "uh" and "um" are used to mark filled pauses. The exact written form of these fillers is given on page 40.

Blocking —   ^

Speakers with marked language disfluencies often engage in a form of word attack known as "blocking" (Bernstein-Ratner et al., 1996). This form of word attack is marked by a caret or up arrow placed directly before the word.

7.6   The Comma

Transcriptions of spontaneous interactions have often tended to overuse the comma. It has often been used to mark five major utterance features at once: syntactic juncture, conceptual juncture, pausing, intonational drop, and even clause boundary. CHAT attempts to mark each of these functions differently. For example, pausing is marked by #; utterance and clause boundaries are marked by periods and question marks; and a level intonational contour is marked by the -, symbol. Once all of these functions have been broken out, there is then a clear and legitimate role for the comma as a marker of the standard forms of syntactic juncture, such as appositives and nonrestrictive relatives.

Syntactic Juncture — ,

The comma is used to mark syntactic juncture in standard English orthography. However, the comma and syntactic juncture are often closely associated with slight pauses and level to falling intonations at the end of phrasal groups.

Tag Question — „

A double comma can be used to mark tag questions for easy retrieval.

```
*MOT:   you're coming home soon,, aren't you?
```

7.7   Pauses

Transcribers frequently want to be able to mark the pauses that occur both within and between tone units. Pauses that are marked only by silence are coded on the main line with the symbol #.

Unfilled Pause — #

Longer pauses can be represented as ## and a very long pause as ###. Alternatively, you can add an estimate of pause length by adding a word after the # symbol as in #long. This example illustrates these forms:

```
*SAR:   I don't # know -.
*SAR:   #long what do you ### think -?
```

If you want to be exact, you can code the exact length of the pauses, following the # in minutes, seconds, and parts of seconds. The minutes are placed before a colon with the seconds following the colon. Parts of seconds are given after an underscore symbol. If there is no colon, it is assumed that the pause lasts under a minute. If there is no underscore, it is assumed that milliseconds are not being measured. However, a number for the seconds is obligatory. The following example codes pauses lasting .5 seconds, 1 minute and 13.41 seconds, and 2 seconds, respectively:

```
*SAR:   I don't #0_5 know -.
*SAR:   #1:13_41 what do you #2 think -?
```

Researchers may wish to distinguish fluent pauses from disfluent pauses. Fluent pauses occur at grammatical junctures where commas are general used. They also occur at other sites that are determined by discourse rules. Pauses that occur elsewhere are typically considered to be disfluent. Disfluent pauses can be marked with the symbol #d. Making overt the distinction between fluent and disfluent pauses helps to guarantee the correct use of a marker for fluent pauses. Here are some examples:

```
*CHI:    well -.
*CHI:    # how I felt about that -?
*CHI:    I had to //put #d in my arms -.
*CHI:    because I had to //put on a special coat -.
*MOT:    we'll see -.
*MOT:    #long maybe to//morrow -.
*CHI:    my brother does-'nt //sleep #dlong so much now -.
```

Lengthening —   **-:**

This symbol is used to indicate lengthening or drawling of the previous word.

7.8   Special Utterance Terminators

In addition to the three basic utterance terminators, CHAT provides a series of more complex utterance terminators to mark various special functions. These special terminators all begin with the + symbol and end with one of the three basic utterance terminators.

Trailing Off —   **+...**

The trailing off or incompletion marker is the terminator for an incomplete, but not interrupted, utterance. Trailing off occurs when speakers shift attention away from what they are saying, sometimes even forgetting what they were going to say. Usually the trailing off is followed by a pause in the conversation. After this lull, the speaker may continue with another utterance or a new speaker may produce the next utterance. Here is an example of an uncompleted utterance:

```
*SAR:    smells good enough for +...
*SAR:    what is that?
```

If the speaker does not really get a chance to trail off before being interrupted by another speaker, then use the interruption marker +/. rather than the incompletion symbol. Do not use the incompletion marker to indicate either simple pausing #, repetition [/], or retracing [//]. Note that utterance fragments coded in this way will be counted as complete utterances for analyses such as MLU, MLT, and CHAINS. If your intention is to avoid treating these fragments as complete utterances, then you should use the symbol [/-] discussed later.

Trailing Off of a Question —   **+..?**

If the utterance that is being trailed off has the shape of a question, then this symbol should be used.

Question With Exclamation — +!?

When a question is produced with great amazement or puzzlement, it can be coded using this symbol. The utterance is understood to constitute a question syntactically and pragmatically, but an exclamation intonationally.

Interruption — +/.

This symbol is used for an utterance that is incomplete because one speaker is interrupted by another speaker. Here is an example of an interruption:

```
*MOT:    what did you +/.
*SAR:    Mommy.
*MOT:    +, with your spoon.
```

Some researchers may wish to distinguish between an invited interruption and an uninvited interruption. An invited interruption may occur when one speaker is prompting his addressee to complete the utterance. This should be marked by the ++ symbol for other-completion, which is given later. Uninvited interruptions should be coded with the symbol +/. at the end of the utterance. A particular advantage of using +/. instead of +... is that programs like MLU are able to piece together the two segments and treat it as a single utterance when a segment with +/. is then followed, after the intervening interruption, by a segment beginning with +,
(XXX this clarification was added on January 18, 2000)

Interruption of a Question — +/?

If the utterance that is being interrupted has the shape of a question, then this symbol should be used.

Self-Interruption — +//.

Some researchers wish to be able to distinguish between incompletions involving a trailing off and incompletions involving an actual self-interruption. When an incompletion is not followed by further material from the same speaker, the +... symbol should always be selected. However, when the speaker breaks off an utterance and starts up another, the +//. symbol can be used, as in this example:

```
*SAR:    smells good enough for +//.
*SAR:    what is that?
```

There is no hard and fast way of distinguishing cases of trailing off from self-interruption. For this reason, some researchers prefer to avoid making the distinction. Researchers who wish to avoid making the distinction should use only the +... symbol.

Self-Interrupted Question —   +//?

If the utterance being self-interrupted is a question, you can use the +//? symbol.

Quotation on Next Line —   +"/.

During story reading and similar activities, a great deal of talk may involve direct quotation. In order to mark off this material as quoted, a special symbol can be used, as in the following example:

```
*CHI:    and then the little bear said +"/.
*CHI:    +" please give me all of your honey.
*CHI:    +" if you do, I'll carry you on my back.
```

The use of the +"/. symbol is linked to the use of the +" symbol. Breaking up quoted material in this way allows us to maintain the rule that each separate utterance should be on a separate line. This form of notation is only used when the material being quoted is a complete clause or sentence. It is not needed when single words are being quoted in noncomplement position. In those cases the ["] symbol can be used. Note that, from the viewpoint of syntactic analysis, the first line in the previous example is not a complete utterance, because the complement is contained in the material quoted on the following lines.

Quotation Precedes —   +".

This symbol is used when the material being directly quoted precedes the main clause, as in the following example:

```
*CHI:    +" please give me all of your honey.
*CHI:    the little bear said +".
```


7.9   Utterance Linkers

There is another set of symbols that can be used to mark other aspects of the ways in which utterances link together into turns and discourse. These symbols are not utterance terminators, but utterance initiators, or rather "linkers." They indicate various ways in which an utterance fits in with an earlier utterance. Each of these symbols begins with the + sign.

Quoted Utterance —   +"

This symbol is used in conjunction with the +"/. and +". symbols discussed earlier. It is placed at the beginning of an utterance that is being directly quoted.

Quick Uptake —   +^

Sometimes an utterance of one speaker follows quickly on the heels of the last utterance of the preceding speaker without the customary short pause between utterances. An example of this is:

```
*MOT:   why did you go?
*SAR:   +^ I really didn't.
```

Lazy Overlap Marking —   +<

If you don't want to mark the exact beginning and end of overlaps between speakers and only want to indicate the fact that two turns overlap, you can use this code at the beginning of the utterance that overlaps a previous utterance, as in this example:

```
*CHI:   we were taking them home.
*MOT:   +< they had to go in here.
```

This marking simply indicate that the mother's utterance overlaps the previous child utterance. It does not indicate how much of the two utterances overlap. For more precise overlap marking, use the scoped form of overlap marking given on page 74.

Self-Completion —   +,

The symbol +, can be used at the beginning of a main tier line to mark the completion of an utterance after an interruption. In the following example, it marks the completion of an utterance by CHI after interruption by EXP. Note that the incompleted utterance must be terminated with the incompletion marker.

```
*CHI:   so after the tower +...
*EXP:   yeah.
*CHI:   +, I go straight ahead.
```

Other-Completion —   ++

A variant form of the +, symbol is the ++ symbol which marks "latching" or the completion of another speaker's utterance, as in the following example:

```
*HEL:   if Bill had known +...
*WIN:   ++ he would have come.
```

Clause Delimiter —   [c]

If you wish to conduct analyses such as MLU and MLT based on clauses rather than utterances as the basic unit of analysis, you should mark the end of each clause with this symbol.

8:   Scoped Symbols

Up to this point, the symbols we have discussed are inserted at single points in the transcript. They refer to events occurring at particular points during the dialogue. There is another major class of symbols that refers not to particular points in the transcript, but to stretches of speech. These symbols are enclosed in square brackets and the material to which they relate can be enclosed in angle brackets. The material in the square brackets functions as a descriptor of the material in angle brackets. If a scoped symbol applies only to the single word preceding it, the angle brackets need not be marked, because CLAN considers that the material in square brackets refers to a single preceding word when there are no angle brackets. Depending on the nature of the material in the square brackets, the material in the angle brackets may be automatically excluded from certain types of analysis, such as MLU counts and so forth. Scoped symbols are useful for marking a wide variety of relations, including paralinguistics, explanations, and retracings.

8.1   Audio and Video Time Marks

In order to link segments of the transcript to stretches of digitized audio and video, CHAT uses the following notation:

Time Alignment —   •%mov:"file.mov"_0_1073•

This marker can include either %mov information for a digitized video file or %snd information for a digitized audio file. The numbers represent time in milliseconds. If you use the escape-4 command in the editor, all of this information is hidden and you see a single bullet. Each set of time alignment information has an implicit scope that includes all of the material to the left up to the next set of bullets.

8.2   Paralinguistic Scoping

Paralinguistic Material —   [=! text]

Paralinguistic events, such as "coughing," "laughing," or "yelling" can be marked by using square brackets, the =! symbol, a space, and then text describing the event.

```
    *CHI:    that's mine [=! cries].
```

This means that the child cries while saying the word "mine." If the child cries throughout, the transcription would be:

```
    *CHI:    <that's mine> [=! cries].
```

In order to indicate crying with no particular vocalization, you can use the 0 symbol, as in this example:

```
*CHI:   0 [=! crying].
```

However, use of the 0 symbol is not necessary and many transcribers find it distracting. The above example could just as well be coded as simply:

```
*CHI:   [=! crying].
```

Alternatively, laughing and other similar vocalizations can be marked using the %par line which is discussed later. This same format of [=! text] can also be used to describe prosodic characteristics such as "glissando" or "shouting" that are best characterized with full English words. Paralinguistic effects such as soft speech, yelling, singing, laughing, crying, whispering, whimpering, and whining can also be noted in this way. For a full set of these terms and details on their usage, see Crystal (1969) or Trager (1958). Here is another example:

```
*NAO:   watch out [=! laughs].
```

Stressing —   [!]

This symbol can be used without accompanying angle brackets to indicate that the preceding word is stressed. The angle brackets can also mark the stressing of a string of words, as in this example:

```
*MOT:   Billy, would you please <take your shoes off> [!].
```

Contrastive Stressing —   [!!]

This symbol can be used without accompanying angle brackets to indicate that the preceding word is contrastively stressed. If a whole string of words is contrastively stressed, they should be enclosed in angle brackets.

8.3   Explanations and Alternatives

Explanation —   [= text]

This symbol is used for brief explanations on the text tier. This symbol is helpful for specifying the deictic identity of objects and people.

```
*MOT:   don't look in there [= closet]!
```

Explanations can be more elaborate as in this example:

```
*ROS:   you don't scare me anymore [= the command "don't scare me any-
        more!"].
```

An alternative form for transcribing this is:

```
*ROS:    you don't scare any more.
%exp:    means to issue the imperative "Don't scare me anymore!"
```

Replacement —   [: text]

On page 31 we discussed the use of a variety of nonstandard forms such as "gonna" and "hafta." On page 52 we examined ways of morphemicizing words directly on the main line. However, words such as "gonna" and irregular forms such as "went" cannot easily be morphemicized as they stand. In order to morphemicize such words, the transcriber can use a replacement symbol that allows CLAN to substitute a morphemicized form for the form actually produced. Here is an example:

```
*BEA:    when ya gonna [: go-ing to] stop doin(g) that?
*CHA:    whyncha [: why do-'nt you] just be quiet!
```

In this example, "gonna" is followed by its morphemicized replacement in brackets. The colon that follows the first bracket tells CLAN that the material in brackets should replace the preceding word. There must be a space following the colon, in order to keep this symbol separate from other symbols that use letters after the colon. This example also illustrates two other ways in which CHAT and CLAN deal with nonstandard forms. The lexical item "ya" is treated as a lexical item distinct from "you." However, the semantic equivalence between "ya" and "you" is maintained by the formalization of a list of dialectal spelling variations. The string "doin(g)" is treated by CLAN as if it were "doing." This is done by simply having the programs ignore the parentheses, unless they are given instructions to pay attention to them, as discussed in in the CLAN manual. From the viewpoint of CLAN, a form like "doin(g)" is much like an incomplete form such as "broth(er)."

In order for replacement to function properly, nothing should be placed between the replacing string and the string to be replaced. For example, one should use the form:

```
go-ed [: went] [*]
```

rather than:

```
go-ed [*] [: went]
```

Translation —   [:=x text]

This symbol is used to translate words spoken in a secondary language. Here is an example from Leopold (1949):

```
*HIL:    spiel@s [:=g game] house, knock down.
```

There is no space here between the colon and the equals sign. In this example, the German word *Spiel* (game) is first given a special form marker @s which indicates that it is a second-language form. Then the English translation is given in brackets. The :=g symbol indicates that the word comes from German. If there are several languages being mixed in a transcript, each can be given its own letter, but this must be marked in the 00readme.cdc file.

Alternative Transcription — [=? text]

Sometimes it is difficult to choose between two possible transcriptions for a word or group of words. In that case an alternative transcription can be indicated in this way:

```
*CHI:   we want <one or two> [=? one too].
```

Dependent Tier on Main Line — [%xxx: text]

The various dependent tiers discussed on page 81 can be placed directly on the main line. This is useful when it is important to refer to a particular set of words, rather than the utterance as a whole, as in this example:

```
*RES:   would all of you <who have not had seconds>
        [%gpx: looks at Timmy] come up to the front of the line?
```

Comment on Main Line — [% text]

Instead of placing comment material on a separate %com line, it is possible to place comments directly on the main line using the % symbol in brackets. Here is an example of this usage:

```
*CHI:   I really wish you wouldn't
        [% said with strong raising of eyebrows] do that.
```

A word of warning regarding comments on the main line. Overuse of this particular notational form can make a transcript difficult to read and analyze. Because placing a comment directly onto the main line tends to highlight it, this form should be used only for material that is crucial to the understanding of the main line.

Quotation Mark — ["]

This symbol marks a metalinguistic reference to a word or phrase. The metalinguistic reference must be surrounded by angle brackets, if it is more than a single word long. Here is an example of its use:

```
*MAR:   what does <unca banana> ["] mean?
```

This symbol is not intended for use in marking complete direct quotations. When a speaker cites a whole utterance from some other speaker as quoted, use the +"/. and +" symbols discussed on page 66.

Code on Main Line —   **[$text]**

We do not recommend that you include codes on the main line. However, if you find it necessary to place codes directly onto the main line, you should enclose them in square brackets. By default, they will apply to the immediately preceding word. If you want them to refer to a longer stretch of material, you should enclose that material in angle brackets. This form of notation is used by the SALTIN command to translate in-line SALT codes. Here is an example:

```
*ADA:   All of them [$TRO] go in here.
```

Best Guess —   **[?]**

Often audiotapes are hard to hear because of interference from room noise, recorder malfunction, vocal qualities, and so forth. Nonetheless, transcribers may think that, through the noise, they can recognize what is being said. The fact that there is some residual uncertainty about this "best guess" is indicated by using this symbol to mark either the single preceding word or the previous group of words enclosed in angle brackets.

```
*SAR:   I want a frog [?].
```

In this example, the word that is unclear is "frog." In general, when there is a symbol in square brackets that takes scoping and there are no preceding angle brackets, then the single preceding word is the scope. When more than one word is unclear, you can surround the unclear portion in angle brackets as in the following example:

```
*SAR:   <going away with my mommy> [?] ?
```

8.4   Retracing and Overlap

Overlap Follows —   **[>]**

During the course of a conversation, speakers often talk at the same time. Transcribing these interactions can be trying. This and the following two symbols are designed to help sort out this difficult transcription task. The "overlap follows" symbol indicates that the text enclosed in angle brackets is being said at the same time as the following speaker's bracketed speech. They are talking at the same time. This code must be used in combination with the "overlap precedes" symbol, as in this example:

```
*MOT:   no # Sarah # you have to <stop doing that> [>] !
*SAR:   <Mommy I don't like this> [<].
*SAR:   it is nasty.
```

Using these overlap indicators does not preclude making a visual indication of overlap in the following way:

```
*MOT:   no # Sarah # you have to <stop doing that> [>] !
*SAR:                        <Mommy I don't like this> [<].
*SAR:   it is nasty.
```

CLAN ignores the series of spaces, treating them as if they were a single space.

Overlap Precedes —   [<]

The "overlap precedes" symbol indicates that the text enclosed in angle brackets is being said at the same time as the preceding speaker's bracketed speech. This code must be used in combination with the "overlap follows" symbol. Sometimes several overlaps occur in a single sentence. It is then necessary to use numbers to identify these overlaps, as in this example:

```
*SAR:   and the <doggy was> [>1] really cute and
        it <had to go> [>2] into bed.
*MOT:   <why don't you> [<1] ?
*MOT:   <maybe we could> [<2].
```

If this sort of intense overlapping continues, it may be necessary to continue to increment the numbers as long as needed to keep everything straight. However, once one whole turn passes with no overlaps, the number counters can be reinitialized to "1."

Sometimes it is necessary to break up the standard flow of the interaction in order to code utterances on separate lines. For example, the following transcription is not legal in CHAT:

```
*SAR:   <I +/.
*EXP:   that's great.
*MOT:   +, bought a> [//] I just bought a helmet.
```

Instead, this passage should be transcribed as:

```
*SAR:   <I [>] bought a> [//] I just bought a helmet.
*EXP:   [<] that's great.
```

In the last analysis, researchers who want to capture overlaps in absolutely full detail should rely on the facilities of "sonic CHAT" that are described for the editor, rather than attempting to capture overlaps by using complex embeddings of pair delimiters.

Overlap Follows and Precedes —   <text> [<>]

This symbol indicates that the text enclosed in angle brackets is being overlapped by the bracketed speech of the following speaker and by the bracketed utterance of the preceding speaker. It must be used in conjunction with the previous two symbols to indicate the overlapped utterances of more than two speakers. The three symbols, used together, would look like this:

```
    *ROS:   well then # four +/.
    *MAR:   hey wait.
    *MAR:   you were <scared> [>].
    *ROS:   +, [//] <five> [<>]
    *MAR:   <I> [<] wasn't really scared.
```

Using spacing to provide additional clarity, these overlaps could be represented in this way:

```
    *ROS:   well then # four +/.
    *MAR:   hey wait.
    *MAR:   you were <scared> [>]
    *ROS:   +,           [//] <five> [<>]
    *MAR:    <I> [<] wasn't really scared.
```

Constructing transcripts with this careful spatial representation of overlap is a time-consuming business. However, if you want to include a visual representation of this type, it is best to do so using the space bar, rather than tabs, because using tabs in the middle of the line can cause problems for CLAN.

Overlap Enumeration —   **[>N] [<N]**

When there are several overlapping overlaps, you can use a number N to mark which pieces are overlapped. Here is an example:

```
   *CHI:   If I had taken <all of my medicine> [>1], I would have gotten
           <sick from the tablets>[>2].
   *ADU:   <why wouldn't you>[<1}, <since you had it> [<2}.
```

Retracing Without Correction —   **[/]**

Often speakers repeat words or even whole phrases (Goldman-Eisler, 1968; MacWhinney & Osser, 1977). The [/] symbol is used in those cases when a speaker begins to say something, stops and then repeats the earlier material without change. The material being retraced is enclosed in angle brackets. If there are no angle brackets, CLAN assumes that only the preceding word is being repeated. In a retracing without correction, it is necessarily the case that the material in angle brackets is the same as the material immediately following the [/] symbol. Here is an example of this:

```
   *BET:   <I wanted> [/] I wanted to invite Margie.
```

If there are pauses and fillers between the initial material and the retracing, they should be placed after the retracing symbol, as in:

```
   *HAR:   it's [/] # um # it's [/] it's like # a um # dog.
```

When a word or group of words is repeated several times with no fillers, all of the repetitions except for the last are placed into a single retracing, as in this example:

```
*HAR:    <it's it's it's> [/] it's like # a um # dog.
```

By default, all of the CLAN commands except MLU, MLT, and MODREP include repeated material. This default can be changed by using the +r6 switch. An alternative way
of indicating several repetitions of a single word uses this form:

```
*HAR:    it's(*4) like # a um # dog.
```

This form indicates the fact that a word has been repeated four times. If this form is
used, it is not possible to get a count of the repetitions to be added to MLU. However, because this is not usually desirable anyway, there are good reasons to use this more compact
form when single words are repeated. For some illustrations of the use of this type of coding
for the study of disfluencies such as stuttering, consult Bernstein Ratner, Rooney, and
MacWhinney (1996).

Retracing With Correction —   [//]

This symbol is used when a speaker starts to say something, stops, repeats the basic
phrase, changes the syntax but maintains the same idea. Usually, the correction moves closer to the standard form, but sometimes it moves away from it. The material being retraced
is enclosed in angle brackets. If there are no angle brackets, CLAN assumes that only the
preceding word is being retraced. In retracing with correction, it is necessarily true that the
material in the angle brackets is different from what follows the retracing symbol. Here is
an example of this:

```
*BET:    <I wanted> [//] uh I thought I wanted to invite Margie.
```

Retracing with correction can combine with retracing without correction, as in this example:

```
*CHI:    <the fish are> [//] the [/] the fish are swimming.
```

Sometimes retracings can become quite complex and lengthy. This is particularly true in
speakers with language disorders. It is important not to underestimate the extent to which
retracing goes on in such transcripts. By default, all of the CLAN commands except MLU,
MLT, and MODREP include retraced material. This default can be changed by using the
+r6 switch.

Retracing With Reformulation —   [///]

Sometimes retracings involve full and complete reformulations of the message without
any specific corrections. Here is an example of this type:

```
*BET:    all of my friends had [///] uh we had decided to
              go home for lunch.
```

When none of the material being corrected is included in the retracing, it is better to use the

[///] marker than the [//] marker.

False Start Without Retracing —   [/-]

In some projects that place special emphasis on counts of particular disfluency types, it may be more convenient to code retracings through a quite different method. For example, the symbols [/] and [//] are used when a false start is followed by a complete repetition or by a partial repetition with correction. If the speaker terminates an incomplete utterance and starts off on a totally new tangent, this can be coded with the [/-] symbol:

```
*BET:   <I wanted> [/-] uh when is Margie coming?
```

If the material is coded in this way, CLAN will count only one utterance. If the coder wishes to treat the fragment as a separate utterance, the +... and +//. symbols that were discussed on page 66 should be used instead. By default, all of the CLAN programs except MLU, MLT, and MODREP include repeated material. This default can be changed by using the +r6 switch.

Unclear Retracing Type —   [/?]

This symbol is used primarily when reformatting SALT files to CHAT files, using the SALTIN command. SALT does not distinguish between filled pausing (#) repetitions ([/]), and retracings ([//]); all three phenomena and possible others are treated as "mazes." Because of this, SALTIN uses the [/?] symbol to translate SALT mazes into CHAT hesitation markings.

Omissions —   [0 text]

On page 38, we used the symbols 0word, 0*word, and 00word to code for omitted words, incorrectly omitted words, and ellipsed words. However, some users may find this form of coding difficult to read. To solve this problem, it is possible to use the forms [0 text], [0* text], and [00 text] instead. The two forms are equivalent.

Error Marking —   [*]

Most of the work of coding for errors is done on the %err line. However, all errors that are to be coded on the %err line must be marked with the [*] symbol on the main line. This symbol can be given multiword scope. However, most often the scope of the error is a single word and the scope can be omitted. Usually, this symbol occurs right after the error. In repetitions and retracing with errors in the initial part of the retracing, the [*] symbol is placed before the [/] mark. If the error is in the second part of the retracing, the [*] symbol goes after the [/]. In error coding, the form actually produced is placed on the main line and the target form is given on the %err line.

The corrections made by retracings are sometimes errors themselves. Here are two examples from aphasic patients:

```
*PAT:   the boy was on the <tree stamp> [*] [//] tree stump.
*PAT:   <he's vacuu(m)ing the> [//] # he's vadgering [*] the grass.
```

8.5   Final Codes

The symbols we have discussed so far in this chapter usually refer to words or groups of words. CHAT also allows for codes that refer to entire utterances. These codes are placed into square brackets following the final utterance delimiter. They always begin with a + sign.

Postcodes —   [+ text]

Postcodes are symbols placed into square brackets at the end of the utterance. They should include the plus sign and a space after the left bracket. There is no predefined set of postcodes. Instead, postcodes can be designed to fit the needs of your particular project. Postcodes differ from the scoped codes that were discussed on page 70. Unlike scoped codes, postcodes must apply to the whole utterance, as in this example:

```
*CHI: not this one. [+ neg] [+ req] [+ inc]
```

Postcodes are helpful in including or excluding utterances from analyses of turn length or utterance length by MLT and MLU. The postcodes, [+ bch] and [+ trn], when combined with the -s and +s+ switch, can be used for this purpose. When the SALTIN command translates codes from SALT format to CHAT format, it treats them as postcodes, because the scope of codes is not usually defined in SALT.

Excluded Utterance —   [+ bch]

Sometimes we want to have a way of marking utterances that are not really a part of the main interaction, but are in some "back channel." For example, during an interaction that focuses on a child, the mother may make a remark to the investigator. We might want to exclude remarks of this type from analysis by MLT and MLU, as in this interaction:

```
*CHI:   here one.
*MOT:   no -, here.
%sit:   the doorbell rings.
*MOT:   just a moment. [+ bch]
*MOT:   I'll get it. [+ bch]
```

In order to exclude the utterances marked with [+ bch], the -s"[+ bch]" switch must be used with MLT and MLU.

Included Utterance —   **[+ trn]**

The [+ trn] postcode can force the MLT command to treat an utterance as a turn when it would normally not be treated as a turn. For example, utterances containing only "0" are usually not treated as turns. However, if one believes that the accompanying nonverbal gesture constitutes a turn, one can note this using [+ trn], as in this example:

```
*MOT:   where is it?
*CHI:   0. [+ trn]
%act:   points at wall.
```

Later, when counting utterances with MLT, one can use the +s+"[+ trn]" switch to force counting of actions as turns, as in this command:

```
mlt +s+"[+ trn]" sample.cha
```

9:   Dependent Tiers

In the previous chapters, we have examined how CHAT can be used to create file headers and to code the actual words of the interaction on the main line. The third major component of a CHAT transcript is the ancillary information given on the dependent tiers. Dependent tiers are lines typed below the main line that contain codes, comments, events, and descriptions of interest to the researcher. It is important to have this material on separate lines, because the extensive use of complex codes in the main line would make it unreadable. There are many codes that refer to the utterance as a whole. Using a separate line to mark these avoids having to indicate their scope or cluttering up the end of an utterance with codes.

It is important to emphasize that no one expects any researcher to code all tiers for all files. CHAT is designed to provide options for coding, not requirements for coding. These options constitute a common set of coding conventions that will allow the investigator to represent those aspects of the data that are most important. It is often possible to transcribe the main line without making much use at all of dependent tiers. However, for some projects, dependent tiers are crucial.

All dependent tiers should begin with the percent symbol (%) and should be in lowercase letters. As in the main line, dependent tiers consist of a tier code and a tier line. The dependent tier code is the percent symbol, followed by a three-letter code ID and a colon. The dependent tier line is the text entered after the colon that describes fully the elements of interest in the main tier. Except for the %mor and %syn tiers, these lines do not require ending punctuation. Here is an example of a main line with two dependent tiers:

```
*MOT:    well go get it!
%spa:    $IMP $REF $INS
%mor:    ADV|well V|go&PRES V|get&PRES PRO|it!
```

The first dependent tier indicates certain speech act codes and the second indicates a morphemic analysis with certain part of speech coding. Coding systems have been developed for some dependent tiers. Often, these codes begin with the symbol $. If there are more than one code, they can be put in strings with only spaces separating them, as in:

```
%spa:    $IMP $REF $INS
```

Multiple dependent tiers may be added in reference to a single main line, giving you as much richness in descriptive capability as is needed.

9.1   Standard Dependent Tiers

Users can make up any new dependent tier that they need for their analyses. Each dependent tier should be used to code consistently for a particular type of data. The shape of any new tiers should be discussed in detail in the 00readme.cdc file. New tiers also have to be added to the "depfile" used by CHECK, as discussed in the section on CHECK in the

CLAN Manual.

Most users will find that they can simply use the dependent tiers that are predefined in this chapter. Here we list all of the dependent tier types that have been proposed for child language data. It is unlikely that a given corpus would ever be transcribed in all of these ways. The listing that follows is alphabetical.

Action Tier —   %act:

This tier describes the actions of the speaker or the listener. Here is an example of text accompanied by the speaker's actions

```
*ROS: I do it!
%act: runs to toy box
```

The %act tier can also be used in conjunction with the 0 symbol when actions are performed in place of speaking:

```
*ADA: 0.
%act: kicks the ball
```

On page 71 we saw how this could also be coded as:

```
*ADA: 0 [%act: kicks the ball].
```

And if one does not care about preserving the identification of the information as an action, the following form can be used:

```
*ADA: 0 [% kicks the ball].
```

The choice among these three forms depends on the extent to which the coder wants to keep track of a particular type of dependent tier information. The first form preserves this best and the last form fails to preserve it at all. Actions also include gestures, such as nodding, pointing, waving, and shrugging.

Addressee Tier —   %add:

This tier describes who talks to whom. Use the three-letter identifier given in the participants header to identify the addressees.

```
*MOT: be quiet.
%add: ALI, BEA
```

In this example, Mother is telling Alice and Beatrice to "be quiet." A simpler way of coding addressee is to use combined speaker ID's such as *MOT-ALI or *MOT-BEA or even *MOT-BEI for various combinations of speakers and addressees. The decision to use either a full %add line or these combined codes is up to the transcriber.

Alternate transcription tier — %alt:

This tier is used to provide an alternative possible transcription. If the transcription is intended to provide an alternative for only one word, it may be better to use the main line form of this coding tier in the form [=? text].

Coding Tier — %cod:

This is the general purpose coding tier. It can be used for mixing codes into a single tier for economy or ease of entry. Here is an example.

```
*MOT: you want Mommy to do it?
%cod: $MLU=6 $NMV=2 $RDE $EXP
```

Cohesion Tier — %coh:

This tier is used to code text cohesion devices.

Comment Tier — %com:

This is the general purpose comment tier. One of its many uses is to note occurrence of a particular construction type, as in this example:

```
*EVE: that's nasty # is it?
%com: note tag question
```

Notations on this line should usually be in common English words, rather than codes. If special symbols and codes are included, they should be placed in quotation marks, so that CHECK does not flag them as errors.

Definitions Tier — %def:

This tier is needed only for files that are reformatted from the SALT system by the SALTIN command.

English Rendition Tier — %eng:

This line provides a fluent, nonmorphemicized English translation for non-English data.

```
*MAR: yo no tengo nada.
%eng: I don't have anything.
```

Error coding Tier —   **%err:**

This tier codes errors using the system discussed in depth on <u>page 142</u>.

Explanation Tier —   **%exp:**

This tier is useful for specifying the deictic identity of objects or individuals. Brief explanations can also appear on the main line, enclosed in square brackets and preceded by the = sign and followed by a space, as discussed on <u>page 71</u>.

Facial Gesture Tier —   **%fac:**

This tier codes facial actions. Ekman and Friesen (1969; 1978) have developed a complete and explicit system for the coding of facial actions. This system takes about 100 hours to learn to use and provides extremely detailed coding of the motions of particular muscles in terms of facial action units. Kearney and McKenzie (1993) have developed computational tools for the automatic interpretation of emotions using the system of Ekman and Friesen.

Flow Tier —   **%flo:**

This tier codes a "flowing" version of the transcript that is as free as possible of transcription conventions and that reflects a minimal number of transcription decisions. Here is an example of a %flo line:

```
*CHI:    <I do-'nt> [//] I do-'nt wanna [: want to] look
         in a [*] badroom [*] or Bill-'s room.
%flo:    I don't I don't wanna look in a badroom or Bill's room.
%err:    a /A/ -> the /DA/ ;
         badroom /baedrUm/ -> bathroom /baeTrUm/
```

Most researchers would agree that the %flo line is easier to read than the *CHI line. However, it gains readability by sacrificing precision and utility for computational analyses. The %flo line has no records of retracings; words are simply repeated. There is no regularization to standard morphemes. Standard English orthography is used to give a general impression of the nature of phonological errors. There is no need to enter this line by hand, because there is a CLAN command that can enter it automatically by comparing the main line to the other coding lines. However, when dealing with very difficult speech such as that of Wernicke's aphasics (particularly in other languages), the transcriber may find it useful to first type in this line as a kind of notepad from which it is then possible to create the main line and the %err line.

Gloss Tier —   **%gls:**

This tier can be used to provide a "translation" of the child's utterance into the adult language. Unlike the %eng tier, this tier does not have to be in English. It should use an explanation in the target language. This tier differs from the %flo tier in that it is being used not to simplify the form of the utterance but to explain what might otherwise be unclear. Finally, this tier differs from the %exp tier in that it is not used to clarify deictic reference or the general situation, but to provide a target language gloss of immature learner forms.

Gestural–Proxemic Tier — %gpx:

This tier codes gestural and proxemic material. Some transcribers find it helpful to distinguish between general activity that can be coded on the %act line and more specifically gestural and proxemic activity, such as nodding or reaching, which can be coded on the %gpx line.

Intonational Tier — %int:

This tier codes intonations, using standard language descriptions.

Language Tier — %lan:

This tier can be used to code the nature of the language of the utterance, the language of the preceding speaker and the dominant language of the speaker and addressee. For example, a code such as $DGDG or $D:G:D:G might indicate an utterance by a Dutch speaker in response to another Dutch speaker who had used German. See the discussion of the %add tier for other approaches to this coding. The exact shape of the codes on this tier will probably be project-specific. For a good example of a system of this type see De Houwer (1990).

Model Tier — %mod:

This tier is used in conjunction with the %pho tier to code the phonological form of the adult target or model for each of the learner's phonological forms.

Morphosyntax Tier — %mor:

This tier codes morphemic semantics in accord with the system outlined on page 156. Here is an example of the %mor tier:

```
*MAR: I wanted a toy.
%mor: PRO|I&1S V|want-PAST DET|a&INDEF N|toy.
```

Movie Tier — %mov:

This is the tier used to code the onset and offset of a segment in a digitized video record.

Paralinguistics Tier —   **%par:**

This tier codes paralinguistic behaviors such as coughing and crying.

Phonology Tier —   **%pho:**

This dependent tier is used to describe phonological phenomena. When the researcher is attempting to describe phonological errors, the %err line should be used instead. The %pho line is to be used when the entire utterance is being coded or when there is no reason to interpret some nonstandard speech string as an error. Coding can use either the UNIBET or IPA format. The chapter on page 120 explains how to use this system. Here is an example of the %pho tier in use. The symbols in the tier line are in UNIBET.

```
*SAR: I got a boo+boo.
%pho: /ai gat V bubu/
```

There are two main uses for the %pho line. One use is the transcription of occasional difficult stretches that the transcriber can render phonemically, but which have no obvious morphemic analysis. The other use is for a more extended transcription of a complete text on the phonemic level as in the work of Carterette and Jones (1974).

For more serious phonological analysis, you can use the symbols of the International Phonetic Alphabet with the IPAPhon font constructed by Henry Rogers of Toronto and distributed both on the CHILDES CD-ROM and through the CHILDES Web site. Complete documentation for installing and use of that font is provided in the package created by Rogers. When using the IPAPhon font, you need to set the font for each %pho line in the editor. CLAN is designed to recognize this font.

Situational Tier —   **%sit:**

This tier describes situational information relevant only to the utterance. There is also an @Situation header. Situational comments that relate more broadly to the file as a whole or to a major section of the file should be placed in a @Situation header.

```
*EVE: what that?
*EVE: woof@o woof@o.
%sit: dog is barking
```

Sound Tier —   **%snd:**

This is the coding tier used by sonic CHAT for marking the onset and offset of a digitized sound segment.

Speech Act Tier — %spa:

This tier is for speech act coding. Many researchers wish to transcribe their data with reference to speech acts. Speech act codes describe the function of sentences in discourse. Often researchers express a preference for the method of coding for speech acts. Many systems for coding speech acts have been developed. A set of speech act codes adapted from a more general system devised by Ninio and Wheeler is provided on page 151.

Syntax Tier — %syn:

This tier is used to code syntactic structure, as discussed on page 156.

Timing Tier — %tim:

This tier is for time stamp coding. Often it is necessary to give time readings during the course of taping. These readings are given relative to the time of the first utterance in the file. The time of that utterance is taken to be time 00:00:00. Its absolute time value can be given by the @Time Start header. Elapsed time from the beginning of the file is given in hours:minutes:seconds. Thus, a %tim entry of 01:20:55 indicates the passage of 1 hour, 20 minutes, and 55 seconds from time zero. If you only want to track time in minutes and seconds, you can use the form minutes:seconds, as in 09:22 for 9 minutes and 22 seconds.

```
*MOT: where are you?
%tim: 00:00:00

... (40 pages of transcript follow and then)

*EVE: that one.
%tim: 01:20:55
```

If there is a break in the interaction, it may be necessary to establish a new time zero. This is done by inserting a new @Time Start header.

You can also use this tier to mark the beginning and end of a time period by using a form such as:

```
*MOT: where are you?
 %tim: 04:20:23-04:21:01
```

9.2 Creating Additional Dependent Tiers

There are no restrictions on the creation of additional dependent tiers. Researchers have found tiers, such as %par for paralinguistics or %gpx for gestural–proxemic, to be extremely useful. For a transcript of language on a farm, one might want to make up a tier for animal noises and call it %ani. When devising additional tiers, the codes and markings should always be based on printing ASCII symbols. In addition, use the $ symbol to indicate unitary codes. The names for new tiers and the codes for those tiers must also be entered into the depfile used by CHECK.

9.3   Synchrony Relations

For dependent tiers whose codes refer to the entire utterance, it is often important to distinguish whether events occur before, during, or after the utterance.

Occurrence Before —   **< bef >**

If the comment refers to something that occurred immediately before the utterance in the main line, you may use the symbol <bef>, as in this example:

```
*MOT:    it is her turn.
%act:    <bef> moves to the door
```


Occurrence After —   **< aft >**

If a comment refers to something that occurred immediately after the utterance, you may use the form <aft>. In this example, Mother opened the door after she spoke:

```
*MOT:    it is her turn.
*MOT:    go ahead.
%act:    <aft> opens the door
```

If neither < bef > or < aft > are coded, it is assumed that the material in the coding tier occurs during the whole utterance or that the exact point of its occurrence during the utterance is not important.

Although CHAT provides transcribers with the option of indicating the point of events using the %com tier and <bef> and <aft> scoping, it may often be best to use the @Comment header tier instead. The advantage of using the @Comment header is that it indicates in a clearer manner the point at which an activity actually occurs. For example, instead of the form:

```
*MOT:    it is her turn.
%act:    <bef> moves to the door
```

one could use the form:

```
@Comment: Mot moves to the door.
*MOT:    it is her turn.
```

The third option provided by CHAT is to code comments in square brackets right on the main line, as in this form:

```
*MOT:    [% Mot moves to the door] it is her turn.
```

Of these alternative forms, the second seems to be the best in this case.

Following Sentences — $=n

When material on a dependent tier refers to a whole string of utterances, the scope of its application may be indicated by using the symbol $=n , where **n** is the number of following utterances to which the tier refers. For example, in the following excerpt, the mother has her arms extended to the child throughout three utterances, including the first utterance and the following two utterances.

```
*MOT:    want to come sit in my lap?
%act:    $=2 MOT extends arms in direction of CHI
*MOT:    come on.
*MOT:    hop up.
```

Scope on Main Tier — $sc=n

When you want a particular dependent tier to refer to a particular word on the main tier, you can use this additional code to mark the scope. For example, here the code marks the fact that the mother's words 4 through 7 are imitated by the child.

```
*MOT:    want to come sit in my lap?
*CHI:    sit in my lap.
%act:     $sc=4-7 $IMIT
```

10: CA Transcription

With the help of Chris Ramsden (Kent), Michael Forrester (Kent), and Johannes Wagner (Odense), we recently implemented an alternative to transcription using CHAT. This alternative is known as Conversational Analysis or simply CA. It is a system originally devised by Sacks, Schegloff, and Jefferson (1974) for the purpose of understanding the construction of conversational turns and sequencing. It is now used by hundreds of researchers internationally to study conversational behavior. Recent applications and formulations of this approach can be found in Ochs, Schegloff, and Thompson (1996), as well as the related "GAT" formulation of Selting (1998). Workers in this tradition find CA notation easier to use than CHAT, because the conventions of this system provide a clearer mapping of features of conversational sequencing. On the other hand, CA transcription has many limits in terms of its ability to represent conventional morphemes, orthography, and syntactic patterns.

The CHILDES tools support CA transcription in three ways. First, we have codified a core set of CA conventions in this chapter. Second, the CLAN editor has been modified to permit transcription with characters and formatting that are unique to CA transcription. This is known as CA mode. This mode allows CA analysts to link their transcripts to audio and video recordings, using the sonic and video modes in the editor. Third, many of the CLAN programs have been modified so that they can track the various patterns of CA notation. For example, it is possible to use the KWAL program to search for the occurrence of particular words in a CA transcript. Because CA is not designed to represent words in a uniform way, some of the CLAN programs are not appropriate for the analysis of a CA transcript. However, we believe that practitioners of CA will find that transcription and analysis inside the CHILDES framework opens up many useful new avenues for research and analysis.

The following table summarizes the basic features of CA that have been implemented in CHAT and CLAN:

Table 16: Features of CA Transcription

Features	Transcription	Comment
Speaker ID	Number:Speaker:<whitespace>	at line beginning
timed intervals	(2.0)	
short interval	(.)	
time between utts.	(3.0)	on its own line
short time between utts.	blank line	less than .5 seconds
latching at end of utt.	word=	
latching at begin of utt.	=word	

Table 16: Features of CA Transcription

Features	Transcription	Comment
drawling, stretching	do::g	after sound drawled
emphasis	underlining	formatting in editor
more emphasis	underlining + caps	formatting in editor
tone jumps up	↑	special character
tone jumps down	↓	special character
fall to low	.	period
comment	((text))	inside utterance
utterances start together	[[	beginning of utterances
begin overlap	[	inside utterances
close overlap	]	inside utterances
glottal cut off	do-	at end of word
fall not to low	,	comma
animated tone	!	exclamation mark
creaky voice	*	asterisk
lowered volume	°text°	superscripted zeros
out-breath	hhh	
in-breath	·hhh	raised dot
half raise	¿	inverted question mark
full raise	?	question mark

In addition to these features that are basic to CA, our implementation requires transcribers to begin their transcript with an @Begin line and to end it with an @End line. Also, comments can be added using the @Comment format. In addition, transcribers should use the @Participants header in this form:

```
@Participants:   geo, mom, tim
```

This line uses only three-letter codes for participant names. By adding this line, it is possible to have quicker entry of speaker codes inside the editor.

11: Signed Language — BTS

The Berkeley Sign Language Acquisition Project has designed a system for transcribing videotapes of sign language interactions. The system was developed using data of adult–child interaction in American Sign Language (ASL) and Sign Language of the Netherlands (SLN). It is intended to be applicable to all sign languages and to all genres of signing. The Berkeley Transcription System (BTS) is modeled on extensive experience with computerized transcription and analysis of child speech, and is explicitly designed to be compatible with the accepted international standards in that field. At the same time, BTS strives to present a consistently morphological analysis of each sign language under study. Support for this work has been provided by the Linguistics Program of the National Science Foundation under grant SBR-97-27050, "Can a Deaf Child Learn to Sign from Hearing Parents?" to Dan I. Slobin and Nini Hoiting. The transcription system is the joint effort of the following:

Dan I. Slobin (Psychology, University of California, Berkeley)
Nini Hoiting (Royal Institute for the Deaf "H.D. Guyot," Haren, Netherlands)
Michelle Anthony (Psychology, University of California, Berkeley)
Yael Biederman (Education, University of California, Berkeley)
Marlon Kuntze (Education, Stanford University, Calif.)
Reyna Lindert (Psychology, University of California, Berkeley)
Jennie Pyers (Psychology, University of California, Berkeley)
Helen Thumann (Education, University of California, Berkeley)
Amy Weinberg (Education, University of California, Berkeley)

The BTS group hopes that this guide will provide the reader with sufficient information and motivation to try out BTS. We expect to receive many questions, objections, and constructive suggestions. Our aim is to continue to refine BTS, in international collaboration, to the point that it can serve as a standard for transcription and analysis of spoken languages. We also hope that the practice of extending BTS will contribute to the morphological analysis of various sign languages. Please send comments to Dan Slobin at slobin@cogsci.berkeley.edu or to Department of Psychology, 3210 Tolman #1650, University of California, Berkeley, CA 94720-1650, USA.

This guide begins with an outline of BTS. This outline describes the motivation for this specific approach to transcription. The presentation of the main body of the transcription conventions begins on page 101.

11.1   Outline of BTS

The goal of all transcription is to produce a permanent, written record of communicative events, allowing for analysis and re-analysis. The goals of analysis are critical in determining the appropriate level and scope of transcription (Ochs, 1979; Slobin, 1993). BTS is designed to capture children's emerging grasp of meaning components and combinatorial possibilities in the exposure language. At the same time, the multi-tiered format allows investigators to add tiers for the transcription and coding of other levels, such as phonology, syntax, and pragmatics.

The most basic aim of every system of notation of behavior is to help researchers see patterns in the data—that is, to facilitate their human pattern-recognition devices. The task of transcription and subsequent data summaries is to present information in various forms, so that one may identify regularities that may not be evident while directly observing the behavior in question. In the domain of communicative interaction, the data must be amenable to both qualitative and quantitative exploration.

For purposes of qualitative analysis, one needs a transcript that makes it possible to follow the interaction as it unfolded in time, scanning for features that are relevant to one's guiding theoretical questions. Thus the transcript must be legible, allowing the trained reader to mentally represent the actual behavior. At the same time, it must be sufficiently schematized to make it possible to scan the data in significantly less time than required to watch the original videotape. It must also highlight units of analysis that may not be immediately evident to the viewer of the video.

For purposes of quantitative analysis, the transcript must be divisible into units that can be automatically extracted, counted, and combined in various ways. Statistical summaries are necessary in order to reveal patterns that are only evident when one compares numerous instances of particular behaviors. This sort of pattern recognition cannot be evoked online or in sequential reading of a transcript, because it requires summing across numerous scattered instances. Some quantitative information can be extracted from transcribed utterances; however, all transcripts must also be coded for levels of analysis that are not evident on the lexical/morphological level. BTS does not include guidelines for coding of transcripts; these must flow from the needs of each individual research project.

BTS is designed to provide a transcription format for signed languages that is fully compatible with CHAT guidelines, and thereby accessible to analysis using CLAN programs. In the long run, we would hope that the CHILDES database will include corpora of child signing, eventually supported by digitized video archives. In the introduction to CHAT coding on page 11, there is a word of caution regarding "the dominance of the written word." This warning applies with even greater force to the transcription of signed languages. In this case, the danger is to treat the sign language in terms of the written language of the surrounding speech community. All too often, scientific studies of sign language are based on uppercase glosses in the local spoken language, supplemented by descriptions of handshapes or discursive notes when a spoken-language equivalent is not readily available. The result is a hybrid of different types of information: lexical, phonological, gestural, pragmatic. A transcript of this sort is not consistent with CHAT format, and is therefore not amenable to CLAN analysis. In addition, on the linguistic level, it all too often leads the analyst to treat the sign language in terms of the written language used in glossing, rather than in its own terms.

11.1.1   Consistently Morphological Representation

Sign language communication poses additional problems for transcription, due to the simultaneous presentation of manual and nonmanual information, movement through space, and the use of gestures along with conventional signs. These problems have been approached in various ways in the literature, but all current solutions require the use of varying font sizes, diacritics, special characters, superscripts and subscripts, and horizontal lines drawn across sequences of elements to indicate the scope of nonmanuals. None of these formats can be simply and directly reproduced on the keyboard, using only ASCII characters in a single font size and typeface. Nor are there any clear guidelines for using such notations, as indicated by inconsistency from publication to publication. An ASL classifier might be indicated as VEHICLE in one paper or as 3-CL in another; a nonmanual feature might be indicated with an English word or abbreviation if it corresponds to an English category (e.g., neg, nod, rhetq), or by a phonological notation if it does not easily map onto a single English word (e.g., th, puff.cheeks, tight lips). Motion might be described geometrically (e.g., move to lf) or discursively (e.g., swerve to lf to miss rabbit). Such heterogeneity of transcription impedes systematic linguistic comparison between reported data in various publications.

BTS requires a consistent notation for all manual, nonmanual, and movement components of utterances. The notation must be consistently morphological, as discussed in detail below. Furthermore, an utterance must be represented in linear fashion, on a continuous typed line, using only ASCII characters in one font size and typeface. We will not present each of the BTS conventions here; they are readily available to the reader in the appended Manual or online in subsequent updated versions. Rather, we will point out the ways in which BTS is based on linguistic analysis and discourse considerations.

11.1.2   Keyboard Conventions

All content elements (lexical items, specific meaning components) are given in capitals and bounded by spaces. A sign is represented by at least two upper-case letters. This convention makes it possible to search for and count lexical items. Grammatical categories are indicated in lower-case, immediately bound to the content item. For example, cl'VEH indicates a vehicle classifier. The distinction between uppercase and lowercase allows for separate searches for function and content elements. Within a complex item, components are separated by hyphens. When necessary, the underscore is used to keep all parts of an item together as a unit bound by spaces, as in PNT_1 'point to self'. Information provided in parentheses is not included as part of an item. Thus, SIGN(1h) indicates that a normally two-handed sign was produced with one hand. Further conventions will be introduced in the discussion of specific topics.

11.1.3   Points, Indexes, and Pronouns

BTS uses the symbol PNT 'point' for all instances of pointing to a physically present referent or person, whether serving as signer (PNT_1), addressee (PNT_2), or another person or object (PNT_3). PNT_3 is followed by a parenthetical indication of the referent, as in PNT_3(visitor), PNT_3(ball), or PNT_3(picture_of_ball). The symbol IX 'index' is reserved for reference to a spatial locus that represents a person or object in signing space.

11.1.4 Polycomponential Signs

A major strength of BTS is its attempt to represent each of the several components of a sign. However, we attend only to those components that can be productively used to create meaningful complex signs in the language. Consider three types of ASL examples:

1. A plain verb, such as 'love,' is formed by crossed arms moving against the chest with two S-hands, palms inward. These components are fixed and do not vary to change the meaning of 'love.' This sort of verb has no morphological components. Signs of this sort are represented in the usual manner in BTS, using uppercase letters: LOVE.

2. Another sort of verb demonstrates agreement by moving in space, but, like LOVE, has no internal morphology. Consider ASL HELP, which consists of an A-hand resting on a palm-up base hand, moving between the helper and the helpee. The movement component is clearly meaningful, in that a variety of personal loci can fill the two roles. However, the configuration of the two hands consists of a single unit in the BTS analysis, because neither handshape can be substituted for another while still retaining the meaning 'help'. Again, an uppercase gloss HELP- for the lexical element is sufficient, but it will have affixed path morphemes.

3. Verbs of object transfer and manipulation, such as 'give' and 'put' have path movement components and handshape "classifiers" that can be substituted to specify the transfered or manipulated object. Such verbs are richly polycomponential or polymorphemic, and it would be grossly misleading to transcribe them as GIVE, PUT, and the like. For such verbs, BTS provides an expanded analysis.

11.1.5 Paths of Movement

BTS also provides a uniform analysis of verbs that move from one spatial locus to another, whether that locus be conceptualized as a place or a person. Path is one of many potential verb components, each of which is indicated by an initial hyphen. A verb that is not monomorphemic, in contrast to a monomorphemic verb such as LOVE, consists of a collection of components. The format for all such components is a lower-case indication of the component, followed by an apostrophe and an upper-case indication of the particular instantiation of the component. Thus, for example, -pth'Z indicates a zigzag path. Path elements can be combined, as in -pth'ZUF ('zigzag up forward'), but any combination still represents a single path component and is treated as a single content element. There are four types of path of movement:

1. Path, the simplest, indicates motion without further specification of either source or goal, as in -pth'ZUF.

2. When a path begins at a specified place (locus or contact), the source is noted as -src'X, where X indicates the starting point of the path. BTS conceives of -src as a type of path, and not just the starting point; that is, -src'X means 'move away

from X'.

3.   When a path ends at a specified place (locus or contact), the goal is noted as -gol'X. Again, this is considered to be a type of path, specifying 'move to X'.

4.   A path can move relative to a fixed referent object—that is, the moving figure can pass or pass through a landmark, barrier, or the like (doorway, bridge, tunnel, etc.). This sort of path is indicated by -rel'X.

11.1.6   Figures and Grounds

Verbs of motion (self-movement, caused-movement, object transfer) are polycomponential, including handshapes or body parts that indicate the figure, the ground, or both, as they are involved in the motion event. BTS considers signed languages in typological perspective, treating them as head-marked and polymorphemic. The transcription of classifier constructions is richly detailed in BTS.

The element that specifies or classifies figure or ground is always indicated in semantic terms. That is, an inverted-V handshape is transcribed as cl'TL 'two-legged animate being,' and never as V-CL, inverted-V, or the like. If both figure and ground are part of a verb, the order of notation is always ground before figure, following the logic of manual representation of such events.

Verbs of motion in signed languages (at least in ASL and SLN, the languages we have worked with in detail), consist of components of ground, figure, path, and various additional movement elements indicating features such as aspect and manner. Such verbs cannot be directly glossed in English, or the other Indo-European, dependent-marking languages that are characteristic of the surrounding speech communities that have been most extensively studied. Consider, for example, an ASL verb with the following components: the nondominant hand is held vertically, with flat palm, fingers extended forward (cl'VP 'vertical plane'); the dominant hand is in an inverted-V position (cl'TL 'two-legged animate being') and it moves to the top of the nondominant hand (gol'VP_TOP 'move to top of vertical plane') to straddle the hand (pst'STR 'posture straddle'). This verb could refer to a range of events, such as a cowboy mounting a horse or a boy sitting up on a fence. It can be represented as a verb with four meaning components ("morphemes"), as indicated by four hyphens:

```
-cl'VP-cl'TL-gol'VP_TOP-pst'STR
```

This is, in fact, a sufficient transcription linguistically, but it lacks legibility—at least for hearing readers. We would like to be reminded of a comparable English verb, but we do not want such a gloss to influence our transcription or analysis. To solve this problem, BTS allows the transcriber to begin a verb with a parenthetical, lower-case possible equivalent. Thus one might type:

```
(mount)-cl'VP-cl'TL-gol'VP_TOP-pst'STR
```

The parenthetical gloss is not a conventional part of the system, and each transcriber can provide a suitable equivalent. For example, this verb could also be glossed as (get_up_on_horse) or (mount_straddling), or whatever seems useful to the transcriber. The parenthetical glosses stand outside of the analyses, and function only to facilitate reading. If more contextual detail is needed, it can be provided on a dependent tier, under the utterance line. For example, one can add a %gls "gloss" tier. The utterance line begins with an asterisk and an identifying code for the speaker in three upper-case letters, while dependent tiers begin with a percent sign and lower-case ID:

```
*MOT:   COWBOY (mount)-cl'VP-cl'TL-gol'VP_TOP-pst'STR .
%gls:   the cowboy got up on the horse's back
```

The transcription is thus based on linguistic analysis, often resulting in initially nonobvious decomposition of complex signs. This work cannot be done without the active participation of native signers. At almost every point in the development of BTS, the native signers have helped us to discover contrasts, nuances, and possibilities that may not have been evident to second-language signers.

Segmentation of a sign into meaning components depends on the availability of contrasts in the language. For example, our analysis of 'mount' is based on the possibilities of contrasting the ground (by use of a horizontal plane to indicate movement onto a different sort of ground), the figure (by reference to an animal, such as a cat, mounting a horse), and the posture (by contrast with a person standing on a horse's back). The search for contrasts is essential to the analysis, and contrasts are not always obvious without careful examination of a range of potential scenarios and their signed descriptions.

To continue the demonstration of this method, note that 'mount' is part of a collection of verbs that have a derivational relationship with one another, as revealed by the addition or removal of a meaning component.

1.   If the path component (-gol-) is replaced by a static component (-loc-), the result is a verb describing a static configuration:

```
(be_mounted)-cl'VP-cl'TL-loc'VP_TOP-pst'STR
```

    Again, the parenthetical gloss is not part of the analysis. This verb could describe a man seated on a horse, a boy seated astraddle on a fence, and so on.

2.   If a movement pattern (-mvt-) is added to 'be_mounted' the resulting verb is dynamic: 'ride'. BTS is not concerned with a phonological description of the particular movement pattern, because it does not contrast with other movement patterns; its only function is to indicate that this configuration has the meaning of 'ride'. Therefore we simply designate the forward rotational movement of this verb as mvt'LEX, where LEX refers to the movement pattern that identifies this particular verb. That pattern is pointed to parenthetically: mvt'LEX(ride). (This is similar to transcription in English, such as 'walk-PAST' or 'run-PAST,' where the reader can provide 'walked' or 'ran' on the basis of knowledge of the language.) With regard to the parenthetical gloss, note that ASL has a different verb for riding in a vehicle, so we indicate the verb we are transcribing here as

'ride_mounted':

```
(ride_mounted)-cl'VP-cl'TL-loc'VP_TOP-pst'STR-mvt'LEX(ride)
```

3.   Once we have a dynamic verb of motion, we can then add further components
      of manner and aspect. For example, the following extended notation indicates
      the referent event was rapid (-mod'RAP-) and that it came to an end (-asp'CES
      'cessive'):

```
(ride_mounted)-cl'VP-cl'TL-loc'VP_TOP-pst'STR-mvt'LEX(ride)-
        mod'RAP-asp'CES
```

These relationships are not evident in the English glosses for each of the verbs discussed
above. That is, if one relied on glosses as the central element of transcription, there would
be no reason to see the regular relationships that hold between three verbs describing a human being mounting, straddling, and riding a horse: GET_ON, BE_LOCATED, and RIDE.

Sign language researchers with experience in typological linguistics should not be sur-
prised by the elaborateness of BTS transcriptions of polycomponential verbs. Such relatively opaque morpheme-by-morpheme glosses are familiar in papers dealing with a wide
range of agglutinative and polysynthetic languages. Consider the following example from
Inuktitut, spoken by a child of 2;5. Here we have an entire sentence in one polycomponential utterance (Crago & Allen, in press).
suna -tuq   -juq -viniq -u   -vunga
what -consume   -NOM -former -be -IND.1SG
     'What did I have to eat before [=I am one who had what to eat before].'

Note that the morpheme-by-morpheme gloss (what-consume-NOM-former-be-
IND.1SG) is uninterpretable without knowledge of Inuktitut, just as BTS utterance-line
transcriptions are uninterpretable without knowledge of the particular sign language. Because BTS is designed for investigators who know the sign language, however, the utterance line should generally be sufficient. The %gls line, like the line in single quotes above,
is always available for clarification.

11.1.7   Amalgams

BTS relies heavily on criteria of morphological productivity for the analysis of a sign
into components. However, children who are learning a language may not yet have carried
out the adult analyses reflected in the transcription. This problem is a familiar one in child
language, where it is well known that children's early forms may be unanalyzed amalgams
that correspond to more fully analyzed adult forms. One way to determine if a particular
morphological analysis is productive for a given child is to locate cases of overgeneraliza-
tions. When an English-speaking child says "breaked," one has evidence for the productivity of the past-tense inflection. This evidence can then be used to argue indirectly that
"jumped" is not an amalgam, but a productive combination. Alternatively, one can present
the child with new lexical items in contexts that should elicit a particular form. If an English-speaking child is presented with a nonce verb, shc as "wug," and says that someone

"wugged" yesterday, this can be taken as evidence for productivity. These same tests can be applied to children learning signed languages.

Analyses of adult signing, however, often treat complex lexical items as if they were frozen or unananlyzed. Again, we appeal to our criterion of substitutability in a lexical frame. A simple example may help to clarify this central issue in the design and use of BTS. Consider the ASL sign 'give', which is similar to signs for 'give' in other sign languages. In the nonspecific form, the handshape (flattened-O, palm up) does not specify the nature of the transferred object. The path components (-src- and -gol-) indicate the giver and recipient. One might conclude that the handshape is not a classifier, because it does not classify. However, in the BTS analysis, the generic handshape is just that: a generic classifier, corresponding to generic classifiers in many spoken languages. It is fully a meaning component of the verb. Furthermore, it contrasts with flattened-O, palm down, which means 'put' in ASL, using the same path component. In BTS such generic elements are labeled LEX—that is, their function is to indicate the particular lexical category (e.g., 'give' vs. 'put'). The transcription of generic 'give', in the frame 'from me to you', is therefore:

```
(give)-cl'LEX(give)-src'1-gol'2
```

LEX(give) should be read as "the generic handshape that specifies the lexical item as 'give'." Replacing cl'LEX with a specific "classifier" handshape adds specification. For example, if the transferred object is a glass, cl'LEX is replaced by cl'CYL (cylinder). Thus the notation would be:

```
(give)-cl'CYL-src'1-gol'2
```

We will not give further examples of the use of LEX here. But we wish to underscore the importance of searching for contrasting examples, with native-signing co-workers, in order to determine if a sign should be transcribed componentially or simply with an upper-case word in the corresponding written language. In our experience, this is often a difficult issue, requiring a good deal of exploration and discussion before a satisfactory analysis is reached for a particular lexical item or set of related items.

11.1.8 Temporal Marking

The temporal dimension is central to signed languages, thanks to the use of two moving articulators and simultaneous information conveyed by parts of the face, body parts, and shifts in gaze and posture. All such components are treated as meaning components in BTS, without deciding on the ultimate linguistic status of each dimension of signed communication. The two hands can do different things at the same time. For example, a child signs CANDY with the dominant hand, while pointing on a picture in a book with the nondominant hand (nh).

```
*CHI:    { CANDY PNT(nh)(on_book) } .
```

BTS indicates temporally co-occurring elements by enclosing them between curly brackets.

11.1.9   Nonmanual Components

A central feature of signed languages is the use of the face and/or body to add meaning to ongoing manual signing. BTS marks four distinct types of nonmanual components. These can occur simultaneously with a single sign, or can last across over several signs. The carat ^ is used to indicate onset and offset of a nonmanual feature which has scope (corresponding to the horizontal line drawn across glosses in most sign language transcriptions).

A grammatical operator has scope over a phrase or clause (negation, question, topic, relative clause, conditional, etc.). The notation is ^opr'X ... ^ . For example, the following indicates negation of a proposition:

```
*CHI:    ^opr'NEG WANT BOOK ^ .
```

Note that opr counts as a grammatical element, similar to cl, pth, and so forth; NEG counts as a content element—that is, a lexical or meaning-bearing element, along with other upper-case elements. The same is true of other nonmanual components.

Nonmanual components can also be employed to modify the referential meaning of a lexical item or proposition by adding a dimension—through the articulation of the sign and/ or accompanying facial expression—such as augmented or diminished size or rate, intensity, and so forth. The notation is ^mod'X ... ^ . To give a simple example, an SLN-signing 2-year-old wanted her mother to draw a big house. She greatly extended the sign HOUSE (AUG=augmented):

```
*CHI:    HOUSE-^mod'AUG .
```

In this example, the nonmanual component is part of a word. (There is no offset carat because such a nonmanual ends with the end of the word sign.) Modification, of course, can extend over longer stretches of signing as well.

Another use of mouth, face, and body is to provide affective accompaniment to an utterance, indicating the signer's attitudinal stance towards the situation being communicated (e.g., disgust, surprise, excitement). The notation is ^aff'X ... ^ . For example, in SLN, a teacher asks a child to do something and the child agrees, though with some worried concern:

```
*CHI:    ^aff'WORRIED CAN PNT_1 ^ .
```

While it may seem unorthodox to treat such affective coloring on a par with other components of the language, we believe that such concerns are based on a narrow and conventional definition of what is "linguistic." In comparable situations in spoken languages, affective prosody has a marginal role in most linguistic analyses, while affective particles and inflections are considered more "linguistic."

Nonmanual markers are also used to regulate the flow of discourse, corresponding to discourse particles and intonation contours in spoken languages. Such markers have interpersonal functions such as checking if the addressee has comprehended, has agreed, and so forth. The format is ^dis'X ... ^ . In the following example, a Deaf SLN-signing mother responds to her 2-year-old's labeling of the lights on a picture of an ambulance. Note that there are two types of nonmanual elements in this utterance. The first is an operator, indicating confirmation (YES); the second is a discourse marker checking whether the child agrees (CONF = confirmation check). The operator (repeated head-nodding) extends throughout the utterance, including the discourse marker (a sort of questioning facial expression). The offset timing of the two nonmanuals coincides (^ ^).

```
*MOT:   ^opr'YES CAR ^dis'CONF LIGHTSIGNALS ^ ^ .
```

Sign language communication includes many subtle shifts of gaze and posture that allow the signer to convey the utterances, thoughts, or actions of other people. This part of sign language needs much more careful study, and BTS does not present a fine-grained analysis of role shift at this time. However, we do consider it to be a meaningful element, and one that follows conventional, linguistic patterns. At this point, we simply indicate role shift by RS. Note that we use capital letters for this element, treating role shift as a meaning component in an utterance. We do not use the carat ^ to indicate onset and offset of role shift, because we want to search separately for nonmanual features and role-shifting. Instead, we use the reverse apostrophe for this function: 'RS ... ' . For example, in a book-reading activity, a Deaf ASL-signing mother points out a picture of a dog, and then role shifts into the dog to indicate that the dog is excited.

```
*MOT: DOG 'RS(dog) EXCITE-^aff'INTENSE ' .
```

She signs EXCITE with an accompanying nonmanual indicating the dog's affect. The notation 'RS(dog) indicates that she has taken on the role of the dog. Note that ^aff can co-occur with role shift.

11.2   Manual Signs

Having completed our survey of the major theoretical considerations in BTS, we now present the specific conventions of the system, beginning with the conventions for manual signs. Lexical items are written in capitals and bounded by spaces. Because of this distinctive use of capitalization, searches in CLAN must use the +k switch to recognize the distinction between uppercase and lowercase. A sign is represented by at least two uppercase letters. There can be no spaces within a lexical item. The component morphemes of polymorphemic lexical items are separated by hyphens. Other elements are joined by underscore or parentheses without spaces. An utterance line ends with a period or question mark, preceded by a space.

11.2.1   Features of Individual Signs

SIGN # SIGN	pause between SIGNs
SIGN(*2)	SIGN repeated rapidly, twice
SIGN(*N)	SIGN repeated rapidly, multiple times

SIGN_SIGN	contracted SIGNs, treated as a single new word
SIGN-SIGN	contracted SIGNs, treated as two words
&SIGN	uncompleted SIGN
<SIGN> [?]	uncertain transcription
XX	unintelligible but definite sign, to be included in word counts
xxx	unintelligible sign or gesture, to be excluded from word counts
SIGN(fs)	SIGN is a fingerspelled loan sign
S_I_G_N(fs)	SIGN is fingerspelled, not a loan sign

11.2.2   Modifications

SIGN:	SIGN is held
SIGN(prx)	SIGN directed to close/proximate location
SIGN(mid)	SIGN directed to intermediate location
SIGN(dis)	SIGN directed to distant location

11.2.3   Additional Specifications

SIGN(1h)	one-handed SIGN (if usually 2h)
SIGN(2h)	two-handed SIGN (if usually 1h)
SIGN(nh)	non-dominant-handed SIGN (if anomalous)
SIGN(dh)	dominant-handed SIGN (if anomalous)

Note: If marking both number of hands and which hand(s), the number of hands comes first, for example, SIGN(1h)(nh). If SIGN is (1h), only mark which hand if the nondominant hand is used.

SIGN(v)	SIGN is a verb (if ambiguous)
SIGN(n)	SIGN is a noun (if ambiguous)
SIGN	citation form
SIGN2	alternative form (e.g., WHERE, WHERE2)
X@ns	name sign (with X handshape)
X@is	idiosyncratic/invented sign (with X handshape)
X@hs	home sign (with X handshape)

11.3   Points, Indexes, and Pronominals

PNT_1	point to self
PNT_2	point to interlocutor
PNT_3(person)	point to third person, if present
PNT_3(obj)	point to object, if present
IX_3(person/object)	index a person or object in signing space, if not present
PNT_1_2	1st & 2nd pers sing ('me and you')
PNT_1_3	1st & 3rd pers sing ('me and him/her', 'two of us')
PNT_1+	1st pers pl ('me and somebody', generic 'we')

PNT_S	selective
PNT_M	multiple (sweep)
PNT_N	numbered (jabs)
PNT_1_2_S	1st & 2nd pers pl, selective ('me and some of you')
PNT_1_2_M	1st & 2nd pers pl, multiple/sweep ('me and all of you')
PNT_1_2_N	1st & 2nd pers pl, numbered/jabs ('me and each of you')
PNT_1_3_S	1st & 3rd pers pl, selective ('me and some others')
PNT_1_3_M	1st & 3rd pers pl, multiple ('me and all others')
PNT_1_3_S_M	1st & 3rd pers pl, selective, multiple ('me and some others')
PNT_1_2_S_N	1st & 3rd pers pl, selective, numbered ('me and certain others')
PNT_1_E	1st pers pl, exclusive ('we', excluding addressees)
PNT_1_I	1st pers pl, inclusive ('we', including addressees)
POSS_1	1st pers sg, possessive
POSS_2	2nd pers sg, possessive
POSS_3	3rd pers sg, possessive

Examples of more complex pronouns:

PNT_1 PNT_2	1st pers, 2nd pers, in succession ('me, you')
PNT_1_2*2	1st & 2nd pers (2) ('me and you two')
PNT_1_2*3	1st & 2nd pers (3) ('me and you three')
PNT_2_3*2	1st & 3rd pers (2) ('you and them two')

11.4 Polycomponential Signs

In the fullest possible elaboration, a polycomponential construction includes:

1. a gloss, indicated in lower case letters enclosed in parentheses to avoid counting it as a lexical item

2. paths of movement in the form -pth'X (also -src, -gol, and -rel)

3. figures and grounds in the form -cl'X

4. locations in the form -loc'X and -pos'X

5. posture in the form -pst'X

6. movement patterns in the form -mvt'X

7. non-manual elements in the form -mod'X (also -opr, -aff, and -dis)

8. aspect in the form -asp'X

Only the gloss and one classifier are obligatory. Locations, movement patterns, and paths of movement may be absent or may have several entries. There can only be one aspect entry. These component morpheme types are indicated in lower case, followed by an apostrophe and specification of the content component; e.g., -cl'TL indicates a two-legged animate being. The order of the components is: parenthetical gloss, classifier(s) (ground/figure), location/movement, modification, aspect (see examples).

Each of the eight possible components of polycomponential verb transcription is presented below, with examples at the end of this section.

11.4.1   Gloss

The first symbol in the verb transcription is the approximate English gloss (e.g., jump, dismount, ride_seated, ride_mounted). The elements within a gloss are separated by underscores, in order to retrieve them as units.

11.4.2   Paths of Movement

The notation -pth'X indicates a movement path of type X. In some instances, a verb of motion will indicate path, without further identification of either source or goal. In this case, path (pth) is indicated alone. If the movement is anchored, indication is also made of source (src), goal (gol), or both. A movement can also simply begin or end at a particular position in signing space (pos). The forms of the entries for path, source, goal, and position are as follows:

-pth'X	path of movement, when semantically meaningful
-src'X	movement from a place or from contact
-gol'X	movement to a place or to contact
-pos'X	position in space

The components of path, source, goal, and position are indicated by uppercase letters from the following list:

1. Shape (path only):
I	line
A	arc
C	circle
W	wandering
Z	zigzag

2. Vertical direction:
U	up
D	down

3. Front/back direction:
F	forward
B	backward

4. Lateral direction:
S	side

5. Body-oriented direction:
R	right
L	left

6. Oscillating direction:

BF   back-and-forth

7. Other directions:

OUT   out

IN   in

EO   two classifiers moving towards each other (e.g., -gol'EO)

OBJ(ref)real-world object referent (e.g., -gol'OBJ(paper))

X_cl'X location/direction in relation to classifier

        (e.g., L_cl'TBL 'left of two bent legs')

11.4.3   Figures and Grounds

The notation -cl'X indicates a classifier of type X. The following list of classifier types is partial; note that classifiers are given semantic (e.g., 'two-legged animate being') rather than phonological (e.g., 'V') definitions. When two classifiers are part of a single verb, the order of notation is **ground** followed by **figure**.

VP	vertical plane
HP	horizontal plane
NHP	narrow horizontal plane
PL	plane (nonspecific orientation)
IP	inclining plane
DP	declining plane
RHP	rounded horizontal plane
TL	two-legged animate being
TBL	two bent legs
TBL_D	two bent legs, dorsal (lying on back)
TBL_V	two bent legs, ventral (lying on stomach)
FD	flat disk
CN	container
CYL	cylindrical object
TR	tree
STK	stick-like object
GRASP	grasping an object
HO	hold real object, for example HO(toy)
LID	lid, put a lid on
BLOCK	shape of a block
OGRASP	open grasp
OBJ	marker for classifier type not yet determined
FL	four-legged creature, object (two-handed classifier)
FBL	four bent legs (two-handed classifier)
SHLDR'B	shoulder ('B indicates the signer's body part is used, in contrast to a manual representation of that same body part)
HEAD'B	head
CL'B	element of a body classsifier (the 'B is used for each element of the BCL)

Some signs have a "frozen" handshape that serves only to indicate the lexical item; for example, GIVE versus PUT. Each of these verbs can replace the frozen handshape with a classifier that specifies characteristics of a moving or moved entity (e.g., size, shape). Because the frozen handshape has no specific semantic content beyond lexical specification, it is indicated as -cl'VERB, following the gloss. Thus, (give)-cl'GIVE indicates the citation form for "give," whereas (give)-cl'CN indicates "give_container." This notation makes it possible to count cl'VERB as a morpheme for some types of analysis, while excluding it from others. Examples of signs that fall under this category are:

GIVE	'give' handshape, palm up
PUT	'put' handshape, palm down
LOOK	'V' handshape, palm up

11.4.4 Locative Relations

The notation -loc'X indicates a locative relation between figure and ground of type X. Locative components are used to indicate the location of the figure classifier with respect to the ground classifier, or of two classifiers to one another. A partial list of locative relations is:

INT	interior ('inside')
SUP	superior ('above')
INF	inferior ('below')
TOP	top ('upper surface')
BOT	bottom ('under surface')
EDG	edge
FRO	front
BAC	back
PAR	parallel
NXT	two classifiers articulated next to each other which do not indicate a figure/ground relationship, but may instead indicate two figures

Two locative components can be combined, as in FRO_EDG (front edge). For example, a verb indicating a two-legged being that is mounted on and riding an animal (e.g., man on horse, boy on dog) includes classifiers for ground (VP) and figure (TL), a location of the two (TOP), and a lexical movement element (VERB), resulting in a four-morpheme verb: (ride_mounted)-cl'VP-cl'TL-loc'TOP-mvt'RIDE. If, in addition, the movement is rapid, a second mvt element is given resulting in a five-morpheme verb: (ride_mounted)-cl'VP-cl'TL-loc'TOP-mvt'RIDE-mvt'RAP.

11.4.5 Posture

The component "posture" (pst'X) indicates the posture of the figure for the subset of polycomponential verbs which indicate posture. Examples of such verbs are sit, stand, lie, mount, and ride. The following posture components have been defined:

ERC	erect

RCL	reclining
STR	straddling
SIT	sitting

11.4.6   Movement Patterns

The notation -mvt'X indicates a movement of pattern X. The following partial list of movement patterns includes both lexically-defining movement patterns and manner of movement.

-mvt'VERB	movement that defines a lexical item but gives no further meaning; e.g., the verb RIDE (on an animal) consists of classifiers indicating the configuration of ground (vertical plane) and figure (two-legged creature), plus a nondirectional component of movement (see elaboration below, after presentation of location).
-mvt'WIG	wiggling movement
-mvt'RAP	rapid movement
-mvt'PIV	pivot (rotation of wrist)
-mvt'BOUNCE	bouncing movement
-mvt'CLOSE	hand closing movement
-mvt'HOLD	item is held
-mvt'JAB	short, jabbing movement
-mvt'LONG	showing long object, e.g. shelf or bed
-mvt'BEND	bending movement
-mvt'TWIST	twisting movement

Indication of manner of movement is often accompanied by nonmanual (facial) elements. Such elements are counted as constituent elements of the verb. Nonmanuals are indicated by a carat (^) and are preceded by a hyphen (-) in order to represent their status as a separate morpheme.

| -mvt'MNR-^NM | manner of movement with appropriate nonmanual (e.g., -mvt'RAP-^IM 'rapid manner, intense mouth') |

11.4.7   Nonmanual Components

See the next major section for an explanation of non-manual components and a list of non-manual components that may be included as part of a polycomponential construction.

11.4.8   Aspect

The notation -asp'X indicates an aspect of type X. Various aspects can be superimposed on a verb. A full list is not yet ready. Example codes are:

| CES | cessive |

ITR   iterative
ITR_CUM   iterative cumulative (e.g., a stack of blocks, one on top of another)

A single verb can indicate that riding was rapid and came to an end, resulting in a seven-morpheme verb:

(ride_mounted)-cl'VP-cl'TL-loc'TOP-mvt'RIDE-mvt'RAP-asp'CES

11.4.9   Other Features

A configuration of classifiers can act as a unit with respect to another element, including real-world objects. Curly brackets are used to indicate simultaneity. With regard to verbs, a configuration can move to a new location; for example, a doll on top of a board is moved to be located on a table:

(put){-cl'HP-cl'TL-loc'TOP}-gol'OBJ(table)

In a series of utterances, a configuration can be held or continued from a previous utterance. For example, if the doll-on-board had already been set up in a previous utterance, the tilde (~) is used for each component that is continued, to indicate that this compoent was not created anew in the following utterance:

(put){-~cl'HP-~cl'TL-~loc'TOP}-gol'OBJ(table)

In addition, the component may serve as a different element in the second utterance, e.g. -src'INT can become -~loc'INT in the next utterance. This means the element with the tilde is continue for the end product of the previous utterance.

The percent sign (%) is used when the hand shape changes to form a new sign which adds meaning, yet the configuraiton is held over from the previous utterance. In the following example, in the first construction the cl'HEAD is formed with one handshape, but in the second construction the index and middle finger sare extended foreward to form cl'%LOOK.

(head_move)-cl'CN-cl'HEAD-src'INT-pth'U-gol'OUT-cl'HEAD'B-mvt'
    ULR'B-^AFF'B.
(look_around)-~cl'CN-cl%'LOOK-~loc'INT_SUP-mvt'LR-cl'HEAD'B-mvt'
    LR'B-^AFF'B

11.4.10   Examples

The following are examples of verbs of motion, with possible translations in parentheses. Note that this analysis reveals derivational relationships between verbs of location and verbs of movement. Some examples are:

(sit_on)-cl'-VP-cl'TL-loc'TOP   'sit on a horse'

(mount)-cl'VP-cl'TL-gol'VP	'get on a horse'
(ride_mounted)-cl'VP-cl'TL-loc'TOP-mvt'RIDE	'ride a horse'
(dismount)-cl'VP-cl'TL-loc'TOP-src'VP	'get off of a horse'
(mount_seated)-cl'CN-cl'BL-gol'CN	'get into a car'
(ride_seated)-cl'CN-cl'BL-loc'TOP-mvt'RIDE	'ride in a car'
(jump)-cl'HP-cl'TL-mvt'JUMP	'jump up and down'
(jump)-cl'HP-cl'TL-loc'TOP-src'HP-gol'HP	'jump from one point to another on a horizontal plane'
(jump)-cl'HP-cl'TL-src'HP	'jump off of a horizontal plane'
(get_on)-cl'HP-pos'USL-cl'BL-gol'HP	'cat getting on a high, left table'
(give)-cl'GIVE-src'3-gol'1	'give from her to me'
(give)-cl'CYL-src'3-pth'A-gol'1	'give something cylindrical from her to me in an arc'

11.4.11 Verb agreement

Verb agreement is indicated by the same conventions as used for transcribing directionality in verbs of motion (i.e., by use of src/goal and numeric indications, as in the preceding examples of GIVE). Although this has not yet been worked out in detail, it seems that an English gloss is sufficient to specify the lexical content of the verb. For example, "You show me": (show)-cl'SHOW-src'2-gol'1.

11.5 Temporal Components of Signs

11.5.1 Manual Simultaneity

11.5.1.1 Simultaneity within an utterance

Single curly brackets surrounded by spaces enclose elements that co-occur in an utterance. For example, a child signs CANDY while pointing on a book with the non-dominant hand:

```
*CHI:              { CANDY PNT(nh)(on_book) } .
```

Indicate which sign is on the non-dominant hand; the default is the dominant hand. Curly brackets are surrounded by spaces. To indicate earlier onset of one sign in curly brackets, append (o) to the sign, e.g.:

```
*CHI:              { CANDY(o) PNT(nh)(on_book) } .
```

11.5.1.2 Simultaneity between utterances

Overlaps are coded in the standard CHAT fashion. If a signed utterance is grammatical, break the utterance by proposition or clause boundaries. If a signed utterance is ungrammatical, break the utterance by prosody (indicated by pauses, placing the hands down, etc.).

11.5.2 Manual–Nonmanual Simultaneity

Non-manual elements are indicated by a carat (^). There are four types, as described below: operator (^opr), modification (^mod), affect (^aff), and discourse marker (^dis). Such an element can be added to a single sign; however, if the non-manual element has scope over several signs, this is indicated using the following conventions:

SIGN-^opr'X	non-manual element associated with a single sign
^opr'X SIGN SIGN ^	non-manual element has scope over several signs

If two different non-manuals are superimposed on a single sign or utterance, each has its own carat, using the following conventions:

{^opr'X ^mod'X} SIGN	simultaneous onset of two non-manuals
SIGN ^ ^	simultaneous offset of two non-manuals
^opr'X ^mod'X SIGN	sequential onset of two non-manuals
^aff'X ^opr'X SIGN opr^ SIGN aff^	sequential offset of two non-manuals
SIGN-^opr'NEG	non-manual which adds a component to a sign

11.5.2.1 Operators

^opr'X	grammatical operator which operates on a whole phrase or clause (e.g. negation, yes/no or wh- question, topical marker, relative clause marker, conditional marker) (partial list)

^opr'NEG	negation
^opr'YNQ	yes/no question
^opr'WHQ	wh- question
^opr'TOP	topical marker
^opr'REL	relative clause marker
^opr'COND	conditional marker

11.5.2.2 Modification

^mod'X	modifies the referential meaning being expressed by adding a dimension (e.g., augmented/diminished size, rate, intensity) (partial list)
^mod'RAP	rapid movement
^mod'DUR	durative activity, situation
^mod'AUG	augmented size, rate, or intensity

11.5.2.3 Affect

^aff'X	freely varying affective accompaniment to a lexical item or ut-

terance to indicate the signer's attitudinal stance towards the situation being communicated (e.g., disgust, surprise) (partial list)

^aff'DISGUST   disgust
^aff'SURPRISE   surprise
^aff'ANGER   anger

11.5.2.4   Discourse markers

^dis'X   markers which regulate the flow of discourse (e.g., checking for agreement, comprehension, confirmation) (partial list)
^dis'CONF   confirmation check
^dis'AGR   agreement

11.5.2.5   Role shift

The signer can shift into the role of someone referred to, using various means of body and gaze shift into and out of the neutral position. Onset and offset of role shift are indicated by a reverse apostrophe (left single quote, grave accent) and indication of the person represented by the role shift is indicated in parentheses:

    'RS(person) SIGN ... '

For example, a child role-shifts into his mother to indicate that she prohibited him from having a cookie:

```
    *CHI:           WANT COOKIE 'RS(mom) NO ' .
```

Note that 'RS is in capital letters, since it is a meaningful element.

11.5.2.6   Gaze

It is often essential to know where signers direct their gaze while signing. Gaze direction is indicated by an asterisk (*) and an indication, in lower case, of the object of gaze:

*mot   looks at mother
*book   looks at book

Gaze direction is indicated only when the transcriber considers that it is relevant to analysis of the interaction. Special notations are used to indicate a recipient's view of particular signs, indicated by backslashes (\). Such information is especially important for assessing a child's comprehension.

\- SIGN \   recipient does not see SIGN
\@ SIGN \   signer modifies location of SIGN outside its normal location
\q SIGN \   unsure whether recipient sees SIGN
\@\- SIGN ...   simultaneous onset of two recipient markings
... SIGN \\   simultaneous offset of two recipient markings
... SIGN @\ -\   sequential offset of two recipient markings

For any modification other than the extension of neutral signing space, insert a %com line to explain how the SIGN is modified.

11.6 Extralinguistic Communicative Behavior

11.6.1 Gestures and actions

If part of an utterance consists of non-signed but meaningful activity, notations of such activity is included as main line commentary in square brackets, as follows:

[%ges: identification]   identifies the gesture and lexical interpretation for gestures occurring without the use of any object or prop, and/or outside of typical signing space (e.g., [%ges: write])

[%act: identification]   identifies the activity that replaces some or all of an utterance, performed with or on some object (e.g., [%act: throws doll])

11.6.2 Attention-getting devices

Various means are used to get the attention of the recipient. These devices are indicated by @ag. The @ag is part of the utterance line. The following attention getting-devices have been identified:

t@ag	tap on person
w@ag	wave at person
g@ag	grab person
f@ag	touch face of person
p@ag	pound on surface

11.7 Performance and Contextual Situation

11.7.1 Interruption

Interruption and continuation after interruption are coded in the standard CHAT fashion. For example:

```
*MOT:   WANT /+ .
*CHI:   PNT_3(on_book) .
*MOT:   +, READ BOOK .
```

11.7.2 Errors

An error is indicated by [*], in the standard CHAT fashion. If an entire utterance is ungrammatical, with no localizable error within the utterance, [*] is placed at the beginning of the line. If an error can be localized, the intended SIGN is given in square brackets with an equal sign, followed by [*]; for example:

```
*CHI:   DAD CHAIR [= SIT] [*] HERE .
```

Explanations of errors are given on a %err dependent tier, using codes including the following:

$agr	agreement error
$cl	classifier error (wrong classifier used)
$hs	handshape error
$lex	sign error (wrong sign used)
$loc	location error
$mvt	movement error
$po	palm orientation error
$syn	syntax error (ungrammatical utterance)

If there is more than one error on a line, separate each explanation with a semicolon bounded by spaces. For example, if the child used the wrong handshape for DAD and signed CHAIR with a movement pattern that means SIT, the transcription and error coding would be as follows:

```
*CHI:   DAD [*] CHAIR [= SIT] [*] HERE .
%err:   DAD $hs ; CHAIR $mvt = SIT ;
```

In words with multiple morphemes, use the [*] with a number to indicate which morpheme has the error. However, if the child confuses src and gol, mark this as an error with the * symbol only on the first component, and then add a [*] at the end of the classifier construction to mark the error; for example:

```
*CHI:   BOY (grab)-cl'GRAB-src'3-gol'1 [*].
%err:   src'3-gol'1 $agr = src'1-gol'3 ;
```

[*q]	possible error
[*u]	unspecified error not tied to one particular SIGN

11.7.3   Retracing

Standard CHAT conventions are used for retracing and retracing with correction, as in these examples:

```
*CHI:   <MOTHER> [/] MOTHER LEAVE .
```

```
*CHI:   <BEAR> [*] [//] BEAR .
%err:   BEAR $mov
```

11.7.4   Empty Utterance Line

If a turn consists of a definite but nonsigned response, use the standard CHAT convention of beginning the utterance line with zero (e.g., *CHI: 0). The zero is used when the interlocutor uses only an attention-getter (*@ag), action, or gesture.

11.7.5 Utterance Segmentation

If a signed utterance is grammatical, break the utterance by proposition or clause boundaries. If a signed utterance is ungrammatical, break the utterance by prosody (indicated by pauses, placing the hands down, etc.).

11.7.6 Gestures and Communicative Actions

If part of an utterance consists of nonsigned but meaningful activity, notations of such activity is included as main line commentary in square brackets, as follows:

[%ges: lex. interp.]   codes the gesture and lexical interpretation for gestures occurring without the use of any object or prop, and/or outside of typical signing space (e.g., [%ges: write])

[%act: explanation]   codes the action and explanation of action(s) that replace some or all of an utterance, performed with or on some object

11.8 Dependent Tiers

The following dependent tiers are being developed for transcription of sign language:

%act   modifies the preceding utterance line, describing actions of signer or recipient that are necessary for the understanding of the transcription

%att   describes participants' attention (e.g., CHI and MOT not attending to one another)

%eng   English translation (for particularly complex utterance lines)

%ges   phonological description of gesture

%pho   phonology

%mor   morphology

%sem   semantics

%spa   speech act

11.9 Examples

11.9.1 SLN (Sign Language of the Netherlands)

This is a segment of joint drawing activity between a mother and her daughter of 2;8 (data of Nini Hoiting):

```
*MOT:   PNT(nh)(with_pen_on_slate) < FATHER > [>] .
*CHI:   < MAN > [<] FATHER PNT_3(on_slate) .
*MOT:   t@ag MAN .
*CHI:   MAN .
*MOT:   PNT_3(at_drawing) .
*CHI:   PNT_3(at_drawing) PNT_1 [%ges: long ears] .
```

```
*MOT:    PNT_2 PNT_3(on_slate) .
*CHI:    PNT_3(on_slate) GRANDPARENTS .
*MOT:    GRANDMOTHER .
*CHI:    PNT_3(on_slate)(*N) < A_LOT(*N) > [>] .
*MOT:    <^HN A_LOT FACES > [<] A_LOT FACES ^ .
```

11.9.2   ASL (American Sign Language)

This is a segment of book reading between a mother and her daughter of 1;9 (data of
Reyna Lindert):

```
*MOT:    t@ag(*2) w@ag ^KB SEE WHAT(1h) ^ ?
*CHI:    MOUSE(*N) .
*MOT:    t@ag g@ag(nh): \- ^KB WHAT(1h) ^ \ ?
*CHI:    0 [%act: lifts panel in book] *mot .
*MOT:    ^KB WHAT(1h) ^ ?
*CHI:    < PNT_3[on book] >m > [>] .
*MOT:    < ^KB WHAT(1h)(*2) ^ > [<] ?
*MOT:    ^BR \- CAT \ t@ag(nh) CAT PNT_3(at cat in book) ^ < CAT > [>] ?
*CHI:    < ^HS > [<] [%ges: don't know/not me] .
%ges:    open 5s, wrists rotate out
*MOT:    ^KB WHAT(1h) ^ ?
*CHI:    <BEAR> [*] [//] BEAR .
%err:    BEAR $mvt
```

12:   Extending CHAT

The CHAT system is designed to provide the transcriber with a toolbox of codes that can be adapted as needed to match the special needs involved in individual research projects. In this chapter, we examine several special topics for which specific adaptions of CHAT can be recommended. These include code-switching and the simultaneous use of signed and spoken language.

12.1   Code-Switching and Voice-Switching

Transcription is easiest when speakers avoid overlaps, speak in full utterances, and use a single standard language throughout. However, the real world of conversational interactions is seldom so simple and uniform. One particularly challenging type of interaction involves code-switching between two or even three different languages. In some cases, it may be possible to identify a default language and to mark a few words as intrusions into the default language. In other cases, mixing and switching are more intense.

CHAT provides several ways of dealing with code-switching. The selection of some or all of these methods of notation depends primarily on the user's needs for retrieval of codes during analysis.

1.   The languages spoken by the various participants can be noted with the @Language of XXX header tier.

2.   As noted on page 32, individual words may be identified with the @s terminator to indicate their second language status. The exact identity of the second language can be coded as needed. For example, words in French could be noted as @f and words in German as @g. In the limiting case, it would be possible to mark every single word in a French-German bilingual transcript as either @f or @g. Of course, doing this would be tedious, but it would provide a complete key for eventual retrieval and study.

3.   If needed, the @f and @g markers can be further expanded with replacement symbols as discussed on page 71. For example, one can have:

    ```
    spiel@g [:=g game]
    ```

4.   It is possible to use the six-letter code for the main tier as an easy way of indicating the matrix language being used for each utterance. For example, *CHIGG could indicate the child speaking German to a German speaker and *CHIGF could indicate the child speaking German to a French speaker. Retrieval during analysis would then rely on the use of the +t switch, as in +t*CHIG*, +t*CHUGG, and +t*CHI*.

5.   The %lan dependent tier can be used to code the status of the main language of each utterance and the presence of additional material. If desired, aspects of the %add tier can be coded together with the %lan tier to indicate the primary language of the addressees.

6.   The system of gem markers can also be used to indicate the beginnings and ends of segments of discourse in particular languages.

7.   A large database may consist of files in certain well-specified interaction types. For example, conversations with the mother may be in German and those with the father in French. If this is the case, the careful selection of file names such as ger01.cha and fre01.cha can be used to facilitate analysis.

These techniques are all designed to facilitate the retrieval of material in one language separately from the other. The choice of one method over another will depend on the nature of the material being transcribed and the eventual goals of the analysis.

Problems similar to those involved in code-switching occur in studies of narratives where a speaker may assume a variety of roles or voices. For example, a child may be speaking either as the dragon in a story or as the narrator of the story or as herself. These different roles are most easily coded by marking the six-character main line code with forms such as *CHIDRG, *CHINAR, and *CHISEL for child-as-dragon, child-as-narrator, and child-as-self. However, the other forms discussed above for noting code-switching can also be used for these purposes.

12.2   Elicited Narratives and Picture Descriptions

Often researchers use a set of structured materials to elicit narratives and descriptions. These may be a series of pictures in a story book, a set of photos, a film, or a series of actions involving objects. The transcripts that are collected during this process can be studied most easily by making full use of the method of gem notation introduced on page 21. In the simplest form of this system, a set of numbers are used for each picture or page of the book. Here is an example from the beginning of an Italian file from the Bologna frog story corpus:

```
@g:      1
*AND:    questo e' un bimbo poi c' e' il cane e la rana.
*AND:    questa e' la casa.
@g:      2
*AND:    il bimbo dorme.
```

The first @g marker indicates the first page of the book with the boy, the dog, and the frog. The second @g marker indicates the second page of the book with the boy sleeping.

When using this lazy gem type of marking, it is assumed that the beginning of each new gem is the end of the previous gem. Programs such as GEM and GEMLIST can then be used to facilitate retrieval of information linked to particular pictures or stimuli.

12.3   Written Language

CHAT can also be adapted to provide computerized records of written discourse. Typically, researchers are interested in transcribing two types of written discourse: (1) written productions produced by school students, and (2) printed texts such as books and newspapers. For printed texts, the Text Encoding Initiative (TEI) group of the Association for Computational Linguistics (ACL) has produced a set of SGML (Standard Generalized Mark-up Language) guidelines for computerization (Sperberg-McQueen & Burnard, 1992). However, researchers in the field of language learning will probably prefer to use an adapted form of CHAT to code written productions by school children. In order to use CHAT effectively for this purpose, the following adaptations or extensions can be used.

The basic structure of a CHAT file should be maintained. The @Begin and @End fields should be kept. However, the @Participant line should look like this:

```
@Participants:   TEX Writer's_Name Text
```

Then, each sentence should be transcribed on a separate line with the *TEX: field at the beginning. Additional @Comment and @Situation fields can be added to add descriptive details about the writing assignment and other relevant information.

For research projects that do not demand a high degree of accurate rendition of the actual form of the written words, it is sufficient to transcribe the words on the main line in normalized standard-language orthographic form. However, if the researcher wants to track the development of punctuation and orthography, the normalized main line should be supplemented with a %spe line. Here are some examples:

```
*TEX:   Each of us wanted to get going home before the Steeler's
        game let out .
%spe:   etch of _us wanted too git goin home *,
        before the Stillers game let out 0.
```

This example indicates several points. First, there is a one-to-one correspondence between the main line and the %spe line that can be used to facilitate the use of MODREP in the analysis of orthographic errors. Second, the words on the main line are all given in their standard target-language orthographic form. For clarity, final punctuation on the main line is preceded by a space. Third, there are certain special symbols on the %spe line that are used to indicate divergences from the standard form. In this example, we see several misspellings, a failure to capitalize the first word of the sentence, an extraneous comma, and an extra space in front of "us." Here are the symbols for coding these types of errors:

Table 17: Errors in Writing

Function	Example	Coding
omitted space	mydog	my/dog
extra space	moon light	moon_light
complete erasure	~~basket~~	basket [:= 0]
partial erasure	baseket	baseket [:= basket]
mishyphenization	pre-pare	pre*-pare

Table 17: Errors in Writing

Function	Example	Coding
omitted apostrophe	dont	don0't
blank for apostrophe	don t	don_0't
apostrophe for blank	will'not	will*'/not
extra apostrophe	wan't	wan*'t
extra punctuation	extra comma	*,
omitted punctuation	missing comma	0,

Additional symbols of this type for other diacritics, ligatures, or punctuation marks can be added as needed. For example, a set parallel to those for the apostrophe could be developed for word-internal hyphens. The goal of all of these symbols is the creation of a good one-to-one correspondence between the main *TEX line and the %spe line, while still preserving the details of the actual orthographic forms.

The conventions discussed so far have focused on the writing of individual words. However, it may also be necessary to note larger features of composition. When the student crosses off a series of words and rewrites them, it makes sense to use the standard CHAT conventions for retracing with scoping marked by angle brackets and the [//] symbol. If you want to mark page breaks, you can use a header such as @Stim: Page 3. If you wish to mark a shift in ink, or orthographic style, you can use a general @Comment field.

12.4   Children With Disfluencies

Bernstein Ratner, Rooney, and MacWhinney (1996) have proposed a specific set of CHAT adaptations that are designed to facilitate the study of children with disfluencies. Each of these extensions to CHAT is discussed elsewhere in this manual. The major modifications to standard coding include:

1.   The use of a notation of the form ba(&3be)by to explicitly code the fact that the first syllable of the word "baby" is repeated three times.

2.   A similar form for multiple word repetitions. For example, four repetitions of the word "that's" are coded as that's(*4).

3.   Use of the special form marked @fp to explicitly mark even standard English words as filled pauses. This use extends also to phrases, which are coded as, for example, "you+know@fp."

4.   Addition of a special symbol to mark blocks. This is the caret placed before the word, as in "^I tend to have blocks early in sentences."

For further suggestions regarding the coding of disfluencies and for specific ways of using the CLAN to tabulate repetitions, please see the article by Bernstein Ratner et al.

13:   UNIBETs

Young children's phonological productions often differ from the adult standard in interesting and important ways. Sometimes a researcher may not want to assume that the sounds made by a child correspond to any adult forms at all. In such cases, researchers may wish to code the phonological shapes of words or word-like strings.

Earlier versions of CLAN relied heavily on systems for coding phonological data in ASCII characters. However, two major changes in the programs have decreased the extent to which transcribers need to rely on ASCII characters for transcription. The first change is the modification of the text editor to permit inclusion of characters in fonts based on the International Phonetic Alphabet or IPA (Pullum & Ladusaw, 1986). Rather than coding these characters in ASCII, it is now possible to code them directly in IPA. Second, the ability of the editor to make reference to full digitized sound makes it less important in some cases to have a full phonological transcription.

Despite these changes, it is still often useful to have a simple way of representing phonemes in ASCII. One reason for the continuing use of a simplified ASCII character set is the fact that there has not yet been any standardization of a font for IPA. In addition, by using standard ASCII, researchers can avoid installation of the complete IPA font and having to mark particular lines in a transcript as taking a special font. We use the term UNIBET to refer to systems that permit transcription on the phonemic level using standard ASCII characters. In this chapter, we present UNIBET systems for several languages. In the first two editions of this manual, we used a home-grown UNIBET. In this edition, we include a UNIBET based on SAMPA coding from Appendix B of Gibbon, Moore, and Winski (1997), because this is a more widely recognized standard ASCII encoding that resembles the earlier UNIBET proposals in many ways.

UNIBET strings on the main line are marked by @u, as noted on page 32. The use of UNIBET on the main line is intended to be fairly limited. Any extensive transcription with UNIBET should be done on the %pho line. When making use of UNIBET on the main line, none of the utterance delimiter symbols such as ! or ? should be included in UNIBET strings. In order to permit coding of the glottal stop within main line UNIBET strings, we use the number 7. Similarly, 8 is used instead of & to represent the "ash," because use of & would block counting of the word by commands such as MLU.

When using COMMANDS such as FREQ or COMBO with UNIBET strings, it is important to remember that UNIBET is case-sensitive. The UNIBET "N" and "n" symbols refer to two different phonemes. The CLAN programs are set up so that, for the %pho and %mod tiers, the default analyses are case-sensitive.

13.1   SAMPA Tables

The SAMPA system provides a set of vowel and consonant symbols that are fairly consistent across languages. This was not true of the earlier UNIBET proposal. The following tables, based on Appendix B of Gibbon et al. (1997), summarize the system. First, there are the SAMPA vowels and consonants.

Table 18: SAMPA Vowels

IPA	SAMPA	ASCII	Openness	Front–Back	Round
a	a	97	open	front	-
ɑ	A	65	near-open	back	-
æ	{	123	near-open	central	-
ɒ	Q	81	open	back	+
ɔ	O	79	open-mid	back	+
e	e	101	close-mid	front	-
ɛ	E	69	open-mid	front	-
ə	@	64	mid	central	-
ɜ	3	51	mid	central	-
i	i	105	close	front	-
ɪ	I	73	near-close	front	-
o	o	111	close-mid	back	+
ø	2	50	close-mid	front	+
œ	9	57	open-mid	front	+
Œ	&	38	open	front	+
u	u	117	close	back	+
U	U	85	near-close	back	+
ʉ	}	125	close	central	+
ʌ	V	86	open-mid	back	-
y	y	121	close	front	+
ʏ	Y	89	near-close	front	+

Table 19: SAMPA Consonants

IPA	SAMPA	ASCII	Voicing	Place	Manner
b	b	98	voice	palatal	plosive
c	c	99	voiceless	palatal	plosive
ç	C	67	voiceless	palatal	fricative
d	d	100	voiced	dent/alv	plosive
ð	D	68	voiced	dental	fricative
f	f	102	voiceless	labiodental	fricative
g	g	103	voiced	velar	plosive
ɣ	G	71	voiced	velar	fricative
h	h	104	voiceless	glottal	fricative
j	j	106		palatal	approximant
k	k	107	voiceless	velar	plosive
l	l	108		dent/alv	lat/approx
ʎ	L	76		palatal	lat/approx
m	m	109		bilabial	nasal
n	n	110		dent/alv	nasal
ɲ	J	74		palatal	nasal
ŋ	N	78		velar	nasal
p	p	112	voiceless	bilabial	plosive
r	r	114		alveolar	trill
ʀ, ʁ	R	82		uvular	trill
s	s	115	voiceless	alveolar	fricative
ʃ	S	83	voiceless	postalveolar	fricative
t	t	116	voiceless	den/alveolar	plosive
θ	t	84	voiceless	dental	fricative
v	v	118	voiced	labiodental	fricative
w	w	119		labiovelar	approximant

Table 19: SAMPA Consonants

IPA	SAMPA	ASCII	Voicing	Place	Manner
x	x	120	voiceless	velar	fricative
ɥ	H	72		labiopalatal	approximant
z	z	122	voiced	alveolar	fricative
ʒ	Z	122	voiced	alveolar	fricative
ʔ	?	63		glottal stop	

In addition, SAMPA provides certain two-character symbol types:

Table 20: Two Character Symbols in SAMPA

IPA	SAMPA	Comment
ɛ	e~	nasalized vowel
aɪ	aI	diphthong
tʃ	tS	affricate
ɖ	rd	retroflex consonant
ɵ	uO	Swedish vowel
n̩	=n	syllabic /n/
	E/	indeterminacy for /e/

Table 21: SAMPA Boundary and Prosodic Features

SAMPA	ASCII	Comment
:	58	length mark
"papa	34	primary stress
""papa	34, 34	accent II words
%papa	37	secondary stress
-papa	45	level tone
'papa	39	rising tone
`papa	96	falling tone
`'papa	96,39	fall-rise
'`	39,96	rise-fall
$	36	syllable boundary
|	124	tone group boundary
-	45	separator

Although SAMPA does not provide a truly universal symbol set for all possible sounds, these symbols can be used to indicate the phonemes of prosodies of many of the languages in the CHILDES database. The next sections show how SAMPA can be applied to individual languages.

13.2   SAMPA UNIBET for English

This list includes symbols from SAMPA, IPA, the earlier CHAT UNIBET system, and the pronouncing dictionary of the CMU Speech Group. The CMU dictionary, used by the phonology programs, has only capital letters. Syllables stress is marked after the vowel as 2 (strong), 1 (mid), and 0 (weak). Segments are separated by spaces.

Table 22: English Consonants

SAMPA	UNIBET	IPA	CMU	Word	Transcription
p	p	p	P	pin	pIn
b	b	b	B	bin	bIn
t	t	t	T	tin	tIn
d	d	d	D	din	dIn
k	k	k	K	kin	kIn
g	g	g	G	give	gIv
tS	tS	tʃ	CH	chin	tSIn
dZ	dZ	dʒ	JH	gin	dZIn
f	f	f	F	fin	fIn
v	v	v	V	vim	vIm
T	T	θ	TH	thin	TIn
D	D	ð	DH	this	DIs
s	s	s	S	sin	sIn
z	z	z	Z	zing	zIN
S	S	ʃ	SH	shin	SIn
Z	Z	ʒ	ZH	measure	"meZ@
h	h	h	HH	hit	hIt
m	m	m	M	mock	mQk
n	n	n	N	knock	nQk
N	N	ŋ	NG	thing	TIN
r	r	r	R	wrong	rQN
l	l	l	L	long	lQN
w	w	w	W	wasp	wQsp
-	W	ʍ	-	which	WItS
j	j	j	Y	yacht	jQt

Table 23: English Vowels

SAMPA	UNIBET	CMU	Word	Transcription
I	I	IH	pit	pIt
e	e	EH	pet	pet
{	8	AE	pat	p{t
Q	a	AA	pot	pQt
V	A	AH	cut	kVt
U	U	UH	put	pUt
@	6	AH	another	@"nVD@
i:	i	IY	ease	i:z
eI	e	EY	raise	reIz
aI	ai	AY	rise	raIz
OI	oi	OY	noise	nOIz
u:		UW	lose	lu:z
@U	6U	OW	nose	n@uz
aU		AW	rouse	raUz
3:	3r	ER	furs	f3:z
A:	ar	AA R	stars	stA:z
O:		AO	cause	kO:z
I@	ir	IH R	fears	fI@z
e@	er	EH R	stairs	ste@z
U@	ur	UH R	cures	tjU@z
i	i	IY	happy	"ha{pi
u	u	UW	into	"Intu

Scottish English has the same consonants as other varieties of English, but also uses a velar fricative, as in "Loch" which can be represented with "x." Scottish English also has a reduced set of vowels.

13.3 SAMPA UNIBET for Dutch

Table 24: Dutch Consonants

SAMPA	Word	Transcription
p	pak	pAk
b	bak	bAk
t	tak	tAk
d	dak	dAk
k	kap	kAp
g	goal	go:l
f	fel	fEl
v	vel	vEl
s	sein	SEin
z	zijn	zEin
x	toch	tOx
G	goed	Gut
h	hand	hAnt
Z	bagage	bAga:Z(@)
S	show	So:u
m	met	mEt
n	net	nEt
N	bang	bAN
l	land	lAnt
r	rand	rAnt
w	wit	wIt
j	ja	ja:

Table 25: Dutch Vowels

SAMPA	Word	Transcription
I	pit	pIt
E	pet	pEt
A	pat	pAt
O	pot	pOt
Y	put	pYt
@	gemakkeliljk	G@"mAk@l@k
i	vier	vir
y	vuur	vyr
u	voer	vur
a:	naam	na:m
e:	veer	ve:r
2:	deur	d2:r
o:	voor	vo:r
Ei	fijn	fEin
9y	huis	h9ys
Au	goud	xAut
a:i	draai	"dra:i
o:i	mooi	"mo:i
ui	roeiboot	"ruibo:t
iu	nieuw	"niu
yu	duw	"dyu
e:u	sneeuw	"sne:u

13.4   Six UNIBETs for Dutch

Steven Gillis of the University of Antwerp has contributed the following table of correspondences between six UNIBETs for Dutch. We are recommending use of the SAMPA format for CHILDES data.

Table 26: Six UNIBETs for Dutch

IPA	YAPA	SAMPA	CELEX	CPA	DISC	CHAT	Example
p	p	p	p	p	p	p	put
b	b	b	b	b	b	b	bad
t	t	t	t	t	t	t	tak
d	d	d	d	d	d	d	dak
k	k	k	k	k	k	k	kat
g	g	g	g	g	g	g	goal
ŋ	N	N	N	N	N	N	lang
m	m	m	m	m	m	m	mat
n	n	n	n	n	n	n	nat
l	l	l	l	l	l	l	lat
R, r	r	r	r	r	r	r	rat
f	f	f	f	f	f	f	fiets
v	v	v	v	v	v	v	vat
s	s	s	s	s	s	s	sap
z	z	z	z	z	z	z	zat
ʃ	S	S	S	S	S	S	sjaal
ʒ	Z	Z	Z	Z	Z	Z	ravage
j	j	j	j	j	j	j	jas
x	x	x	x	X	x	X	licht
c	G	G	G	G	G	G	regen
h	h	h	h	h	h	h	had
ʊ	w	w	w	w	w	w	wat
dʒ	dZ	dZ	dZ	J/	_	dZ	jazz

Table 26: Six UNIBETs for Dutch

IPA	YAPA	SAMPA	CELEX	CPA	DISC	CHAT	Example
i:	i	i:	i:	i:	i	i	liep
y	y	y:	y:	y:	y	y	buut
e:	e	e:	e:	e:	e	e	leeg
ø:	&	2:	&:	q:	|	3	deuk
a:	a	a:	a:	a:	a	a	laat
o:	o	o:	o:	o:	o	o	boom
u:	u	u:	u:	u:	u	u	boek
ɪ	I	I	I	I	I	I	lip
ɛ	E	E	E	E	E	E	leg
ɑ	A	A	A	A	A	A	lat
ɔ	O	O	O	O	O	O	bom
œ	Y	}	U	Y/	}	Y	put
ə	@	@	@	@	@	6	gelijk
		i::	i::	i::	!		analyse
		y:	y:	y:	(		centrifuge
	E:	E:	E;	E;	)		scene
		/:	U:	Q:	*		freule
		Q:	O:	o:	<		zone
θɛi	E:j	Ei	EI	y/	K	8	wijs
œy	@:9	/I	UI	q/	L	8y	huis
ɑu	O:w	Au	AU	A/	M	Au	koud
c						c	petje

13.5   SAMPA UNIBET for French

Table 27: French Consonants

SAMPA	Word	Transcription
p	pont	po~
b	bon	bo~
t	temps	ta~
d	dans	da~
k	quand	ka~
g	gant	ga~
f	femme	fam
v	vent	va~
s	sans	sa~
z	zone	zon
S	champ	Sa~
Z	gens	Za~
j	ion	jo~
m	mont	mo~
n	nom	no~
J	oignon	oJo~
N	camping	ka~piN
l	long	lo~
R	rond	Ro~
w	coin	kwe~

Table 28: French Vowels

SAMPA	Word	Transcription
i	si	si
e	ses	se
E	seize	sEz
a	patte	pat
A	pâte	pAt
O	comme	kOm
o	gros	gRo
u	doux	du
y	du	dy
2	deux	d2
9	neuf	n9f
@	justement	Zyst@ma~
e~	vin	ve~
a~	vent	va~
o~	bon	bo~
9~	brun	bR9~

13.6   SAMPA UNIBET for German

Table 29: German Consonants

SAMPA	Word	Transcription
p	Pein	paIn
b	Bein	baIn
t	Teich	taIC
d	Deich	daIC
k	Kunst	kUnst
g	Gunst	gUnst
?	Verein	fE6"?aIn
pf	Pfahl	pfa:l
ts	Zahl	tsa:l
tS	deutsch	dOYtS
dZ	Dschungel	"dZUN=l
f	fast	fast
v	was	vas
s	Tasse	"tas@
z	Hase	"ha:z@
S	waschen	"vaS=n
Z	Genie	Ze"ni:
C	sicher	"zIC6
j	Jahr	ja:6
h	Hand	hant
m	mein	maIn
m	nein	naIn
N	Ding	dIN
l	Leim	laIm
R	Reim	RaIm

Table 30: German Vowels

SAMPA	Word	Transcription
I	Sitz	zIts
E	Gesetz	g@"zEts
a	Satz	zats
O	Trotz	trOts
U	Schutz	SUts
Y	hübsch	hYpS
9	plötzlich	"pl9tslIC
i:	Lied	li:t
e:	Beet	be:t
E:	spät	SpE:t
a:	Tat	ta:t
o:	rot	ro:t
u:	Blut	blu:t
y:	süß	zy:s
2:	blöd	bl2:t
aI	Eis	aIs
aU	Haus	haUs
OY	Kreuz	krOYts
@	bitte	"bIt@

13.7   SAMPA UNIBET for Italian

Table 31: Italian Consonants

SAMPA	Word	Transcription
p	pane	"pane
b	banco	"banko
t	tana	"tana
d	danno	"danno
k	cane	"kane
g	gamba	"gamba
ts	zitto	"tsitto
dz	zona	"dzOna
tS	cena	"tSena
dZ	gita	"dZita
f	fame	"fame
v	vano	"vano
s	sano	"sano
z	sbaglio	"zbaLLo
S	scendo	"Sendo

For the long consonants, the single character symbols are just doubled, as in "pp." The two-character symbols have the first character doubled as in "tts."

Table 32: Italian Vowels

UNIBET	IPA	Orthography	Example	Example
a	a	a	altro	"altro
e	e	e	pesca	"peska
E	ɛ	e	pesca	"pEska
i	i	i	spianti	"spianti
j	j	i	spianti	"spjanti
o	o	o	botte	"bot:e
O	ɔ	o	botte	"bOt:e
u	u	u	acuita'	akuit"a
w	w	u	equita'	ekwit"a

13.8   UNIBET for Japanese

Double letters are marked by colons and palatalization by "j".

Table 33: Japanese UNIBET - from Yashushi Terao

UNIBET	IPA	Word	Transcription
p	p	papa	papa
b	b	banana	banana
m	m	mame	mame
t	t	taki	taki
d	d	daiku	daiku
n	n	nami	nami
k	k	kagami	kagami
g	g	gakkoo	gak:o:
N	n(moraic)	san	saN
F	f	fune	Fune
s	s	sakana	sakana
z	z	zasshi	zaS:i
S	ʃ	shinsetsu	SiNsetsu
Z	dʒ	junjo	ZuNjo
ts	ts	kutsu	kutsu
tS	tʃ	kuchi	kutSi
h	h	hana	hana
x	h	hiza	xiza
w	w	watashi	wataSi
dt	r	remon	dtemoN
j	y	yama	jama
T	T	so:deTu@u	so:deTu
D	D	Dodtayaki	Dodtajaki
i	i	ike	pond
e	e	eki	station
u	u	uma	horse
o	o	obake	ghost
a	a	atama	head
6	ə	6ko:ki@b	airplane

13.9 SAMPA UNIBET for Portuguese

Table 34: Portuguese Consonants

SAMPA	Word	Transcription
p	pai	pai
b	barco	"barku
t	tenho	"teJu
d	doce	"dos@
k	com	ko~
f	falo	"falu
v	verde	"verd@
s	céu	sEw
z	case	"kaz6
S	chapéu	S6"pEw
Z	jóia	"ZOj6
m	mar	mar
n	nada	"nad6
J	vinho	"viJu
l	lanche	"l6nS@
L	trabalho	tr6"baLu
r	caro	"karu
R	rua	"Ru6

Table 35: Portuguese Vowels

SAMPA	Word	Transcription
i	vinte	"vint@
e	fazer	f6"zer
E	belo	"bElu
a	falo	"falu
6	cama	"k6m6
O	ontem	"Ont6~j~
o	lobo	"lobu
u	jus	Zus
@	felizes	f@liz@S
i~	fim	fi~
e~	emprego	e~"pregu
6~	irmã	ir"m6
u~	um	u~
aw	mau	maw
aj	mais	majS
6~j~	têm	t6~j~

The last three vowel symbols can also be combined with i, e, E, O, and o.

13.10   SAMPA UNIBET for Spanish

Table 36: Spanish UNIBET

SAMPA	Word	Transcription
p	padre	"paDre
b	vino	"bino
t	tomo	"tomo
d	donde	"donde
k	casa	"kasa
g	gata	"gata
tS	mucho	"mutSo
jj	hielo	"jjelo
f	fácil	"faTil
B	cabra	"kaBra
T	cinco	"Tinko
D	nada	"naDa
s	sala	"sala
x	mujer	"muxer
G	luego	"lweGo
m	mismo	"mismo
n	nunca	"nunka
J	año	"aJo
l	lejos	"lexos
L	caballo	ka"baLo
r	pure	"puro
rr	torre	"torre
j	pie	pje
w	deuda	"dewDa
i	pico	"pico
e	pero	"pero
a	valle	"baLe
o	toro	"toro
u	duro	"duro

13.11   Romanization of Cyrillic

Comrie and Corbett (1992) have summarized the Cyrillic characters of Ukrainian, Serbian, Macedonian, Russian, Belorussian, and Bulgarian. To their list we have added a set of ASCII forms. The meanings of the column headers are as follows:

Cyril: This is the Cyrillic character in uppercase and lowercase.

Lang: This is the language that uses this character. The dash symbol means that all of the languages in question use this character.

CHAT: This is the character string that will be stored in a CHAT file by the editor. We recommend use of the Macintosh Unicode fonts for Cyrillic, such as Latinski which are now built into the Macintosh operating system. For Windows, there is no clear standardization of fonts yet.

ASC: This is the form that some users may decide to use if they are restricted to using ASCII characters and are not hoping to see Cyrillic characters in their CHAT files.

C&C: These are the transliteration symbols used by Comrie and Corbett (1992). Some are ASCII characters, but some are non-ASCII Roman-based characters.

The abbreviations for languages are as follows:
R = Russian
U = Ukrainian
M = Macedonia
Bu = Bulgarian
Be = Belorussian
S = Serbian

Table 37: Cyrillic Characters

Cyr	Lang	CHAT	ASC	C&C	Cyr	Lang	CHAT	ASC	C&C
Аа	-	a	a	a	Њњ	M S	^nj	nj	nj
Бб	-	b	b	b	Оо	-	o	o	o
Вв	-	v	v	v	Пп	-	p	p	p
Гг	Bu M R S	g	g	g	Рр	-	r	r	r
Гг	Be U	h	h	h	Сс	-	s	s	s
Ѓѓ	U	g	g	g	Тт	-	t	t	t
Дд	-	d	d	d	Ћћ	S	^c'	c'	c'
Ђђ	S	^dh	dh	ð	Ќќ	M	^k'	k'	k'
Ѓѓ	M	^g'	g'	g'	Уу	-	u	u	u
Ее	-	e	e	e	Ўў	Be	^uc	u'	u°
Ёё	Be R	^jo	jo	ё	Фф	-	f	f	f
Єє	U	^je	je	je	Хх	Be Bu R U	x	x	x
Жж	-	^zh	zh	z=	Хх	M S	h	h	h
Ѕѕ	M	^dz	dz	dz	Цц	-	c	c	c
Зз	-	z	z	z	Чч	-	^ch	ch	c=
Ии	Bu M R S	i	i	i	Џџ	M S	^dz	dzh	dz=
Йй	U	y	y	y	Шш	-	^sh	sh	s=
Іі	Be U	i	i	i	Щщ	R U	^sc	sch	s=c=
Її	U	^i"	i"	ï	Щщ	Bu	^st	sht	s=t
Јј	M S	j	j	j	Ъъ	R	"	"	"
Йй	Be Bu R U	j	j	j	Ъъ	Bu	^ac	ac	a°
Кк	-	k	k	k	Ыы	Be R	y	y	y
Лл	-	l	l	l	Ьь	Be Bu R U	'	'	'
Љљ	M S	^lj	lj	lj	Ээ	Be R	^e'	e'	è
Мм	-	m	m	m	Юю	Be Bu R U	^ju	ju	ju
Нн	-	n	n	n	Яя	Be Bu R U	^ja	ja	ja

14: Error Coding

The CHAT error coding system was designed with the assistance of Joseph Stemberger. All of the examples of speech errors used in this chapter come from Stemberger's collection of natural speech errors (Stemberger, 1985). In the previous version of this error coding system, errors were always inserted on the main line. The problem with this method of coding is that it interferes with accurate lexical retrieval. In the current version of the system, errors are given on the main line when they are standard lexical forms. However, when they involve phonological changes, the target lexical form is given on the main line and the phonological error is coded on the %err line.

The [*] symbol is used to mark the presence of an error on the main line and this error is then analyzed and categorized in detail on the %err line. The CHAT system for error coding is designed with several goals in mind:

1. the system must indicate what the speaker actually said,

2. the system must indicate in some way that what the speaker said was an error,

3. the system must allow the transcriber to indicate what the correct or target forms should have been,

4. the coding should facilitate retrieval oriented both toward target forms and actually produced forms, and

5. the system must allow the analyst to indicate theoretically interesting aspects of the error by delineating the source of the error, the processes involved, and the type of the error in theoretical terms.

Researchers who are not trained in speech error theory will want to focus primarily on the first four goals. If the initial transcription meets these first four goals, then it will always be possible to produce new theoretical analyses at some later date.

14.1 Coding Format

On the main line, the transcriber places the [*] symbol after the error to indicate that the form preceding it was an error. If the error results in the misarticulation of a word, you should enter the target word on the main line, rather than the error. Doing this allows you to use the transcript for lexical searches. Let us consider some examples from an aphasic patient. If the patient describes a picture of a dog with the word "cat," we code this on the main line as follows:

```
*PAT: a cat [*].
```

The shape of the target is coded on the %err line in the following way.

```
*PAT: a cat [*].
%err: cat = dog
```

Here, the sequence of elements on the %err line is:

```
erroneous form = target form
```

Often errors are corrected by the speaker. In such cases we need to code both the presence of an error and the nature of the retracing. For example, in the following example, the error is marked with the asterisk and the retracing is marked by angle brackets:

```
*PAT:    a <cat [*] uh> [//] dog
```

If the error involves more than just the word before the [*], it is necessary to use angle brackets to indicate the complete error.

The transcriber must make sure that each error is followed immediately by the [*] symbol, and that each error is coded separately on the %err line. It is not absolutely necessary to code errors on the %err line. However, if the %err line is used, it is crucial to mark each error with the [*] symbol on the main line. Every error marked on the main line by an asterisk must be coded separately on the %err line. If this is not done, CLAN will not be able to construct the proper correspondence between the two lines. The following elements must always be present in the error analysis on the %err line:

1. the form actually said,
2. the symbol =,
3. the target,
4. a series of statements regarding possible sources that may have induced the error, using the $= symbol and parentheses to indicate the focus of the source,
5. various codes for the error, and
6. the semicolon symbol to mark the end of the codes for an error.

If the error involves nonstandard phonological forms, the transcriber should put the UNIBET representation of the actual form and the target in slashes directly after them. There is no need to provide UNIBET representations for standard lexical items unless the error involves a phonological change between standard lexical items. Let us take as an example of a phonological error a case where a subject is describing a picture of a boy hitting a dog and says "higging" for "hitting." In this case, the target form is entered on the main line, as shown here:

```
*PAT:    a boy hitting [*] a dog.
%err:    higging /hIgIN/ = hitting /hItIN/ $=hItI(N)
                $PHO $ANT ;
```

When the target is not clear, it can be followed by a question mark in brackets [?]. If the coder has no idea at all what the target might be, the [?] alone is sufficient. For example, the patient may respond to a question from the doctor saying in Italian "doctore fare" where the verb "fare" (= to do) could have as its target "ha fatto," "fa," or any of a number of the other forms in the conjugational paradigm for the verb. Here, we cannot really know what the target is. We may put down "ha fatto" as our best guess, but we realize that other forms are possible. Here is an example of the coding of these errors:

```
*PAT:    dottore fare [*]
%err:    fare = ha fatto [?] ;
```

Finally, consider the case where the patient is describing in English a picture of a mouse crying and says "eagles, eagles going." There is no clear relation between "eagles" and any aspect of the picture. In this case, we code the target as simply [?]:

```
*PAT:    eagles [*] [/] eagles [*] going
%err:    eagles = [?] ; eagles = [?] ;
```

Note that each separate occurrence of the same error is coded in full. The semicolon separates the two codings. If you want to avoid having to enter and analyze repeated error entries for repeated errors, you can use this form of notation instead:

```
*PAT:    eagles(*2) [*] going
%err:    eagles = [?] ;
```

In general, any number of errors may be coded on a single %err line, as long as there is one [*] symbol for each error and each coding on the %err line is separated by a semicolon.

So far, the types of errors we have been discussing are all **substitutions** that involve the use of one form for another. The other major types of morphemic error are **loss** and **addition**. "Loss" is just another name for "omission" or "deletion." Here is an example of loss:

```
*CHI:    I want two candy [*].
%err:    candy = candies $MOR $LOS ;
```

And here is an example of addition:

```
*CHI:    I want a candies [*].
%err:    candies = candy $MOR $ADD
```

Occasionally, a single form involves two major types of errors. For example, the following error from an Italian child involves both a phonological and an inflectional error. In this case, the second level of the error is coded after an additional = after which appears the second level of the target at the same locus. The second = symbol is not preceded by a second transcription of the error.

```
*CHI:    sei [*] (c)aduto [*].
%err:    tei /tei/ = sei /sei/
         $PHO $SUB $CON = sono $NFL ;
         (c)aduto = caduto $PHO $LOS
```

Here the singular form "sei" was used instead of the correct verb "sono." In addition, "sei" was misarticulated as "tei" and "caduto" was misarticulated as "aduto."

If there is a clearly identifiable lexical or phonological source for the error, the identity of this source can be coded by using the $= symbol. If the source is a whole word, insert the whole word after the $=. If the source is one or more parts of a word, surround those parts with parentheses as in $=(l)asts. An example of this is the following exchange error:

```
*SHE:   in the lakes [*] cities [*].
%err:   lakes /leiks/ = late /leit/ $=/si(ks)tiz/=cities
        $PHO $EX1 $CC ;
        cities /sItiz/ = sixties /sIkstiz/
        $PHO $EX2 $CC
```

In this example, the source is itself a target that never appears. The notation $=/si(ks)tiz/ =cities is to be read as follows: the source of the error is the target of the form "cities" which has the phonological shape /sikstiz/ for which the particular source is the sequence /ks/ noted by the parentheses. In most cases there is no reason to include the form after the second = sign. However, in some complicated errors it is nice to have this option so that the nature of the source is made maximally clear. When there are two or more sources for an error, as typically happens in blends, the various sources are listed separated only by commas (see the following examples). Admittedly, coding of the sources of errors is not an easy matter. If the transcriber prefers, the task of identifying sources can be left to others. However, if this is done, a note to this effect should be put in the 00readme.cdc file or in an @Warning header.

14.2   Error Codes

Having completed the coding of the error up to this point, the transcriber can choose whether or not to further analyze the error in terms of particular error codes. For those who wish to do further analysis, this section provides an initial set of codes. Researchers will surely wish to add to this set. If they do add new codes, they will also need to enter these codes in the "depfile" used by CHECK. The codes are given in capital letters, but they can be entered in lower case, if this is easier. Except for the symbols in the UNIBET systems, CHAT coding is not case-sensitive.

Level codes distinguish between different linguistics levels, including phonology, lexicon, morphology, and syntax. If both phonological and lexical influences are suspected, both codes can be used.

Table 38: Error Level Codes

Code	Usage
$PHO	error involving specific phonological units
	example: gutter = butter
$LEX	choice of the wrong word on a semantic basis
	example: coat = sweater
$SYN	syntactic error, accommodation, stranding, etc.
$MOR	omissions, additions, and substitutions of closed-class items
	example: jump = jumped

Table 38: Error Level Codes

Code	Usage
$ALL	morphophonological errors in allosegments or allomorphs
	example: guve = gave
$CWFA	complex word finding attempts as in Wernicke's aphasia
	example: a binny, a figgy, a fig, no an eagey
$MAL	malapropism (mix of phonological and lexical sources)
	example: croutons = coupons
$INT	intonational error usually detected during a retraced false start
$NW	nonword with an unknown or unclear basis
	example: griff
$CIR	circumlocution, as in Wernicke's aphasia
	example: do with car = drive

After the general codes, the analyst should classify the error into at least one of the following error types.

Table 39: Error Type Codes

Code	Error Type	Example
$ADD	addition	blunch = bunch
$LOS	loss (also use the 0 symbol)	garet = garnet
$SUB	substitution	batter = tatter
$HAP	haplology	Sancisco -> San Francisco
$BLE	a blend	flaste = flavor + taste
$EX1	first part of an exchange error	broudy klight = cloudy bright
$EX2	second part of an exchange error	broudy klight = cloudy bright
$SH1	first part of a shift error	people same = same people
$SH2	second part of a shift error	people same = same people
$ANT	anticipation – an item is produced early	bould be = would be
$PER	perseveration – an item is produced late	would we = would be

Table 39: Error Type Codes

Code	Error Type	Example
$A/P	anticipation and perseveration	thingle = single thing
$ACH	A anticipates B which anticipates C	
$PCH	C perseverates B which perseverates A	
$INC	the production is incomplete	
$UNC	unclear how to classify the error type	

Phonological codes are used to further characterize $PHO errors.

Table 40: Phonological Error Codes

Code	Usage	Example
$VOW	error involving a vowel or diphthong	bonny = bunny
$CON	error involving consonants	munny = bunny
$CC	error involving consonant clusters	tickle = trickle
$SYL	the target or source are full syllables	perfacial performance = spatial performance
$FEA	error involving particular features	munny = bunny
$STS	error involving stress	capiTULate = caPITulate
$MRA	moraic error	
$TON	error involving tone	

Morphological codes are used to further characterize $MOR errors.

Table 41: Morphological Error Codes

Code	Usage	Example
$PRE	error involving prefix	misforgiving = unforgiving
$SUF	error involving suffix	taked = taken
$NFX	error involving infix	
$NFL	error involving inflection	taked = taken
$DER	error involving derivation	misforgiving = unforgiving

Table 41: Morphological Error Codes

Code	Usage	Example
$RED	error involving reduplication	sevenses = sevens
$AGA	error of agreement, agreer is wrong	el palma
$AGC	error of agreement, controller is wrong	la palmo
$AGB	error with both wrong	el palmo
$REG	regularization	eated = ate
$FUL	full regularization	throwed = threw
$PAR	partial regularization	threwed = threw
$HAR	vowel harmony error	ablakek = ablakok

Syntactic codes are used to further characterize $SYN errors

Table 42: Syntactic Error Codes

Code	Usage	Example
$ACC	error with accommodation	a apper = an 'A'
$STR	error where affixes are stranded	the flood was roaded = the road was flooded
$SBL	syntactic blend	thingle = single thing
$POS	position error	gave it him = gave him it

14.3   Hesitation Codes

CHAT allows you to code hesitation phenomena directly on the main line, using symbols such as # for pause or [//] for retracing. Some researchers may also want to indicate these various hesitation phenomena by separate codes on the %err line.

Table 43: Hesitation Code List

Code	Usage
$ISR	initial segment repetition
$WR	word repetition
$MWR	multiple word repetition
$RFS	retraced false start
$UNP	unfilled pause
$FIP	filled pause
$FRG	word fragment

14.4   Error Codes for Coder's Editor

The coding of speech errors can be facilitated by the use of the Coder's Editor facility. This facility allows the user to automatically step through a pre-determined set of codes that can be constructed in a hierarchical fashion. The codes.cut file that we could use to do this is as follows. This file is distributed with CLAN as the file codes.err. Also, the +s1 switch declared in the first line allows us to avoid repeated entry of codes under categories. For further details on this type of coding, see the description of Coder's Editor in the CLAN manual.

14.5   Examples

This section provides a series of examples that show how the codes given in this chapter are intended to be used.

```
*JOE:    is it cloudy [*] bright [*] ?
%err:    broudy /braUdi/ = cloudy /klaUdi/
         $=/(br)aIt/ = klight $PHO
         $EX1 $CC ; klight /klaIt/ = bright /braIt/
         $=/(kl)aUdi/= broudy $PHO $EX2 $CC

*SHE:    I got <a paper> [*] on my test [*].
%err:    a paper = an A $=paper=test $LEX $EX1 $ACC ;
         test = paper $LEX $EX2 $SUB

*SHE:    the flood [*] was roaded [*].
%err:    flood = road $=flooded=roaded $STE $EX1 $STR ;
         roaded = flooded $=road=flood $STE $EX2 $STR

*SHE:    he would [*] &re [*] real +...
```

```
%err:    bould /bUd/ = would /wUd/ $=/(b)i/=re $PHO $ANT $CHN ;
         re / ri/ = be /bi/ $=/(r)il/
         $PHO $SUB $DANT $CON $CHN

*SHE:    you think Purina [*] Cat [*] Chow lasts +...
%err:    Pulina /pulin6/ = Purina /purin6/ $=(l)&sts
         $PHO $ANT $SUB $CON ;
         Lat /l&t/ = Rat /r&t/
         $=(l)&sts $PHO $ANT $SUB $CON

*JIM:    +... in the bite [*] block experiment.
%err:    blite /blaIt/ = bite /baIt/ $=/b(l)Qk/ $PHO $ANT $ADD $CON

*BEA:    oh # we plant [*] peas every spring.
%err:    pant /pAnt/ = plant /plAnt/ $=/p()iz/ $PHO $ANT $LOS $CON
*KAT:    perfacial [*] performance.
%err:    perfacial /p3feISVl/ = spatial /speISVl/
         $=/(p3f)ormVns/ $PHO $ANT $SUB $CON $SYL $MIX

*SHE:    you don't act [*] mad.
%err:    atk /&tk/ = act /&kt/ $PHO $SH1 $SH2 $CON

*SHE:    I knit my sweater [*] Michelle a scarf.
%err:    sweater = sister $=scarf $ANT $SUB $LEX<7> $SND<4>

*SHE:    it has a very nice taste [*].
%err:    flaste /fleIst/ = taste /teIst/ $=flavor,taste $LEX $BLN

*SHE:    I haven't found a single [*] yet.
%err:    thingle /TiNgl/ = single thing /siNglTiN/$=single thing
         $LEX $SBL $A/P

*SHE:    he relax [*] when you go away.
%err:    relax = relaxes $LOS $SUF $NFL

*SHE:    I carefully looked at them and
         <choosed [*]>[//] chose that one.
%err:    choosed = chose $MOR $SUF $NFL $REG $FUL

*SPE:    it took [*] a while.
%err:    tooked = took $MOR $SUF $NFL $SUB $REG $PAR

*JEA:    the infant <tucks [*]> [//] touches the nipple.
%err:    tucks = touches $PHO $SUB $ACC

*JOE:    did a lot of people [*] different [*] see it?
%err:    people = different $=people=different $LEX $SH1 ;
                 different = people $=different=people $LEX $SH2

*SHE:    uhoh # where it [*] is [*]?
%err:    it = is $LEX $SH1 ; is = it $LEX $SH2
```

15:   Speech Act Codes

One way of coding speech acts is to separate the component of illocutionary force from those aspects that deal with interchange types. One can also distinguish a set of codes that relate to the modality or means of expression. Codes of these three types can be placed together on the %spa tier. One form of coding precedes each code type with an identifier, such as "x" for interchange type and "i" for illocutionary type. Here is an example of the combined use of these various codes:

```
*MOT:    are you okay?
%spa:    $x:dhs $i:yq
```

Alternatively, one can combine the codes in a hierarchical system, so that the previous example would have only the code $dhs:yq. Choice of different forms for codes depends on the goals of the analysis, the structure of the coding system, and the way the codes interface with CLAN.

Users will often need to construct their own coding schemes. However, one scheme that has received extensive attention is one proposed by Ninio and Wheeler (1986). Ninio, Snow, Pan, and Rollins (1994) provided a simplified version of this system called INCA-A, or Inventory of Communicative Acts – Abridged. The next two sections give the categories of interchange types and illocutionary forces in the proposed INCA-A system.

15.1   Interchange Types

Table 44: Interchange Type Codes

Code	Function	Explanation
CMO	comforting	to comfort and express sympathy for misfortune
DCA	discussing clarification of action	to discuss clarification of hearer's nonverbal communicative acts
DCC	discussing clarification of communication	to discuss clarification of hearer's ambiguous verbal communication or a confirmation of the speaker's understanding of it
DFW	discussing the fantasy world	to hold a conversation within fantasy play
DHA	directing hearer's attention	to achieve joint focus of attention by directing hearer's attention to objects, persons, and events
DHS	discussing hearer's sentiments	to hold a conversation about hearer's nonobservable thoughts and feelings

Table 44: Interchange Type Codes

Code	Function	Explanation
DJF	discussing a joint focus of attention	to hold a conversation about something that both participants are attending to, e.g., objects, persons, ongoing actions of hearer and speaker, ongoing events
DNP	discussing the nonpresent	to hold a conversation about topics that are not observable in the environment, e.g., past and future events and actions, distant objects and persons, abstract matters (excluding inner states)
DRE	discussing a recent event	to hold a conversation about immediately past actions and events
DRP	discussing the related-to-present	to discuss nonobservable attributes of objects or persons present in the environment or to discuss past or future events related to those referents
DSS	discussing speaker's sentiments	to hold a conversation about speaker's nonobservable thoughts and feelings
MRK	marking	to express socially expected sentiments on specific occasions such as thanking, apologizing, or to mark some event
NCS	negotiate copresence and separation	to manage the transition
NFA	negotiating an activity in the future	to negotiate actions and activities in the far future
NIA	negotiating the immediate activity	to negotiate the initiation, continuation, ending and stopping of activities and acts; to direct hearer's and speaker's acts; to allocate roles, moves, and turns in joint activities
NIN	noninteractive speech	to engage in private speech or produces utterances not addressed to present hearer
NMA	negotiate mutual attention	to establish mutual attentiveness and proximity or withdrawal
PRO	performing verbal moves	to perform moves in a game or other activity by uttering the appropriate verbal forms
PSS	negotiating possession of objects	to discuss who is the possessor of an object
SAT	showing attentiveness	to demonstrate that speaker is paying attention to the hearer

Table 44: Interchange Type Codes

Code	Function	Explanation
TXT	reading written text	to read or recite written text aloud
OOO	unintelligible	to mark unintelligible utterances
YYY	uninterpretable	to mark uninterpretable utterances

15.2   Illocutionary Force Codes

15.2.1   Directives

AC   Answer calls; show attentiveness to communications.
AD   Agree to carry out an act requested or proposed by other.
AL   Agree to do something for the last time.
CL   Call attention to hearer by name or by substitute exclamations.
CS   Counter-suggestion; an indirect refusal.
DR   Dare or challenge hearer to perform an action.
GI   Give in; accept other's insistence or refusal.
GR   Give reason; justify a request for an action, refusal, or prohibition.
RD   Refuse to carry out an act requested or proposed by other.
RP   Request, propose, or suggest an action for hearer, or for hearer and speaker.
RQ   Yes/no question or suggestion about hearer's wishes and intentions
SS   Signal to start performing an act, such as running or rolling a ball.
WD   Warn of danger.

15.2.2   Speech Elicitations

CX   Complete text, if so demanded.
EA   Elicit onomatopoeic or animal sounds.
EI   Elicit imitation of word or sentence by modelling or by explicit command.
EC   Elicit completion of word or sentence.
EX   Elicit completion of rote-learned text.
RT   Repeat or imitate other's utterance.
SC   Complete statement or other utterance in compliance with request.

15.2.3   Commitments

FP   Ask for permission to carry out act.
PA   Permit hearer to perform act.
PD   Promise.
PF   Prohibit/forbid/protest hearer's performance of an act.
SI   State intent to carry out act by speaker; describe one's own ongoing activity.
TD   Threaten to do.

15.2.4   Declarations

DC   Create a new state of affairs by declaration.
DP   Declare make-believe reality.
ND   Disagree with a declaration.
YD   Agree to a declaration.

15.2.5   Markings

CM   Commiserate, express sympathy for hearer's distress.
EM   Exclaim in distress, pain.
EN   Express positive emotion.
ES   Express surprise.
MK   Mark occurrence of event (thank, greet, apologize, congratulate, etc.).
TO   Mark transfer of object to hearer.
XA   Exhibit attentiveness to hearer.

15.2.6   Statements

AP   Agree with proposition or proposal expressed by previous speaker.
CN   Count.
DW   Disagree with proposition expressed by previous speaker.
ST   Make a declarative statement.
WS   Express a wish.

15.2.7   Questions

AQ   Aggravated question, expression of disapproval by restating a question.
AA   Answer in the affirmative to yes/no question.
AN   Answer in the negative to yes/no question.
EQ   Eliciting question (e.g., hmm?).
NA   Intentionally nonsatisfying answer to question.
QA   Answer a question with a wh-question.
QN   Ask a product-question (wh-question).
RA   Refuse to answer.
SA   Answer a wh-question with a statement.
TA   Answer a limited-alternative question.
TQ   Ask a limited-alternative yes/no question.
YQ   Ask a yes/no question.
YA   Answer a question with a yes/no question.

15.2.8   Performances

PR   Perform verbal move in game.
TX   Read or recite written text aloud.

15.2.9 Evaluations

AB	Approve of appropriate behavior.
CR	Criticize or point out error in nonverbal act.
DS	Disapprove, scold, protest disruptive behavior.
ED	Exclaim in disapproval.
ET	Express enthusiasm for hearer's performance.
PM	Praise for motor acts, i.e. for nonverbal behavior.

15.2.10 Demands for clarification

RR	Request to repeat utterance.

15.2.11 Text editing

CT	Correct, provide correct verbal form in place of erroneous one.

15.2.12 Vocalizations

YY	Make a word-like utterance without clear function.
OO	Unintelligible vocalization.

There are some other, more general, speech act codes that have been widely used in child language research and which can be encountered in some of the corpora in the CHILDES database. These general codes should not be combined with the more detailed INCA-A codes. They include ELAB (Elaboration), EVAL (Evaluation), IMIT (Imitation), NR (No Response), Q (Question), REP (Repetition), N (Negation), and YN (Yes/No Question).

16:   Morphosyntactic Coding

Many students of child language are interested in examining the role of universals in language acquisition. To test for the impact of universals, researchers need to examine the development of grammatical marking and syntax in corpora from different languages. If such research is to be conducted efficiently, it must be made available to computational analysis. This requires that there be a level of representation that uses a standard set of morphosyntactic codings. This chapter presents a system for constructing such a representation, using the %mor and the %syn tiers.

16.1   Morphological Coding

It is now possible to automatically generate a %mor tier from a main tier by using the MOR command. At present, MOR grammars exist for English, Dutch, German, Japanese, and Spanish. The grammars for Dutch and German are based on full listings of forms, rather than morphological analysis by parts. MOR creates a %mor tier with a one-to-one correspondence between words on the main line and words on the %mor tier. In order to achieve this one-to-one correspondence, the following rules are observed:

1.   Each word on the %mor line is separated by spaces to correspond to a space-delimited word on the main line.

2.   Utterance delimiters are preserved on the %mor line to facilitate readability and analysis.

3.   Retracings and repetitions are excluded from this one-to-one mapping, as are nonwords such as xxx or strings beginning with &. When word repetitions are marked in the form word(*3), the material in parentheses is stripped off and the word is considered as a single form.

4.   When a replacing form is indicated on the main line with the form [: text], the material on the %mor line corresponds to the replacing material in the square brackets, not the material that is being replaced. For example, if the main line has **gonna [: going to],** the %mor line will code **going to.**

5.   The [*] symbol that is used on the main line to indicate errors is not duplicated on the %mor line. However, morphological errors of omission and commission can be coded on the %mor line using the symbols *0 and *text respectively. If a morphological error can be coded on the %mor line without using the %err line, there is no need to insert the [*] on the main line.

The basic scheme for coding of words on the %mor line is:

```
part-of-speech|
stem
&fusionalsuffix
#prefix
-suffix
=english (optional)
```

Items of this shape can be further combined using the delimiter + is for words in a compound and the delimiter ~ for clitics.

When a word has several prefixes and/or several suffixes, these should be listed in the order of their occurrence within the word. The English translation of the stem is not a part of the morphology, but is included for convenience in retrieval and data entry.

Now let us look in greater detail at the nature of each of these types of coding. Throughout this discussion, bear in mind that all coding is done on a word-by-word basis.

16.2 Part of Speech Codes

The morphological codes on the %mor line begin with a part-of-speech code. The basic scheme for the part-of-speech code is:

```
syntactic category:sub-category
```

Additional fields can be added, using the colon character as the field separator. The sub-category fields contain information about syntactic features of the word that are not marked overtly. For example, you may wish to code the fact that Italian "andare" is an intransitive verb even though there is no single morpheme that signals intransitivity. You can do this by using the part-of-speech code **v:intrans**, rather than by inserting a separate morpheme.

In order to avoid redundancy, information that is marked by a prefix or suffix is not incorporated into the part-of-speech code, as this information will be found to the right of the | delimiter. These codes can be given in either uppercase, as in **ADJ**, or lowercase, as in **adj**. In general, CHAT codes are not case-sensitive.

The particular codes given below are the ones that MOR uses for automatic morphological tagging of English. Individual researchers will need to define a system of part-of-speech codes that correctly reflects their own research interests and theoretical commitments. Languages that are typologically quite different from English may have to use very different part-of-speech categories. Quirk, Greenbaum, Leech, and Svartvik (1985) explain some of the intricacies of part-of-speech coding. Their analysis should be taken as definitive for all part-of-speech coding for English. However, for many purposes, a more coarse-grained coding can be used.

The following set of top-level part-of-speech codes is the one used by the MOR program. Additional refinements to this system can be found by studying the organization of the lexicon files for that program For example, in MOR, numbers are coded as types of determiners, because this is there typically usage. The word "there" is coded as either a locative adverb (adv:loc) or an existential pronoun (pro:exist). Further distinctions can be found by looking at the MOR lexicon.

Table 45: Major Parts of Speech

Category	Code
Adjective	ADJ
Adverb	ADV
Communicator	CO
Conjunction	CONJ
Determiner	DET
Filler	FIL
Infinitive marker *to*	INF
Noun	N
Proper Noun	N:PROP
Number	DET:NUM
Particle	PTL
Preposition	PREP
Pronoun	PRO
Quantifier	QN
Verb	V
Auxiliary verb, including modals	V:AUX
WH words	WH

16.3   Stems

Every word on the %mor tier must include a "lemma" or stem as part of the morpheme analysis. The stem is found on the right hand side of the | delimiter, following any pre-clitics or prefixes. If the transcript is in English, this can be simply the canonical form of the word. For nouns, this is the singular. For verbs, it is the infinitive. If the transcript is in another language, it can be the English translation. A single form should be selected for each stem. Thus, the English indefinite article is coded as `det|a` with the lemma "a" whether or not the actual form of the article is "a" or "an." When the stem is a special word, such as a nonce form marked with the @n symbol, then the full nonce form together with its @n should be put after the | symbol, as in `N|bahbi@n`.

When English is not the main language of the transcript, the transcriber must decide whether to use English stems. Using English stems has the advantage that it makes the corpus more available to English-reading researchers. To show how this is done, take the German phrase "wir essen":

```
*FRI:    wir essen.
%mor:    pro|wir=we v|ess=eat-INF.
```

Some projects may have reasons to avoid using English stems, even as translations. In this example, "essen" would be simply **v|ess-INF**. Other projects may wish to use only English stems and no target-language stems. Sometimes there are multiple possible translations into English. For example, German "Sie"/sie" could be either "you," "she," or "they." Choosing a single English meaning helps fix the German form. However, when it is not clear which form to choose, the alternatives can be indicated by a second = sign, as in "=she=they."

16.4   Affixes

Affixes and clitics are coded in the position in which they occur with relation to the stem. The morphological status of the affix should be identified by the following delimiters: - for a suffix, # for a prefix, ~ for a clitic, and & for fusional or infixed morphology. These four markers have the same meaning on the %mor tier as in the main line morphemicization system presented on page 52.

The **&** is used to mark affixes that are not realized in a clearly isolable phonological shape. For example, the form "men" cannot be broken down into a part corresponding to the stem "man" and a part corresponding to the plural marker, because one cannot say that the vowel "e" marks the plural. For this reason, the word is coded as **n|man&PL**. The past forms of irregular verbs may undergo similar ablaut processes, as in "came," which is coded **v|come&PAST**, or they may undergo no phonological change at all, as in "hit", which is coded **v|hit&PAST**. Sometimes there may be several codes indicated with the **&** after the stem. For example, the form "was" is coded **v|be&PAST&13s**. Affix and clitic codes are based either on Latin forms for grammatical function or English words corresponding to particular closed-class items. MOR uses the following set of affix codes for automatic morphological tagging of English.

Table 46: Inflectional Affixes for English

Function	Code
adjective suffix *er, r*	CP
adjective suffix *est, st*	SP
noun suffix *ie*	DIM

Table 46: Inflectional Affixes for English

Function	Code
noun suffix *s, es*	PL
noun suffix *'s, '*	POSS
verb suffix *s, es*	3S
verb suffix *ed, d*	PAST
verb suffix *ing*	PROG
verb suffix *en*	PERF

Table 47: Derivational Affixes for English

Function	Code
adjective and verb prefix *un*	UN
adverbializer *ly*	LY
nominalizer *er*	ER
noun prefix *ex*	EX
verb prefix *dis*	DIS
verb prefix *mis*	MIS
verb prefix *out*	OUT
verb prefix *over*	OVER
verb prefix *pre*	PRE
verb prefix *pro*	PRO
verb prefix *re*	RE

16.5   Clitics

Clitics are marked by a tilde, as in `v|parl=speak&IMP:2S~pro|DAT:MASC:SG` for Italian "parlagli" and `pro|it~v|be&3s` for English "it's." Note that part of speech codingwith the | symbol is repeated for clitics after the tilde. Both clitics and contracted elements are coded with the tilde. The use of the tilde for contracted elements extends to forms like "sul" in Italian, "ins" in German, or "rajta" in Hungarian in which prepositions are merged with articles or pronouns.

Table 48: Clitic Codes for English

Clitic	Code
noun phrase post-clitic *'d*	v:aux|would, v|have&PAST
noun phrase post-clitic *'ll*	v:aux|will
noun phrase post-clitic *'m*	v|be&1S, v:aux|be&1S
noun phrase post-clitic *'re*	v|be&PRES, v:aux|be&PRES
noun phrase post-clitic *'s*	v|be&3S, v:aux|be&3S
verbal post-clitic *n't*	neg|not

16.6   Compounds

On <u>page 52</u> we discussed the marking of compounds on the main line. For coding on the %mor line, we will want to make further, more precise differentiations. Here are some words that we might want to treat as compounds: *San+Diego+Zoo*, *Mister+Frog*, *sweat+shirt*, *tennis+court*, *bathing+suit*, *high+school*, *play+ground*, *choo+choo+train*, *rock+'n+roll*, and *High+street*. There are also many idiomatic phrases that could be best analyzed as compounds. Here are some examples: *a+lot+of*, *all+of+a+sudden*, *at+last*, *for+sure*, *kind+of*, *of+course*, *once+and+for+all*, *once+upon+a+time*, *so+far*, and *lots+of*.

On the %mor tier it is necessary to assign a part-of-speech label to the entire compound, and to identify the constituent stems, plus any inflectional affixes or clitics. For example, the word *choo+choo+trains* is coded on the %mor tier as **n|choo+choo+train-PL**.

In order to preserve the one-to-one correspondance between words on the main line and words on the %mor tier, words that are not marked as compounds on the main line should not be coded as compounds on the %mor tier. For example, if the words "come here" are used as a rote form, then they should be written as "come+here" on the main tier. On the %mor tier this will be coded as **v|come+here**. It makes no sense to code this as **v|come+adv|here**, because that analysis would contradict the claim that this pair functions as a single unit. It is sometimes difficult to assign a part-of-speech code to a morpheme. In the usual case, the part-of-speech code should be chosen from the same set of codes used to label single words of the language. For example, some of the these idiomatic phrases can be coded as compounds on the %mor line.

Table 49: Phrases Coded as Compounds

Phrase	Phrase
qn|a+lot+of	adv|all+of+a+sudden
co|for+sure	adv:int|kind+of
adv|once+and+for+all	adv|once+upon+a+time
adv|so+far	qn|lots+of.

16.7   Sample Morphological Tagging for English

The following table describes and illustrates a more detailed set of word class codings for English. The %mor tier examples correspond to the labellings MOR produces for the words in question. It is possible to augment or simplify this set, either by creating additional word categories, or by adding additional fields to the part-of-speech label, as discussed previously.

Table 50: Word Classes for English

Class	Examples	Coding of Examples
adjective	big	adj|big
adjective, comparative	bigger, better	adj|big-CP, adj|good&CP
adjective, superlative	biggest, best	adj|big-SP, adj|good&SP
adverb	well	adv|well
adverb, ending in ly	quickly	adv|quick-ADVR
adverb, intensifying	very, rather	adv:int|very, adv:int|rather
adverb, post-qualifying	enough, indeed	adv|enough, adv|indeed
adverb, locative	here, then	adv|here, adv|then
communicator	aha	co|aha
conjunction, coordinating	and, or	conj:coord|and, conj:coord|or
conjunction, subord.	if, although	conj:subord|if, conj:subord|although
conjunction, pragmatic	but	conj:prag|but
determiner, indefinite	some, any, no	det|some, det|any, det|no

Table 50: Word Classes for English

Class	Examples	Coding of Examples
determiner, singular	a, the, this	det|a, det|this
determiner, plural	these, those	det|these, det|those
determiner, conjunctive	either, neither	det|either, det|neither
determiner, possessive	my, your, her	det:poss|my
infinitive marker	to	inf|to
noun, common	cat, coffee	n|cat, n|coffee
noun, plural	cats	n|cat-PL
noun, possessive	cat's	n|cat-POSS
noun, plural possessive	cats'	n|cat-PL-POSS
noun, proper	Mary	n:prop|Mary
noun, proper, plural	Marys	n:prop|Mary-PL
noun, proper, possessive	Mary's	n:prop|Mary-POSS
noun, proper, pl. poss.	Marys'	n:prop|Mary-PL-POSS
noun, adverbial	home, west	n:adv|home, n:adv|west
number, cardinal	two	num|two
number, ordinal	second	adj|second
particle	up	ptl|up
preposition	in	prep|in
pronoun, personal	I, me, we, us, he	pro|I, pro|me, pro|we, pro|us
pronoun, reflexive	myself, ourselves	pro:refl|myself
pronoun, possessive	mine, yours, his	pro:poss|mine, pro:poss|his
pronoun, demonstrative	that, this, these	pro:dem|that
pronoun, indefinite	everybody, nothing	pro:indef|everybody
pronoun, indefinite, poss.	everybody's	pro:indef|everybody-POSS
pronoun. existential	there	pro:exist|there
quantifier	half, all	qn|half, qn|all
verb, base form	walk, run	v|walk, v|run

Table 50: Word Classes for English

Class	Examples	Coding of Examples
verb, 3rd singular present	walks, runs	v|walk-3S, v|run-3S
verb, past tense	walked, ran	v|walk-PAST, v|run&PAST
verb, present participle	walking, running	v|walk-PROG, v|run-PROG
verb, past participle	walked, run	v|walk-PAST, v|run&PERF
verb, modal auxiliary	can, could, must	v:aux|can, v:aux|could, v:aux|must

Since it is sometimes difficult to decide what part of speech a word belongs to, we offer the following overview of the different part-of-speech labels used in the standard English grammar.

Adjectives modify nouns, either prenominally, or predicatively. Unitary compound modifiers such as **good-looking** should be labeled as adjectives.

Adverbs cover a heterogenous class of words including: manner adverbs, which generally end in **-ly**; locative adverbs, which include expressions of time and place; intensifiers that modify adjectives; and post-head modifiers, such as **indeed** and **enough.**

Communicators are used for interactive and communicative forms which fulfill a variety of functions in speech and conversation. Many of these are formulaic expressions such as **hello, good-morning, good-bye, please, thank-you**. Also included in this category are words used to express emotion, as well as imitative and onomatopeic forms, such as **ah, aw, boom, boom-boom, icky, wow, yuck,** and **yummy.**

Conjunctions conjoin two or more words, phrases, or sentences. Coordinating conjunctions include: **and, but, or,** and **yet**. Subordinating conjunctions include: **although, because, if, unless,** and **until.**

Determiners include articles, and definite and indefinite determiners. Possessive determiners such as **my** and **your** are tagged **det:poss.**

The Infinitive marker is the word "to" which is tagged **inf|to.**

Nouns are tagged with **n** for common nouns, and n:**prop** for proper nouns (names of people, places, fictional characters, brand-name products).

The Negative marker is the word "not" which is tagged **neg|not.**

Numbers are labelled **num** for cardinal numbers. The ordinal numbers are adjectives.

Particles are words that are often also prepositions, but are serving as verbal particles.

Prepositions are labelled **prep.** When classifying a word as a preposition, make sure that it is part of a prepositional phrase. When a preposition is not a part of a phrase, it should be coded as a particle or an adverb.

Quantifiers include **each, every, all, some,** and similar items.

16.8   Error Coding on the %mor Tier

When an item on the main line is incorrect in either phonological or semantic terms, the coding of that item on the %mor line should be based on its target, as given in the %err line. If there is no clear target, the form should be represented with xxx, as in the following example:

```
*PAT:    the catty [*] was on a eaber [*].
%mor:    det|the *n|kitty v|be&PAST prep|on
                   det|a *n|xxx.
%err:    catty - kitty $BLE $=cat,kitty ; eaber = [?]
```

In this example the symbol * on the %mor line indicates the presence of an error, in this case a stem error. The detailed analysis of this error should be conducted on the %err line. In order to facilitate the analysis of overuse and underuse of grammatical markers, the symbol *0 can be used to indicate omission and the symbol * can be used to indicate incorrect usage, as in the following examples:

```
*CHI:    dog is eat.
%mor:    *0det|the n|dog v:aux|be&PRES v|eat-*0PROG.

*PAT:    the dog was eaten [*] the bone.
%mor:    det|the n|dog v:aux|be&PAST&3S v|eat-*PERF det|the n|bone.
%err:    eaten = eating $MOR $SUB
```

Here is an example of coding on the %mor line that indicates how the omission of an auxiliary is coded:

```
*BIL:    he going.
%mor:    pro|he *0v|be&3S v|go-prog.
```

Note that the missing auxiliary is not coded on the main line, because this information is available on the %mor line. If a noun is omitted, there is no need to also code a missing article. Similarly, if a verb is omitted, there is no need to also code a missing auxiliary.

16.9   Coding Syntactic Structure

The syntactic role of each word can be notated before its part of speech on the %mor line. However, in order to capture syntactic groupings, it is better to code syntactic structure on the %syn line. Clauses are enclosed in angle brackets and their type is indicated in square brackets, as in the following example:

```
*CHI:   if I don't get all the cookies you promised to give me,
        I'll cry.
%syn:   <C S X V M M D < S V < R V I > [CP] > [RC] > [CC] <S    V    >
        [MC].
```

In this notation, each word plays some syntactic role. The rules for achieving one-to-one correspondence to words on the main line apply to the %syn line also. Higher order syntactic groupings are indicated by the bracket notation. The particular syntactic codes used in this example come from the following list. This list is not complete and researchers may need to devise additional codes, particularly for languages other than English.

Table 51: Syntactic Codes

Code	Category	Code	Category
A	Adverbial Adjunct	V	Verb
C	Conjunction	X	Auxiliary
D	Direct Object	AP	Appositive Phrase
I	Indirect Object	CC	Coordinate Clause
M	Modifier	CP	Complement
P	Preposition	MC	Main Clause
R	Relativizer/Inf	PP	Prepositional Phrase
S	Subject	RC	Relative Clause

The proposals for syntactic coding given in this section are extremely preliminary and will need significant further development.

16.10   Codes for Grammatical Morphemes

It is not possible to provide an exhaustive list of all of the concepts expressed in all of the morphological systems of the world's languages. However, abbreviations for the names of some of the most frequent concepts can be found in a list first constructed by Lehmann (1982). The codes are given in capital letters, but they can also be used in lowercase, because CHAT coding is not case sensitive. Codes that refer to parts of speech, rather than grammatical markings, are noted with asterisks.

Table 52: Universal Morphological Codes

Code	Meaning	Code	Meaning	Code	Meaning
1	first person	INESS	inessive (in X)	2	second person
INF	infinitive*	3	third person	INFER	inferential
1S	first singular	INJ	injunctive	2S	second singular
INSTR	instrumental	3S	third singular	INTNS	intensifier
1P	first plural	INT	interrogative	1PI	1P inclusive
INTENT	intentive	1PE	1P exclusive	INTERJ	interjection*
2P	second plural	INTRANS	intransitive	3P	third plural
INVIS	invisible	ABESS	abessive (without)	IO	indirect object
ABL	ablative(from)	IPFV	imperfective	ABS	absolutive
IRR	irrealis	ABST	abstract	ITER	iterative
ACC	accusative	JUSS	jussive	ACH	achieve
LAT	lative (moving to)	ACT	active	LOC	locative
ADESS	adessive(toward)	MAIN	main	ADJ	adjective*
MAN	manner	ADJR	adjectivalizer	MASC	masculine
ADP	adposition*	MASS	mass	ADV	adverb(ial)*
MEAS	measure	ADVR	adverbializer	MP	mediopassive
ADVN	adverbial noun*	MDL	modal	ADVERS	adversative
MOD	modifier	ADVR	adverbializer	N	noun*
AFFECT	affective	NARR	narrative	AFF	affirmative
NEG	negative	AGTV	agentive	NEUT	neuter
AG	agent	NEUTRA	neutral	AGR	agreement
NR	nominalizer	AL	alienable	NOM	nominative
ALL	allative	NOML	nominal	ALLOC	allocutive
NH	nonhuman	ANA	anaphoric	NONPAST	nonpast
ANI	animate	NONVIR	nonvirile	ANT	antipassive
NUM	numeral, numeric	AORIST	aorist	OBJ	object
APPL	applicative	OBL	oblique	ART	article*
OBLIG	obligatory	ASP	aspect	OPT	optative
ASS	assertive	ORD	ordinal (first)	AT	attributor

Table 52: Universal Morphological Codes

Code	Meaning	Code	Meaning	Code	Meaning
OTHER	other	ATTEN	attenuative	PART	participle*
AUG	augmentative	PARTIT	partitive	AUX	auxiliary*
PASS	passive	BEN	benefactive	PAST	past
CARD	cardinal number	PASTPT	past participle	CAT	catenative
PAT	patient	CAUS	causative	PEJ	pejorative
CESS	cessive "stop"	PERF	perfect	CGN	conjugational
PFV	perfective	CIRC	circumstantial	PERM	permissive
CLFR	classifier	PL	plural	CLIT	clitic*
PLACE	place	CMPLR	complementizer	POL	polite
CMN	common	POSS	possessive (X's)	CMPLX	complex
POST	postposition*	COLL	collective	POT	potential
COM	comitative	PP	past participle	COMPL	completive
PRE	prefix	CONC	concessive	PREP	preposition*
COND	conditional	PRES	present	CONJ	conjunction*
PRESPT	present participle	CONN	connective	PRESUM	presumptive
CONSEC	consecutive	PRH	prohibitive	CONT	continuative
PRO	pronoun*	COO	coordinating	PROG	progressive
COP	copula*	PROL	prolative (along)	CORR	correlative
PROP	proper	COU	count	PROS	prospective
CP	comparative	PROT	protracted	DAT	dative
PRET	preterite	DCLN	declensional	PROX	proximal
DECL	declarative	PSBL	possible	DEF	definite
PTL	particle*	DEICT	deictic	PURP	purposive
DEM	demonstrative	QUE	question	DESID	desiderative
QUANT	quantifier*	DET	determiner*	QUOT	quotative
DIM	diminutive	REAL	realized, nonfuture	DIREC	directional
RECENT	recent	DIST	distal	RECIP	reciprocal
DISTR	distributive	REFL	reflexive	DO	direct object
REL	relative*	DU	dual	REM	remote
DUB	dubitative	REPET	repetition	DUR	durative

Table 52: Universal Morphological Codes

Code	Meaning	Code	Meaning	Code	Meaning
REPORT	reportative	DYN	dynamic	RES	resultative
ELAT	elative (out of X)	RETRO	retrospective	EMPH	emphatic
SEQ	sequential	EMPTY	empty	SG	singular
EPIT	epithet	SIMUL	simultaneous	ERG	ergative
SS	same subject	ESS	essive (as X)	SPEC	specific
EVE	event	STAT	stative	EV	evidential
SUBJ	subject	EXCL	exclusive	SUBJV	subjunctive
EXIST	existential	SUBL	sublative (onto X)	FACT	factive
SUBOR	subordinating	FEM	feminine	SUFF	suffix
FIN	finite	SUG	suggestive	FNL	final (goal)
SUPER	superessive (on X)	FOC	focus	SP	superlative
FREQ	frequentative	TANG	tangible	FUT	future
TEMP	temporal, time	GEN	genitive (of X)	TERM	terminative
GENER	generic	TNS	tense	GER	gerund
TOP	topic	HAB	habitual	TRANS	transitive
HE	head	TRANSL	translative	HON	honorific
TRY	try to achieve	HORT	hortative	USIT	usitative
HUM	human	VAL	validator	ILL	illative (into)
VR	verbalizer	IMM	imminent	VIS	visible
IMP	imperative	V	verb*	IMPF	imperfective
VIR	virile	IMPRS	impersonal	VOC	vocative
INAL	inalienable	VOL	volitional	INANI	inanimate
WH	wh-question word	INCPT	inceptive	YN	yes-no word
INCH	inchoative	INCL	inclusive	INDEF	indefinite

16.11   Parts of Speech and Markedness Conventions

The codes for the grammatical morphemes should be taken from the basic set given in the last section wherever possible. New elements for grammatical concepts not in Lehmann's list can be made up by using capitalized abbreviations as in POSSR for the Hungarian possessor genitive. For each language, markedness conventions can be set up so that zero morphs need not be rendered in the %mor line. These conventions should be included in the file entitled 0morcodes.cdc attached to the corpus. For example, the unmarked form of the noun in English is the singular and it is prefereable to avoid entering -SG for every singular noun in English. Another type of markedness statement refers to the neutralization of a distinction. For example, the gender distinction is neutralized in the plural in German. Thus one can code German plural possessive "der" as DET|der&DEF:GEN:PL|. These marking conventions should be stated in the file 0morcodes.cdc attached to the corpus. This file should also have a complete listing of the grammatical morphemes of the language and their proper transcription in the %mor line. Examples of transcribed forms should also be discussed in this 0morcodes.cdc file. Examples of markedness conventions are given later.

In addition to these quasi-universal codes, we have also developed some special codes for German and Hungarian. These codes, which are given in the next two subsections, are provided as illustrations of how systems of morphological coding can be elaborated for morphologically complex languages.

16.11.1   Specialized Codes for Hungarian

The following codes assume that the unmarked N, ADJ, ART is sg, nom, indef; that the unmarked possessed is sg; that the V is indef, pres, indic, 3S; that the person of the V agrees with the subject and that the conjugation of the V agrees with the object.

Table 53: Hungarian Nominal Derivation (képzök)

Ending	Code	Example
-s	DAA	futós
-s	DNA	erös
-és	DVN	fözés
-ság	DAN	szabadság
-ó	DVN	fogó
-atlan	ABSE	erötlen (absentative)
-andó	PROG	teendö
-va	COMPL	futva
-ék	FAMIL	Paliék
-né	WIFE	Nagyné
-cska, -ka	DIM	fiúcska
-ú	DNA	kezü

Table 54: Hungarian Case Markings (ragok)

Ending	Code	Ending	Code
-m	POSSR:1S	-é	POSS:NM
-d	POSSR:2S	-i	POSS:PL
-ja	POSSR:3S	-ban	INESS
-nk	POSSR:1P	-nál	ADESS
-tok	POSSR:2P	-on	SUPER
-juk	POSSR:3P	-tól	ABL
-nak	DAT	-ról	DEL
-val	INSTR	-hoz	ALL
-t	ACC	-ba	ILL
-ig	TERM	-ból	ELAT
-kor	TEMP	-ra	SUB
-szor	MULT		

Example Codings:

csinál-tam volna	V | do-1S:PAST PART | COND
láss-átok	V | see&IMP-2P
kér-ni fog-ok	V | ask-INF V | FUT-1S
áll-t-am	V | stand-PAST-DEF:1S
igyál	V | drink&IMP:2S
lett	V | COP&PAST
meg#esz-em	V | #COMP+eat&DEF-1S
dolgoz-ni fog-ok	V | work-INF V | FUT-1S
el fogok menni	PART | away V | FUT-1S V | go-INF
edd	V | eat&2S:IMP:DEF
ettem	V | eat&1S:PAST

Table 55: Hungarian Verb Inflections

Ending	Code	Ending	Code	Ending	Code
-ok	1S	-tam	1S:PAST:DEF	-nék	1S:COND
-sz	2S	-tad	2S:PAST:DEF	-nál	2S:COND
-ik	3S (ikes)	-ta	3S:PAST:DEF	-na	3S:COND
-unk	1P	-tuk	1P:PAST:DEF	-nánk	1P:COND
-tok	2P	-tátok	2P:PAST:DEF	-nátok	2P:COND
-nak	3P	-ták	3P:PAST:DEF	-nának	3P:COND
-om	1S:DEF	-jak	1S:IMP	-nám	1S:DEF:COND
-od	2S:DEF	-jál	2S:IMP	-nád	2S:DEF:COND
-ja	3S:DEF	-jon -j	3S:IMP (ikes)	-ná	3S:DEF:COND
-juk	1P:DEF	-junk	1P:IMP	-nánk	1P:DEF:COND
-játok	2P:DEF	-jatok	2P:IMP	-nátok	2P:DEF:COND
-ják	3P:DEF	-janak	3P:IMP	-nák	3P:DEF:COND
-jam	1S:DEF:IMP	van	COP	-tam	1S:PAST
-jad	2S:DEF:IMP	volna	COND	-tál	2S:PAST
-d	3S:DEF:IMP	-ja	POSSD:3S	-t	3S:PAST
-juk	1P:DEF:IMP	-om	POSSD:1S	-tunk	1P:PAST
-játok	2P:DEF:IMP			-tatok	2P:PAST
-ják	3P:DEF:IMP			-tak	3P:PAST

16.11.2   Specialized Codes for German

These codings assume that N is singular, PRO is nominative, V is present indicative, and person is unknown in the strong past and the plural.

Table 56: German Inflections

Nominal	Marking	Verbal	Marking
PL	-s	INF	-en
PL	-en	PAST	-t
PL	-e	1S	-e
PL	umlaut-e	2S	-(e)st
1P	-en	3S	-(e)t

Table 57: German Articles

Article	Codes	Adj. Ending	Codes
der	DEF:MASC:NOM:SG	-er	MASC:NOM:SG
	DEF:FEM:GEN:SG		FEM:GEN:SG
	DEF:NEU:GEN:PL		GEN:PL
	DEF:GEN:PL	-e	FEM:NOM:SG
die	DEF:FEM:NOM:SG		NOM:PL
	DEF:NOM:PL		ACC:PL
	DEF:ACC:PL		weak declension
das	DEF:NEU:NOM:SG	-es	NEU:NOM:SG
	DEF:NEU:ACC:SG		NEU:ACC:SG
dem	DEF:MASC:DAT:SG	-em	MASC:DAT:SG
	DEF:NEU:DAT:SG		NEU:DAT:SG
den	DEF:MASC:ACC:SG	-en	MASC:ACC:SG
	DEF:DAT:PL		DAT:PL
des	DEF:MASC:GEN:SG		weak declension
	DEF:NEU:GEN:SG	-es	MASC:GEN:SG
			NEU:GEN:SG

17: Word Lists

This chapter provides word lists for some of the most important lexical groups in English. Some of the lists were constructed from a search of the million-word spoken language corpus of Francis and Kucera (1982). However, there are some forms that exist in the language that did not turn up in that corpus. Please use these lists only as suggestive starting points, not as definitive characterizations.

Adjectives (Interrogative): what, whatever, which, whichever, whose.

Adverbs (Interrogative): how, however, howsabout, when, whenever, where, whereby, wherever, wherefore, wherein, whereof, whereon, wherever, wherewith, why.

Adverbs (Nominal): afar, here, then, downtown, Monday, Tuesday, Wednesday, Thursday, Friday, Saturday, Sunday, home, north, south, east, west, northeast, southeast, northwest, southwest, left, right, today, tomorrow, tonight, yesterday.

Adverbs (Phrasal): about, across, after, down, in , off, on, out, over, through, up.

Auxiliaries (Copula): ain't, am, are, aren't, be, been, being, is, isn't, was, wasn't, were, weren't.

Auxiliaries (Do): did, didn't, do, does, doesn't, doing, don't, done.

Auxiliaries (Have): had, hadn't, hafta, has, hasn't, have, haven't, having.

Auxiliaries (Modal): can, can't, could, couldn't, dare, may, might, must, need, needn't, ought, shall, should, shouldn't, will, won't, would, wouldn't.

Cardinal Numbers: zero, one, two, three, four, five, six, seven, eight, nine, ten, eleven, twelve, thirteen, fourteen, fifteen, sixteen, seventeen, eighteen, nineteen, twenty, twenty+one, twenty+two, thirty, forty, fifty, sixty, seventy, eighty, ninety, hundred, two+hundred+twenty+six, thousand, million, billion, trillion, quadrillion, quintillian, sextillion, septillion, octillion.

Conjunctions: after, again, against, albeit, although, and, as, (be)cause, before, but, during, either, else, except, for, if, lest, like, likewise, minus, neither, nevertheless, nor, notwithstanding, once, only, or, otherwise, plus, provided, providing, save, seeing, since, so, still, supposing, than, that, then, though, unless, (un)til, when, whence, whenever, where, whereas, whereupon, wherever, whether, while, whilst, without, yet.

Contractions: -'is, -'nt, -'re, -'s, -'d, -'t, -'ve.

Determiners: a, an, another, any, both, each, either, every, few, fewer, fewest, half, many, more, most, nary, neither, no, one, only, several, some, such, that, the, them, these, this, those.

Fused Forms: See page 44 for the treatment of forms like wanna and gimme.

Interactive and Communicative Markers: abracadabra, adieu, ah, aha, ahah, ahem, ah-hah, ahoy, alas, all-right, alright, amen, anyway, atta-boy, augh, auh, aw, awoh, ay, aye, bah, bang, blimey, bong, boo, boohoo, boom, boom-boom-boom, bounce, bow-wow, boy, bravo, bullshit, bye-bye, careful, certainly, cheerio, cheers, chrissake, christ, come-on, crap, creepers, crunch, da-da-da-dum, daddy, dammit, damn, darling, darn, dear, doggone, drat, eek, egad, eh, farewell, fiddle-sticks, fiddlesticks, for-pete's-sake, gad, gawdamighty, gee, gee-up, glory, glory-be, go-ahead, god, goddam-mit, goddamn, golly, good, good-bye, good-morning, good-night, goodby, goodbye, goodmorning, goodnight, goody, gosh, guck, gucky, h'm, ha, hah, haha, hallelujah, hallo, haw, haw-haw, heehee, heh, hell, hello, help, hey, hi, hmm, hmpf, ho, honey, hoo, hooray, how, howdy, hubba, huh, huh-uh, hullo, hum, humbug, humph, hunhunh, hunmmm, hup, hurrah, hurray, hush, hush-hush, ick, icky, indeed, it-appears-so, it's-okay, jee, jeepers, jesus, kaboom, la, look, man, ma'am, mew, mhm, miaow, mmhm, mommy, morning, mum, mush, mushy, nah, never, no, nope, not-at-all, now, nuhuh, occasionally, of-course, oh, oh-good-right, oh-nuts, oh-oh, oh-yeah, oho, ok, okay, oops, ouch, out, ow, pah, perhaps, phew, phooey, please, poof, pooh, presto, probably, pshaw, pss, pugh, rah, roger, say, scrunch, see, see-here, sh, shalom, shh, shit, shoo, shucks, shush, sir, smoosh, so, sonuvabitch, ssh, sure, sure-sure, sweetie, ta, ta-ta, te-hee, thank-you, that's wrong, that's-not-right, that's-ok, that's-right, there, thud, to-some-extent, toot, toot-toot, truly, tsk, tush, tut, tut-tut, tweet, ugh, um, umph, up-a-daisy, welcome, well, what, whee, whew, whirr, whoa, whoo, whoopee, whoosh, wo, woa, woof, wow, yah, yay, yea, yeah, yeah-sure, yeahhuh, yeek, yeh, yep, yes, yesiree, yick, yicky, yikes, yippee, yo, yoho, yoicks, you-see, yow, yuck, yucky, yum, yummy, yumyum, yup, zounds, zowie.

Particles: about, across, after, down, in , off, on, out, over, through, up.

Prefixes: a-, an-, anti-, arch-, auto-, be-, bi-, bio-, co-, contra-, counter-, de-, demi-, di-, dis-, double-, em-, en-, ex-, extra-, fore-, hemi-, hyper-, hypo-, il-, im-, in-, inter-, ir-, long-, lower-, mal-, mid-, middle-, mini-, mis-, mono-, multi-, neo-, non-, out-, over-, paleo-, pan-, poly-, post-, pre-, pro-, proto-, psuedo-, re-, semi-, short-, sub-, super-, tele-, tran-, tri-, ultra-, un-, under-, uni-, upper-, ur-, vice-.

Prepositions: aboard, about, above, abroad, according, across, afore, after, again, against, aloft, along, alongside, alongst, amid, amidst, among, amongst, and, anti, around, as, aside, astride, at, atop, before, behind, below, beneath, beside, besides, between, be-twixt, beyond, but, by, concerning, considering, consisting, cross, depending, despite, down, downward, during, except, excepting, excluding, following, for, from, gainst, in, including, infra, inside, inter, into, involving, less, like, mid, midst, midway, minus, more, near, nearer, nearest, neath, next, notwithstanding, o'er, of, off, on, only, onto, opposite, or, out, outside, over, past, pending, per, plus, post, pursuant, rather, regard-ing, respecting, round, save, since, spite, than, through, throughout, thru, till, times, to, together, toward, towards, under, underneath, unless, unlike, until, unto, up, upon, upward, upwards, versus, via, vis-a-vis, with, within, without.

Pronouns (Interrogative): that, what, whatsoever, who, whoever, whom, whosoever.

Pronouns (Nominal): anybody, anyone, anything, everybody, everyone, everything, naught, no-one, nobody, none, nothing, one, somebody, someone, something.

Pronouns (Object): her, him, it, you, us, them, me.

Pronouns (Possessive): his, her, its, my, our, your, their.

Pronouns (Predicate Possessives): hers, his, mine, ours, theirs, yours.

Pronouns (Reflexive): herself, himself, itself, myself, oneself, ownself, yourself.

Pronouns (Subject): he, she, it, I, we, you, they, y'all, younz.

Qualifiers (General): These include hundreds of adverbs ending in -ly along with the following: all, almost, already, altogether, always, amply, any, aptly, as, awful, best, better, brand, close, cracking, damn, darned, dead, downright, even, ever, extra, far, farther, fast, flat, full, goddamn, great, half, half-way, halfway, head-and-shoulders, how, ill, indeed, just, kinda, least, less, little, long, lot, lots, many, midway, mighty, more, most, much, near, never, next, no, only, plain, plumb, pretty, quite, rather, raving, real, right, ruddy, second, so, soaking, softly, some, somewhat, sound, stark, still, straight, such, that, this, thus, too, two-thirds, very, way, well, wide, yet.

Qualifiers (Interrogative): how, however.

Qualifiers (Post): enough, indeed, still.

Quantifiers: all, any, both, each, either, enough, every, few, fewer, fewest, half, lots, many, more, most, much, neither, only, other, plenty, several, some, such.

Suffixes (inflectional): -s, -es, -ed, -ing.

Suffixes (derivational): -(i)an, -able, -age, -al, -ally, -ant , -ate, -atic, -ation, -ative, -dom, -ed, -ee, -eer, -en, -eous, -er, -ery, -es, -ese, -esque, -ess, -ette, -ful, -fy, -hood, -ial, -ic, -ible, -ical, -ify, -ine, -ing, -ious, -ise, -ish, -ism, -ist, -ity, -ive, -ize, -less, -let, -like, ly, -ling,, -ment, -ness, -ocracy, -or, -ous, -ren, -ry, -s, -ship, -ster, -uble, -ward(s), -ways, -wise, -y.

Irregular Plural Nouns:

1.   Final -y -> -ies
2.   Final -f, -fe -> -ves
3.   Final -ex -> -ices

4.   Final -us -> -i

5.   Final -um -> -a

6.   Special forms: brother – brethren, child – children, die – dice, man – men, foot – feet, goose – geese, louse – lice, mouse – mice, tooth – teeth, woman – women.

Table 58: Irregular Verbs in English

Present	Past	Participle
bear	bore	borne
beat	beat	beaten/beat
bend	bent	bent
bet	bet/betted	bet/betted
bid	bad/bade/bid	bade/bid/bidden
hide	bode	bode
bind	bound	bound
bite	bit	bitten/bit
bleed	bled	bled
blow	blew	blown
break	broke	broken
breed	bred	bred
bring	bought	brought
build	built	built
burn	burnt/burned	burnt/burned
burst	burst	burst
bust	bust/busted	bust/busted
buy	brought	bought
cast	cast	cast
catch	caught	caught
chide	chid/chided	chidden/chid/chided
choose	chose	chosen
cleave	cleft/clove/cleaved	cleft/cloven/cleaved

Table 58: Irregular Verbs in English

Present	Past	Participle
cling	clung	clung
come	came	come
cost	cost	cost
creep	crept	crept
cut	cut	cut
deal	dealt	dealt
dig	dug	dug
dive	dived/dove	dived
do/does	did	done
draw	drew	drawn
dream	dreamt/dreamed	dreamt/dreamed
drink	drank	drunk
drive	drove	driven
dwell	dwelt/dwelled	dwelt/dwelled
eat	ate	eaten
fall	fell	fallen
feed	fed	fed
feel	felt	felt
fight	fought	fought
find	found	found
fit	fit/fitted	fit/fitted
flee	fled	fled
fling	flung	flung
fly	flew	flown
freeze	froze	frozen
get	got	got/gotten
give	gave	given

Table 58: Irregular Verbs in English

Present	Past	Participle
go	went	gone
grind	ground	ground
grow	grew	grown
hang	hung/hanged	hung/hanged
have/has	had	had
hear	heard	heard
heave	heaved/hove	heaved/hove
hew	hewed	hewn/hewed
hide	hid	hidden/hid
hit	hit	hit
hold	held	held
hurt	hurt	hurt
inset	inset	inset
keep	kept	kept
kneel	knelt/kneeled	knelt/kneeled
knit	knit/knitted	knit/knitted
know	knew	known
lay	laid	laid
lead	led	led
lean	leant/leaned	leant/leaned
leap	leapt/leaped	leapt/leaped
learn	learnt/learned	learnt/learned
leave	left	left
lend	lent	lent
let	let	let
lie	lay	lain
light	lit/lighted	lit/lighted

Table 58: Irregular Verbs in English

Present	Past	Participle
lose	lost	lost
make	made	made
mean	meant	meant
meet	met	met
mow	mowed	mown/mowed
pay	paid	paid
plead	pleaded/pled	pleaded/pled
prove	proved	proved/proven
put	put	put
quit	quit/quitted	quit/quitted
read	read	read
rend	rent	rent
rid	rid/ridded	rid/ridded
ride	rode	ridden
ring	rang/rung	rung
rise	rose	risen
run	ran	run
saw	sawed	sawn/sawed
say	said	said
see	saw	seen
seek	sought	sought
sell	sold	sold
send	sent	sent
set	set	set
sew	sewed	sewn/sewed
shake	shook	shaken
shave	shaved	shaved/shaven

Table 58: Irregular Verbs in English

Present	Past	Participle
shear	sheared	shorn/sheared
shed	shed	shed
shew	shewed	shewn
shine	shone/shined	shone/shined
shit	shit/shat	shit
shoe	shod/shoed	shod/shoed
shoot	shot	shot
show	showed	shown/showed
shred	shredded/shred	shredded/shred
shrink	shrank	shrunk
shrive	shrived/shrove	shrived/shriven
shut	shut	shut
sing	sang	sung
sink	sank	sunk
sit	sat	sat
slay	slew, slayed	slain
sleep	slept	slept
slide	slid	slid
sling	slung	slung
slink	slunk	slunk
slit	slit	slit
smell	smelt/smelled	smelt/smelled
smite	smote	smitten
sow	sowed	sowed/sown
speak	spoke	spoken
speed	sped/speeded	sped/speeded
spell	spelt/spelled	spelt/spelled

Table 58: Irregular Verbs in English

Present	Past	Participle
spend	spent	spent
spill	spilt/spilled	spilt/spilled
spin	spun/span	spun
spit	spat/spit	spat/spit
split	split	split
spoil	spoilt/spoiled	spoilt/spoiled
spread	spread	spread
spring	sprang/sprung	sprung
stand	stood	stood
steal	stole	stolen
stick	stuck	stuck
sting	stung	stung
stink	stank/stunk	stunk
strew	strewed	strewn/strewed
stride	strode	stridden/strid/strode
strike	struck	struck
string	strung	strung
strive	strove/strived	striven/strived
swear	swore	sworn
sweat	sweat/sweated	sweat/sweated
sweep	swept	swept
swell	swelled	swollen/swelled
swim	swam/swum	swum
swing	swang/swung	swung
take	took	taken
teach	taught	taught
tear	tore	torn

Table 58: Irregular Verbs in English

Present	Past	Participle
tell	told	told
think	thought	thought
thrive	thrived/throve	thrived/thriven
throw	threw	thrown
thrust	thrust	thrust
transfer	transferred	transferred
tread	trod	trodden/trod
wake	woke/waked	woken/waked
wear	wore	worn
weave	wove	woven
wed	wedded/wed	wedded/wed
weep	wept	wept
wet	wet/wetted	wet/wetted
win	won	won
wind	wound	wound
wring	wrung	wrung
write	wrote	written

Verbs with derivational prefixes behave like their stem. This includes: abide, arise, awake, become, befall, beget, begin, behold, bereave, beseech, beset, bestride, broadcast, deep-freeze, forbear, forbid, forecast, foresee, foretell, forget, forgive, forgo, forsake, forswear, gainsay, hamstring, miscast, misdeal, misgive, mishear, mislay, mislead, misspell, misspend, mistake, misunderstand, offset, outbid, outdo, outfight, outgrow, outrun, outshine, overbear, overcast, overcome, overdo, overeat, overfeed, override, overrun, oversee, overshoot, oversleep, overtake, overthrow, partake, rebind, redo, recast, rebuild, remake, repay, reread, rerun, reset, restring, retell, rethink, rewind, rewrite, telecast, unbend, unbind, undo, unmake, unfreeze, unwind, uphold, upset, underbid, undergo, understand, undertake, underwrite, waylay, withdraw, withhold, withstand.

18:   Recording Techniques

This chapter offers some suggestions on techniques and equipment for recording, digitizing, and transcribing. Four pieces of advice stand out as most important. First, it is important to structure the recording session in a way that maximizes the naturalness of the interaction. Second, it is crucial to avoid excessive background noise. Third, the production of a high-quality transcript requires the use of high-quality recording and playback equipment. Fourth, it is important to learn to use the editor for transcription and coding. In this chapter, we also recommend specific types of equipment for recording and transcription.

18.1   Audio Recording

The best recordings are those produced by digital devices such as DAT tape recorders. However, a high-quality portable casette tape recorder can produce reasonably good recordings. It is important to avoid using the microphone that is built into the tape recorder. Instead, use a small external microphone, preferably one that is omnidirectional to allow for movement of your sound source. If the tape recorder is running on internal batteries, make sure to check their level before the recording session.

Use a volume level that is well below the distortion level. The needle should never cross over into the red area. At the same time, the level should be as high as possible, as long as there is no distortion. You may wish to accept the occasional distortion produced by yells or toy crashes in order to maintain a sufficiently high recording level. Try to avoid adjusting the tape recorder during the session. If you know your equipment well, you will not have to worry about its functioning. Simply set it in place and then try to forget about it. After the session, listen to the recording immediately to determine if you need to change the recording level for the next session.

Try to avoid recording near traffic or other external noises. Rooms with carpets have fewer echoes and floor noises than rooms with hard floors. Ongoing noise from televisions, radios, stereos, and other appliances can ruin a recording. Try to minimize spurious background noises or noises caused from bumping the microphone onto hard surfaces or jostling the microphone cord. Try to keep the microphone out of clear view so that the child will not try to talk directly into it.

You can also use the tape recorder as a notebook. You can record commentary directly onto the tape when the child is not talking and you are in a different room. You can begin each casette with a statement of the date, the year, the name of the child, the nature of the setting, and so on. This practice is very helpful in identifying tapes that have been otherwise mislabeled.

If you wish to record mobile groups of children, you will need to associate a particular microphone and a particular recording channel with each child separately. If you have only two children, you can use a single stereo recorder. If you want to study more children, you will need separate recorders. You will then have the problem of trying to time-lock the multiple tape sources when you come to transcription.

When children are mobile, it is often difficult to follow each child about with a tape recorder. A solution to this problem is to use a transmitting microphone with a receiver connected to a stationary tape recorder.

In some social situations, speakers will become self-conscious when they know they are being recorded. This even occurs with children. One solution to this problem is to record without the knowledge of the people being recorded. However, this solution may run afoul of Human Subject institutional review board rules in some countries. If you record in a clandestine manner, it is imperative that you explain this later to your informants and explicitly request their permission to use the recording. If they do not give you this permission, you will need to erase the recording. Much of the British National Corpus was recorded in this way (Crowdy, 1993).

18.2   Recording Equipment

In the earlier days of audio recording, high quality portable equipment was expensive and difficult to locate. Now, good quality equipment is cheap and widely available. For ease of use and quality of recording, the Sony walkman, stereo cassette recorder WM-DC6 is an excellent choice. If you prefer to use a DAT (Digital Audio Tape) recorder, a good choice is the Sony TCD. Some features to look for in a audiocassette recorder are: a tape footage counter, a high signal/noise ratio, and a wide frequency response range. In some cases you may want to have a VU meter to monitor volume, but paying too much attention to this will interfere with the naturalness of the recording situation.

It is important never to use the built-in microphone in a tape recorder. These microphones inevitably pick up the motor noise of the recorder itself. A good choice for an external microphone is the SONY ECM-909A low-impedance electret condensor microphone. The batteries for the ECM-909A are standard AA cell batteries. With small portable sets of this type, it is easy to turn recordings on and off without interfering with the natural flow of the interaction. Decisions about when to sample speech and whether to attempt to keep the recording equipment out of the child's view depend highly on the goals of the project. For some discussions of these issues, see Clark (1976).

Be careful to avoid low-quality tapes, even those from well-known manufacturers. Instead, try to select high-quality nonmetallic tapes. Metal tape can be used on the Walkman, but it requires setting a special switch. Metal cassette tapes are fairly expensive and add little quality beyond that available from very high-quality nonmetallic tape. The best length for most purposes is the 90-minute length that is also the most readily available in stores. Never use microcassettes.

18.3   Transcribing Equipment

Audiotapes can be played back either through headphones or through sound systems. The cheapest way to get high-quality playback is to use headphones. Moreover, playing back the cries and yells common in interactions with children over a sound system can lead to complaints from office mates and neighbors. People differ in their preferences for transcribing headphones. Some prefer lightweight headphones. These are comfortable, but they allow in ambient noise, which can interfere with listening. Most people doing transcribing for long periods prefer the padded headphones. You can often get units that are well-padded, but still lightweight and comfortable. A crucial factor in deciding which type of headphones to use is the environment in which the transcription will take place. If the room will be fairly quiet, then the lightweight ones are probably better. If there will be other noise or talking in the room while you are transcribing, the heavier headphones may be necessary.

It is important to use a high-quality transcribing machine. A good machine allows you to repeat sections of the tape easily. A feature that aids in this repeated playback is a foot pedal with a backwards winding action. The pedal is operated with your foot so that you do not have to remove your hands from the keyboard to operate the transcriber. When you remove your foot from the pedal, the tape automatically moves back a small specified amount. Using a foot pedal and the automatic replay facility, one can repeatedly play back short stretches of speech to identify difficult words. The Sony BM-77, or its current model replacement, is a reliable machine that allows you to control the amount of tape that will rewind each time you stop. It also allows you to slow down the replay for accuracy in transcription.

An even better system for transcribing involves the use of computer digitized sounds and the "sonic CHAT" mode of the editor. The use of this system is discussed in the CLAN manual.

18.4   Audio Digitization

This section outlines the general process of audio digitization. The details of this process vary depending on the specific hardware you are using. However, the overall shape of the process is the same in all cases. We will use the process of digitization using SoundEdit™ 16 on the Macintosh as our example, however the steps involved are much the same for all programs.

18.4.1   Components for Digitizing

The hardware and software components that you need are:

1.   **An audio sound source.** The two types of sound sources are analog sources such as reel-to-reel and cassette, or digital, such as DAT or minidisk. Digital sources are better than analog sources. However, analog sources are acceptable for many purposes. In many cases, your sound source or playback unit will be the same unit that you used to make the recordings. However, any unit can be

used that has external audio outputs.

2. **Power supplies.** You need power supplies for the audio playback unit and the computer.

3. **A computer with a 16-bit sound card.** All PPC Macintosh machines have built-in 16-bit digitization facilities. Most Windows computers come installed with Sound Blaster™ 16-bit cards as standard.

4. **Cables.** You need to connect your playback unit to your computer's audio input ports. The inputs to your computer are usually either mini or RCA format, and the outputs from your audio playback unit may also be mini, RCA, or a variety of less common formats.

5. **Digitization software.** We recommend use of either SoundEdit or PeakLE programs on the Macintosh. SoundEdit is sold by Macromedia, but may be phased out soon. PeakLE is sold by Berkeley Systems. For Windows, commonly used programs include Goldwave (www.goldwave.com) and Cool Edit (www.syntrillium.com/cooledit).

6. **Headphones.** Usually you will want to monitor the digitized sound at the computer. However, you will sometimes also want to monitor the sound at the source.

18.4.2   Connecting the Sound Source to the Computer

The most difficult step in digitizing a sound file is figuring out how to connect your playback unit to the computer. It is easy enough to find a cable that will make the connection. However, you also need to insure that the voltage level coming into the computer sound card is at the right level to achieve high-quality digitization. On the audio playback unit, you usually have a choice of coming out of either the line output or the headphones jack. For superior sound quality we recommend going through the line output and not the headphones. The major drawback to using the line output is that you cannot control output level or volume on many machines (although some have a control for this). If the output level of the line output of your machine does not match that required by the computer, you will overdrive the input and get bad results. This is one reason to use a device to control line output level. Another reason to have a device to control line output level is that, if the tapes are of poor quality or contain a large range of volume levels, you will need to adjust the sound manually at various points in the tape in order to prevent clipping. (See the discussion of the monitoring of sound levels below.)

There are four methods for controlling line output levels: using an amplifier, using a mixer, using the headphones jack on the tape recorder, or adjusting the volume in Sound Edit. The best option is to use a mixer. The Studio Master 42DC, a very inexpensive device, can be purchased from Full Compass Audio (800 356-5844). Audio technicians tell us that mixers are better than amplifiers. However, we have not noticed an audible difference. Running the output from the tape recorder through an amplifier or mixer allows you to control the volume in order to maintain good sound quality. If an amplifier or mixer is not available, the next best alternative is going through the headphones jack on the tape recorder. However, this might degrade the sound quality. The remaining alternative is to control the volume in SoundEdit. Macromedia recommends against this and we agree with their recommendation.

The cabling connections you need to make vary depending on the hardware you are using. We will describe three alternative cases:

1.   The first scenario involves a connection from the lineout connector of your portable tape recorder to the Macintosh. This connection will only work if your recording has been made at a fairly high level. For this connection, you use a mini-mini stereo cable from the tape recorder to the Macintosh audio input. Plug one end into the line output of the tape recorder. Plug the other end into the Mac's microphone jack. Then, plug your headphones into the Mac's headphones jack. Open up SoundEdit — you don't have to start recording yet. Just have it open. Start playing the tape and listen to the sound. You can control the sound level with the SoundEdit volume controls.

2.   The second scenario is the one we recommend. In this scenario, we will assume that you are using an amplifer or a mixer. We will assume that your amplifer or mixer has RCA connector plugs. We will assume that your tapecorder has either a mini or a pair of RCA line outputs. If you have a mini output on your tape recorder, you need a mini-dual-RCA cable. If you have a dual RCA output on your tape recorder, you need a double RCA cable. Plug the correct end of one of these cables into your tapecorder's line output. Plug the other end of one of these cables into your mixer or amplifier's line in. Now you need another cable to connect to your Mac. This should be a dual RCA to mini cable. Plug the one pair of RCA plugs into the mixer's line output. Plug the mini jack into the Macintosh. Plug your headphones into the Mac's headphones jack. Open up SoundEdit — you don't have to start recording yet. Just have it open. Start playing the tape and listen to the sound. You can control the sound level with the amplifier or mixer volume controls.

3.   In the third scenario, we will assume that you are taking your sound out of the headphones output of your sound playback unit. In this case, plug a mini-mini audio cable into the headphones jack on the tape recorder. Plug the other end into the Mac's microphone jack. Plug headphones into Mac's headphones jack. Open up SoundEdit — you don't have to start recording yet. Just have it open. Start playing the tape and listen to the sound. You can control the sound level with the tape recorder volume controls.

18.4.3   Using the Digitizing Software

In this section, we will explain how to use the SoundEdit™16 digitization program. These instructions are specific to the Macintosh and SoundEdit. The steps involved are these:

1.   In the **Control Panels** pop up window, select **Sound**. If your system is older than 8.0, refer to the owner's manual for information on setting Sound Input.

2.   In the **Sound** window, click on the **Sound** button.

3.   Set the Sound Input to **Microphone** or **External Mic**.

4.   Check "Listen."

5.   Set the sound output quality to 22.050 kHz.

6.   Click on SoundEdit to open the application.

7.   SoundEdit should then display a window called **Untitled-1**. This is your recording window.

8.   Under the **Sound** menu select **Sound Format** and set the recording to 16 bit and 22050 kHz. The recording will be monophonic by default. Then click the box that makes these setttings the default.

9.   Use the pulldown file menu to select **Preferences**. In **Preferences** select: Document, AIFF file format, 22,050 kHz sample rate, 16-bit sample size, no compression, and no stereo. If you are digitizing on Windows, select the WAV file format.

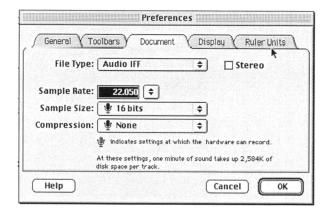

10.   Hit the OK button to close the Preferences file.

11.   Set your input source under the **Sound** menu in the **Recording Options** to microphone. This is a double-check of step 3.

12.   Open the **Controls** palette from the **Windows** menu. Press **Record** on the **Controls** palette, as shown here.

13.   While the recording continues, check to see that the volume stays in the green

area and only seldom or never enters into the red. The **Levels** window allows you to monitor and control the recording and playback levels in Sound Edit. Make sure to set the L/R volume to –16.

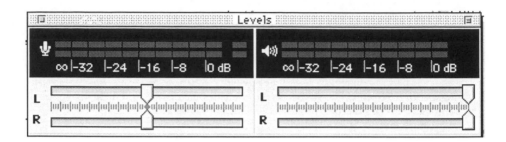

If a red dot or red block appears in the recording levels area, the sound is being clipped. Clipping is defined by SoundEdit as the amplitude of a sample exceeding the quantization range. For example, if a child is sitting too close to the microphone and starts to scream the top and bottom of the waveform will be cut off. This results in a very poor digitized sample. To control for clipping, adjust the volume of the source (i.e., amplifier, mixer, or tapecorder) until the red light or dot no longer appears in the **Levels** window. You can also control the volume using the input or volume controls in the **Levels** window. Sound Edit does not recommend this method because the sound quality may be sacrificed.

14. Erase your test record by highlighting everything using the -A key and then hit the delete key.

15. Now go ahead and record a few minutes for your first file. You should decide which segment you want to record and how much.

16. When you are finished, select "stop" in the **Controls** palette and then save the file.

17. Quit SoundEdit.

18.5   Video Digitization

This section provides some basic pointers for researchers who wish to digitize videotaped interactions for analysis in the editor. These instructions are designed to produce a basic low-end video digitization. For higher-end digitization, you will need more elaborate and expensive hardware. For the basic level of digitization, you need these materials:

1. **A FireWire video source**. There are two types of FireWire sources. If you are recording new material, you will want to use a digital camcorder with a FireWire output. Most Sony and Canon units have this type of output. Prices range from $700 to $5000. For basic observational work, lower priced models are probably good enough. The other possible video source is a VHS videotape. In order to take this as input to a FireWire port, you will want to purchase the Sony DVMC-

DA1 convertor for about $500 or its equivalent.

2. **A computer with FireWire inputs**. The default here is the DV (digital video) iMac. This machine is equipped with the software, cables, and other hardware that you need to create digital video movies. Alternatively, you can use a Windows machine with an add-on video digitization card.

3. **Software**. The DV iMac provides iMovie, an integrated software solution for producing digital video.

4. **Storage**. Because the video files produced by the digitization software are so large, you will need to write them out to some form of removable storage. The choice here is between the inexpensive, low capacity (650 MB) CD-ROM format and the more expensive, high capacity (5.2 GB) DVD-ROM format. CD-ROMs currently cost about $2 each, whereas each DVD-ROM disk costs about $25.

19:   Symbol Summary

Obligatory Headers on page 21

@**Begin**	marks the beginning of a file - page 22
@**End**	marks the end of the file - page 23
@**ID**:	code for a larger database - page 23
@**Participants**:	lists actors in a file - page 22

Constant Headers on page 23

@**Age of XXX:**	marks a speaker's age - page 24
@**Birth of XXX:**	shows date of birth of speaker - page 24
@**Coder:**	people doing transcription and coding - page 25
@**Coding:**	version of CHAT coding - page 25
@**Education of XXX:**	indicates educational level of speaker - page 25
@**Filename:**	shows name of file - page 25
@**Font:**	sets the default font for the file -page 25
@**Group of XXX:**	indicates the subject's group in group studies - page 26
@**Language:**	the principal language of the transcript - page 26
@**Language of XXX:**	language(s) spoken by a given participant -page 26
@**SES of XXX:**	ndicates socioeconomic status of speaker - page 26
@**Sex of XXX:**	indicates gender of speaker - page 26
@**Stim:**	indicates stimulus for elicited production - page 26
@**Transcriber:**	gives the transcriber's name or initials - page 26
@**Warning:**	marks defects in file - page 27

Changeable Headers on page 27

@**Activities:**	component activities in the situation - page 27
@**Bg** and @**Bg:**	begin gem - page 27
@**Bck:**	backgrounding information - page 27
@**Comment:**	comments - page 28
@**Date:**	date of the interaction - page 28
@**Eg** and @**Eg:**	end gem - page 28
@**g:**	simple gems - page 28
@**Location:**	geographical location of the interaction - page 29
@**New Episode:**	point at which a new episode begins and old one ends - page 29
@**Room Layout:**	configuration of furniture in room - page 29
@**Situation:**	general atmosphere of the interaction - page 29
@**Tape Location:**	footage markers from tape - page 30
@**Time Duration:**	beginning and end times - page 30
@**Time Start:**	beginning time - page 30

Words on page 31

@	special form markers - page 32
xxx	unintelligible speech, not treated as a word - page 36
xx	unintelligible speech, treated as a word - page 36

yyy	unintelligible speech transcribed on %pho line, not treated as a word - page 36
yy	unintelligible speech transcribed on %pho line, treated as a word - page 36
www	untranscribed material - page 36
0	actions without speech - page 37
&	phonological fragment - page 37
[?]	best guess - page 38
()	noncompletion of a word - page 38
0word	omitted word - page 38
0*word	ungrammatical omission - page 39
00word	(grammatical) ellipsis - page 39

Morphemes on page 52

-	suffix marker - page 52
#	prefix marker - page 52
+	compound or rote form marker - page 52
~	clitic marker - page 53
&	fusion marker page 53
-0	omitted affix - page 53
-0*	incorrectly omitted affix - page 54

Basic Utterance Terminators on page 60

.	period - page 60
?	question - page 60
!	exclamation - page 61

Tone Unit Marking on page 61

-?	rising final contour - page 61
-!	final exclamation contour - page 62
-.	falling final contour - page 62
-'.	rise-fall final contour - page 62
-,.	fall-rise final contour - page 62
-,	level nonfinal contour - page 62
-_	falling nonfinal contour - page 63
-	low level contour - page 63
-'	rising nonfinal contour - page 63
,	syntactic juncture - page 65
"	tag question - page 65
#	pause between words - page 65
-:	previous word lengthened - page 66

Prosody Within Words on page 63

/	stress - page 63
//	accented nucleus - page 63

///	contrastive stress - page 64	
:	lengthened syllable - page 64	
::	pause between syllables - page 64	
^	blocking - page 64	

Special Utterance Terminators on page 66

+...	trailing off - page 66
+..?	trailing off of a question - page 66
+!?	question with exclamation - page 66
+/.	interruption - page 67
+/?	interruption of a question - page 67
+//.	self-interruption - page 67
+//?	self-interruption of a question - page 68
+"/.	quotation follows on next line - page 68
+".	quotation precedes - page 68
+"	quoted utterance follows - page 68
+^	quick uptake - page 68
+<	"lazy" overlap marking - page 69
+,	self-completion - page 69
++	other-completion - page 69
[c]	clause delimiter - page 69

Scoped Symbols on page 70

•%mov:"*"_0_1073•	time alignment marker - page 70
[=! text]	paralinguistics, prosodics - page 70
[!]	stressing - page 71
[!!]	contrastive stressing - page 71
["]	quotation marks - page 73
[= text]	explanation - page 71
[: text]	replacement - page 72
[0 text]	omission - page 78
[:=x text]	translation - page 72
[=? text]	alternative transcription - page 73
[%xxx: text]	dependent tier on main line - page 73
[% text]	comment on main line - page 73
[$text]	code on main tier - page 74
[?]	best guess - page 74
[>]	overlap follows - page 74
[<]	overlap precedes - page 75
<text> [<>]	overlap follows and precedes - page 75
[>number][<number]	overlap enumeration - page 76
[/]	retracing without correction - page 76
[//]	retracing with correction - page 77
[///]	retracing with reformulation - page 77
[-]	false start without retracing - page 78
[/?]	unclear retrace type - page 78

[*]	error marking - page 78
[+ text]	postcode - page 79
[+ bck]	excluded utterance - page 79
[+ trn]	included utterance - page 80

Dependent Tiers on page 81

%act:	actions - page 82
%add:	addressee - page 82
%alt:	alternative transcription - page 83
%cod:	general purpose coding - page 83
%coh:	cohesion tier - page 83
%com:	comments by investigator - page 83
%def:	codes from SALT - page 83
%eng:	English translation - page 83
%err:	error coding - page 83
%exp:	explanation - page 84
%fac:	facial actions - page 84
%flo:	flowing version - page 84
%gls:	target language gloss for unclear utterance - page 84
%gpx:	gestural and proxemic activity - page 85
%int:	intonation - page 85
%lan:	language - page 85
%mod:	model or target phonology - page 85
%mor:	morphemic semantics - page 85
%mov:	movie tier - page 85
%par:	paralinguistics - page 86
%pho:	phonetic transcription - page 86
%sit:	situation - page 86
%snd:	sonic CHAT sound tier - page 86
%spa:	speech act coding - page 87
%syn:	syntactic structure notation - page 87
%tim:	time stamp coding - page 87

Dependent Tier Special Codes on page 81

$	indicates codes - page 81
$=N	occurs for N following utterances - page 89
$sc=N-M	codes refer to words N through M on the main tier - page 89
<bef>	occurrence before an utterance - page 88
<aft>	occurrence after an utterance - page 88

Error Coding on page 142

$=	source of an error in the %err line - page 142
=	placed between error and target - page 142
;	separates errors on %err line - page 142

Morphosyntactic Coding on page 156

| | follows part-of-speech on %mor line - <u>page 156</u>

&   nonconcatenated morpheme in %mor line - <u>page 159</u>

prefix delimiter on %mor line - <u>page 159</u>

+ (Plus)   compound delimiter on %mor line - <u>page 161</u>

- (Dash)   suffix delimiter on %mor line - <u>page 159</u>

:   feature fusion on %mor line - <u>page 157</u>

~ (Tilde)   clitic delimiter on %mor line - <u>page 159</u>

0   precedes omitted element - <u>page 165</u>

0*   precedes incorrectly omitted element - <u>page 165</u>

20: References

Allen, G. D. (1988). The PHONASCII system. *Journal of the International Phonetic Association, 18,* 9–25.

Ament, W. (1899). *Die Entwicklung von Sprechen und Denken beim Kinder.* [The development of speech and language in the child.] Leipzig: Ernst Wunderlich.

Augustine. (1952). *The Great Books.* (Vol. 18: The Confessions of St. Augustine). Chicago: Encyclopedia Britannica.

Bates, E., & MacWhinney, B. (1982). Functionalist approaches to grammar. In E. Wanner & L. Gleitman (Eds.), *Language acquisition: The state of the art* (pp. 173-218). New York: Cambridge University Press.

Bernstein Ratner, N., Rooney, B., & MacWhinney, B. (1996). Analysis of stuttering using CHILDES and CLAN. *Clinical Linguistics and Phonetics, 10,* 169-187.

Bloom, L., & Lahey, M. (1973). *Language development and language disorders.* New York: John Wiley & Sons.

Bloom, L., Lightbown, P., & Hood, L. (1975). Structure and variation in child language. *Monographs of the Society for Research in Child Development, 40,* (whole no. 2).

Bolinger, D. (1986). *Intonation and its parts: Melody in spoken English.* Stanford, CA: Stanford University Press.

Branigan, G. (1979). Some reasons why successive single word utterances are not. *Journal of Child Language, 6,* 411-421.

Brown, R. (1973). *A first language: The early stages.* Cambridge, MA: Harvard University Press.

Carterette, E. C., & Jones, M. H. (1974). *Informal Speech: Alphabetic and phonemic texts with statistical analyses and tables.* Berkeley, CA: University of California Press.

Chafe, W. (Ed.). (1980). *The Pear stories: Cognitive, cultural, and linguistic aspects of narrative production.* Norwood, NJ: Ablex.

Clark, E. (1987). The Principle of Contrast: A constraint on language acquisition. In B. MacWhinney (Ed.), *Mechanisms of Language Acquisition* (pp. 1–34). Hillsdale, NJ: Lawrence Erlbaum Associates.

Clark, R. (1976). A report on methods of longitudinal data collection. *Journal of Child Language, 3,* 457–461.

Comrie, B., & Corbett, G. (Eds.) (1992). *The Slavonic languages.* London: Routledge.

Crago, M. B., & Allen, S. E. M. (in press). Acquiring Inuktitut. In L. Leonard & O. Taylor (Eds.), *Language acquisition in North America: Cross-cultural and cross-linguistic perspectives.* San Diego, CA: Singular Publishing.

Crowdy, S. (1993). *Spoken corpus design and transcription.* Harlow, UK: Longman.

Crystal, D. (1969). *Prosodic systems and intonation in English.* Cambridge: Cambridge University Press.

Crystal, D. (1975). *The English tone of voice: Essays in intonation, prosody and paralanguage.* London: Edward Arnold.

Darwin, C. (1877). A biographical sketch of an infant. *Mind, 2,* 292–294.

De Houwer, A. (1990). *The acquisition of two languages: A case study.* New York: Cambridge University Press.

Edwards, J. (1992). Computer methods in child language research: four principles for the use of archived data. *Journal of Child Language, 19,* 435–458.

Ekman, P., & Friesen, P. (1969). The repertoire of nonverbal behavior: Categories, origins, usage, and coding. *Semiotica, 1,* 47–98.

Ekman, P., & Friesen, P. (1978). *Facial action coding system: Investigator's guide.* Palo Alto, CA, Consulting Psychologists Press.

Elbers, L., & Wijnen, F. (1993). Effort, production skill, and language learning. In C. Ferguson, L. Menn, & C. Stoel-Gammon (Eds.), *Phonological development* (pp. 337–368). Timonium, MD: York.

Fletcher, P. (1985). *A child's learning of English.* Oxford: Blackwell.

Francis, W., & Kucera, H. (1982). *Frequency analysis of English usage: Lexicon and grammar.* Boston: Houghton Mifflin.

Gerken, L. (1991). The metrical basis for children's subjectless sentences. *Journal of Memory and Language, 30,* 431–451.

Gerken, L., Landau, B., & Remez, R. E. (1990). Function morphemes in young children's speech perception and production. *Developmental Psychology, 26*(2), 204–216.

Gibbon, D., Moore, R., & Winski, R. (Eds.). (1997). *Handbook of standards and resources for spoken language systems.* Berlin: Mouton de Gruyter.

Goldman-Eisler, F. (1968). *Psycholinguistics: Experiments in spontaneous speech.* New York: Academic Press.

Gvozdev, A. N. (1949). *Formirovaniye u rebenka grammaticheskogo stroya.* Moscow: Akademija Pedagogika Nauk RSFSR.

Halliday, M. (1966). Notes on transitivity and theme in English: Part 1. *Journal of Linguistics, 2,* 37–71.

Halliday, M. (1967). Notes on transitivity and theme in English: Part 2. *Journal of Linguistics, 3,* 177–274.

Halliday, M. (1968). Notes on transitivity and theme in English: Part 3. *Journal of Linguistics, 4,* 153–308.

Jefferson, G. (1984). Transcript notation. In J. Atkinson & J. Heritage (Eds.), *Structures of social interaction: Studies in conversation analysis* (pp. 134–162). Cambridge: Cambridge University Press.

Kearney, G. & McKenzie, S. (1993). Machine interpretation of emotion: Design of memory-based expert system for interpreting facial expressions in terms of signaled emotions. *Cognitive Science, 17,* 589–622.

Kenyeres, E. (1926). *A gyermek elsö szavai es a szófajók föllépése.* [The child's first words and the appearance of parts of speech.] Budapest: Kisdednevelés.

Lehmann, C. (1982). Directions for interlinear morphemic translations. *Folia Linguistica,* 16, 119-224.

Leopold, W. (1939). *Speech development of a bilingual child: a linguist's record: Vol. 1. Vocabulary growth in the first two years.* (Vol. 1). Evanston, IL: Northwestern University Press.

Leopold, W. (1947). *Speech development of a bilingual child: a linguist's record: Vol. 2. Sound-learning in the first two years.* Evanston, IL: Northwestern University Press.

Leopold, W. (1949a). *Speech development of a bilingual child: a linguist's record: Vol. 3. Grammar and general problems in the first two years.* Evanston, IL: Northwestern University Press.

Leopold, W. (1949b). *Speech development of a bilingual child: a linguist's record: Vol. 4. Diary from Age 2.* Evanston, IL: Northwestern University Press.

LIPPS Group. (2000). The LIDES Coding Manual: A document for preparing and analyzing language interaction data. *Journal of Bilingualism, 4,* whole no. 2.

Low, A. A. (1931). A case of agrammatism in the English language. *Archives of Neurology and Psychiatry, 25,* 556–597.

MacWhinney, B. (1989). Competition and lexical categorization. In R. Corrigan, F. Eckman, & M. Noonan (Eds.), *Linguistic categorization* (pp. 195–242). New York: Benjamins.

MacWhinney, B., & Osser, H. (1977). Verbal planning functions in children's speech. *Child Development, 48,* 978–985.

Massone, M. I. (1993). *Lengua de Señas Argentina: Diccionario bilingüe.* [Argentine Sign Language: Bilingual dictionary]. Buenos Aires: Editorial Sopena Argentina.

Miller, J., & Chapman, R. (1983). *SALT: Systematic analysis of language transcripts, User's manual.* Madison, WI: University of Wisconsin Press.

Moerk, E. (1983). *The mother of Eve as a first language teacher.* Norwood, N.J.: Ablex.

Ninio, A., Snow, C., Pan, B., & Rollins, P. (1994). Classifying communicative acts in children's interactions. *Journal of Communication Disorders, 27,* 157–188.

Ninio, A., & Wheeler, P. (1986). A manual for classifying verbal communicative acts in mother–infant interaction. *Transcript Analysis, 3,* 1–83.

Ochs, E. (1979). Transcription as theory. In E. Ochs & B. Schieffelin (Eds.), *Developmental pragmatics.* New York: Academic.

Ochs, E. A., Schegloff, M., & Thompson, S. A. (1996). *Interaction and grammar.* Cambridge, UK: Cambridge University Press.

Oshima-Takane, Y., & MacWhinney, B. (1995). *Japanese CHAT manual.* Tokyo: Tokyo University Press.

Parrish, M. (1996). Alan Lomax: Documenting folk music of the world. *Sing Out!: The Folk Song Magazine, 40,* 30–39.

Pick, A. (1913). *Die agrammatischer Sprachstörungen.* [Agrammatical speech disorders.] Berlin: Springer-Verlag.

Preyer, W. (1882). *Die Seele des Kindes.* [The soul of the child.] Leipzig: Grieben's.

Pullum, G., & Ladusaw, W. (1986). *Phonetic symbol guide.* Chicago: University of Chicago Press.

Quirk, R., Greenbaum, S., Leech, G., & Svartvik, J. (1985). *A comprehensive grammar of the English language.* London: Longman.

Rivero, M., Gràcia, M., & Fernández-Viader, P. (1998). Including non-verbal communicative acts in the mean length of turn analysis using CHILDES. In A. Aksu Koç, E. Taylan, A. Özsoy, & A. Küntay (Eds.), *Perspectives on language acquisition* (pp. 355–367). Istanbul: Bogaziçi University Press.

Sacks, H., Schegloff, E., & Jefferson, G. (1974). A simplest systematics for the organization of turn-taking for conversation. *Language, 50,* 696–735.

Selting, M. (1998). Gesprächsanalytisches Transkriptionssystem (GAT). *Linguistische Berichte, 173,* 91–122.

Slobin, D. (1977). Language change in childhood and in history. In J. Macnamara (Ed.), *Language learning and thought* (pp. 185–214). New York: Academic Press.

Slobin, D. I. (1993). Coding child language data for crosslinguistic analysis. In J. A. Edwards & M. D. Lampert (Eds.), *Talking data: Transcription and coding in discourse research* (pp. 207–219). Hillsdale, NJ: Lawrence Erlbaum Associates.

Sokolov, J. L., & Snow, C. (Eds.). (1994). *Handbook of research in language development using CHILDES*. Hillsdale, NJ: Lawrence Erlbaum Associates.

Sperberg-McQueen, C. M., & Burnard, L. (Eds.). (1992). *Guidelines for electronic text encoding and interchange*. Waterloo: University of Waterloo.

Stemberger, J. (1985). *The lexicon in a model of language production*. New York: Garland.

Stern, C., & Stern, W. (1907). *Die Kindersprache*. [Child language.] Leipzig: Barth.

Svartvik, J., & Quirk, R. (Eds.). (1980). *A corpus of English conversation*. Lund: Gleerup/ Liber.

Szuman, S. (1955). Rozwój treści słownika u dziece. *Studia Pedagogicane, 2*.

Talmy, L. (1985). Lexicalization patterns: Semantic structure in lexical forms. In T. Shopen (Ed.), *Language typology and semantic description: Vol. 3. Grammatical categories and the lexicon* (pp. 36-149). Cambridge, UK: Cambridge University Press.

Trager, G. (1958). Paralanguage: A first approximation. *Studies in Linguistics, 13*, 1–12.

Wernicke, C. (1874). *Die Aphasische Symptomenkomplex*. [The aphasic symptom complex.] Breslau: Cohn & Weigart.

21: Index

Part 2: The Programs

Contents of Part 2

1:   Introduction

This manual describes the use of the CLAN program. The acronym CLAN stands for Computerized Language Analysis. It is a program that is designed specifically to analyze data transcribed in the format of the Child Language Data Exchange System (CHILDES). CLAN was written by Leonid Spektor at Carnegie Mellon University. The current version uses a graphic user interface and runs on both Macintosh and Windows machines. Earlier versions also ran on DOS and Unix without a graphic user interface. CLAN allows you to perform a large number of automatic analyses on transcript data. The analyses include frequency counts, word searches, co-occurrence analyses, mean length of utterance (MLU) counts, interactional analyses, text changes, and morphosyntactic analysis.

This chapter explains how to install and learn CLAN. Chapter 2, <u>Tutorial on page 3,</u> provides a tutorial on how to begin using CLAN. Chapter 3, <u>The Editor on page 15,</u> explains how to use the editor. Chapter 4, <u>Features on page 32</u>, explains some additional features, how to access help, and how to report bugs. Chapter 5, <u>Analysis Commands on page 35</u>, provides detailed descriptions of each of the CLAN commands. Chapter 6, <u>Options on page 134</u>, provides details regarding particular command options. Chapter 7, <u>Exercises on page 144</u>, gives some exercises for learning CLAN.

1.1   Learning CLAN

In order to learn CLAN, you will want to first work through the <u>Tutorial on page 3</u>. That tutorial will give you a basic understanding of the program. After going through these initial steps, you will want to explore the features of the editor by working through the chapter on <u>The Editor on page 15</u>. Then you will want to learn each of the various analytic commands that are described in the chapter on <u>Analysis Commands on page 35</u>, concentrating first on the five basic commands illustrated in the tutorial.

1.2   Installing CLAN

CLAN can be retrieved from http://childes.psy.cmu.edu using a Web Browser or it can be copied from the CHILDES CD-ROM. On the Internet, Macintosh CLAN is distributed in a StuffIt file with the extension .sit. You will need to have a copy of StuffIt Expander™ to expand it. You drop this file onto StuffIt Expander and it will expand. The CD-ROM version of Macintosh CLAN can be dragged onto your desktop.

Windows CLAN is distributed in a file called clanwin.exe. You can copy this file to your hard drive from either the Internet or the CD-ROM. You then click on the file and it will run InstallShield which then installs CLAN in c:\childes\clan.

1.3   Starting CLAN

In order to start CLAN, you can either click on the program icon, select the startup item, or click on a file that is linked to or "opened by" CLAN. On Windows, the installer configures the system to allow files with the extensions .cha, .cdc, and .cut to be opened by CLAN. When first learning to use CLAN, it may be safest to begin by opening the program directly by clicking on its icon. A small window titled **Commands** should open up and you can type commands into this window. If the window does not open automatically, then just type *Control-d* on Windows or *⌘-d* on the Macintosh.

2: Tutorial

After you have installed CLAN according to the instructions in the previous chapter, you start it by double-clicking on its icon. The window that comes up is called the **Commands** window. Here is what the **Commands** window looks like:

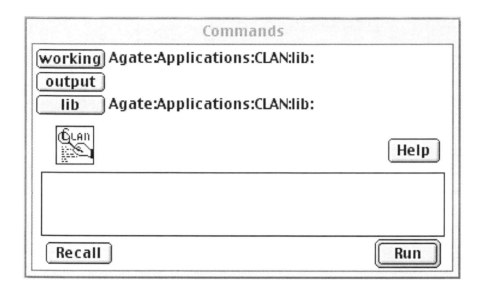

2.1   Commands Window

This window controls many of the functions of CLAN. It remains active in the background until the program is terminated. The main components of the **Commands** window are the command box in the center and the several buttons. The first thing you need to do when running CLAN is to set the **working** and **lib** directories.

Setting the Working Directory

The working directory is the place where the files you would like to work with are located. For this tutorial, we will use the CLAN library directory as both our Working directory and our Library directory. To set the working directory:

1.   Press the **working** button (see Figure 1).

2.   Locate the directory that contains the desired files. Use the **lib** directory inside the CLAN directory.

3.   Press the **Select Current Directory** button (see next screen image).

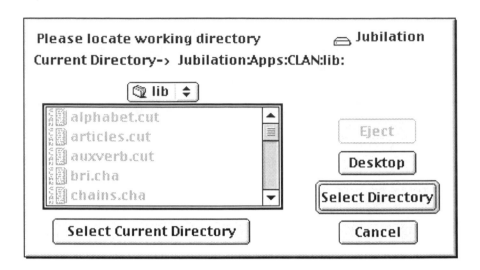

After selecting the current directory, you will automatically return to the **Commands** window. Please note that the selected directory will be listed to the right of the **working** button. This is useful because you will always know what directory you are working in without having to leave the **Commands** window.

After you have set the working directory, go through the same process to set the library directory. You do not need to worry about setting the output directory. By default, it is the same as the working directory. In order to see if CLAN is working, type "freq sample.cha" into the **Commands** window. The window should then look like this:

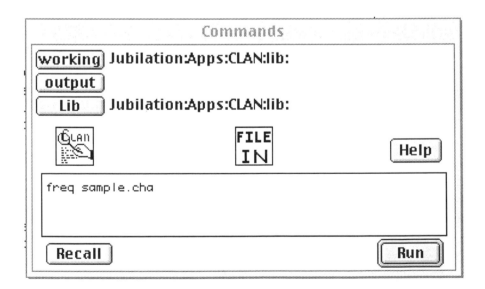

After typing in "freq sample.cha" you can either hit the return key or press the **Run** button. You should get the following output:

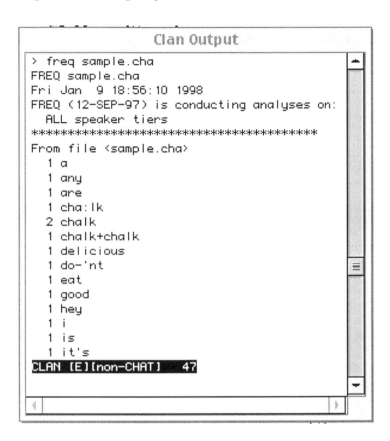

The output continues down the page. The exact shape of this window will depend on how you have sized it.

The Recall Button

If you want to see some of your old commands, you can use the recall function. Just hit the **Recall** button and you will get a window of old commands. The **Recall** window contains a list of the last 20 commands entered into the **Commands** window. These commands can be automatically entered into the **Commands** window by double-clicking on the line. This is particularly useful for repetitive tasks and tracking command strings. Another way to access previously used commands is by using the ↑ arrow on the keyboard. This will enter the previous command into the **Commands** window each time the key is pressed. In the Windows version of CLAN, the recall function is implemented by allowing you to scroll up and down to access old commands.

The HELP Button

The **Help** button can also give you some basic information about file and directory commands that you may find useful. These commands may be used by entering them into the command box. To test these out, just try typing *dir* into the **Commands** window. You should get something like this in the **CLAN Output** window:

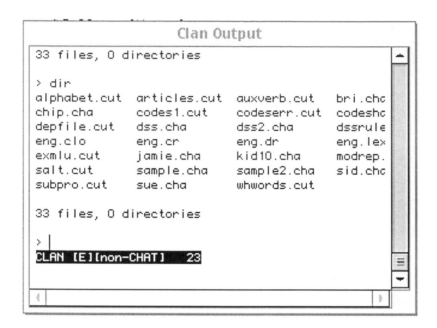

You may want to resize this window if text is being cut off.

The CLAN Button

The CLAN button gives you a list of CLAN analytic commands you can run. If you already know which command you want to run, you may find it faster just to type the name in the **Commands** window. However, just for practice, try clicking this button and then selecting the FREQ command. The name of the command will then be inserted into the **Commands** window.

The Files In Button

Once you have selected the FREQ command, you now see that the **Files In** button becomes available. Click on this button and you will get a dialog that asks you to locate some input files in your working directory. It should look like this:

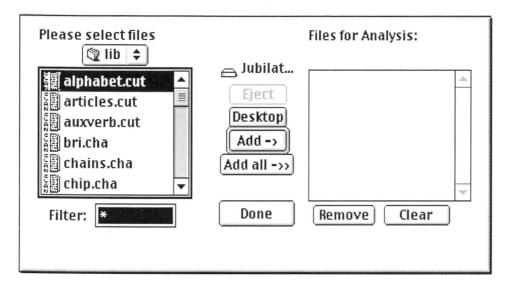

Scroll down to the file sample.cha and double-click on it to move it to the right. The files on the right will be the ones used for analysis. The **Remove** button that appears under the **Files for Analysis** scrolling list is used to eliminate files from the selected data set before it is read in by CLAN. The **Clear** button removes all the files you have added. The **Filter** text box shows the file extension of the selected data set. Those files with an extension other than the one shown will not be visible to the user. In order to see all available files, you will want to have the * symbol in the filter box. When you are finished adding files for analysis, hit **Done**. After the files are selected and you have returned to the **Commands** window, an @ is appended onto the command string. This symbol represents the set of files listed.

2.2   Typing Command Lines

There are two ways to build up commands. You can build commands using buttons and menus. Alternatively, you can just type them in. Let's try entering a command just by typing. Suppose we want to run an MLU analysis on the sample.cha file. Let us say that we also want to restrict the MLU analysis so that it looks only at the child's utterances. To do this, we enter the following command into the window:

```
mlu +t*CHI sample.cha
```

In this command line, there are three parts. The first part gives the name of the command; the second part tells the program to look at only the *CHI lines; and the third part tells the program which file to analyze as input. If we type this directly in the window, the window will look like this:

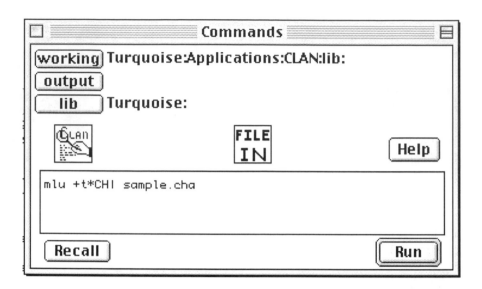

If you press the return key after entering this command, you should see a **CLAN Output** window that gives you the result of this particular MLU analysis. Of course, you must learn how to use the various options, such as +t or +f. One way to learn the options is to use the various buttons in the graphic user interface as a way of learning what CLAN can do. Once you have learned these options, it is often easier to just type in this command directly. However, in other cases, it may be easier to use buttons to locate rare options that are hard to remember. The decision of whether to type directly or to rely on buttons is one that is left to each user.

What if you want to send the output to a permanent file and not just to the temporary **CLAN Output** window? To do this you add the +f switch:

```
mlu +t*CHI +f sample.cha
```

Try entering this command, ending with a carriage return. You should see a message in the **CLAN Output** window telling you that a new file called sample.mlu.cex has been created. If you want to look at that file, type ⌘-*o* or *Control-o* for Open File and you can use the standard navigation window to locate the sample.mlu.cex file. It should be in the same directory as your sample.cha file.

You do not need to worry about the order in which the options appear. In fact, the only order rule that is used for CLAN commands is that the command name must come first. After that, you can put the file name or any switch in any order you wish.

Wildcards

A wildcard uses the asterisk symbol (*) to take the place of something else. For example, if you want to run this command across a group of ten files all ending with the extension .cha, you can enter the command in this form:

```
mlu +t*CHI +f *.cha
```

wildcards can be used to refer to a group of files (*.cha), a group of speakers (CH*), or a group of words with a common form (*ing). To see how these could work together, try out this command:

```
freq *.cha +s*ing
```

This command runs the FREQ program on all the .cha files in the LIB directory and looks for all words ending in "-ing." The output is sent to the **CLAN Output** window and you can set your cursor there and scroll back and forth to see the output. You can print this window or you can save it to a file.

Output Files

When you run the command

```
mlu +f sample.cha
```

the program will create an output file with the name sample.mlu.cex. It drops the .cha extension from the input file and then adds a two-part extension to indicate which command has run (.mlu) and the fact that this is CLAN output file (.cex). If you run this command repeatedly, it will create additional files such as sample.ml0.cex, sample.ml1.cex, sample.ml2.cex, and the like. You can add up to three letters after the +f switch, as in:

```
mlu +fmot sample.cha
```

If you do this, the output file will have the name "sample.mot.cex." As an example of a case where this would be helpful, consider how you might want to have a group of output files for the speech of the mother and another group for the speech of the father. The mother's files would be named *.mot.cex and the father's files would be named *.fat.cex.

Redirection

Instead of using the +f switch for output, you may sometimes want to use the redirect symbol (>). This symbol sends all of the output to a single file. The individual analysis of each file is preserved and grouped into one output file that is named in the command string. The use of the redirect syntax is illustrated in the following examples:

```
freq sample.cha > myanalyses
freq sample.cha >> myanalyses
freq sample.cha >& myanalyses
```

These three forms have slightly different results.

1.   The single arrow overwrites material already in the file.

2. The double arrow appends new material to the file, placing it at the end of material already in the file.

3. The single arrow with the ampersand writes both the analyses of the program and various system messages to the file.

If you want to analyze a whole collection of files and send the output from each to a separate file, use the +f switch instead.

2.3   Sample Runs

Now we are ready to try out a few sample runs with the five most basic CLAN commands – FREQ, MLU, COMBO, KWAL, and GEM.

2.3.1   Sample FREQ Runs

FREQ counts the frequencies of words used in selected files. It also calculates the type–token ratio typically used as a measure of lexical diversity. In its simplest mode, it generates an alphabetical list of all the words used by all speakers in a transcript along with the frequency with which these words occur. The following example looks specifically at the child's tier. The output will be printed in the CLAN window in alphabetical order:

```
freq +t*CHI 0042.cha
```

The output is:

```
> freq +t*CHI 0042.cha
FREQ +t*CHI 0042.cha
Wed May 5 16:30:13 1999
FREQ (04-May-99) is conducting analyses on:
 ONLY speaker main tiers matching: *CHI;
*****************************************
From file <0042.cha>
 1 ah
 1 pow wow
 1 bow+wow@
10 uh
 1 vroom@o
------------------------------
 5 Total number of different word types used
   14 Total number of words (tokens)
0.357 Type/Token ratio
```

A statistical summary is provided at the end. In the above example there were a total of 14 words or tokens used with only five different word types. The type–token ratio is found by dividing the total of unique words by the total of words spoken. For our example, the type–token ratio would be 5 divided by 14 or a ratio of 0.357.

The +f option can be used to save the results to a file. CLAN will automatically add the .frq.cex extension to the new file it creates. By default, FREQ excludes the strings xxx, yyy, www, as well as any string immediately preceded by one of the following symbols: 0, &, +, -, #. However, FREQ includes all retraced material unless otherwise commanded. For example, given this utterance:

```
*CHI: the dog [/] dog barked.
```

FREQ would give a count of two for the word "dog," and one each for the words "the" and "barked." If you wish to exclude retraced material, use the +r6 option.

2.3.2   Sample MLU Run

The MLU command is used primarily to determine the mean length of utterance of a specified speaker. It also provides the total number of utterances and of morphemes in a file. The ratio of morphemes over utterances (MLU) is derived from those two totals. The following command would perform an MLU analysis on the mother's tier (+t*MOT) from the file 0042.cha:

```
mlu +t*MOT 0042.cha
```

The output from this command looks like this:

```
> mlu +t*MOT 0042.cha
MLU +t*MOT 0042.cha
Wed May 5 16:31:13 1999
MLU (04-May-99) is conducting analyses on:
 ONLY speaker main tiers matching: *MOT;
*****************************************
From file <0042.cha>
MLU for Speaker: *MOT:
counts xxx and yyy are EXCLUDED from the utterance and morpheme
        Number of: utterances = 514, morphemes = 1553
        Ratio of morphemes over utterances = 3.021
        Standard deviation = 2.155
```

Thus, we have the mother's MLU or ratio of morphemes over utterances (3.021) and her total number of utterances (514).

2.3.3   Sample COMBO Run

COMBO is a powerful program that searches the data for specified combinations of words or character strings. For example, COMBO will find instances where a speaker says both *kitty* and *cat* within a single utterance. The following command would search the mother's tiers (+t*MOT) of the specified file 0042.cha:

```
combo +t*MOT +s"kitty^kitty" 0042.cha
```

Here, the string +t*MOT selects the mother's speaker tier only for analysis. When searching for a particular combination of words with COMBO, it is necessary to precede the combination with +s (e.g., +s"kitty^cat") in the command line. The symbol ^ specifies that the word *kitty* is immediately followed by the word *cat*. A portion of the output of the command used above would be as follows:

```
> combo +t*MOT +s"kitty^kitty" 0042.cha
((kitty^kitty))
COMBO +t*MOT +skitty^kitty 0042.cha
Mon May 17 12:40:37 1999
COMBO (04-May-99) is conducting analyses on:
  ONLY speaker main tiers matching: *MOT;
***************************************
From file <0042.cha>
-----------------------------------------
*** File "0042.cha": line 2548.
*MOT:   kitty kitty kitty .
        1     1
-----------------------------------------
*** File "0042.cha": line 2610.
*MOT:   and kitty kitty .
            1     1


Strings matched 2 times
```

2.3.4   Sample KWAL Run

KWAL searches data for user-specified words and outputs those keywords in context. The +s option is used to specify the words to be searched. The context or cluster is a combination of main tier and the selected dependent tiers in relation to that line. The following command searches for the keyword "bunny" and shows both the two sentences preceding it, and the two sentences following it in the output.

```
kwal +sbunny -w2 +w2 0042.cha
```

The -w and +w options indicate how many lines of text should be included before and after the search words. The output is as follows:

```
> kwal +sbunny -w2 +w2 0042.cha
KWAL +sbunny -w2 +w2 0042.cha
Wed May 5 16:31:59 1999
KWAL (04-May-99) is conducting analyses on:
 ALL speaker tiers
***************************************
From file <0042.cha>
-----------------------------------------
*** File "0042.cha": line 2304. Keyword: bunny
*CHI:   0.
*MOT:   see ?
*MOT:   is the bunny rabbit jump-ing ?
*MOT:   okay .
*MOT:   wanna [: want to] open the book ?
-----------------------------------------
*** File "0042.cha": line 2422. Keyword: bunny
*MOT:   <<one chick break-es out of its shell> ["]> [>]  .
```

```
*CHI:    <0> [<] .
*MOT:    <and a bunny go-es by hoppety+hoppety+hop@> ["] .
*MOT:    <<baby koala bear ride-s on mother-'s back> ["]> [>] .
*CHI:    <0> [<] .
-----------------------------------------
*** File "0042.cha": line 2564. Keyword: bunny
*CHI:    0.
*MOT:    hmm ?
*MOT:    <the bunny> [>] .
*CHI:    <0> [<] .
*MOT:    <hop hop bunny> [>] .
-----------------------------------------
*** File "0042.cha": line 2568. Keyword: bunny
*MOT:    <the bunny> [>] .
*CHI:    <0> [<] .
*MOT:    <hop hop bunny> [>] .
*CHI:    <0> [<] .
*MOT:    you like that book ?
```

2.3.5   Sample GEM Run

GEM searches for previously tagged passages for further analyses. For example, we might want to divide the transcript according to different social situations. By dividing the transcripts in this manner, separate analyses can be conducted on each situation type. One way of doing this is by "piping." Piping directs the output from one command to another.

```
gem +t*CHI +d 0012.cha | freq
```

The output is as follows:

```
> gem +t*CHI +d 0012.cha | freq
GEM +t*CHI +d 0012.cha
Wed May 5 16:33:56 1999
GEM (04-May-99) is conducting analyses on:
 ONLY speaker main tiers matching: *CHI;
 and ONLY header tiers matching: @BG:; @EG:;
*****************************************
From file <0012.cha>
FREQ
Wed May 5 16:33:57 1999
FREQ (04-May-99) is conducting analyses on:
 ALL speaker tiers
*****************************************
From pipe input
 2 box
 1 bye+bye
 1 do
 1 go-ing
 1 here
 6 kitty
 2 no+no
 2 oh
```

```
   5 this
   1 to
------------------------------
  10 Total number of different word types used
  22 Total number of words (tokens)
0.455 Type/Token ratio
```

The majority of the effort involved in using GEM is in the coding of the gem entries. There are three levels of coding:

1. Lazy GEM is the simplest form of GEM. It needs no @eg because each gem begins with one @g and ends with the next @g.

2. The next level is basic GEM. It can be used when the gem is surrounded by unwanted material. It should be marked with @bg at the beginning and with @eg at the end. Make sure all gems begin with @bg and end with @eg.

3. Tagged gems require the highest degree of care. They are good for identifying speech segments defined by the activities they accompany. They may be embedded with other segments but must be delineated by gem coding with tags to differentiate them from surrounding GEM material.

By using the +t option in the command, you may limit the search to a specific speaker or include the dependent tiers in the output. For example:

```
gem +t"*MOT" sample.cha
```

The output would be as follows:

```
> gem +t"*MOT" sample.cha
GEM +t*MOT sample.cha
Wed May 5 16:28:00 1999
GEM (04-May-99) is conducting analyses on:
 ONLY speaker main tiers matching: *MOT;
 and ONLY header tiers matching: @BG:; @EG:;
*****************************************
From file <sample.cha>
***** From file sample.cha; line 13.
@bg
*MOT:   you wanna [: want to] see # a [*] more toy+s ?
*MOT:   oh # I see .
@eg
***** From file sample.cha; line 25.
@bg
*MOT:   what's that ?
*MOT:   is there any delicious cha:lk ?
@eg
```

3:   The Editor

CLAN includes an editor that is specifically designed to work cooperatively with CHAT files. To open up an editor window, either type ⌘-n (*Control-n* on Windows) for a new file or ⌘-o to open an old file (*Control-o* on Windows). This is what a new text window looks like on the Macintosh:

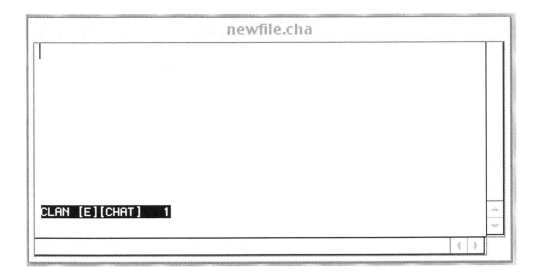

You can type into this editor window just as you would in any text editor.

3.1   The Modes

The editor works in several modes, each corresponding to a different function. The selection of different modes is done from the **Mode** pulldown menu.

1.   **Text Mode.** There are three editor modes — Text Mode, CHAT Mode, and CA Mode. In Text Mode, the editor functions as a basic ASCII editor. To indicate that you are in Text Mode, the bar at the bottom of the editor window displays [E][Text]. To enter Text Mode, you have to uncheck the CA Mode and CHAT Mode buttons on the **Mode** pulldown menu.

2.   **CHAT Mode.** In CHAT Mode, the editor facilitates the typing of new CHAT files and the editing of existing CHAT files. If your file has the extension .cha, you will automatically be placed into CHAT Mode when you open it. To indicate that you are in CHAT Mode, the bar at the bottom of the editor window displays [E][CHAT]. The use of this mode is described in the section on CHAT Mode on page 16.

3.   **CA Mode.** As an alternative to CHAT, you may wish to use CA format. This mode is intended for use by researchers working in the field of Conversation Analysis and should not be used for data in the CHILDES database or for data

that will be added to the CHILDES database. If your file has the extension .ca, you will automatically be placed into CA Mode when you open it. To indicate that you are in CA Mode, the bar at the bottom of the editor window displays [E][CA].The use of this mode is described in the section on <u>CA Mode on page 27</u>.

4.   **Coder Mode.** In Coder Mode [C], the editor provides a systematic interface for inserting codes onto a new coding line from a predefined coding menu. The use of this mode is described in the section on <u>Coder Mode on page 23</u>.

5.   **Disambiguator Mode.** When the editor is in Disambiguator Mode, it is possible to disambiguate the output of the MOR program on the %mor line. You can select Disambiguator Mode from the Mode menu or by typing Esc-2. The use of this mode is described in the section on <u>Disambiguator Mode on page 22</u>.

6.   **Sonic Mode.** In Sonic Mode (with the waveform displayed), you can link the transcript in your file to a digitized sound file. A wave form is displayed at the bottom of the screen and the beginnings and ends of sounds are indicated in the transcript with millisecond values. Once these links are made, sounds may be directly played from the transcript. The use of Sonic Mode is described in the section on <u>Sonic Mode on page 28</u>.

7.   **Continuous Playback Mode.** There are two continuous playback modes — one for sonic playback and the other for movie playback. They operate in similar ways. In Continuous Sonic Playback Mode, the waveform display is turned off and the machine plays back the entire transcript, one utterance after another, while moving the cursor and adjusting the screen to continually display the current utterances. This has somewhat the effect of "following the bouncing ball" as in the old sing-along cartoons. In Continuous Movie Playback Mode, the video is played as the cursor highlights utterances in the text. The use of Continuous Sonic Playback Mode is described in the section on <u>Continuous Playback Mode on page 29</u>.

8.   **Video Mode.** Just as it is possible to link transcripts to digitized audio, it is also possible to link them to digitized video with audio. The section on <u>Video Mode on page 30</u> describes the use of this mode.

You can use the options in the **Mode** pulldown menu to turn these modes on and off.

3.2   CHAT Mode

When you are first learning to use the editor, it is best to begin in CHAT mode. When you start CLAN, it automatically opens up a new window for text editing. By default, this file will be opened using CHAT mode. You can use this editor window to start learning the editor or you can open an existing CHAT file using the option in the **File** menu. It is probably easiest to start work with an existing file. To open a file, type ⌘-*o* on Macintosh or *Control-o* on Windows. You will be asked to locate a file. Try to open up the sample.cha file that you will find in the Lib directory inside the CLAN directory or folder. This is just a sample file, so you do not need to worry about accidentally saving changes.

You should stay in CHAT mode until you have learned the basic editing commands. You can insert characters by typing in the usual way. Movement of the cursor with the mouse and arrow keys works the same way in this editor as it does in most graphic editors. Functions like scrolling, highlighting, cutting, and pasting also work in the standard way. You should try these functions right away. Use them to move around in the sample.cha file. Try cutting and pasting sections and using the scroll bar, the arrow keys, and the page up and page down keys. Try to type a few sentences.

3.2.1   File, Edit, and Font Menus

The basic functions of opening files, printing, cutting, undoing, and font changing are common to all window-based text editors. These commands can be found under the **File, Edit,** and **Font** menus in the menu bar. The keyboard shortcuts for pulling down these menu items are listed next to the menu options.

3.2.2   Setting Special Colors

Within the Font Menu, you will find options for setting the style of areas as "smaller", "larger", "underline", "italic", or "color keyword". It is best to avoid using these formatting features unless necessary, since they tend to complicate the shape of the CHAT file. However, underlining is a crucial component of CA transcription and must be used when you are working in that format. You may also find it important to set the color of certain tiers to improve the readability of your files. For the Macintosh, you can do this in the following way. Select the "Color Keywords" option. In the dialog that appears, type the tier that you want to color in the upper box. For example, you may want to have %mor or *CHI in a special color. Then click on "add to list" and edit the color to the type you wish. The easiest way to do this is to use the crayon selector. Then make sure you select "color entire tier." To learn the various uses of this dialog, try selecting and applying different options.

3.2.3   Searching

In the middle of the **Edit** menu, you will find a series of commands for searching. The **Find** command brings up a dialog that allows you to enter a search string and to perform a reverse search. The **Find Same** command allows you to repeat the find multiple times. The **Go To** command allows you to move to a particular line number. The **Replace** command allows you to find a particular string and replace it. There is a dialog on both Macintosh and Windows that allows you to enter your search string, your replacement string, along with tabs or returns. When you need to perform a large series of different replacements, you can set up a file of replacement forms in the two-column form used by CHSTRING on page 51. You then are led through the words in this replacement file one by one. On the Macintosh, you have to use the following keyboard commands which are described at the bottom of the editor screen:

!	replace all of them
n	do not replace current occurrence
spacebar	replace the current occurrence
Control-g	abort this command

3.2.4   Keyboard Commands

In addition to the mouse and the arrow keys, there are many keyboard movement commands based on the EMACS editor. However, most users will prefer to use mouse movements and the commands available in the menu bar. For those familiar with EMACS, a list of these commands can be written out by typing *Esc-h*. This creates a file called keys list which you can then read, save, or print out. If you want to change the binding of a key, you go through these steps:

1.   Type *Esc-k*.

2.   Enter a command name, such as "cursor-down."

3.   Enter a key, such as F4.

4.   Then F4 should move the cursor down.

3.2.5   Tiers Menu

When you open a CHAT file with an @Participants line, the editor looks at each of the participants declared for the file and inserts their codes into the Tiers menu. Each speaker is associated with a keyboard command that lets you enter the name quickly. Similarly, you can add up to four dependent tier names on the @Dependent header tier. The line should look something like this:

```
@Dependent:  spa, add, acc
```

If you make changes to the @Participants or @Dependent line, you can press the Update button at the bottom of the menu to reload new speaker names.

3.2.6   Hiding Tiers

The function *Esc-4* allows you to hid certain tiers. For example, if you want to exclude the %mor tier, you type *Control-x Control-t* (hold down the control key and type x and then t). Then you type *e* to exclude a tier and *%mor* for the morphological tier. If you want to exclude all tiers, you type just *%*. To reset the tiers and to see them all, you type *Esc-4* and then *r*.

3.2.7   Running CHECK Inside the Editor

You can run CHECK from inside the editor. You do this by typing *Esc-L* or selecting **Check Opened File** from the **Mode** menu. If you are in CHAT Mode, CHECK will look for the correct use of CHAT. If you are in CA Mode, CHECK will look for the correct use of CA transcription. The use of CHECK is described in the section on <u>CHECK on page 41.</u>

3.3   Special Characters

Both Macintosh and Windows systems provide extensive support for keyboards and character sets that match up with different languages. On the Macintosh, you can run the desk accessory called "KeyFinder" to understand the placement of particular keys on your particular keyboard. If you do not have a copy of KeyFinder, you can use KeyCaps, although it is a bit harder to use. You use KeyCaps by pressing the shift, option, or command keys to check out the full character set. On Windows, you can use the accessory called "Character Map." There are special keyboard drivers and extensions on Windows that may interfere with the use of some editor commands, particularly those involving the command key. The Macintosh OS9 version of the operating system introduced consistent support for keyboards and scripts in all major world languages. This consistent support makes the use of non-Roman scripts particularly easy.

The CLAN editor provides extensive support for the display of non-ASCII Roman-based characters such as á, ñ, or ç, as well as non-Roman characters from Cyrillic, Japanese, Chinese and other languages. This support is available for Windows and Macintosh systems, using either system fonts, or special fonts available from vendors.

3.3.1   Roman-Based Character Sets

Many languages use the basic characters of the Roman alphabet, along with some additional characters and special diacritics. The basic characters of Roman are all present in the 128 character ASCII set. The characters of ASCII are:

```
a b c d e f g h i j k l m n o p q r s t u v w x y z
A B C D E F G H I J K L M N O P Q R S T U V W X Y Z
1 2 3 4 5 6 7 8 9 0 - = [ ] ' ` ; / \ . ,
! @ # $ % ^ & * ( ) _ + { } " ~ : ? | > <
```

This core set of characters is constant across computers, but the next 128 characters used on many computers are not standardized. These additional 128 characters are called *extended ASCII*. The exact assignment of special characters such as Spanish "ñ" to a particular extended ASCII value varies from font to font on different systems. By default, CHAT files use the Monaco font values on Macintosh and the Courier font values on Windows. Languages with characters outside the extended set can be represented by using special fonts.

The editor can display these various symbols by loading special fonts that are unique to each machine. Here is an example of a file in Spanish:

```
@Begin
@Participants: CHI Target_Child, MOT Mother
*CHI:    hasta mañana
*MOT:    ¿qué? creo que sí.
@End
```

This file will look fine in other text editors on the Macintosh. However, if you move it to another platform, the special characters will not look right unless you run the file through MAKEDATA, as described in the section on MAKEDATA on page 89. If you plan to use MAKEDATA, you must use a font recognized by MAKEDATA.

3.3.2   Non-Roman Scripts

For scripts that are not based on Roman, we are even more dependent on particular fonts that are supplied for particular machines. For example, when working with Cyrillic, one can use the editor to create a file like this:

```
@Begin
@Participants: CHI Target_Child, MOT Mother
*CHI: молоко?
*MOT: нет.
@End
```

This file is produced using the Apple Latinskij font. When this file is viewed without this font installed, it will look like this:

```
@Font: Latinskij:9
@Begin
@Participants: CHI Target_Child, MOT Mother
*CHI: ïóîóíó?
*MOT: ìâú.
@End
```

Fonts for Cyrillic, Korean, Chinese, Arabic, Hebrew, Japanese, and a variety of Indian and European languages are now included with Mac OS9. For Windows, language kits are produced by various companies. A useful source for Asian languages for Windows is Twinbridge, which has a web page at http://www.twinbridge.com. Our testing of Asian language kits for Windows has been restricted to those from Twinbridge. We have verified that the Twinbridge Japanese Partner 4.5 and Chinese Partner 4.5 work with Windows 95/98 and NT, although separate products are needed for these two variations of Windows. However, some of the characters in the CHILDES Cantonese corpus are not included in the Twinbridge character set. Before installing the Twinbridge products, you need to shut down all other Windows programs using *Control-alt-del*.

3.3.3   Font Definitions

Each CHAT file includes a first line that declares the nature of the font used in the file. In most cases, this font name also indicates the platform (Macintosh or Windows). The default fonts for Chinese and Japanese are:

Table 1: Default Fonts

Language	Mac	Windows
Chinese	Taipei:12	Win95:Chn System:-13
Japanese	Osaka:12	Win95:Jpn System:-13

You can change these defaults by explicitly setting the font inside the editor. However, if you plan to use other fonts, please tell us, so that we can include them in the cross-platform font translation table we use with MAKEDATA that helps us maintain the database.

In order to set the correct font for your file, use ⌘-a or *Control-a* to select the whole file. Then go into the **Font** menu and select the correct font. Your file should now appear in the correct font. When you save the file, a hidden first line will be inserted that tells CLAN what font to use and whether the file is a Macintosh or Windows file. You will also see the name of the font in the black line at the bottom of the editor window. If you fail to set font in this way under Windows, you will think that all is well until you attempt to take the file to Macintosh. At this point, Macintosh CLAN will think your file is in Courier and the non-Roman fonts will be all wrong. On the Macintosh, it is impossible to make this mistake, because the setting of fonts is tightly linked to the operating system which provides the correct information about the file to CLAN.

The use of special fonts on both Macintosh and Windows is usually linked to the use of a special keyboard. For non-Roman scripts, such as those of Japanese or Korean, you use a special entry method and keyboard which you can turn on or off. Turning the script and keyboard on and off is done through the "auto-script" menu item in the Fonts menu or, on the Macintosh, by pressing the option key twice.

3.4 Preferences and Options

You can set preferences by pulling down the **Edit** menu and selecting **Options**. The following dialog box will pop up:

```
Checkpoint every:   [0     ]   0 - turns off checkpoint
[ Codes file: ]      No file selected
[ Key-bind file: ]   No file selected
Limit of lines in CLAN Output      [500    ]  0 - no limit
Tier for disambiguation:       [%MOR:           ]
[ ] Open Commands window at startup
[✓] No backup file      [ ] Start in CHAT Coder mode
[ ] Start in CA Mode
[ ] Show cursor position in percentages
[ ] Auto-wrap in TEXT Mode   [✓] Auto-wrap CLAN output
[ ] Recognize prosodic delimiters [ ] Check for @ID tier
[ ] Check words for illegal characters

    [   OK   ]                   [ Cancel ]
```

These options control the following features:

1. Checkpoint frequency. This controls how often your file will be saved. If you set the frequency to 50, it will save after each group of 50 characters that you enter.

2. Codes file. This file is used to specify a set of codes for Coder Mode, as described in the section on <u>Coder Mode on page 23</u>. You can select this file by hand when you start Coder Mode. However, if you select it here, you will have it load automatically whenever you start Coder Mode.

3. Key-bind file. This file specifies a set of custom key bindings for specific commands. If you are happy with the standard key bindings, you do not need to use this file.

4. Limit of lines in CLAN output. This determines how many output lines will go to your CLAN output screen. It is good to use a large number, since this will allow you to scroll backwards through large output results.

5. Tier for disambiguation. This is the default tier for the Disambiguator Mode function, which is described in the section on <u>Disambiguator Mode on page 22.</u>

6. Open Commands window at startup. Selecting this option makes it so that the **Commands** window comes up automatically whenever you open CLAN.

7. No backup file. By default, the editor creates a backup file, in case the program hangs. If you check this, CLAN will not create a backup file.

8. Start in CHAT Coder mode. Checking this will start you in Text Mode when you open a new text window.

9. Start in CA Mode. Checking this will start you in CA Mode, as described in the section on <u>CA Mode on page 27</u>, when you open a new text window.

10. Show cursor position in percentages. By default, the cursor position is shown in terms of absolute line numbers.

11. Auto-wrap in Text Mode. This will wrap long lines when you type.

12. Auto-wrap CLAN output. This will wrap long lines in the output.

13. Recognize prosodic delimiters. This is a special option used by CHECK. It allows you to use delimiters such as -?, rather than the standard question mark.

14. Check for @ID tier. This option instructs CHECK to look for the @ID field that is used by commands like STATFREQ.

15. Check words for illegal characters. Checking this option forces the CHECK program, which is described in the section on <u>CHECK on page 41</u>, to look inside words for possible illegal characters.

3.5   Disambiguator Mode

Disambiguation is a special facility that is used to "clean up" the ambiguities in the %mor tier that are created by MOR (see the description of <u>MOR on page 104</u>). Toggling the **Disambiguator Mode** option in the **Mode** menu allows you to go back and forth between Disambiguator Mode and standard Editor Mode. In Disambiguator Mode, you will see each ambiguous interpretation on a %mor line broken into its alternative possibilities at the bottom of the editor screen. The user double-clicks on the correct option and it is inserted. An ambiguous entry is defined as any entry that has the ^ symbol in it. For example, the form N|back^Prep|back is ambiguously either the noun "back" or the preposition "back."

By default, Disambiguator Mode is set to work on the %mor tier. However, you may find it useful for other tiers as well. To change its tier setting, select the **Edit** menu and pull down to **Options** to get the **Options** dialog box. Set the disambiguation tier to the tier you want to disambiguate. To test all of this out, edit the sample.cha file, reset your default tier, and then type *Esc-2*. The editor should take you to the second %spa line which has:

```
%spa:    $RES:sel:ve^$DES:tes:ve.
```

At the bottom of the screen, you will have a choice of two options to select. Once the correct one is highlighted, you hit a carriage return and the correct alternative will be inserted. If you find it impossible to decide between alternative tags, you can select the UND or undecided tag, which will produce a form such as "und|drink" for the word drink, when you are not sure whether it is a noun or a verb.

3.6   Coder Mode

Once you have learned to use CHAT Mode, you may wish to learn Coder Mode. Just double-click on a file. Near the bottom of the text window is a line like this:

```
CLAN [E] [chat] sid.cha 1
```

The [E] entry indicates that you are in editor mode and the [chat] entry indicates that you are in CHAT Mode. In order to begin coding, you first want to set your cursor on the first utterance you want to code. In the sid.cha file, this would be the first *MOT utterance, beginning "I-'ll tell you what." Once you have placed the cursor anywhere on this line, you are ready to leave CHAT Mode and start using Coder Mode. Type Esc-e and you should be placed into Coder Mode. You will be asked to load a codes file. Just navigate to your library directory and select one of the demo codes files beginning with the word "code." We will use codes1.cut for our example.

3.6.1   Entering Codes

Now the coding tier that appears at the top line of the codes1.cut file is shown at the bottom of the screen. In this case it is %spa:. If you click on the tier symbol with the mouse, the editor will automatically insert the appropriate coding tier header (e.g. %spa), a colon and a tab on the line following the main line. It will also display all the codes at the top level of your coding scheme. In this case, they are $POS and $NEG. Let's select $POS and enter a carriage return. Next, we see the second level of the coding scheme, as in the following screen shot.

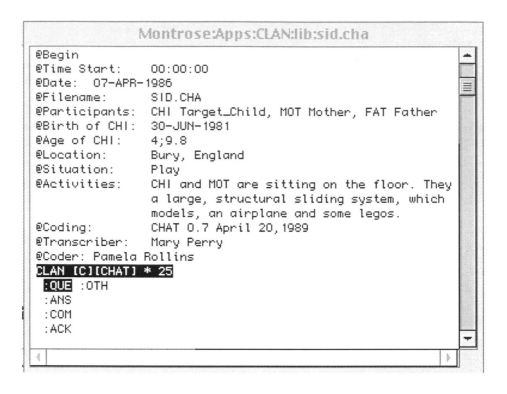

To get a quick overview of your coding choices, type *Esc-s* several times in succession and you will see the various levels of your coding hierarchy. Then return back to the top level to make your first selection. When you are ready to select a top-level code, double-click on it with your mouse. Once you have selected a code on the top level of the hierarchy, the coder moves down to the next level and you repeat the process until that complete code is constructed. To test this out, try to construct the code $POS:COM:VE.

The coding scheme entered in codes1.cut is hierarchical, and you are expected to go through all the decisions in the hierarchy. However, if you do not wish to code lower levels, type *Esc-c* to signal that you have completed the current code. You may then enter any subsequent codes for the current tier.

Once you have entered all the codes for a particular tier, type *Esc-c* to signal that you are finished coding the current tier. You may then either highlight a different coding tier relevant to the same main line, or move on to code another main line. To move on to another main line, you may use the arrow keys to move the cursor or you may automatically proceed to next main speaker tier by typing *Control-t*. Typing *Control-t* will move the cursor to the next main line, insert the highlighted dependent coding tier, and position you to select a code from the list of codes given. If you want to move to yet another line, skipping over a line, type *Control-t* again. Try out these various commands now to get a sense of how they work.

If you want to code data for only one speaker, you can restrict the way in which the *Control-t* feature works by using *Esc-t* to reset the set-next-tier-name function. For example, you confine the operation of the coder to only the *CHI lines, by typing *Esc-t* and then entering *CHI*. You can only do this when you are ready to move on to the next line.

If you receive the message "Finish coding current tier" in response to a command (as, for example, when trying to change to editor mode), use *Esc-c* to extricate yourself from the coding process. At that point, you can reissue your original command. Here is a summary of the commands for controlling the coding window.

Command	Function
Control -c	insert highlight code at cursor
Esc-c	finish coding current code
Esc-c	finish coding current tier
Control-t	finish coding current tier and go to the next
Esc-t	restrict coding to a particular speaker
Esc-Esc	go on to the next speaker
Esc-s	show subcodes under cursor
Control-g	cancel illegal command

3.6.2   Setting Up Your Codes File

When you are ready to begin serious coding, you will want to create your own codes file to replace our sample. When editing your codes file, make sure that you are in Text Mode and not CHAT Mode. The first line of your codes.cut file should be something like:

\ +b50 +d +l1 +s1

The options on the main line were described in the previous section on editor options. In this example, the +b option sets the checkpoint buffer (that is, the interval at which the program will automatically back up the work you have done so far in that session). If you find the interval is too long or too short, you can adjust it by changing the value of b. The +d option tells the editor not to keep a ".bak" backup of your original CHAT file. The +l option reorders the presentation of the codes based on their frequency of occurrence. There are three values of the +l option:
0   leave codes without frequency ordering
1   move most frequent code to the top
2   move codes up one level by frequency

If you use the +s option, the program assumes that all of the codes at a particular level have the same codes symmetrically nested within them. For example, consider the following codes.cut file:

```
\ +ll +s1 +b50
%spa:
$MOT
 :POS
         :Que
         :Res
 :NEG
$CHI
```

This file is a shorthand for the following complete listing of code types:

```
$MOT:POS:Que
$MOT:POS:Res
$MOT:NEG:Que
$MOT:NEG:Res
$CHI:POS:Que
$CHI:POS:Res
$CHI:NEG:Que
$CHI:NEG:Res
```

It is not necessary to explicitly type out each of the eight combinations of codes. With the +s1 switch turned on, each code at a particular level is copied across the branches so that all of the siblings on a given level have the same set of offspring. A more extensive example of a file that uses this type of inheritance is given in the chapter on speech error coding in the CHAT manual.

If you want to include a real space character at the beginning of one of your codes, you should precede it with a quote. For example, to include spaces before the $MOT and $CHI codes, the previous short form of the codes.cut file should be changed to look like this:

```
\ +ll +s1 +b50
%spa
' $MOT
 :POS
   :Que
   :Res
 :NEG
' $CHI
```

If not all codes at a given level occur within each of the codes at the next highest level, each individual combination must be spelled out explicitly in codes.cut and the +s option should not be used. The second line in the file should declare the name for your dependent tier. It should end with a tab, so that the tab is inserted automatically in the line you are constructing. A single codes.cut file can include coding systems for many different dependent tiers with each system in order in the file and beginning with an identifier such as $spa:.

Setting up the codes.cut file properly is the trickiest part of Coder Mode. Once properly specified, however, it rarely requires modification. If you have problems getting the editor to work, chances are the problem is with your codes.cut file.

3.7 CA Mode

A major alternative to the use of CHAT Mode for transcription is the system of CA (Conversation Analysis) coding developed by Sacks, Schegloff, Jefferson (1974) and their students. The CHAT manual describes the basic features of CA transcription. The iimplementation of CA inside CLAN was guided by suggestions from Johannes Wagner of Odense University and Chris Ramsden and Michael Forrester of the University of Nottingham. Inside CLAN, the use of CA Mode is very much like the use of CHAT Mode. All of the same basic editor functions, such as cut, paste, searching, replacing, and cursor movement, work in both modes. In addition, it is possible to underline words in accord with CA format. Here are some step-by-step instructions for learning to use CA Mode in CLAN.

1. Retrieve a current version of CLAN and the CA font from childes.psy.cmu.edu or your CD-ROM.

2. For Macintosh, you need to drag the CA font onto the System Folder to install it. For Windows, the font will be installed along with the rest of CLAN. This font includes symbols such as ↑ that are important components of CA transcription.

3. In the **Edit** menu, open the CLAN options and check the box that says "Start in CA Mode."

4. Open the file sample.ca.

5. Open and close the bullets that link to the sound or movie tiers by typing *Esc-A* once and then once more to close them.

6. Click on a bullet while holding down the command on the Macintosh or the control key for the PC to play a sound or movie segment.

7. Each turn-constructional unit of a CA file is identified with a line number, followed by a colon, and a participant code followed by a colon. Place your cursor at the beginning of a line and press the F2 function key. This will insert a new line number. Move the old line down by entering a carriage return. Then type F3 and the line numbers will automatically be updated to reflect the new insertion. You can do this at the end of the file too.

8. If your sample file has an @Participants line, you can use the **Tiers** menu to insert turn numbers and participant codes automatically using the numbers listed in that menu. After doing this, try typing F3 again to reorder numbers. The form of this line is:

```
@Participants:    fi, geo, do, car
```

9. Run CHECK by typing *Esc-L*. If you have made changes to the file, CHECK may ask you to correct some of them.

10. CHECK looks for a few basic structural features in your CA files. They are:
    The presence of a speaker code after the turn number.
    The use of paired parentheses around pause durations.
    Paired latching.
    Paired parentheses around comments.
    Paired overlap markers.

Paired superscripted zeroes.

11.   The CA font allows you to enter three special symbols for CA Mode:

Table 2: CA Symbols

Symbol	Macintosh	Windows
↑	Alt-6	Control-↑
↓	Alt-v	Control-↓
°	Alt-0	Control-0
.	Alt-8	Control-*

3.8   Sonic Mode

In addition to the various modes for text editing, the CLAN editor provides methods for linking the transcript to digitized audio and video. These modes are called Sonic Mode and Video Mode. We will begin with a description of Sonic Mode. In order to use Sonic Mode, you need to have a digitized audio file. For instructions on how to create a digitized audio file, please consult the CHAT manual. Once you have created a digitized sound file for the material you wish to transcribe, you are ready to start using sonic CHAT.

To begin, you should launch CLAN and open a new file. Type in your basic header tiers first. Then, go to the **Mode** pulldown menu and select "Sonic Mode" and you will be asked to locate the digitized sound file. Once you have selected your file, the waveform comes up, starting at the beginning of the file. Several functions are available at this point:

1.   **Sound playing from the waveform.** You can drag your cursor over a segment of the waveform to highlight it. When you release your mouse, the segment will play. As long as it stays highlighted, you can replay it by holding down the shift key and clicking the mouse. At this point, it does not matter where your cursor is positioned.

2.   **Waveform demarcation.** You can move the borders of a highlighted region by holding down the shift key and clicking your mouse to place the cursor at the place to which you wish the region to move. You can use this method to either expand or contract the highlighted region.

3.   **Transcription.** While you are working with the wave form, you can repeatedly play the sound by using shift-click. This will help you recognize the utterance you are trying to transcribe. You then go back to the editor window and type out the utterance that corresponds to the highlighted segment.

4.   **Linking.** When you believe that the highlighted waveform corresponds correctly to the utterance you have transcribed, you can click on the "s" button to the left of the waveform display and a bullet will be inserted. This bullet contains information regarding the exact onset and offset of the highlighted segment. You can achieve the same effect using ⌘-I (insert time code).

5. **Changing the waveform window.** The **+V** and **-V** buttons on the left allow you to increase or decrease the amount of time displayed in the window. The **+H** and **-H** buttons allow you to control the amplitude of the wave form.

6. **Scrolling.** At the bottom of the sound window is a scroll-bar that allows you to move forward or backward in the sound file (please note that scrolling in the sound file can take some time as the sound files for long recordings are very large and take up processing capacity).

7. **Waveform activation.** In order to highlight the section of the waveform associated with a particular utterance, you need to triple-click on the bullet following the utterance you want to replay. The waveform will redisplay. Then you can replay it by using shift-click. Here is an example of a file with associated waveform.

8. **Expanding and hiding the bullets.** If you want to see the exact temporal references that are hiding inside the bullet symbols, you can type *Esc-A* to expand them. Typing *Esc-A* again will hide them again.

9. **Time duration information.** Just above the waveform, you will see the editor mode line. This is the black line that begins with the word "CLAN". If you click on this line, you will see three additional numbers. The first is the beginning and end time of the current window in seconds. The second is the position of the cursor in hours:minutes:seconds.milliseconds. The third is the beginning and end of the current selection in seconds. If you click once again on the mode line, you will see sampling rate information for the audio file.

3.9   Continuous Playback Mode

If you have a file that has been fully transcribed and then linked in Sonic Mode or Video Mode, you can use Continuous Playback Mode to play through each utterance in a file in sequence, highlighting each utterance as it goes. This allows you to hear the transcript as you read it. You can turn on "Continuous Sonic Playback" or "Continuous Movie Playback" from the **Modes** menu. Before turning on Continuous Sonic Playback, you have to turn off Sonic Transcriber Mode. If you do not, the editor will complain and ask you to turn it off. A single mouse-click pauses Continuous Playback and a double-click terminates Continuous Playback and throws you back to your previous mode. You can start Continuous Playback again by positioning the cursor where you want it and selecting the mode again.

If you only want to listen to a single utterance, rather than lots of utterances in sequence, you can do this by positioning your cursor on the bullet of the utterance you want to listen to and using ■-mouseclick or *Control-mouseclick*. As in Continuous Playback, you need to have Sonic Transcriber Mode turned off to do this.

3.10   Sonic Commands

3.10.1   Waveform window

+V / -V buttons   decreases/increases the length of the displayed sound wave
+H / -H buttons   increases/decreases the display of the sound wave
S-button or Esc-i: links selected sound segment to utterance at cursor position
Scrollbar at bottom: move backwards/forwards in the sound file

Shift + click   plays selected sound segment
Shift + drag   changes the borders of a selected sound segment

3.10.2   Editor window

Esc-A   expands bullet, reduces bullet
Esc-1   plays the sound segment associated with an utterance (cursor
                            needs to be right in front of the bullet's position, or in front
                            of the %snd-symbol in an expanded bullet)
triple-click on bullet   highlights respective segment of the waveform

3.10.3   Continuous Playback Mode

(Note: Sonic mode needs to be turned off)
Esc-8   turn on continuous playback
any key   stops continuous playback
click   pauses continuous playback

3.11   Video Mode

Video Mode works very much like Sonic Mode. In order to run Video Mode, you need to first create a digitized video file. The instructions for doing this are given in the CHAT manual. There are several sample movie files that we distribute over the Internet. These are distributed along with transcription files. You may wish to use one of these sample file sets. We will call the movie file sample.mov and the transcript file sample.cha.

To play a file that has already been linked to a movie, you open the transcript file and click on the bullet following the utterance you wish to play. This will open the movie and play the segment. You can also use Continuous Playback Mode to play all the segments in the file. If you want to link your transcript to a movie or create a new transcript that is linked to a movie, you follow this procedure:

1.   Start CLAN by clicking on your transcript file. If you are creating a new file from scratch, just start CLAN and then open a new file for editing.

2.   Select **Play Movie** from the **Mode** menu. You will be asked to find your movie file.

3.   In your movie file, drag the slider to the position you wish to begin the playback.

4.   Press right pointing arrow to the left of the slider.

5.   When the segment is finished, quickly click the mouse.

6.   Put your cursor on this line and press command-mouseclick. This will play the first few seconds of your video. The numbers for a 10 minute video clip will reach up to about 300,000 at the end.

7.   Put in additional %mov: tiers for each new segment you transcribe.

4:   Features

4.1   Shell Commands

CLAN provides two types of commands. The first are the Shell commands. These are utility commands like those in the old-style DOS or Unix shells. These commands are available inside the **Commands** window. The set of shell commands is particularly extensive for Macintosh. The following commands allow you to change your folder or directory, display information, or launch a new program.

accept   This command applies only to Macintosh. If you only want to have CLAN look at files that the Macintosh calls TEXT files, then type: accept text. If you want to set this back to all files, type *accept all*.

batch   You can place a group of commands into a text file which you then execute as a batch. The word *batch* should be followed by the name of a file in your working directory. Each line of that file is then executed as a CLAN command.

cd   This command allows you to change directories. With two dots, you can move up one directory. If you type a folder's name and the folder is in the current folder, you can move right to that folder. If you type a folder's absolute address, you can move to that folder from any other folder. For example, the command **cd HardDisk:Applications:**CLAN on the Macintosh will take you to the CLAN directory.

copy   If you want to copy files without going back to the Finder, you can use this command. The -q option asks to make sure you want to make the copy.

del   This command allows you to delete files. Using this in combination with the +re switch can be very dangerous. In this combination, the command *del ** can delete all files from your current working directory and those below it. **Please be careful!**

dir   This command lists all the files in your current directory.

info   This command displays the available programs and commands.

list   This command lists the files that are currently in your input files list.

rmdir   This command deletes a directory or folder.

ren   This command allows you to change file names in a variety of ways. The rename command can use the asterisk as a wildcard for files in which there is a period. You can change case by using -u for upper and -l for lower. You can change extensions by using wildcards in file names. The -c and -t switches allow you to change the creator signature and file types recognized by Macintosh. Usually, you will want to have TEXT file types. CLAN produces these by default and you should seldom need to use the

-t option. You will find that the -c option is more useful. On the Macintosh, if you want a set of files to have the icon and ownership for CLAN, you should use this command:

```
ren -cMCED *.cha *.cha
```

If you have spaces in these names, surround them with single quotes. For example, to change ownership to the MPW shell, you would need quotes in order to include the additional fourth space character:

```
ren -c'MPS ' *.cha *.cha
```

Or you could rename a series of files with names like "child.CHA (Word 5)," using this command:

```
ren '*.CHA (Word 5)' '*.cha
```

4.2   Online Help

CLAN has a limited form of online help. To use this help, you simply type the name of the command without any further options and without a file name. The computer will then provide you with a brief description of the command and a list of its available options. To see how this works, just type *freq* and a carriage return and observe what happens. If you need help remembering the various shell commands discussed in the previous section, you can click on the **Help** button at the right of the **Commands** window. If there is something that you do not understand about CLAN, the best thing you can do is to try to find the answer to your problem in this manual.

4.3   Testing CLAN

It is a good idea to make sure that CLAN is conducting analyses correctly. In some cases you may think that the program is doing something different from what it is actually designed to do. In order to prevent misunderstandings and misinterpretations, you should set up a small test file that contains the various features you want CLAN to analyze. For example, if you are running a FREQ analysis, you can set a file with several instances of the words or codes for which you are searching. Be sure to include items that should be "misses" along with those that should be "hits." For example, if you do not want CLAN to count items on a particular tier, make sure you put some unique word on that tier. If the output of FREQ includes that word, you know that something is wrong. In general, you should be testing not for correct performance but for possible incorrect performance. In order to make sure that you are using the +t and +s switches correctly, make up a small file and then run KWAL over it without specifying any +s switch. This should output exactly the parts of the file that you intend to include or exclude.

4.4   Bug Reports

Although CLAN has been extensively tested for years, it is possible that some analyses will provide incorrect results. When this occurs, the first thing to do is to reread the relevant sections of the manual to be sure that you have entered all of your commands correctly. If a rereading of the manual does not solve the problem, then you can send e-mail to macw@cmu.edu to try to get further assistance. In some cases, there may be true "bugs" or program errors that are making correct analyses impossible. Should the program not operate properly, please send e-mail to macw@cmu.edu with the following information:

1. a description of the machine you are using and the operating system you are running,

2. a copy of the file that the program was being run on,

3. the complete command line used when the malfunction occurred,

4. all the results obtained by use of that command, and

5. the date of compilation of your CLAN program, which you can find by clicking on "About CLAN" at the top left of the menu bar on Macintosh or the "Help CLAN" option at the top right of the menu bar for Windows.

Use WinZip or Stuffit to save the input and output files and include them as an e-mail attachment. Please try to create the smallest possible file you can that will still illustrate the bug.

4.5   Feature Requests

CLAN has been designed in response to information we have received from users about the kinds of programs they need for furthering their research. Your input is important, because we are continually designing new commands and improving existing programs. If you find that these programs are not capable of producing the specific type of analysis that you are trying to achieve, contact us and we will do our best to help. Sometimes we can explain ways of using CLAN to achieve your goals. In other cases, it may be necessary to modify the program. Each request must include a simple example of an input file and the output you would like, given this input. Also, please explain how this output will help you in your research. You can address inquiries by email to macw@cmu.edu.

5: Analysis Commands

The analytic work of CLAN is performed by a series of commands that search for strings and compute a variety of indices. These commands are all run from the Commands window. In this section, we will examine each of the commands and the various options that they take. The commands are listed alphabetically. The following table provides an overview of the various CLAN commands.

Table 3: The Analysis Commands

Command	Function
CHAINS on page 37	Tracks sequences of interactional codes across speakers.
CHECK on page 41	Verifies the accuracy of CHAT conventions in files.
CHIP on page 45	Examines parent-child repetition and expansion.
CHSTRING on page 51	Changes words and characters in CHAT files.
COMBO on page 56	Searches for complex string patterns.
COOCUR on page 63	Examines patterns of co-occurence between words.
DATES on page 64	Uses the date and birthdate of the child to compute age.
DIST on page 65	Examines patterns of separation between speech act codes.
DSS on page 66	Computes the Developmental Sentence Score.
FREQ on page 72	Computes the frequencies of the words in a file or files.
FREQMERG on page 79	Combines the outputs of various runs of FREQ.
FREQPOS on page 80	Tracks the frequencies in various utterance positions.
GEM on page 81	Finds areas of text that were marked with gem markers.
GEMFREQ on page 83	Computes frequencies for words inside gem markers.
GEMLIST on page 84	Lists the pattern of gem markers in a file or files.
ID on page 85	Adds an ID tier to a file.
KEYMAP on page 85	Lists the frequencies of codes that follow a target code.
KWAL on page 87	Searches for word patterns and prints the line.
MAKEDATA on page 89	Converts data formats for CHAT files across platforms.
MAXWD on page 91	Finds the longest words in a file.
MLT on page 92	Computes the mean length of turn.

Table 3: The Analysis Commands

Command	Function
MLU on page 95	Computes the mean length of utterance.
MODREP on page 101	Matches the child's phonology to the parental model.
MOR on page 104	Inserts a new tier with part-of-speech codes.
PHONFREQ on page 120	Computes the frequency of phonemes in various positions.
POST on page 121	Probabilistic disambiguator for the %mor line
POSTLIST on page 123	Displays the patterns learned by POSTTRAIN
POSTTRAIN on page 123	Trains the probabilistic network used by POST
RELY on page 124	Measures reliability across two transcriptions.
SALTIN on page 125	Converts SALT files to CHAT format.
STATFREQ on page 126	Formats the output of FREQ for statistical analysis.
TEXTIN on page 127	Converts straight text to CHAT format.
TIMEDUR on page 127	Uses the numbers in sonic bullets to compute overlaps.
VOCD on page 128	Computes the VOCD lexical diversity measure.
WDLEN on page 132	Computes the length of utterances in words.

5.1   CHAINS

CHAINS is used to track sequences of interactional codes. These codes must be entered by hand on a single specified coding tier. In order to test out CHAINS, you may wish to try the file chains.cha which contains the following sample data.

```
@Begin
@Participants:CHI Sarah Target_child, MOT Carol Mother
*MOT:    sure go ahead [c].
%cod:    $A
%spa:    $nia:gi
*CHI:    can I [c] can I really [c].
%cod:    $A $D. $B.
%spa:    $nia:fp $npp:yq.
%sit:    $ext $why. $mor
*MOT:    you do [c] or you don't [c].
%cod:    $B $C.
%spa:    $npp:pa
*MOT:    that's it [c].
%cod:    $C
%spa:    $nia:pa
@End
```

The symbol [c] in this file is used to delimit clauses. Currently, its only role is within the context of CHAINS. The %cod coding tier is a project-specific tier used to code possible worlds, as defined by narrative theory. The %cod, %sit, and %spa tiers have periods inserted to indicate the correspondence between [c] clausal units on the main line and sequences of codes on the dependent tier.

To change the order in which codes are displayed in the output, create a file called codes.ord. This file could be located in either your working directory or in the \childes\clan\lib directory. CHAINS will automatically find this file, no option is required. If the file is not found then the codes are displayed in alphabetical order, as before. In the codes.ord file, list all codes in any order you like, one code per line. You can list more codes than could be found in any one file. But if you do not list all the codes, the missing codes will be inserted in alphabetical order. All codes must begin with the $ symbol.

5.1.1   Sample Runs

For our first CHAINS analysis of this sample file, let us look at the %spa tier. If you run the command:

```
chains +t%spa chains.cha
```

you will get a complete analysis of all chains of individual speech acts for all speakers, as in the following output:

```
> chains +t%spa chains.cha
CHAINS +t%spa chains.cha
Mon May 17 13:09:34 1999
```

```
CHAINS (04-May-99) is conducting analyses on:
  ALL speaker tiers
and those speakers' ONLY dependent tiers matching: %SPA;
*****************************************
From file <chains.cha>

Speaker markers:  1=*MOT, 2=*CHI
```

$nia:fp	$nia:gi	$nia:pa	$npp:pa	$npp:yq	line #
0	1	0	0	0	3
2	0	0	0	2	6
0	0	0	1	0	10
0	0	1	0	0	13

ALL speakers:

	$nia:fp	$nia:gi	$nia:pa	$npp:pa	$npp:yq
# chains	1	1	1	1	1
Avg leng	1.00	1.00	1.00	1.00	1.00
Std dev	0.00	0.00	0.00	0.00	0.00
Min leng	1	1	1	1	1
Max leng	1	1	1	1	1

Speakers *MOT:

	$nia:fp	$nia:gi	$nia:pa	$npp:pa	$npp:yq
# chains	0	1	1	1	0
Avg leng	0.00	1.00	1.00	1.00	0.00
Std dev	0.00	0.00	0.00	0.00	0.00
Min leng	0	1	1	1	0
Max leng	0	1	1	1	0
SP Part.	0	1	1	1	0
SP/Total	0.00	1.00	1.00	1.00	0.00

Speakers *CHI:

	$nia:fp	$nia:gi	$nia:pa	$npp:pa	$npp:yq
# chains	1	0	0	0	1
Avg leng	1.00	0.00	0.00	0.00	1.00
Std dev	0.00	0.00	0.00	0.00	0.00
Min leng	1	0	0	0	1
Max leng	1	0	0	0	1
SP Part.	1	0	0	0	1
SP/Total	1.00	0.00	0.00	0.00	1.00

It is also possible to use the +s switch to merge the analysis across the various speech act codes. If you do this, alternative instances will still be reported, separated by commas. Here is an example:

```
chains +d +t%spa chains.cha +s$nia:%
```

This command should produce the following output:

```
Speaker markers:   1=*MOT, 2=*CHI

$nia:                                       line #
1 gi                                           3
2 fp                                           6
                                               6
1 pa                                          13

ALL speakers:
          $nia:

# chains   2
Avg leng   1.50
Std dev    0.50
Min leng   1
Max leng   2

Speakers  *MOT:
          $nia:

# chains   2
Avg leng   1.00
Std dev   -0.00
Min leng   1
Max leng   1
SP Part.   2
SP/Total   0.67

Speakers  *CHI:
          $nia:

# chains   1
Avg leng   1.00
Std dev    0.00
Min leng   1
Max leng   1
SP Part.   1
SP/Total   0.33
```

You can use CHAINS to track two coding tiers at a time. For example, one can look at chains across both the %cod and the %sit tiers by using the following command. This command also illustrates the use of the +c switch, which allows the user to define units of analysis lower than the utterance. In the example file, the [c] symbol is used to delimit clauses. The following command makes use of this marking:

```
chains +c"[c]" +d +t%cod chains.cha +t%sit
```

The output from this analysis is:

```
Speaker markers: 1=*MOT, 2=*CHI

$a                $b              $c              $d              line #
1                                                                   3
```

```
 2 $ext $why                                    2 $ext $why        6
           2 $mor                                                  6
           1                     1                                11
                                 1                                14
```

ALL speakers:

	$a	$b	$c	$d
# chains	1	1	1	1
Avg leng	2.00	2.00	2.00	1.00
Std dev	0.00	0.00	0.00	0.00
Min leng	2	2	2	1
Max leng	2	2	2	1

Speakers *MOT:

	$a	$b	$c	$d
# chains	1	1	1	0
Avg leng	1.00	1.00	2.00	0.00
Std dev	0.00	0.00	0.00	0.00
Min leng	1	1	2	0
Max leng	1	1	2	0
SP Part.	1	1	1	0
SP/Total	0.50	0.50	1.00	0.00

Speakers *CHI:

	$a	$b	$c	$d
# chains	1	1	0	1
Avg leng	1.00	1.00	0.00	1.00
Std dev	0.00	0.00	0.00	0.00
Min leng	1	1	0	1
Max leng	1	1	0	1
SP Part.	1	1	0	1
SP/Total	0.50	0.50	0.00	1.00

5.1.2   Unique Options

At the end of our description of each CLAN command, we will list the options that are unique to that command. The commands also use several options that are shared with other commands. For a complete list of options for a command, type the name of the command followed by a carriage return in the Commands window. Information regarding the additional options shared across commands can be found in the chapter on Options on page 134.

+c   The default unit for a CHAINS analysis is the utterance. You can use the +c option to track some unit type other than utterances. The other unit type must be delimited in your files with some other punctuation symbol that you specify after the +c, as in +c"[c]" which uses the symbol [c] as a unit delimiter. If you have a large set of delimiters you can put them in a file and use the form +c@filename. To see how this switch operates try out this command:

```
chains +c"[c]" +d +t%cod chains.cha
```

+d   Use this switch to change zerocs to spaces in the output. The following command illustrates this option:

```
chains +d +t%spa chains.cha +s$nia:%
```

The +d1 value of this option works the same as +d, while also displaying every input line in the output.

+sS   This option is used to specify particular codes to track. For example, +s$b will track only the $b code. A set of codes to be tracked can be placed in a file and tracked using the form +s@filename. In the examples given earlier, the following command was used to illustrate this feature:

```
chains +d +t%spa chains.cha +s$nia:%
```

+wN   Sets the width between columns to N characters.

5.2   CHECK

Checking the syntactic accuracy of a file can be done in two ways. One method is to work within the editor. In the editor, you can start up the CHECK program by just typing *Esc-L*. Alternatively, you can run CHECK as a separate program. The CHECK program checks the syntax of the specified CHAT files. If errors are found, the offending line is printed, followed by a description of the problem.

5.2.1   How CHECK Works

CHECK makes two passes through each CHAT file. On the first pass it checks the overall structure of the file. It makes sure that the file begins with @Begin and ends with @End, that each line starts with either *, @, %, or a tab, and that colons are used properly with main lines, dependent tiers, and headers that require entries. If errors are found at this level, CHECK reports the problem and stops, because further processing would be misleading. If there are problems on this level, you will need to fix them before continuing with CHECK. Errors on the first level can mask the detection of further errors on the second level. It is important not to think that a file has passed CHECK until all errors have been removed.

The second pass checks the detailed structure of the file. To do this, it relies heavily on depfile.cut, which we call the "depfile." The depfile distributed with CLAN lists the legitimate CHAT headers and dependent tier names as well as many of the strings allowed within the main line and the various dependent tiers. When running CHECK, you should have the depfile located either in the directory you are working in or in \childes\clan\lib (or / childes/clan/lib on Unix). On the Macintosh, the depfile should be kept inside the LIB folder. If the programs cannot find the depfile, they will query you for its location.

To get an idea of how CHECK operates, open up the file kid10.cha in the library directory. That file has a large number of CHAT errors. Type *Esc-L*. Try to fix the errors. If you can put the file into correct CHAT format so that it passes cleanly through CHECK, you will have learned how to use CHECK to verify CHAT format.

5.2.2 The Construction of the Depfile

In order to maintain consistency in the use of CHAT across projects, we ask you to avoid modification of the depfile. We occasionally make some additions to the depfile to reflect new uses of CHAT, but we try to be conservative in regards to these changes. If you need to extend CHAT in particular ways, you can create a file called 00depadd.cut which you should place into the same directory as the files being checked. CHECK will automatically pick up the additional codes in this file and use them to amplify the standard depfile. If you use a 00depadd.cut file, it should remain with the data files to which it applies as a form of documentation of the particular divergences from standard CHAT.

In order to work effectively with CHECK, and in order to create lines in a 00depadd file, it is helpful to understand the format of depfile.cut . The depfile is, in effect, a shorthand summary of CHAT. The three components of the file are the definitions for headers, the main line, and the dependent tiers. Some of the details of the rules for making declarations in depfile.cut or 00depadd.cut are as follows:

1. Headers like @Begin that take no additional material are entered in just this form, one on each line.

2. Headers that take additional information like @Comment are entered with a following colon and tab and then an asterisk to allow any word.

3. For headers such as @Age that allow dates, the format is specified by using "y" to indicate the year; "m" to indicate a month; and "d" to indicate a day. Lowercase letters indicate numbers and uppercase letters indicate letters. For dates, the standard form is @d<dd-MMM-yyyy>, as in 14-NOV-1956. For ages, the standard form is @d<yy;mm.dd>, as in 2;5.17. For timing, the standard form is @t<hh:mm-hh:mm>, as in 12:15-4:30. The name of a particular participant such as "MOT" or "CHI" is indicated in headers such as "Age of #" by the # sign.

4. Following the header definitions, the symbol *: appears on the left. This is the marker for the main line. After this tier marker, the following characters indicate possible strings. The first symbol is the asterisk. This allows CHECK to accept all words that begin with alphabetic characters.

5. Next come the main line definitions for various prefixes and suffixes. The standard depfile is oriented toward coding in English and includes many English prefixes and suffixes. These can be changed for other languages. In addition, strings beginning with symbols like the dash and the square bracket must be exhaustively listed. Suffixes are coded by using the notation *-suffix and prefixes are coded by using the notation *prefix#.

6. The main line definition concludes with all the special forms of CHAT.

7. Following the definition for the main line are a series of definitions for the de-

pendent tiers. These have the same form as the definitions for the main line, although they differ in content.

8.   Unlike words on the main tier, words on the dependent tiers are not analyzed into suffixes and prefixes. Because of this, if you want to explicitly include a particular set of suffixes or prefixes on a dependent tier, you should add the code [AFX] to that tier in your 00depadd file. If the main depfile does not have an asterisk for a coding tier and your 00depadd does not have one either, then you must explicitly list all of the word-affix combinations or types that you want to use on that tier in your 00depadd file.

9.   The %mor line includes the special symbol [UTD], which is designed to allow for the inclusion of all utterance delimiters. If you do not want to have utterance delimiters on the %mor line, you need to create a 00depadd.cut file with an entry for the %mor line that includes [-UTD]. Adding this to the 00depadd file will override the [UTD] in the standard depfile. The %mod line includes the special symbol [IGN] which is designed to turn off all checking of characters on a particular dependent tier.

5.2.3   CHECK in CA Mode

CHECK can also be used with files that have been produced using CA Mode (see the section on CA Mode on page 27). The features that CHECK is looking for in CA Mode are:

1.   Each utterance should begin with a number and a speaker code in the form #:speaker:<whitespace>.

2.   There should be paired parentheses around pause numbers.

3.   Numbers marking pause duration are allowed on their own line.

4.   Latching should be paired.

5.   The double parentheses marking comments should be paired.

6.   Overlap markers should be paired.

7.   Superscript zeros should be paired.

8.   The up-arrow, down-arrow, and zeros are allowed inside words.

5.2.4   Running CHECK

There are two ways to run CHECK. If you are working on new data, it is easiest to run CHECK from inside the editor. To do this, you type *Esc-L* and CHECK runs through the file looking for errors. It highlights the point of the error and tells you what the nature of the error is. Then you need to fix the error in order to allow CHECK to move on through the file.

The other way of running CHECK is to issue the command from the commands window. This is the best method to use when you want to check a large collection of files. If you want to examine several directories, you can use the +re option to make CHECK work recursively across directories. It will use the 00depadd.cut files appropriate to each directory it examines. If you send the output of CHECK to the **CLAN Output** window, you can locate errors in that window and then triple-click on the file name and CLAN will take you right to the problem that needs to be fixed. This is an excellent way of working when you have many files and only a few errors.

5.2.5   Some Hints

1.   Use CHECK early and often, particularly when you are learning to code in CHAT. When you begin transcribing, check your file inside the editor using *Esc-L*, even before it is complete. When CHECK complains about something, you can learn right away how to fix it before continuing with the same error.

2.   Learn how to add codes to 00depadd.cut. Try to avoid adding symbols such as * or *$, because you will then lose the ability to trap certain types of errors on coding lines.

3.   If you are being overwhelmed by CHECK errors, you can use the +d1 switch to limit error reports to one of each type. Or you can focus your work first on eliminating main line errors by using the -t% switch.

4.   Learn how to use the query-replace function in your text editor to make general changes and CHSTRING to make changes across sets of files.

5.2.6   Unique Options

+c   By default, CHECK will look in your directory for 00depadd.cut. However, if you wish to use some other name for your depadd file, you need to use this switch and follow it with the name of your file.

+d   This option attempts to suppress repeated warnings of the same error type. It is convenient to use this in your initial runs when your file has consistent repeated divergences from standard CHAT form. However, you must be careful not to rely too much on this switch, because it will mask many types of errors you will eventually want to correct. The +d1 value of this switch represses errors even more severely to only one of each type.

+e   This switch allows the user to select a particular type of error for checking. To find the numbers for the different errors, type:

```
check +e
```

Then look for the error type you want to track, such as error #16, and type:

```
check +e16 *.cha
```

+g1   Setting +g1 turns on the treatment of prosodic contour markers such as -. or -? as utterance delimiters, as discussed in the section on prosodic delimiters in the CHAT manual. Setting -g1 sets the treatment back to the default, which is to not treat these codes as delimiters.

+g2   By default, CHECK requires tabs after the colon on the main line and at the beginning of each line. However, versions of Word Perfect before 5.0 cannot write out text files that include tabs. Other non-ASCII editors may also have this problem. To get around the problem, you can set the -g2 switch in CHECK which stops checking for tabs. If you want to turn this type of checking back on, use the +g2 switch.

+g3   Without the +g3 switch, CHECK does minimal checking for the correctness of the internal contents of words. With this switch turned on, the program makes sure that words do not contain numbers, capital letters, or spurious apostrophes.

CHECK also uses several options that are shared with other commands. For a complete list of options for a command, type the name of the command followed by a carriage return in the Commands window. Information regarding the additional options shared across commands can be found in the chapter on Options on page 134.

5.3   CHIP

CHIP was designed and written by Jeffrey Sokolov. The program analyzes specified pairs of utterances. CHIP has been used to explore parental input, the relation between speech acts and imitation, and individual differences in imitativeness in both normal and language-impaired children. Researchers who publish work based on the use of this program should cite Sokolov and MacWhinney (1990). There are four major aspects of CHIP to be described: (1) the tier creation system, (2) the coding system, (3) the technique for defining substitution classes, and (4) the nature of the summary statistics.

5.3.1   The Tier Creation System

CHIP compares two specified utterances and produces an analysis which it then inserts onto a new coding tier. The first utterance in the designated utterance pair is the "source" utterance and the second is the "response" utterance. The response is compared to the source. Speakers are designated by the +b and +c codes. An example of a minimal CHIP command is as follows:

```
chip +bMOT +cCHI chip.cha
```

We can run this command runs on the following seven-utterance chip.cha file which is distributed with CLAN.

```
@Begin
@Participants:MOT Mother, CHI Child
*MOT: what-'is that?
*CHI: hat.
*MOT: a hat!
*CHI: a hat.
*MOT: and what-'is this?
```

```
*CHI: a hat !
*MOT: yes that-'is the hat .
@End
```

The output from running this simple CHIP command on this short file is as follows:

```
CHIP (04-May-99) is conducting analyses on:
  ALL speaker tiers
***************************************
From file <chip.cha>
*MOT:   what-'is that ?
*CHI:   hat .
%chi:   $NO_REP $REP = 0.00
*MOT:   a hat !
%asr:   $NO_REP $REP = 0.00
%adu:   $EXA:hat $ADD:a $EXPAN $DIST = 1 $REP = 0.50
*CHI:   a hat .
%csr:   $EXA:hat $ADD:a $EXPAN $DIST = 2 $REP = 0.50
%chi:   $EXA:a-hat $EXACT $DIST = 1 $REP = 1.00
*MOT:   and what-'is this ?
%asr:   $NO_REP $REP = 0.00
%adu:   $NO_REP $REP = 0.00
*CHI:   that a hat !
%csr:   $EXA:a-hat $ADD:that $EXPAN $DIST = 2 $REP = 0.67
%chi:   $NO_REP $REP = 0.00
*MOT:   yes that-'is the hat .
%asr:   $NO_REP $REP = 0.00
%adu:   $EXA:that $EXA:hat $ADD:yes $ADD:the $DEL:a $MADD:-'is $DIST
        $REP = 0.50
```

The output also includes a long set of summary statistics which are discussed later. In the first part of this output, CHIP has introduced four different dependent tiers:

%chi   This tier is an analysis of the child's response to an adult's utterance, so the adult's utterance is the source and the child's utterance is the response.

%adu   This tier is an analysis of the adult's response to a child's utterance, so the child is the source and the adult is the response.

%csr   This tier is an analysis of the child's self repetitions. Here the child is both the source and the response.

%asr   This tier is an analysis of the adult's self repetitions. Here the adult is both the source and the response.

By default, CHIP produces all four of these tiers. However, through the use of the -n option, the user can limit the tiers that are produced. Three combinations are possible:

1.   You can use both -ns and -nb. The -ns switch excludes both the %csr tier and the %asr tier. The -nb switch excludes the %adu tier. Use of both switches results in an analysis that computes only the %chi tier.

2.   You can use both -ns and -nc. The -ns switch excludes both the %csr tier and the %asr tier. The -nc switch excludes the %chi tier. Use of both of these switches results in an analysis that computes only the %adu tier.

3.   You can use both -nb and -nc. This results in an analysis that produces only the %csr and the %asr tiers.

It is not possible to use all three of these switches at once.

5.3.2   The Coding System

The CHIP coding system includes aspects of several earlier systems (Bohannon & Stanowicz, 1988; Demetras, Post, & Snow, 1986; Hirsh-Pasek, Trieman, & Schneiderman, 1984; Hoff-Ginsberg, 1985; Moerk, 1983; Nelson, Denninger, Bonvilian, Kaplan, & Baker, 1984). It differs from earlier systems in that it computes codes automatically. This leads to increases in speed and reliability, but certain decreases in flexibility and coverage.

The codes produced by CHIP indicate lexical and morphological additions, deletions, exact matches and substitutions. The codes are as follows:

$ADD	additions of N continuous words
$DEL	deletions of N continuous words
$EXA	exact matches of N continuous words
$SUB	substitutions of N continuous words from within a word list
$MADD	morphological addition based on matching word stem
$MDEL	morphological deletion based on matching word stem
$MEXA	morphological exact match based on matching word stem
$MSUB	morphological substitution based on matching word stem
$DIST	the distance the response utterance is from the source
$NO_REP	the source and response do not overlap
$LO_REP	the overlap is below a user-specified minimum
$EXACT	source-response pairs with no changes
$EXPAN	pairs with additions but no deletions or substitutions
$REDUC	pairs with deletions but no additions or substitutions
$SUBST	source-response pairs with only exact-matches and substitutions
$FRO	an item from the word list has been fronted
$REP	the percentage of repetition between source and response

Let us take the last line of the chip.cha file as an example:

```
*MOT:    yes that-'is the hat .
%asr:    $NO_REP $REP = 0.00
%adu:    $EXA:hat $ADD:yes-that-'is-the $DEL:a $DIST = 1 $REP = 0.25
```

The %adu dependent tier indicates that the adult's response contained an EXAct match of the string "hat," the ADDition of the string "yes-that-'is-the" and the DELetion of "a." The DIST=1 indicates that the adult's response was "one" utterance from the child's, and the repetition index for this comparison was 0.25 (1 matching stem divided by 4 total stems in the adult's response).

CHIP also takes advantage of CHAT-style morphological coding. Upon encountering a word, the program determines the word's stem and then stores any associated prefixes or suffixes along with the stem. During the coding process, if lexical stems match exactly, the program then also looks for additions, deletions, repetitions, or substitutions of attached morphemes.

5.3.3   Word Class Analysis

In the standard analysis of the last line of the chip.cha file, the fact that the adult and the child both use a definite article before the noun *hat* is not registered by the default CHIP analysis. However, it is possible to set up a substitution class for small groups of words such as definite articles or modal auxiliaries that will allow CHIP to track such within-class substitutions, as well as to analyze within-class deletions, additions, or exact repetitions. To do this, the user must first create a file containing the list of words to be considered as substitutions. For example to code the substitution of articles, the file distributed with CLAN called articles.cut can be used. This file has just the two articles *a* and *the*. Both the +g option and the +h (word-list file name) options are used, as in the following example:

```
chip +cCHI +bMOT +g +harticles.cut chip.cha
```

The output of this command will add a $SUB field to the %adu tier:

```
*CHI:    a hat!
*MOT:    yes that-'is the hat.
%adu:    $EXA:that $EXA:hat $ADD:yes $SUB:the $MADD:-'is $DIST = 1 $REP
         =0.50
```

The +g option enables the substitutions, and the +harticle.cut option directs CHIP to examine the word list previously created by the user. Note that the %adu now indicates that there was an EXAct repetition of *hat*, an ADDition of the string *yes that-'is* and a within-class substitution of *the* for *a*. If the substitution option is used, EXPANsions and REDUCtions are tracked for the included word list only. In addition to modifying the dependent tier, using the substitution option also affects the summary statistics that are produced. With the substitution option, the summary statistics will be calculated relative only to the word list included with the +h switch. In many cases, you will want to run CHIP analyses both with and without the substitution option and compare the contrasting analyses.

You can also use CLAN iterative limiting techniques to increase the power of your CHIP analyses. If you are interested in isolating and coding those parental responses that were expansions involving closed-class verbs, you would first perform a CHIP analysis and then use KWAL to obtain a smaller collection of examples. Once this smaller list is obtained, it may be hand coded and then once again submitted to KWAL or FREQ analysis. This notion of iterative analysis is extremely powerful and takes full advantage of the benefits of both automatic and manual coding.

5.3.4   Summary Measures

In addition to analyzing utterances and creating separate dependent tiers, CHIP also produces a set of summary measures. These measures include absolute and proportional values for each of the coding categories for each speaker type that are outlined below. The definition of each of these measures is as follows. In these codes, the asterisk stands for any one of the four basic operations of ADD, DEL, EXA, and SUB.

Total # of Utterances The number of utterances for all speakers regardless of the number of intervening utterances and speaker identification.

Total Responses The total number of responses for each speaker type regardless of amount of overlap.

Overlap The number of responses in which there is an overlap of at least one word stem in the source and response utterances.

No Overlap The number of responses in which there is NO overlap between the source and response utterances.

Avg_Dist The sum of the DIST values divided by the total number of overlapping utterances.

%_Overlap The percentage of overlapping responses over the total number of responses.

Rep_Index Average proportion of repetition between the source and response utterance across all the overlapping responses in the data.

*_OPS The total (absolute) number of add, delete, exact, or substitution operations for all overlapping utterance pairs in the data.

%_*_OPS The numerator in these percentages is the operator being tracked and the denominator is the sum of all four operator types.

*_WORD The total (absolute) number of add, delete, exact, or substitution words for all overlapping utterance pairs in the data.

%_*_WORDS The numerator in these percentages is the word operator being tracked and the denominator is the sum of all four word operator types.

MORPH_* The total number of morphological changes on exactlymatching stems.

%_MORPH_* The total number of morphological changes divided by the number of exactly matching stems.

AV_WORD_* The average number of words per operation across all the overlapping utterance pairs in the data.

FRONTED   The number of lexical items from the word list that have been
                         fronted.

EXACT   The number of exactly matching responses.

EXPAN   The number of responses containing only exact matches and ad-
                         ditions.

REDUC   The number of responses containing only exact-matches and de-
                         letions.

SUBST   The number of responses containing only exact matches and
                         substitutions.

5.3.5 Unique Options

+b   Specify that speaker ID S is an "adult." The speaker does not actually have to be
           an adult. The "b" simply indicates a way of keeping track of one of the speakers.

+c   Specify that speaker ID S is a "child." The speaker does not actually have to be a
           child. The "c" simply indicates a way of keeping track of one of the speakers.

+d   Using +d with no further number outputs only coding tiers, which are useful for
           iterative analyses. Using +d1 outputs only summary statistics, which can then be
           sent to a statistical program.

+g   Enable the substitution option. This option is meaningful in the presence of a
           word list in a file specified by the +h/-h switch, because substitutions are coded
           with respect to this list.

+h   Use a word list file. The target file is specified after the letter "h." Words to be
           included (with +h) or excluded (with -h) are searched for in the target file. The
           use of an include file enables CHIP to compare ADD and DEL categories for any
           utterance pair analyses to determine if there are substitutions within word classes.
           For example, the use of a file containing a list of pronouns would enable CHIP to
           determine that the instances of ADD of "I" and DEL of "you" across a source and
           response utterance are substitutions within a word class.

           Standard CLAN wildcards may be used anywhere in the word list. When the tran-
           script uses CHAT-style morphological coding (e.g., I-'ve), only words from the
           word list file will match to stems in the transcript. In other words, specific mor-
           phology may not be traced within a word list analysis. Note that all of the opera-
           tion and word-based summary statistics are tabulated with respect to the word list
           only. The word list option may be used for any research purpose including gram-

matical word classes, number terms, color terms, or mental verbs. Note also that the -h option is useful for excluding certain terms such as "okay" or "yeah" from the analysis. Doing this often improves the ability of the program to pick up matching utterances.

+n   This switch has three values: +nb, +nc, and +ns. See the examples given earlier for a discussion of the use of these switches in combination.

+qN   Set the utterance window to N utterances. The default window is seven utterances. CHIP identifies the source-response utterances pairs to code. When a response is encountered, the program works backwards (through a window determined by the +q option) until it identifies the most recent potential source utterance. Only one source utterance is coded for each response utterance. Once the source-response pair has been identified, a simple matching procedure is performed.

+x   Set the minimum repetition index for coding.

CHIP also uses several options that are shared with other commands. For a complete list of options for a command, type the name of the command followed by a carriage return in the Commands window. Information regarding the additional options shared across commands can be found in the chapter on Options on page 134.

5.4   CHSTRING

This program changes one string to another string in an ASCII text file. CHSTRING is useful when you want to correct spelling, change subjects' names to preserve anonymity, update codes, or make other uniform changes to a transcript. This changing of strings can also be done on a single file using a text editor. However CHSTRING is much faster and allows you to make a whole series of uniform changes in a single pass over many files.

It is important to note that CHSTRING is string-oriented, as opposed to word-oriented. This means that the program treats *the* as the letters "t", "h", and "e" rather than a single unique word *the.* Searching for *the* with this program will result in retrieving words such as *other, bathe,* and *there.* Using spaces can help you to limit your search. Knowing this will help you to specify the changes that need to be made on words. By default, CHSTRING works only on the text and not on the dependent tiers or the headers.

5.4.1   Unique Options

+b   Work only on material that is to the right of the colon which follows the tier ID.

+c   Often, many changes need to be made in data. You can do this by using a text editor to create an ASCII text file containing a list of words to be changed and what they should be changed to. This file should conform to this format:

```
" old string " " new string "
```

The default name for the file listing the changes is changes.cut. If you don't specify a file name at the +c option, the program searches for changes.cut. If you want
to another file, the name of that file name should follow the +c. For example, if
your file is called mywords.cut, then the option takes the form **+cmywords.cut**.
To test out the operation of CHSTRING, try creating the following file called
changes.cut:

```
" the "  " wonderful "
" eat "  " quark "
```

Then try running this file on the sample.cha file with the command:

```
chstring +c sample.cha
```

Check over the results to see if they are correct. If you need to include the double
quotation symbol in your search string, use a pair of single quote marks around
the search and replacement strings in your include file. Also, note that you can include extended ASCII symbols in your search string. For example, the following
changes.txt file would convert German text with extended ASCII characters to basic ASCII:

```
"ä"        '^a"'
"ö"        '^o"'
"ü"        '^u"'
"ß"        "^ss"
```

+d   This option turns off a number of CHSTRING clean-up actions. It turns off the
         deletion of blank lines, the removal of blank spaces, the removal of empty depen-
         dent tiers, the replacement of spaces after headers with a tab, and the wrapping of
         long lines. All it allows is the replacement of individual strings.

+l   Work only on material that is to the left of the colon which follows the tier ID.

+n   Work only on material that is to the right of the colon which follows the tier ID.

+q   CHAT requires that a three letter speaker code, such as *MOT:, be followed by a
         tab. Often, this space is filled by three spaces instead. Although this is undetect-
         able visually, the computer recognizes tabs and spaces as separate entities. The +q
         option brings the file into conformance with CHAT by replacing the spaces with
         a tab.

+s   Sometimes you need to change just one word, or string, in a file(s). These strings
         can be put directly on the command line following the **+s** option. For example, if
         you wanted to mark all usages of the word *gumma* in a file as child-based forms,
         the option would look like this:

```
+s" gumma " " gumma@c "
```

Please note the format of the previous example command line. The original string *gumma* has spaces around it and is delimited by double quotes. There is a space separating the quotes surrounding the replacement string *gumma@c* from the original. The replacement string is also delimited by double quotes and surrounded by spaces. If either the original or the replacement string contains a double quote ("), then the whole string must be put between single quotes (').

+x   The default setting of CHSTRING does not treat the asterisk (*), the underline (_), and the backslash (\) as metacharacters, because treating them as metacharacters can often lead to bad results. Therefore, if the user really wants to use them as metacharacters, CLAN requires this switch to be overtly set. Using this option will make CHSTRING interpret these characters as metacharacters.

CAUTION: Used incorrectly, CHSTRING can lead to serious losses of important data. You must be quite careful when defining changes. If you do not accurately show the strings to be changed, including spaces, the results can be disastrous. Consider what happens when changing all occurrences of "yes" to "yeah." If you use this command:

```
chstring +s"yes" "yeah" myfile.cha
```

every single occurrence of the sequence of letters y-e-s will be changed. This includes words, such as "yesterday," "eyes," and "polyester," which would become "yeahterday," "eyeah," and "polyeahter," respectively. Spaces should be inserted around strings in order for the program to make the proper changes. A better version of this line would look like this:

```
chstring +s" yes " " yeah " myfile.cha
```

Please note also that this option will cause all possible occurrences of *yes* to be changed. It will also change those occurrences when followed by punctuation, because the program recognizes final punctuation as a space. By default, CHSTRING works only on the text and not on the dependent tiers or the headers.

CHSTRING also uses several options that are shared with other commands. For a complete list of options for a command, type the name of the command followed by a carriage return in the Commands window. Information regarding the additional options shared across commands can be found in the chapter on Options on page 134.

5.5   COLUMNS

When viewing printed versions of CHAT files, it is often helpful to have a visual display that can separate the contributions of the child from those of the other speakers. A traditional way of doing this is to place the child's utterances in the left column, the other speakers' utterances in a middle column, and commentary in the right column. In order to reformat a CHAT file in this way, you can run the COLUMNS program. For example, if you want to get columned output for the first five utterances in the sample file, you can use this command:

```
columns +h +nCHI +z5u sample.cha
```

This should produce output much like this:

```
                              hey Nicky wanna [: want to] see what
                              other neat toy-s there are?
                              %spa: $INI:sel:in $RFI:tes:ve
yeah. [+ Q]
%spa: $RES:sel:ve $DES:tes:ve
toy-s?                        you wanna [: want to] see a [*] more
                              %err: a = some $LEX
                              %spa: $RDE:sel:non $RFI:xxx:in
yeah. [+ Q]
%spa:$RES:sel:in $DES:tes:non
%add:mot
                              oh # I see.
                              %spa: $INI:xxx:non $CR:sel:in
```

In this output, the child's speech is in the left column, the mother's is in the right, with the dependent tiers placed under the main tiers. If you want to have the dependent tiers placed in a separate column, you can add the +d switch, as in this command:

```
columns +h +d +nCHI +z5u sample.cha
```

which will yield this output:

```
                   hey Nicky wanna
                   [: want to] see what
                   other neat toy-s there
                   are?
                                          %spa: $INI:sel:in
                                          $RFI:tes:ve
yeah. [+ Q]
                                          %spa: $RES:sel:ve
                                          $DES:tes:ve
                   you wanna [: want to]
                   see a [*] more toy-s?
                                          %err: a = some $LEX
                                          %spa: $RDE:sel:non
                                          $RFI:xxx:in
yeah. [+ Q]
                                          %spa: $RES:sel:in
                                          $DES:tes:non
                                          %add: mot
                   oh # I see.
                                          %spa: $INI:xxx:non
                                          $CR:sel:in
```

You can add speaker ID codes by omitting the +h switch. You can also suppress the comments column altogether by adding a -t switch. In order to use the space of the omitted comments column, you can change the columns for the second speaker to the second 36 columns by using +b40 and +c76. You can move the mother's utterances to the left column by using the +nMOT switch instead of +nNIC. The next example shows these changes:

```
columns +nMOT -t% +z5u +b40 +c76 sample.cha
```

The output of this version of the command is simply:

```
*MOT: hey Nicky wanna [: want to] see
what other neat toy-s there are?
                                          *CHI: yeah. [+ Q]
*MOT: you wanna [: want to] see a [*]
more toy-s?
                                          *CHI: yeah. [+ Q]
```

Finally, for those who want to see as little CHAT coding and headers as possible, it is possible to pipe the file through FLO using a command such as the following:

```
flo +d sample.cha | columns +nCHI +z5u +h +b40 +c76
```

This command will produce this type of very simple output:

```
                        hey Nicky wanna see what other
                        neat toys there are ?
yeah .
                        you wanna see a more toys ?
yeah .
                        oh I see .
```

5.5.1   Unique Options

+b   Set the column in which the second speaker's utterances should start to N, as in +b40 to start the second speaker in the column 40.

+c   Set the column in which the dependent tiers should start to N, as in +c60 to start the dependent tiers in the sixtieth column.

+d   Display the dependent tiers in a separate column.

+h   Do not include the tier name in the output.

+n   You must always use this switch in order to tell the program which speaker should be placed in the first column. For example, +nCHI will select the speaker.

COLUMNS also uses several options that are shared with other commands. For a complete list of options for a command, type the name of the command followed by a carriage return in the Commands window. Information regarding the additional options shared across commands can be found in the chapter on Options on page 134.

5.6   COMBO

COMBO provides the user with ways of composing Boolean search strings to match patterns of letters, words, or groups of words in the data files. This program is particularly important for researchers who are interested in syntactic analysis. The search strings are specified with either the +s/-s option or in a separate file. Use of the +s switch is obligatory in COMBO. When learning to use COMBO, what is most tricky is learning how to specify the correct search strings.

5.6.1   Composing Search Strings

Boolean searching uses algebraic symbols to better define words or combinations of words to be searched for in data. COMBO uses regular expressions to define the search pattern. These six special symbols are listed in the following table:

Table 4: COMBO Strings

Meaning	Type	Symbol
immediately FOLLOWED by	Boolean	^
inclusive OR	Boolean	+
logical NOT	Boolean	!
repeated character	metacharacter	*
single character	metacharacter	_
quoting	metacharacter	\

Inserting the ^ operator between two strings causes the program to search for the first string followed by the second string. The + operator inserted between two strings causes the program to search for either of the two strings. In this case, it is not necessary for both of them to match the text to have a successful match of the whole expression. Any one match is sufficient. The ! operated inserted before a string causes the program to match a string of text that does not contain that string.

The items of the regular expression will be matched to the items in the text *only* if they directly follow one another. For example, the expression **big^cat** will match only the word *big* directly followed by the word *cat* as in *big cat*. To find the word *big* followed by the word *cat* immediately or otherwise, use the metacharacter * between the items *big* and *cat*, as in **big^*^cat**. This expression will match, for example, *big black cat*. Notice that, in this example, * ends up matching not just any string of characters, but any string of words or characters up to the point where *cat* is matched. Inside a word, such as *go**, the asterisk stands for any number of characters. In the form ^*^, it stands for any number of words. The * alone cannot be used in conjunction with the +g or +x option.

The underscore is used to "stand in for" for any *single* character. If you want to match any single word, you can use the underscore with the asterisk as in +s"_*." which will match any single word followed by a period. For example, in the string *cat.*, the underscore would match *c*, the asterisk would match *at* and the period would match the period.

The backslash (\) is used to quote either the asterisk or the underline. When you want to search for the actual characters * and _, rather than using them as metacharacters, you insert the \ character before them.

Using metacharacters can be quite helpful in defining search strings. Suppose you want to search for the words *weight, weighs, weighing, weighed,* and *weigh.* You could use the string *weigh** to find all of the previously mentioned forms. Metacharacters may be used anywhere in the search string.

When COMBO finds a match to a search string, it prints out the entire utterance in which the search string matched, along with any previous context or following context that had been included with the +w or -w switches. This whole area printed out is what we will call the "window."

5.6.2   Examples of Search Strings

The following command searches the sample.cha file and prints out the window which contains the word "want" when it is directly followed by the word "to."

```
combo +swant^to sample.cha
```

If you are interested not just in cases where "to" immediately follows "want," but also cases where it eventually follows, you can use the following command syntax:

```
combo +s"want^*^to" sample.cha
```

The next command searches the file and prints out any window that contains both "want" and "to" in any order:

```
combo +s"want^to" +x sample.cha
```

The next command searches sample.cha and sample2.cha for the words "wonderful" or "chalk" and prints the window that contains either word:

```
combo +s"wonderful+chalk" sample*.cha
```

The next command searches sample.cha for the word "neat" when it is *not* directly followed by the words "toy" or "toy-s." Note that you need the ^ in addition to the ! in order to clearly specify the exact nature of the search you wish to be performed.

```
combo +s"neat^!toy*" sample.cha
```

In this next example, the COMBO program will search the text for either the word "see" directly followed by the word "what" or all the words matching "toy*."

```
combo +s"see^(what+toy*)" sample.cha
```

You can use parentheses in order to group the search strings unambiguously as in the next example:

```
combo +s"what*^(other+that*)" sample.cha
```

This command causes the program to search for words matching "what" followed by either the word "that" or the word "other." An example of the types of strings that would be found are: "what that," "what's that," and "what other." It will not match "what is that" or "what do you want." Parentheses are necessary in the command line because the program reads the string from left to right. Parentheses are also important in the next example.

```
combo +s"the^*^!grey^*^(dog+cat)" sample2.cha
```

This command causes the program to search the file sample2.cha for *the* followed, immediately or eventually, by any word or words except *grey*. This combination is then to be followed by either *dog* or *cat*. The intention of this search is to find strings like *the big dog* or *the boy with a cat*, and not to match strings like *the big grey cat*. Note the use of the parentheses in the example. Without parentheses around *dog+cat*, the program would match simply *cat*. In this example, the sequence ^*^ is used to indicate "immediately or later." If we had used only the symbol ^ instead of the ^*^, we would have matched only strings in which the word immediately following *the* was not *grey*.

5.6.3   Referring to Files in Search Strings

Inside the +s switch, one can include reference to one, two, or even more groups of words that are listed in separate files. For example, you can look for combinations of prepositions with articles by using this switch:

```
+s@preps^@arts
```

To use this form, you first need to create a file of prepositions called "preps" with one preposition on each line and a file of articles called "arts" with one article on each line. By maintaining files of words for different parts of speech or different semantic fields, you can use COMBO to achieve a wide variety of syntactic and semantic analyses. Some suggestions for words to be grouped into files are given in the chapter of the CHAT manual on word lists. Some particularly easy lists to create would be those including all the modal verbs, all the articles, or all the prepositions. When building these lists, remember the possible existence of dialect and spelling variations such as *dat* for *that*.

5.6.4 Cluster Pairs in COMBO

Most computer search programs work on a single line at a time. If these programs find a match on the line, they print it out and then move on. Because of the structure of CHAT and the relation between the main line and the dependent tiers, it is more useful to have the CLAN programs work on "clusters" instead of lines. The notion of a cluster is particularly important for search programs, such as COMBO and KWAL. A cluster can be defined as a single utterance by a single speaker, along with all of its dependent tiers. By default, CLAN programs work on a single cluster at a time. For COMBO, one can extend this search scope to a pair of contiguous clusters by using the +b switch. However, this switch should only be used when cross-cluster matches are important, because addition of the switch tends to slow down the running of the program.

5.6.5 Searching for Clausemates

When conducting analyses on the %syn tier, researchers often want to make sure that the matches they locate are confined to "clausemate" constituents. Consider the following two %syn tiers:

```
%syn:    ( S V L ( O V ) )
%syn:    ( S V ( S V O ) )
```

If we want to search for all subjects (S) followed by objects (O), we want to make sure that we match only patterns of the type found in the embedded clause in the second example. If we use a simple search pattern such as +sS^*^O", we will match the first example as well as both clauses in the second example. In order to prevent this, we need to add parentheses checking to our search string. The string then becomes:

```
+s"S^*^(!\(+!\))^*^O
```

This will find only subjects that are followed by objects without intervening parentheses. In order to guarantee the correct detection of parentheses, they must be surrounded by spaces on the %syn line.

5.6.6 Tracking Final Words

In order to find the final words of utterances, you need to use the complete delimiter set in your COMBO search string. You can do this with this syntax (\!+?+.) where the parentheses enclose a set of alternative delimiters. In order to specify the single word that appears before these delimiters, you can use the asterisk wildcard preceded by an underline. Note that this use of the asterisk treats it as referring to any number of letters, rather than any number of words. By itself, the asterisk in COMBO search strings usually means any number of words, but when preceded by the underline, it means any number of characters. Here is the full command:

```
combo +s"_*^(\!+?+.)" sample.cha
```

This can then be piped to FREQ if the +d3 switch is used:

```
combo +s"_*^(\!+?+.)" +d3 sample.cha | freq
```

5.6.7   Tracking Initial Words

Because there is no special character that marks the beginnings of files, it is difficult to compose search strings to track items at utterance initial position. To solve this problem, you can run use CHSTRING to insert sentence initial markers. A good marker to use is the ++ symbol, which is only rarely used for other purposes. You can use this command:

```
chstring +c -t@ -t% +t* *.cha
```

You also need to have a file called changes.cut that has this one line:

```
":                    "    ":          ++"
```

In this one-line file, there are two quoted strings. The first has a colon followed by a tab; the second has a colon followed by a tab and then a double plus.

5.6.8   Adding Excluded Characters

COMBO strings have no facility for excluding a particular set of words. However, you can achieve this same effect by (1) matching a pattern, (2) outputting the matches in CHAT format, (3) altering unwanted matches so they will not rematch, and (4) then rematching with the original search string. Here is an example:

```
combo +s"*ing*" +d input.cha | chstring +c +d -f | combo +s"*ing*"
```

The goal of this analysis is to match only words ending in participial *ing*. First, COMBO matches all words ending in *ing*. Then CHSTRING takes a list of unwanted words that end in *ing* like *during* and *thing* and changes the *ing* in these words to *iing*, for example. Then COMBO runs again and matches only the desired participial forms.

5.6.9   Limiting with COMBO

Often researchers want to limit their analysis to some particular group of utterances. CLAN provides the user with a series of switches within each program for doing the simplest types of limiting. For example, the +t/-t switch allows the user to include or exclude whole tiers. However, sometimes these simple mechanisms are not sufficient and the user will have to use COMBO or KWAL for more detailed control of limiting. COMBO is the most powerful program for limiting, because it has the most versatile methods for string search using the +s switch. Here is an illustration. Suppose that, in sample.cha, you want to find the frequency count of all the speech act codes associated with the speaker *MOT when this speaker used the phrase "want to" in an utterance. To accomplish this analysis, use this command:

```
combo +t*MOT +t%spa sample.cha +s"want^to" +d | freq
```

The +t*MOT switch (Unix users should add double quotes for +t"*MOT") tells the program to select only the main lines associated with the speaker *MOT. The +t%spa tells the program to add the %spa tier to the *MOT main speaker tiers. By default, the dependent tiers are excluded from the analysis. Then follows the file name, which can appear anywhere after the program name. The +s"want^to" then tells the program to select only the *MOT clusters that contain the phrase *want to*. The +d option tells the program to output the matching clusters from sample.cha without any non-CHAT identification information. Then the results are sent through a "pipe" indicated by the | symbol to the FREQ program, which conducts an analysis on the main line. The results could also be piped on to other programs such as MLU or KEYMAP or they can be stored in files.

Sometimes researchers want to maintain a copy of their data that is stripped of the various coding tiers. This can be done by this command:

```
combo +s* +o@ -t% +f *.cha
```

The +o switch controls the addition of the header material that would otherwise be excluded from the output and the -t switch controls the deletion of the dependent tiers. It is also possible to include or exclude individual speakers or dependent tiers by providing additional +t or -t switches. The best way to understand the use of limiting for controlling data display is to try the various options on a small sample file.

5.6.10   Unique Options

+b   COMBO usually works on only one cluster at a time. However, when you want to look at a contiguous pair of clusters, you can use this switch.

+d   Normally, COMBO outputs the location of the tier where the match occurs. When the +d switch is turned on you can output only each matched sentence in a simple legal CHAT format. The +d1 switch outputs legal CHAT format along with line numbers and file names. The +d2 switch outputs files names once per file only. The +d3 switch outputs legal CHAT format, but with only the actual words matched by the search string, along with @Comment headers that are ignored by other programs. Try these commands:

```
combo +s"want^to" sample.cha
combo +s"want^to" +d sample.cha
combo +s"want^to" +d1 sample.cha | freq
combo +d2 +s"_*^." sample.cha | freq
```

This final command provides a useful way of searching for utterance final words and tabulating their frequency.

+g   COMBO can operate in either string-oriented or word-oriented mode. The default mode is word-oriented. COMBO can be converted to a string-oriented program by using the +g option. Word-oriented search assumes that the string of characters requested in the search string is surrounded by spaces or other word delimiting characters. The string-oriented search does not make this assumption. It sees a string of characters simply as a string of characters. In most cases, there is no need to use this switch, because the default word-oriented mode is usually more useful.

The interpretation of metacharacters varies depending on the search mode. In word-oriented mode, an expression with the asterisk metacharacter, such as `air*^plane`, will match *air plane* as well as *airpline plane* or *airy plane*. It will not match *airplane* because, in word-oriented mode, the program expects to find two words. It will not match *air in the plane* because the text is broken into words by assuming that all adjacent nonspace characters are part of the same word, and a space marks the end of that word. You can think of the search string *air* as a signal for the computer to search for the expressions: `_air_`, `_air.`, `air?`, `air!`, and so forth, where the underline indicates a space.

The same expression `air*^plane` in the string-oriented search will match *airline plane, airy plane, air in the plane* or *airplane*. They will all be found because the search string, in this case, specifies the string consisting of the letters "a," "i," and "r", followed by any number of characters, followed by the string "p," "l," "a," "n," and "e." In string-oriented search, the expression (`air^plane`) will match *airplane* but not *air plane* because no space character was specified in the search string. In general, the string-oriented mode is not as useful as the word-oriented mode. One of the few cases when this mode is useful is when you want to find all but some given forms. For example if you are looking for all the forms of the verb *kick* except the *ing* form, you can use the expression "kick*^! ^!ing" and the +g switch.

+o   The +t switch is used to control the addition or deletion of particular tiers or lines from the input and the output to COMBO. In some cases, you may want to include a tier in the output that is not being included in the input. This typically happens when you want to match a string in only one dependent tier, such as the %mor tier, but you want all tiers to be included in the output. In order to do this you would use a command of the following shape:

```
combo +t%mor +s"*ALL" +o% sample2.cha
```

+s   This option is obligatory for COMBO. It is used to specify a regular expression to search for in a given data line(s). This option should be immediately followed by the regular expression itself. The rules for forming a regular expression are discussed in detail earlier in this section.

+t   Particular dependent tiers can be included or excluded by using the +t option immediately followed by the tier code. By default, COMBO excludes the header and dependent code tiers from the search and output. However, when the dependent code tiers are included by using the +t option, they are combined with their speaker tiers into clusters. For example, if the search expression is `the^*^kitten`, the match would be found even if *the* is on the speaker tier and *kitten* is on one of the speaker's associated dependent tiers. This feature is useful if one wants to select for analyses only speaker tiers that contain specific word(s) on the main tier and some specific codes on the dependent code tier. For example, if one wants to produce a frequency count of the words *want* and *to* when either one of them is coded as an imitation on the %spa line, or *neat* when it is a continuation on the %spa line, the following two commands could be used:

```
combo +s(want^to^*^%spa:^*^$INI*)+(neat^*^%spa:^*^$CON*)
      +t%spa +f +d sample.cha
freq +swant +sto +sneat sample.cmb
```

In this example, the +s option specifies that the words *want, to,* and *$INI* may occur in any order on the selected tiers. The +t%spa option must be added in order to allow the program to look at the %spa tier when searching for a match. The +d option is used to specify that the information produced by the program, such as file name, line number and exact position of words on the tier, should be excluded from the output. This way the output is in a legal CHAT format and can be used as an input to another CLAN program, FREQ in this case. The same effect could also be obtained by using the piping feature, which is discussed in the section on FREQ on page 72.

+x   COMBO searches are sequential. If you specify the expression **dog^cat**, the program will match only the word "dog" directly followed by the word "cat". If you want to find clusters that contain both of these words, in any order, you need to use the +x option. This option allows the program to find the expressions in both the original order and in reverse order. Thus, to find a combination of "want" and "to" anywhere and in any order, you use this command:

```
combo +swant^to +x sample.cha
```

COMBO also uses several options that are shared with other commands. For a complete list of options for a command, type the name of the command followed by a carriage return in the Commands window. Information regarding the additional options shared across commands can be found in the chapter on Options on page 134.

5.7   COOCUR

The COOCCUR program tabulates co-occurences of words. This is helpful for analyzing syntactic clusters. By default, the cluster length is two words, but you can reset this value just by inserting any integer up to 20 immediately after the +n option. The second word of the initial cluster will become the first word of the following cluster, and so on.

```
cooccur +t*MOT +n3 sample.cha +f
```

The +t*MOT switch tells the program to select only the *MOT main speaker tiers. The header and dependent code tiers are excluded by default. The +n3 option tells the program to combine three words into a word cluster. The program will then go through all of *MOT main speaker tiers in the sample.cha file, three words at a time. When COOCCUR reaches the end of an utterance, it marks the end of a cluster, so that no clusters are broken across speakers or across utterances. Co-ocurrences of codes on the %mor line can be searched using commands such as this example:

```
cooccur +t%mor -t* +s*def sample2.cha
```

5.7.1   Unique Options

+d   Strip the numbers from the output data that indicate how often a particular cluster occurred.

+n   Set cluster length to a particular number. For example, +n3 will set cluster length to 3.

+s   Select either a word or a file of words with @filename to search for.

COOCCUR also uses several options that are shared with other commands. For a complete list of options for a command, type the name of the command followed by a carriage return in the Commands window. Information regarding the additional options shared across commands can be found in the chapter on Options on page 134.

5.8   DATES

The DATES program takes two time values and computes the third. It can take the child's age and the current date and compute the child's date of birth. It can take the date of birth and the current date to compute the child's age. Or it can take the child's age and the date of birth to compute the current date. For example, if you type:

```
dates +a 2;3.1 +b 12-jan-1962
```

you should get the following output:

```
@Age of Child: 2;3.1
@Birth of Child: 12-JAN-1962
@Date: 13-APR-1964
```

5.8.1   Unique Options

+a   Following this switch, after an intervening space, you can provide the child's age in CHAT format.

+b   Following this switch, after an intervening space, you can provide the child's birth date in day-month-year format.

+d   Following this switch, after an intervening space, you can provide the current date or the date of the file you are analyzing in day-month-year format.

DATES also uses several options that are shared with other commands. For a complete list of options for a command, type the name of the command followed by a carriage return in the Commands window. Information regarding the additional options shared across commands can be found in the chapter on <u>Options on page 134</u>.

5.9   DIST

This program produces a listing of the average distances between words or codes in a file. DIST computes how many utterances exist between occurrences of a specified key word or code. The following example demonstrates a use of the DIST program.

```
dist +t%spa -t* +b: sample.cha
```

This command line tells the program to look at the %spa tiers in the file sample.cha for codes containing the : symbol. It then does a frequency count of each of these codes, as a group, and counts the number of turns between occurrences. The -t* option causes the program to ignore data from the main speaker tiers.

5.9.1   Unique Options

+b   This option allows you to specify a special character after the +b. This character is something like the colon that you have chosen to use to divide some complex code into its component parts. For example, you might designate a word as a noun on the dependent tier then further designate that word as a pronoun by placing a code on the dependent tier such as $NOU:pro. The program would analyze each element of the complex code individually and as a class. For the example cited earlier, the program would show the distance between those items marked with a $NOU (a larger class of words) and show the distance between those items marked with $NOU:pro as a subset of the larger set. The +b option for the example would look like this with a colon following the +b:

```
dist +b: sample.cha
```

+d   Output data in a form suitable for statistical analysis.

+g   Including this switch in the command line causes the program to count only one occurrence of each word for each utterance. So multiple occurrences of a word or code will count as one occurrence.

+o   This option allows you to consider only words that contain the character specified by the b option, rather than all codes in addition to those containing your special character.

DIST also uses several options that are shared with other commands. For a complete list of options for a command, type the name of the command followed by a carriage return in the Commands window. Information regarding the additional options shared across commands can be found in the chapter on Options on page 134.

5.10   DSS

This program is designed to provide an automatic computation of the Developmental Sentence Score (DSS) of Lee (1974). This score is based on the assignment of scores for a variety of syntactic, morphological, and lexical structures across eight grammatical domains. The current version of DSS is preliminary and incomplete. A fully automatic computation of the DSS will be possible only when we complete work on the PARS program. Until this additional work is finished, automatic computation of DSS must be carefully supplemented by manual correction of the automatically computed profile.

5.10.1   CHAT File Format Requirements

For DSS to run correctly on a file, the following CHAT conventions must be followed:

1.   All utterances must have delimiters, and imperatives must end with an exclamation mark.

2.   Incomplete or interrupted utterances must end either with the +... or the +/. codes.

3.   Only the pronoun *I* and the first letter of proper nouns should be uppercase.

4.   Utterances that contain a noun and a verb in a subject-predicate relation in an unusual word order must contain a [dss] code after the utterance delimiter.

5.   DSS automatically excludes any child utterances that are imitations of the immediately preceding adult utterance. If, however, the analyst feels that there are additional child utterances that are imitations and should be excluded from the analysis, the [+ imit] postcode must be included for these utterances.

5.10.2   Selection of a 50-sentence Corpus

DSS scores are based on analysis of a corpus of 50 sentences. The DSS program is designed to extract a set of 50 sentences from a language sample using Lee's six inclusion criteria.

1.   **The corpus should contain 50 complete sentences.** A sentence is considered complete if it has a noun and a verb in the subject-predicate relationship. Imperatives such as "Look!" also are included. Imperative sentences must have end with an exclamation mark. Immature sentences containing word order reversals such as "car a garage come out" or "hit a finger hammer Daddy" also should be included. However, these sentences must contain the [dss] code after the utterance delimiter on the main tier to be included in the analysis.

2.   **The speech sample must be a block of consecutive sentences.** To be representative, the sentences constituting the corpora must occur consecutively in a

block, ignoring incomplete utterances. The analyst may use his or her discretion as to which block of sentences are the most representative. The DSS program automatically includes the first 50 consecutive sentences in the transcript. To start the analysis at another point, use the +z switch, perhaps in combination with KWAL and piping to DSS.

3. **All sentences in the language sample must be different.** Only unique child sentences will be included in the corpora. Thus, DSS automatically analyzes each sentence and excludes any repeated sentences .

4. **Unintelligible sentences should be excluded from the corpus.** The DSS program automatically excludes any sentences containing unintelligible segments. Thus, any sentence containing xxx, xx, yyy, and yy codes on the main tier will be excluded from the analysis.

5. **Echoed sentences should be excluded from the corpus**. Any sentence that is a repetition of the adult's preceding sentence is automatically excluded. Additionally, sentences containing a [+ imit] post-code also may be excluded by using the -s option.

6. **Incomplete sentences should be excluded**. Any sentence which has the +... or the +/. sentence delimiters, indicating that they were either incomplete or interrupted, will not be included in the analysis.

7. **DSS analysis can only be used if at least 50% of the utterances are complete sentences as defined by Lee**. If fewer than 50% of the sentences are complete sentences, then the Developmental Sentence Type analysis (DST) is appropriate instead.

5.10.3 Automatic Calculation of DSS

In order to compute DSS, the user must first complete a morphological analysis of the file using the MOR program with the +c option. After completing the MOR analysis, the %mor line should be disambiguated using POST.

Once the disambiguated %mor is created, the user can run DSS to compute the Developmental Sentence Analysis. The DSS program has two modes: automatic and interactive. The automatic mode generates a DSS table *without* a final Developmental Sentence Score. The use of the **+e** option invokes the automatic mode. A basic automatic DSS command has this shape:

```
dss +b*CHI +e sample.mor
```

5.10.4 Interactive Calculation

In the interactive mode, DSS analyzes each sentence in the corpora and then allows the user to add additional sentence points or attempt marks where appropriate. An additional sentence point is assigned to each sentence if it "meets all the adult standard rules" (Lee, p. 137). Sentence points also should be withheld for errors outside the eight categories analyzed by DSS, such as errors in the use of articles, prepositions, plural and possessive markers, and word-order changes. In addition, sentence points should be withheld for semantic errors including neologisms such as "sitting-thing" for "chair" or "letterman" for "mail-man" (Lee, p. 137).

Grammatical category points should be assigned only to those structures that meet all of Lee's requirements. If a grammatical structure is attempted but produced incorrectly then attempt marks should be inserted in the place of a numerical score. When using the interactive mode, the DSS program displays each sentence and asks the user to determine if it should or should not receive the additional sentence point and allows the user the opportunity to add attempt marks or edit the scoring. When assigning the sentence point, the user can assign a point by typing *p*, can assign no sentence point by typing *n*, or can modify the point values for each of the categories by typing *e* and then typing *p* or *n*.

It is also possible to modify the points given for each category. Here is an example of a display of category points:

```
     Sentence        |IP |PP |PV |SV |NG |CNJ|IR |WHQ|

what this say.   | 1 |   |   |   |   |   |   | 2 |
```

To edit this display, you should type the name of the column and a plus or minus with a number for how you want the score raised or lowered. For example, if you wish to raise the IP column by 2 points, you type: ip+2. Adding attempt marks is done in a similar fashion. To add the "-" attempt mark to primary verbs you type: pv+0. To remove the "-" attempt marker from primary verbs, you type pv-0.

For example, in the sentence "what this say" the user might want to add attempt markers to both the primary verb (PV) and the interrogative reversal (IR) categories indicating the nature of the grammatical errors. To add an attempt mark for the primary verb category, the user would type: pv+0 and get the following changes:

```
     Sentence        |IP |PP |PV |SV |NG |CNJ|IR |WHQ|

what this say.   | 1 |   | - |   |   |   |   | 2 |
```

To add an attempt mark for the interrogative reversal category the user would type **ir+0**, which would produce:

```
     Sentence        |IP |PP |PV |SV |NG |CNJ|IR |WHQ|

what this say.   | 1 |   | - |   |   |   | - | 2 |
```

The DSS program allows the user to make multiple changes simultaneously. There should be no spaces between the *ir* the + and the *0*. This interactive component also enables users to add or subtract point values from grammatical categories in the same way as adding or removing attempt marks.

Warning: The automatic form of DSS is unable to correctly assign points for the following three forms. If these forms are present, they would have to be scored using interactive DSS after use of automatic DSS.

1. The pronominal use of "one" as in "One should not worry about one's life." These constructions should receive 7 points as personal pronouns.

2. The distinction between non-complementing infinitive structures (e.g,. I stopped to play) which receives 3 points as secondary verb and later infinitival complement structures (e.g., I had to go), which receive 5 points as secondary verbs. When these constructions occur in the analysis the DSS program presents both the 3 and the 5 point value, and the user needs to differentiate these.

3. Wh-questions with embedded clauses that do not contain a conjunction (e.g., Why did the man we saw yesterday call you?) in contrast to those where the embedded clause is marked with a conjunction (e.g., What did the man *that* we saw yesterday say to you?).

5.10.5   DSS Output

Once all 50 sentences have been assigned sentence points, the DSS program automatically generates a table. For both the automatic and interactive modes, each sentence is displayed on the left hand column of the table with the corresponding point values. For the interactive mode, the attempt markers for each grammatical category, sentence point assignments, and the DSS score also are displayed. The Developmental Sentence Score is calculated by dividing the sum of the total values for each sentence by the number of sentences in the analysis.

The output of the table has specifically been designed for users to determine "at a glance" areas of strength and weakness for the individual child for these eight grammatical categories. The low points values for both the indefinite and personal pronoun (IP, PP) categories in the table below indicate that this child used earlier developing forms exclusively. In addition, the attempt mark for the primary verb (PV) and interrogative reversal (IR) categories suggest possible difficulties in question formulation.

Sentence	IP	PP	PV	SV	NG	CNJ	IR	WHQ	S	TOT
I like this.	1	1	1						1	4
I like that.	1	1	1						1	4
I want hot dog.		1	1						0	2
I like it .	1	1	1						1	4
what this say.	1			-				-	2	0	3

Developmental Sentence Score: 4.2

5.10.6   DSS Summary

DSS has been designed to adhere as strictly as possible to the criteria for both sentence selection and scoring outlined by Lee. The goal is the calculation of DSS scores based upon Lee's (1974) criteria, as outlined below. The numbers indicate the scores assigned for each type of usage.

Indefinite Pronouns (IP)
1   it, this, that
3   no, some, more, all, lot(s), one(s), two (etc.), other(s), another,
                                something, somebody, someone
4   nothing, nobody, none, no one
7   any, anything, anybody, anyone,
                             every, everything, everybody, everyone,
                             both, few, many, each, several, most, least, last, second, third (etc.)

Personal Pronouns (PP)
1   1st and 2nd person: I, me, my, mine, your(s)
2   3rd person: he, him, his, she, her(s)
3   plurals: we, us, our(s) they, them, their, these, those
5   reflexives: myself, yourself, himself, herself, itself, themselves, our-
                                selves
6   Wh-pronouns: who, which, whose, whom, what,, how much
                             Wh-word + infinitive: I know *what* to do, I know *who(m)* to take.
7   (his) own, one, oneself, whichever, whoever, whatever

Main Verb (MV)
1   uninflected verb
                             copula, is or 's
                             is + verb + ing
 2   -s and -ed
                             irregular past
                             copula *am, are, was, were*
                             auxiliary *am, are, was, were*
4   can, will may + verb
                             obligatory do + verb
                             emphatic do + verb
6   could, would, should, might + verb
                             obligatory does, did + verb
                             emphatic does, did +verb
7   passive including with *get* and *be*
                             must, shall + verb
                             have + verb + en
                             have got
8   have been + verb + ing, had been + verb + ing
                             modal + have + verb + en
                             modal + be + verb + ing
                             other auxiliary combinations (e.g., should have been sleeping)

Secondary Verbs (SV)
2   five early developing infinitives

	I wanna see, I'm gonna see, I gotta see, Lemme see, Let's play
3	noncomplementing infinitives: I stopped *to play*
4	participle, present or past: I see a boy *running*
5	early infinitives with differing subjects in basic sentences:
	I want you *to come*
	later infinitival complements: I had *to go*
	obligatory deletions: Make it [*to*] go
	infinitive with wh-word: I know what *to get*
7	passive infinitive with *get:* I have *to get dressed*
	with *be*: I want *to be pulled.*
8	gerund: *Swinging* is fun.

Negative (NG)

1	it, this, that + copula or auxiliary is, 's + not: It's not mine.
	This is not a dog.
4	can't don't
5	isn't won't
7	uncontracted negatives
	pronoun-auxiliary or pronoun-copula contraction
	auxiliary-negative or copula-negative contraction

Conjunction (CNJ)

3	and
5	but, so, and so, so that, or, if
8	where, when, how, while, whether, (or not), till, until, unless, since,
	before, after, for, as, as + adjective + as, as if, like, that, than
	obligatory deletions: I run faster than you [run].
	elliptical deletions (score 0)
	wh-words + infinitive: I know *how* to do it.

Interrogative Reversal (IR)

1	reversal of copula: *isn't it* red?
4	reversal of auxiliary be: *Is* he coming?
6	obligatory -do, -does, -did *Do* they run?
	reversal of modal: *Can* you play?
	tag questions: It's fun *isn't it?*
8	reversal of auxiliary have: *Has he* seen you?
	reversal with two or three auxiliaries: *Has he been* eating?

Wh-question (WHQ)

2	who, what, what + noun
	where, how many, how much, what....do, what....for
5	when, how, how + adjective
7	why, what it, how come, how about + gerund
8	whose, which, which + noun

5.10.7   Unique Options

+b   Designate which speaker to be analyzed.

+c   Determine the number of sentences to be included in analysis. The default for this
option is 50 sentences. These sentences must contain both a subject and a verb, be
intelligible, and be unique and non-imitative. A strict criteria is used in the development of the corpora. Any sentences containing xxx yyy and www codes will be
excluded from the corpora.

+e   Automatically generate a DSS table.

+s   This switch has specific usage with DSS. To include sentences marked with the
[dss] code, the following option should be included on the command line:
+s"[dss]". To exclude sentences with the [+ imit] postcode, the user should include the following option on the command line: -s"<+ imit>". These are the only
two uses for the +s/-s option.

5.11   FLO

The FLO program creates a simplified version of a main CHAT line. This simplified
version strips out markers of retracing, overlaps, errors, and all forms of main line coding.
The only unique option in FLO is +d, which replaces the main line, instead of just adding
a %flo tier.

FLO also uses several options that are shared with other commands. For a complete list
of options for a command, type the name of the command followed by a carriage return in
the Commands window. Information regarding the additional options shared across commands can be found in the chapter on Options on page 134.

5.12   FREQ

One of the most powerful programs in CLAN is the FREQ program for frequency analysis. It is also one of the easiest programs to use and a good program to start with when
learning to use CLAN. The FREQ program constructs a frequency word count for user-
specified files. A frequency word count is the calculation of the number of times a word,
as delimited by a punctuation set, occurs in a file or set of files. The FREQ program produces a list of all the words used in the file, along with their frequency counts, and calculates a type–token ratio. The type–token ratio is found by calculating the total number of
unique words used by a selected speaker (or speakers) and dividing that number by the total
number of words used by the same speaker(s). It is generally used as a rough measure of
lexical diversity. Of course, the type–token ratio can only be used to compare samples of
equivalent size, because, as sample size increases, the increase in the number of types starts
to level off.

5.12.1   What FREQ Ignores

The CHAT manual specifies two special symbols that are used when transcribing difficult material. The xxx symbol is used to indicate unintelligible speech and the www symbol is used to indicate speech that is untranscribable for technical reasons. The FREQ program ignores these symbols by default. Also excluded are all the words beginning with one of the following characters: 0, &, +, -, #. If you wish to include them in your analyses, list them, along with other words you are searching for, in a file and use the +s/-s option to specify them on the command line. The FREQ program also ignores header and code tiers by default. Use the +t option if you want to include headers or coding tiers.

5.12.2   Studying Lexical Groups

The easiest way of using FREQ is to simply ask it to give a complete frequency count for all the words in a transcript. However, FREQ can also be used to study the development and use of particular lexical groups. If you are interested, for example, in how children use personal pronouns between the ages of 2 and 3 years, a frequency count of these forms would be helpful. Other lexical groups that might be interesting to track could be the set of all conjunctions, all prepositions, all morality words, names of foods, and so on. In order to get a listing of the frequencies of such words, you need to put all the words you want to track into a text file and then use the +s switch with the name of the file preceded by the @ sign, as in this example:

```
freq +s@articles.cut +f sample.cha
```

This command would conduct a frequency analysis on all the articles that you have put in the file called articles.cut.

5.12.3   Using Wildcards with FREQ

Some of the most powerful uses of FREQ involve the use of wildcards. Wildcards are particularly useful when you want to analyze the frequencies for various codes that you have entered into coding lines. Here is an example of the use of wildcards with codes. One line of Hungarian data in sample2.cha has been coded on the %mor line for syntactic role and part of speech, as described in the CHAT manual. It includes these codes: N:A|duck-ACC, N:I|plane-ACC, N:I|grape-ALL, and N:A|baby-ALL, where the suffixes mark accusative and illative cases and N:A and N:I indicate animate and inanimate nouns. If you want to obtain a frequency count of all the animate nouns (N:A) that occur in this file, use this command line:

```
freq +t%mor +s"N:A|*" sample2.cha
```

The output of this command will be:

```
1 n:a|baby-all
```

```
1 n:a|ball-acc
```

```
1 n:a|duck-acc
```

Note that material after the **+s** switch is enclosed in double quotation marks to guarantee that wildcards will be correctly interpreted. For Macintosh and Windows, the double quotes are the best way of guaranteeing that a string is correctly interpreted. On Unix, double quotes can also be used. However, in Unix, single quotes are necessary when the search string contains a $ sign.

The next examples give additional search strings with asterisks and the output they will yield when run on the sample file. Note that what may appear to be a single underline in the second example is actually two underline characters.

String	Output
*-acc	1 n:a|ball-acc
	1 n:a|duck-acc
	1 n:i|plane-acc
*-a__	1 n:a|baby-all
	1 n:a|ball-acc
	1 n:a|duck-acc
	1 n:i|grape-all
	1 n:i|plane-acc
N:*|*-all	1 N:A|baby-all
	1 N:I|grape-all

These examples show the use of the asterisk as a wildcard. When the asterisk is used, FREQ gives a full output of each of the specific code types that match.

If you do not want to see the specific instances of the matches, you can use the percentage wildcard, as in the following examples:

String	Output
N:A|%	3 N:A|
%-ACC	3 -ACC
%-A__	3 -ACC
	2 -ALL
N:%|%-ACC	3 N:|-ACC
N:%|%	5 N:|

It is also possible to combine the use of the two types of wildcards, as in these examples:

String	Output
N:%|*-ACC	1 N:|ball-acc
	1 N:|duck-acc

```
                         1 N:|plane-acc
N:*|%                    3 N:A|
                         2 N:I|
```

Researchers have also made extensive use of FREQ to tabulate speech act and interactional codes. Often such codes are constructed using a taxonomic hierarchy. For example,
a code like $NIA:RP:NV has a three-level hierarchy. In the INCA-A system discussed in
the chapter on speech act coding in the CHAT manual, the first level codes the interchange
type; the second level codes the speech act or illocutionary force type; and the third level
codes the nature of the communicative channel. As in the case of the morphological example cited earlier, one could use wildcards in the +s string to analyze at different levels. The
following examples show what the different wildcards will produce when analyzing the
%spa tier. The basic command here is:

```
freq +s"$*" +t%spa sample.cha
```

```
String              Output

$*                  frequencies of all the three-level
                    codes in the %spa tier

$*:%                frequencies of the interchange types

$%:*:%              frequencies of the speech act codes

$RES:*: %           frequencies of speech acts within the
                    RES category

$*:sel:%            frequencies of the interchange types that have SEL
                    speech acts
```

If some of the codes have only two levels rather than the complete set of three levels,
you need to use an additional % sign in the +s switch. Thus the switch

```
        +s"$%:*:%%"
```

will find all speech act codes, including both those with the third level coded and those with
only two levels coded.

5.12.4   Directing the Output of FREQ

When FREQ is run on a single file, output can be directed to an output file by using the
+f option:

```
    freq +f sample.cha
```

This results in the output being sent to sample.frq.cex. If you wish, you may specify a file
extension other than .frq.cex for the output file. For example, to have the output sent to a
file with the extension .mot.cex, you would specify:

```
freq +fmot sample.cha
```

Suppose, however, that you are using FREQ to produce output on a group of files rather than on a single file. The following command will produce a separate output file for each .cha file in the current directory:

```
freq +f *.cha
```

To specify that the frequency analysis for each of these files be computed separately but stored in a single file, you must use the redirect symbol (>) and specify the name of the output file. For example:

```
freq *.cha > freq.all
```

This command will maintain the separate frequency analyses for each file separately and store them all in a single file called freq.all. If there is already material in the freq.all file, you may want to append the new material to the end of the old material. In this case, you should use the form:

```
freq *.cha >> freq.all
```

Sometimes, however, researchers want to treat a whole group of files as a single database. To derive a single frequency count for all the .cha files, you need to use the +u option:

```
freq +u *.cha
```

Again, you may use the redirect feature to specify the name of the output file, as in the following:

```
freq +u *.cha > freq.all
```

5.12.5   Limiting in FREQ

An important analytic technique available in CLAN is the process of "limiting" which allows you to focus your analysis on the part of your data files that is relevant by excluding all other sections. Limiting is based on use of the +s, +t, and +z switches. Limiting is available in most of the CLAN string search programs, but cannot be done within special purpose programs such as CHSTRING or CHECK.

1.   **Limiting by including or excluding dependent tiers.** Limiting can be used to select out particular dependent tiers. By using the +t and -t options, you can choose to include certain dependent tiers and ignore others. For example, if you select a particular main speaker tier, you will be able to choose the dependent tiers of only that particular speaker. Each type of tier has to be specifically selected by the user, otherwise the programs follow their default conditions for selecting tiers.

2.   **Limiting by including or excluding main tiers.** When the -t* option is combined with a switch like +t*MOT, limiting first narrows the search to the utterances by MOT and then further excludes the main lines spoken by MOT. This

switch functions in a different way from -t*CHI, which will simply exclude all of the utterances of CHI and the associated dependent tiers.

3. **Limiting by including or excluding sequential regions of lines or words.** The next level of limiting is performed when the +z option is used. At this level only the specified data region is chosen out of all the selected tiers.

4. **Limiting by string inclusion and exclusion.** The +s/-s options limit the data that is passed on to subsequent programs.

Here is an example of the combined use of the above four limiting techniques. There are two speakers, *CHI and *MOT, in sample.cha. Suppose you want to create a frequency count of all variations of the $ini codes found on the %spa dependent tiers of *CHI only in the first 20 utterances. This analysis is accomplished by using this command:

```
freq +t*CHI +t%spa +s"$INI*" -t* +z20u sample.cha
```

The +t*CHI switch tells the program to select the main and dependent tiers associated only with the speaker *CHI. The +t%spa tells the program to further narrow the selection. It limits the analysis to the %spa dependent tiers and the *CHI main speaker tiers. The -t* option signals the program to eliminate data found on the main speaker tier for NIC from the analysis. The +s option tells the program to eliminate all the words that do not match the $INI* string from the analysis. Quotes are needed for this particular +s switch in order to guarantee correct interpretation of the asterisk. In general, it is safest to always use pairs of double quotes with the +s switch. The +z20u option tells the program to look at only the first 20 utterances. Now the FREQ program can perform the desired analysis. This command line will send the output to the screen only. You must use the +f option if you want it sent to a file. By default, the header tiers are excluded from the analysis.

5.12.6   Studying Unique Words and Shared Words

With a few simple manipulations, FREQ can be used to study the extent to which words are shared between the parents and the child. For example, we may be interested in understanding the nature of words that are used by the child and not used by the mother as a way of understanding the ways in which the child's social and conceptual world is structured by forces outside of the immediate family. In order to isolate shared and unique words, you can go through three steps. To illustrate these steps, we will use the sample.cha file.

1. Run FREQ on the child's and the mother's utterances using these two commands:

    ```
    freq +d1 +t*MOT +f sample.cha
    freq +d1 +t*CHI +f sample.cha
    ```

    The first command will produce a sample.frq.cex file with the mother's words and the second will produce a sample.fr0.cex file with the child's words.

2. Next you should run FREQ on the output files:

    ```
    freq +y +o +u sample.f*
    ```

The output of these commands is a list of words with frequencies that are either 1 or 2. All words with frequencies of 2 are shared between the two files and all words with frequencies of 1 are unique to either the mother or the child.

3.   In order to determine whether a word is unique to the child or the mother, you can run the previous command through a second filter that uses the COMBO program. All words with frequencies of 2 are unique to the mother. The words with frequencies of 1 are unique to the child. Commands that automate this procedure are:

```
freq +y +o +u sample.f*  |  combo +y +s"2" +d  |  freq +y +d1 > shared.frq
freq +y +o +u *.frq
```

The first command has three parts. The first FREQ segment tags all shared words as having a frequency of 2 and all non-shared words as having a frequency of 1. The COMBO segment extracts the shared words. The second FREQ segment strips off the numbers and writes to a file. Then you compare this file with your other files from the mother using a variant of the command given in the second step. In the output from this final command, words with a frequency of 2 are shared and words with a frequency of 1 are unique to the mother. A parallel analysis can be conducted to determine the words unique to the child. This same procedure can be run on collections of files in which both speakers participate, as long as the speaker ID codes are consistent.

5.12.7   Unique Options

+c   Find capitalized words only.

+d   Perform a particular level of data analysis. By default the output consists of all selected words found in the input data file(s) and their corresponding frequencies. The +d option can be used to change the output format. Try these commands:

```
freq sample.cha +d0
freq sample.cha +d1
freq sample.cha +d2 +t@ID=eng.samp.*
```

Each of these three commands produces a different output.

+d0   When the +d0 option is used, the output consists of all selected words found in the input data file(s), their corresponding frequencies, and line numbers where each word is located in the file.

+d1   This option outputs each of the words found in the input data file(s) one word per line with no further information about frequency. Later this output could be used as a word list file for KWAL or COMBO programs to locate the context in which those words or codes are used.

+d2   With this option, the output is sent to a file in a very specific form that is useful for input to STATFREQ. This option also creates a stat.out file to keep track of multiple .frq.cex output files. You do not need to use the +f option with +d2, because this is assumed. Note that you must include a +t specification in order to tell the +d2 option which speaker to track for the STATFREQ analysis. You can provide this specification either in the @ID form or in the +t*CHI form. For further discussion of the @ID codes, see the section on STATFREQ on page 126.

+d3   This output is essentially the same as that for +d2, but with only the statistics on types, tokens, and the type–token ratio. This option also creates a "stat.out" file to keep track of multiple .frq.cex output files. Word frequencies are not placed into the output. You do not need to use the +f option with +d3, since this is assumed.

+d4   This switch allows you to output just the type–token information.

+o   Normally, the output from FREQ is sorted alphabetically. This option can be used to sort the output in descending frequency. The +o1 level will sort to create a reverse concordance.

FREQ also uses several options that are shared with other commands. For a complete list of options for a command, type the name of the command followed by a carriage return in the Commands window. Information regarding the additional options shared across commands can be found in the chapter on Options on page 134.

5.13   FREQMERG

If you have collected a large number of FREQ output files and you want to merge these counts together, you can use FREQMERG to combine the outputs of several runs of the FREQ program. For example, you could run this command:

```
freq sample*.cha +f
```

This would create sample.frq.cex and sample2.frq.cex. Then you could merge these two counts using this command:

```
freqmerg *.frq.cex
```

The only option that is unique to FREQMERG is +o, which allows you to search for a specific word on the main speaker tier. To search for a file that contains a set of words use the form +o@filename.

FREQMERG also uses several options that are shared with other commands. For a complete list of options for a command, type the name of the command followed by a carriage return in the Commands window. Information regarding the additional options shared across commands can be found in the chapter on Options on page 134.

5.14   FREQPOS

The FREQPOS program is a minor variant of FREQ. What is different about FREQ-POS is the fact that it allows the user to track the frequencies of words in initial, final, and second position in the utterance. This can be useful in studies of early child syntax. For example, using FREQPOS on the main line, one can track the use of initial pronouns or auxiliaries. For open class items like verbs, one can use FREQPOS to analyze codes on the %mor line. This would allow one to study, for example, the appearance of verbs in second position, initial position, final position, and other positions.

To illustrate the running of FREQPOS, let us look at the results of this simple command:

```
freqpos sample.cha
```

Here are the first six lines of the output from this command:

```
1 a              initial = 0, final = 0, other = 1, one word = 0
1 any            initial = 0, final = 0, other = 1, one word = 0
1 are            initial = 0, final = 1, other = 0, one word = 0
3 chalk          initial = 0, final = 3, other = 0, one word = 0
1 chalk+chalk    initial = 0, final = 1, other = 0, one word = 0
1 delicious      initial = 0, final = 0, other = 1, one word = 0
```

We see here that the word "chalk" appears three times in final position, whereas the word "delicious" appears only once and that is not in either initial or final position. In order to study occurrences in second position, we must use the +d switch as in:

```
freqpos +d sample.cha
```

5.14.1   Unique Options

+d   Count words in either first, second, or other positions. The default is to count by first, last, and other positions.

+g   Display only selected words in the output. The string following the +g can be either a word or a file name in the @filename notation.

-s   The effect of this option for FREQPOS is different from its effects in the other CLAN programs. Only the negative -s value of this switch applies. The effect of using -s is to exclude certain words as a part of the syntactic context. If you want to match a particular word with FREQPOS, you should use the +g switch rather than the +s switch.

FREQPOS also uses several options that are shared with other commands. For a complete list of options for a command, type the name of the command followed by a carriage return in the Commands window. Information regarding the additional options shared across commands can be found in the chapter on <u>Options on page 134</u>.

5.15   GEM

The GEM program is designed to allow you to mark particular parts of a transcript for further analysis. Separate header lines are used to mark the beginning and end of each interesting passage you want included in your GEM output. These header tiers may contain "tags" that will affect whether a given section is selected or excluded in the output. If no particular tag information is being coded, you should use the header form @bg with no colon. If you are using tags, you must use the colon, followed by a tab. If you do not follow these rules, CHECK will complain.

5.15.1   Sample Runs

By default, GEM looks for the beginning marker @bg without tags and the ending marker @eg, as in this example command:

```
gem sample.cha
```

If you want to be more selective in your retrieval of gems, you need to add code words or tags to both the @bg: and @eg: lines. For example, you might wish to mark all cases of verbal interchange during the activity of reading. To do this, you must place the word "reading" on the @bg: line just before each reading episode, as well as on the @eg: line just after each reading episode. Then you can use the +sreading switch to retrieve only this type of gem, as in this example:

```
gem +sreading sample2.cha
```

Ambiguities can arise when one gem without a tag is nested within another or when two gems without tags overlap. In these cases, the program assumes that the gem being terminated by the @eg line is the one started at the last @bg line. If you have any sort of overlap or embedding of gems, make sure that you use unique tags.

GEM can also be used to retrieve responses to particular questions or particular stimuli used in an elicited production task. The @bg entry for this header can show the number and description of the stimulus. Here is an example of a completed header line:

```
@bg:    Picture 53, truck
```

One can then search for all of the responses to picture 53 by using the +s"53" switch in GEM.

The / symbol can be used on the @bg line to indicate that a stimulus was described out of its order in a test composed of ordered stimuli. Also the & symbol can be used to indicate a second attempt to describe a stimulus, as in 1a& for the second description of stimulus 1a, as in this example:

```
@bg:      1b /
*CHI:     a &b ball.
@bg:      1a /
*CHI:     a dog.
@bg:      1a &
*CHI:     and a big ball.
```

Similar codes can be constructed as needed to describe the construction and ordering of stimuli for particular research projects.

When the user is sure that there is no overlapping or nesting of gems and that the end of one gem is marked by the beginning of the next, there is a simpler way of using GEM, which we call lazy GEM. In this form of GEM, the beginning of each gem is marked by @g: with one or more tags and the +n switch is used. Here is an example:

```
@g:       reading
*CHI:     nice kitty.
@g:       offstage
*CHI:     who that?
@g:       reading
*CHI:     a big ball.
@g:       dinner
```

In this case, one can retrieve all the episodes of "reading" with this command:

```
gem +n +sreading
```

5.15.2   Limiting With GEM

GEM also serves as a tool for limiting analyses. The type of limiting that is done by GEM is very different from that done by KWAL or COMBO. In a sense, GEM works like the +t switches in these other programs to select particular segments of the file for analysis. When you do this, you will want to use the +d switch, so that the output is in CHAT format. You can then save this as a file or pipe it on to another program, as in this command.:

```
gem +sreading +d sample2.cha | freq
```

Note also that you can use any type of code on the @bg line. For example, you might wish to mark well-formed multi-utterance turns, teaching episodes, failures in communications, or contingent query sequences.

5.15.3   Unique Options

+d   The +d0 level of this switch produces simple output that is in legal CHAT format. The +d1 level of this switch adds information to the legal CHAT output regarding file names, line numbers, and @ID codes.

+g   If this switch is used, all of the tag words specified with +s switches must appear on the @bg: header line in order to make a match. Without the +g switch, having just one of the +s words present is enough for a match.

```
gem +sreading +sbook +g sample2.cha
```

This will retrieve all of the activities involving reading of books.

+n   Use @g: lines as the basis for the search. If these are used, no overlapping or nesting of gems is possible and each @g must have tags. In this case, no @eg is needed, but CHECK and GEM will simply assume that the gem starts at the @g and ends with the next @g.

+s   This option is used to select file segments identified by words found on the @bg: tier. Do not use the -s switch. See the example given above for +g. To search for a group of words found in a file, use the form +s@filename.

GEM also uses several options that are shared with other commands. For a complete list of options for a command, type the name of the command followed by a carriage return in the Commands window. Information regarding the additional options shared across commands can be found in the chapter on Options on page 134.

5.16   GEMFREQ

This program combines the basic features of the FREQ and GEM programs. Like GEM, it analyzes portions of the transcript that are marked off with @bg and @eg markers. For example, gems can mark off a section of bookreading activity with *@bg: bookreading* and *@eg: bookreading*. Once these markers are entered, you can then run GEMFREQ to retrieve a basic FREQ-type output for each of the various gem types you have marked. For example, you can run this command:

```
gemfreq +sarriving sample2.cha
```

and you would get the following output:

```
GEMFREQ +sarriving sample2.cha
Wed May 12 15:54:35 1999
GEMFREQ (04-May-99) is conducting analyses on:
  ALL speaker tiers
  and ONLY header tiers matching: @BG:; @EG:;
*******************************************
From file <sample2.cha>
  2 tiers in gem " arriving":
   1 are
   1 fine
   1 how
   1 you
```

5.16.1   Unique Options

+d   The d0 level of this switch produces simple output that is in legal CHAT format. The d1 level of this switch adds information to the legal CHAT output regarding file names, line numbers, and @ID codes.

+g   If this switch is used, all of the tag words specified with +s switches must appear on the @bg: header line in order to make a match. Without the +g switch, having just one of the +s words present is enough for a match.

```
gem +sreading +sbook +g sample2.cha
```

This will retrieve all of the activities involving reading of books.

+n   Use @g: lines as the basis for the search. If these are used, no overlapping or nesting of gems is possible and each @g must have tags. In this case, no @eg is needed, and both CHECK and GEMFREQ will simply assume that the gem starts at the @g and ends with the next @g.

+o   Search for a specific word on the main speaker tier. To search for a file of words use the form +o@filename.

5.17   GEMLIST

The GEMLIST program provides a convenient way of viewing the distribution of gems across a collection of files. For example, if you run GEMLIST on both sample.cha and sample2.cha, you will get this output:

```
From file <sample.cha>
12 @BG
 3 main speaker tiers.
21 @EG
 1 main speaker tiers.
24 @BG
 3 main speaker tiers.
32 @EG
 From file <sample2.cha>
18 @BG: just arriving
 2 main speaker tiers.
21 @EG: just arriving
22 @BG: reading magazines
 2 main speaker tiers.
25 @EG: reading magazines
26 @BG: reading a comic book
 2 main speaker tiers.
29 @EG: reading a comic book
```

GEMLIST can also be used with files that use only the @g lazy gem markers. In that case, the file should use nothing by @g markers and GEMLIST will treat each @g as implicitly providing an @eg for the previous @g. Otherwise, the output is the same as with @bg and @eg markers.

The only option unique to GEMLIST is +d which tells the program to display only the data in the gems. GEMLIST also uses several options that are shared with other commands. For a complete list of options for a command, type the name of the command followed by a carriage return in the Commands window. Information regarding the additional options shared across commands can be found in the chapter on <u>Options on page 134</u>.

5.18   ID

The ID command inserts an @ID header into a data file. It constructs the @ID header from parts provided by the user with the +b option along with information derived from a @Participants header tier and the @Age header tier. The command looks for the speaker name of the participant who has been assigned the role of Target_Child. If there is no Target_Child, it looks for the speaker in the role of Child. It then uses the speaker code to find an @Age header, which should give the age of the target child. This information along with the file name constitutes the last part of the ID tier. The ID command changes the speaker code to CHI throughout the data file.

5.18.1   Unique Options

+a   Use the Target_Adult, instead of Target_Child, as the basis for constructing the @ID line.

+b   This option specifies the first elements of the ID code. For example, if you enter

```
id +bbrown.ad. *.cha
```

then the ID created will have this form for the file adam01.cha:

```
@ID:      brown.ad.adam01.0203=CHI
```

+n   This option allows the program to derive the target child's name for the @ID field from the file name. You should avoid use of this option unless needed.

ID also uses several options that are shared with other commands. For a complete list of options for a command, type the name of the command followed by a carriage return in the Commands window. Information regarding the additional options shared across commands can be found in the chapter on <u>Options on page 134.</u>

5.19   KEYMAP

The KEYMAP program is useful for performing simple types of interactional and contingency analyses. KEYMAP requires users to pick specific initiating or beginning codes or "keys" to be tracked on a specific coding tier. If a match of the beginning code or key is found, KEYMAP looks at all the codes on the specified coding tier in the next utterance. This is the "map." The output reports the numbers of times a given code maps onto a given key for different speakers.

5.19.1   Sample Runs

Here is a file fragment with a set of codes that will be tracked by KEYMAP:

```
*MOT: here you go.
%spa: $INI
*MOT: what do you say?
%spa: $INI
*CHI: thanks.
%spa: $RES
*MOT: you are very welcome.
%spa: $CON
```

If you run the KEYMAP program on this data with the $INI as the +b key symbol, the program will report that $INI is followed once by $INI and once by $RES. The key ($INI in the previous example) and the dependent tier code must be defined for the program. On the coding tier, KEYMAP will look only for symbols beginning with the $ sign. All other strings will be ignored. Keys are defined by using the +b option immediately followed by the symbol you wish to search for. To see how KEYMAP works, try this example:

```
keymap +b$INI* +t%spa sample.cha
```

For Unix, this command would have to be changed to quote metacharacters as follows:

```
keymap +b\$INI\* +t%spa sample.cha
```

KEYMAP produces a table of all the speakers who used one or more of the key symbols, and how many times each symbol was used by each speaker. Each of those speakers is followed by the list of all the speakers who responded to the given initiating speaker, including continuations by the initial speaker, and the list of all the response codes and their frequency count.

5.19.2   Unique Options

+b   This is the beginning specification symbol.

+s   This option is used to specify the code or codes beginning with the $ sign to treat as possible continuations. For example, in the sample.cha file, you might only want to track $CON:* codes as continuations. In this case, the command would be as follows.

```
keymap +b$* +s"$CON:*" +t%spa sample.cha
```

KEYMAP also uses several options that are shared with other commands. For a complete list of options for a command, type the name of the command followed by a carriage return in the Commands window. Information regarding the additional options shared across commands can be found in the chapter on <u>Options on page 134</u>.

5.20 KWAL

The KWAL program outputs utterances that match certain user-specified search words. The program also allows the user to view the context in which any given keyword is used. In order to specify the search words, use the +s option, which allows you to search for either a single word or a whole group of words stored in a file. It is possible to specify as many +s options on the command line as you like.

Like COMBO, the KWAL program works not on lines, but on "clusters." A cluster is a combination of the main tier and the selected dependent tiers relating to that line. Each cluster is searched independently for the given keyword. The program lists all keywords that are found in a given cluster tier. A simple example of the use of KWAL is:

```
kwal +schalk sample.cha
```

The output of this command tells you the file name and the absolute line number of the cluster containing the key word. It then prints out the matching cluster.

5.20.1 Limiting in KWAL

Sometimes you may want to create new files in which some of the information in your original files is systematically deleted. For example, you may wish to drop out certain coding tiers that interfere with the readability of your transcript. In order to drop out a tier of %mor codes, you can use this command:

```
kwal +o@ -t%mor +d +f sample2.cha
```

The +o@ switch will preserve the header tiers. Note that KWAL distinguishes between the +t switch which is used for limiting and the +o switch which is specifically used for formatting the shape of the output. In this process, the main lines and their dependent tiers are preserved by default. The -t%mor switch excludes the %mor tiers. The +d switch specifies that the output should be in CHAT format and the +f switch sends the output to a file. In this case, there is no need to use the +s switch. Try this command with the sample file to make sure you understand how it works.

The user can specify which main speaker and its dependent tiers, if any, are to be included in the cluster. This is done by using the +t options. Only the main speaker tiers are included in the cluster by default. The main lines can be excluded using the -t* switch. However, this exclusion affects only the search process, not the form of the output. It will guarantee that no matches are found on the main line, but the main line will be included in the output. If you want to exclude the main lines from your output, you can use a simple FLO command such as:

```
flo +t*CHI -t* +t%spa sample.cha
```

If you need to do more elaborate limiting, you can combine FLO and KWAL:

```
kwal +t*CHI +t%spa +s"$*SEL*" -t* sample.cha +d |
flo -t* +t%
```

To search for a keyword on the *MOT main speaker tiers and the %spa dependent tiers of that speaker only, include +t*MOT +t%spa on the command line, as in this command.

```
kwal +s"$INI:*" +t%spa +t*MOT sample.cha
```

5.20.2   Unique Options

+a   Sort the output alphabetically. Choosing this option can slow down processing significantly.

+d   Normally, KWAL outputs the location of the tier where the match occurs. When the +d switch is turned on you can output each matched sentence without line number information in a simple legal CHAT format. The +d1 switch outputs legal CHAT format along with file names and line numbers. Try these commands:

```
kwal +s"chalk" sample.cha
kwal +s"chalk" +d sample.cha
kwal +s"chalk" +d1 sample.cha
```

The +d and +d1 switches can be extremely important tools for performing analyses on particular subsets of a text. For example, in one project, a central research question focused on variations in MLU as a function of the nature of the addressee. In order to analyze this, each utterance was given a %add line along with a code that indicated the identity of the addressee. Using sample.cha as an example, the following KWAL line was used:

```
kwal +t%add +t*CHI +s"mot" +d sample.cha | mlu
```

This produced an MLU analysis on only those child utterances that are directed to the mother as addressee.

+o   The +t switch is used to control the addition or deletion of particular tiers or lines from the input and the output to KWAL. In some cases, you may want to include a tier in the output that is not being included in the input. This typically happens when you want to match a string in only one dependent tier, such as the %mor tier, but you want all tiers to be included in the output. In order to do this you would use a command of the following shape:

```
kwal +t%mor +s"*ACC" +o% sample2.cha
```

In yet another type of situation, you may want to include tiers in the KWAL output that are not normally included. For example, if you want to see output with the ages of the children in a group of files you can use this command:

```
kwal +o@Age -t* *.cha
```

+w It is possible to instruct the program to enlarge the context in which the keyword was found. The +w and -w options let you specify how many clusters after and before the target cluster are to be included in the output. These options must be immediately followed by a number. Consider this example:

```
kwal +schalk +w3 -w3 sample.cha
```

When the keyword *chalk* is found, the cluster containing the keyword and the three clusters above (-w3) and below (+w3) will be shown in the output.

KWAL also uses several options that are shared with other commands. For a complete list of options for a command, type the name of the command followed by a carriage return in the Commands window. Information regarding the additional options shared across commands can be found in the chapter on Exercises on page 144.

5.21   LINES

When working with a printed transcript, it is often helpful to be able to refer to parts of a transcript by using line numbers. The LINES program allows you to add line numbers and then remove them. You must remember to remove the line numbers before doing any analysis of your files with CLAN.

The only option unique to LINES is +n which removes all the line/tier numbers that were inserted by an earlier run of LINES. LINES also uses several options that are shared with other commands. For a complete list of options for a command, type the name of the command followed by a carriage return in the Commands window. Information regarding the additional options shared across commands can be found in the chapter on Options on page 134.

5.22   MAKEDATA

This program allows you to take files in Macintosh, DOS, or Unix format and convert them to files in one of the other formats. It is intended to convert whole directories or trees of directories at a single time. It converts all of the files in your current working directory as well as all of the subdirectories contained in that directory. The output of the conversion is stored in a new directory at the same level as the top of the tree being analyzed, so that the originals are not touched. Consider the following command:

```
makedata +w +om
```

This command will take all files in your current working directory and the directories below it. It will assume that they originally came from a Macintosh and that you wish to convert them to Windows format.

Based on information in the command line, font header lines, and the shape of the file, MAKEDATA will take one of three courses of action:

1.   If the file has the extension .cha and is a text file, MAKEDATA will convert it to Windows format and will convert extended ASCII characters or remap font names for two-byte fonts.

2.   If the file is a text file, but has an extension other than .cha, MAKEDATA will only convert the carriage returns to Windows style returns.

3.   If the file is not a text file, MAKEDATA will simply copy the file without changing it.

The folders created by MAKEDATA will often have files of all three types, each processed in one of these three ways. To make sure that MAKEDATA has correctly reformatted files, you may want to run CHECK recursively with the +re switch after running MAKEDATA.

5.22.1   Unique Options

+a   Create data for MAC only.

+b   Override font in original CHAT files with font specified in the +o switch.

+d   Create data for DOS only.

+m   Create data for Macintosh only.

+o   If the font header is missing, define the font according to this scheme:
              +od for standard DOS 850 format
              +op for Portuguese DOS 860 format
              +om for Macintosh Monaco format
              +oc for Macintosh Courier format
              +ow for Windows Courier format

+u   Create data for Unix only.

+w   Create data for Windows only.

MAKEDATA also uses several options that are shared with other commands. For a complete list of options for a command, type the name of the command followed by a carriage return in the Commands window. Information regarding the additional options shared across commands can be found in the chapter on Options on page 134.

5.23   MAXWD

This program locates, measures, and prints either the longest word or the longest utterance in a file. MAXWD reads through a set of files looking for the longest word or utterance. When searching for the longest word, the MAXWD output consists of: the word, its length in characters, the line number on which it was found, and the name of the file where it was found. When searching for the longest utterance with the +g option, the output consists of: the utterance itself, the total length of the utterance, the line number on which the utterance begins, and the file name where it was found. By default, MAXWD only analyzes data found on the main speaker tiers. The +t option allows for the data found on the header and dependent tiers to be analyzed as well. Try out the following command which should report the longest word in sample.cha.

```
maxwd sample.cha
```

You can also use MAXWD to track all of the utterances of a certain length. For example, the following command will locate all of the utterances with only one word in them:

```
maxwd +x1 +g2 sample.cha
```

5.23.1   Unique Options

+b   You can use this switch to either include or exclude particular morpheme delimiters. By default the morpheme delimiters #, ~, and - are understood to delimit separate morphemes. You can force MAXWD to ignore all three of these by using the -b#-~ form of this switch. You can use the +b switch to add additional delimiters to the list.

+c   This option is used to produce a given number of longest items. The following command will print the seven longest words in sample.cha.

```
maxwd +c7 sample.cha
```

+d   The +d level of this switch produces output with one line for the length level and the next line for the word. The +d1 level produces output with only the longest words, one per line, in order in legal CHAT format.

+g   This switch forces MAXWD to compute not word lengths but utterance lengths. It singles out the sentence that has the largest number of words or morphemes and prints that in the output. The way of computing the length of the utterance is determined by the number following the +g option. If the number is 1 then the length is in number of morphemes per utterance. If the number is 2 then the length is in number of words per utterance. And if the number is 3 then the length is in the number of characters per utterance. For example, if you want to compute the MLU and MLT of five longest utterances in words of the *MOT, you would use the following command:

```
maxwd +g2 +c5 +d1 +t*MOT sample.cha | mlu
```

The +g2 option specifies that the utterance length will be counted in terms of numbers of words. The +c5 option specifies that only the five longest utterances should be sent to the output. The +d1 option specifies that individual words, one per line, should be sent to the output. The | symbol sends the output to analysis by MLU.

+j   If you have elected to use the +c switch, you can use the +j switch to further fine-tune the output so that only one instance of each length type is included. Here is a sample command:

```
maxwd +c8 +j sample.cha
```

+o   The +o switch is used to force the inclusion of a tier in the output. In order to do this you would use a command of the following shape:

```
maxwd +c2 +j +o%mor sample2.cha
```

+x   This option allows you to start the search for the longest item at a certain item length. As a result, all the utterances or words shorter than a specified number will not be included in a search. The number specifying the length should immediately follow the +x option. Try this command:

```
maxwd sample.cha +x6
```

MAXWD also uses several options that are shared with other commands. For a complete list of options for a command, type the name of the command followed by a carriage return in the Commands window. Information regarding the additional options shared across commands can be found in the chapter on .

5.24   MLT

The MLT program computes the mean number of utterances in a turn, the mean number of words per utterance, and the mean number of words per turn. A turn is defined as a sequence of utterances spoken by a single speaker. Overlaps are not taken into account in this computation. Instead, the program simply looks for sequences of repeated speaker ID codes at the beginning of the main line. These computations are provided for each speaker separately. Note that none of these ratios involve morphemes. If you want to analyze morphemes per utterances, you should use the MLU program.

5.24.1   MLT Defaults

The exact nature of the MLT calculation depends both on what the program includes and what it excludes. The default principles that it uses are as follows:

1.   MLT excludes material in angle brackets followed by either [/] or [//]. This can be changed by using the +r6 switch or by adding any of these switches:

```
+s"</>"  +s"<//>"
```

2.   In order to exclude utterances with a specific postcode, such as [+ bch], you can use the -s switch:

```
-s"[+ bch]"
```

Similarly, you can use +s to include lines that would otherwise be excluded. For example, you may want to use +s"[+ trn]" to force inclusion of lines marked with [+ trn].

3.   The following strings are also excluded:

```
www  0*  &*  +*  -*  #*  $*.
```

Here the asterisk indicates any material following the first symbol until a delimiter. Unlike the MLU program, MLT does not exclude utterances with *xxx* and *yyy* by default.

4.   The program considers the following symbols to be word delimiters:

```
.  ?  !  ,  ;  [  ]  <  >
```

The space is also a word delimiter.

5.   The program considers the following three symbols to be utterance delimiters:

```
.  !  ?
```

as well as the various complex symbols such as +..., which end with one of these three marks.

6.   The special symbols xxx and yyy are not excluded from the data. Thus if the utterance consists of those symbols only it will still be counted.

7.   Utterances with no speech on the main line can be counted as turns if you add the [+ trn] code, as in this example:

```
CHI:      0. [+ trn]
%spa:     gestures to mother
```

In order to count this utterance as a turn, you can use this switch:

```
+s+"[+ trn]"
```

The second + after the *s* is used to mark the inclusion of something that is usually excluded. This method for including nonverbal activities in MLT was developed by Pan (1994).

5.24.2   Breaking Up Turns

Sometimes speakers will end a turn and no one takes over the floor. After a pause, the initial speaker may then start up a new turn. In order to code this as two turns rather than one, you can insert a "dummy" code for an imaginary speaker called XXX, as in this example from Rivero, Gràcia, and Fernández-Viader (1998):

```
*FAT:   ma::.
%act:   he touches the girl's throat
*FAT:   say mo::m.
@EndTurn
*FAT:   ## what's that?
%gpx:   he points to a picture that is on the floor
*FAT:   what's that?
```

Using the @EndTurn marker, this sequence would be counted as two turns, rather than as just one.

5.24.3   Sample Runs

The following example demonstrates a common use of the MLT program:

```
mlt sample.cha
```

5.24.4   Unique Options

+cS   Look for unit marker S. If you want to count phrases or narrative units instead of sentences, you can add markers such as [c] to make this segmentation of your transcript into additional units. Compare these two commands:

```
mlt sample.cha
mlt +c[c] sample.cha
```

+d   You can use this switch, together with the @ID specification described for STAT-FREQ to produce numbers for a statistical analysis, one per line. The command for the sample file is:

```
mlt +d +t@ID=*=CHI sample.cha
```

The output of this command should be:

```
eng samp sample 0110 CHI   6   6   8 1.333 1.000 1.333
```

This output gives 11 fields in this order: language, corpus, file, age, participant id, number of utterances, number of turns, number of words, words/turn, utterances/turn, and words/utterance. The first five of these fields come from the @ID field. The next six are computed for the particular participant for the particular file. In order to run this type of analysis you must have an @ID header for each participant you wish to track. Alternatively, you can use the +t switch in the form

+t*CHI. In this case, all of the *CHI lines will be examined in the corpus. However, if you have different names for children across different files, you need to use the @ID fields.

+d1   This level of the +d switch outputs data in another systematic format, with data for each speaker on a single line. However, this form is less adapted to input to a statistical program than the output for the basic +d switch. Also this switch works with the +u switch, whereas the basic +d switch does not. Here is an example of this output:

```
*CHI:   6   6   8 1.333 1.000 1.333
*MOT:   8   7  43 6.143 1.143 5.375
```

+g   You can use the +g option to exclude utterances composed entirely of particular words. For example, you might wish to exclude utterances composed only of *hi*, *bye*, or both of these words together. To do this, you should place the words to be excluded in a file, each word on a separate line. The option should be immediately followed by the file name. That is to say, there should not be a space between the +g option and the name of this file. If the file name is omitted, the program displays an error message: "No file name for the +g option specified!"

+s   This option is used to specify a word to be used from an input file. This option should be immediately followed by the word itself. In order to search for a group of words stored in a file, use the form +s@filename. The -s value of this switch excludes certain words from the MLT count. This is a reasonable thing to do. The +s switch bases the count only on the included words. It is difficult to imagine why anyone would want to do such an analysis.

MLT also uses several options that are shared with other commands. For a complete list of options for a command, type the name of the command followed by a carriage return in the Commands window. Information regarding the additional options shared across commands can be found in the chapter on Options on page 134.

5.25   MLU

The MLU program computes the mean length of utterance, which is the ratio of morphemes to utterances. The predecessor of the current MLU measure was the "mean length of response" or MLR devised by Nice (1925). The MLR corresponds to what we now call MLUw or mean length of utterance in Words. Brown (1973) emphasized the value of thinking of MLU in terms of morphemes, rather than words. Brown was particularly interested in the ways in which the acquisition of grammatical morphemes reflected syntactic growth and he believed that MLUm or mean length of utterance in morphemes would reflect this growth more accurately than MLUw. Brown linked growth in MLU to movement through six stages from MLU 1.75 to MLU 4.5. Subsequent research (Klee, Schaffer, May, Membrino, & Mougey, 1989) shows that MLU is correlated with age until about 48 months. Rondal, Ghiotto, Bredart, and Bachelet (1987) found that MLU is highly correlated with increases in grammatical complexity between MLU of 1 and 3. However, after MLU of 3.0, the measure was not well correlated with syntactic growth, as measured by LARSP. A parallel study by Blake, Quartaro, and Onorati (1970) with a larger subject group found that MLU was correlated with LARSP until MLU 4.5. Even better correlations between MLU and grammatical complexity have been reported when the IPSyn is used to measure grammatical complexity (Scarborough, Rescorla, Tager-Flusberg, Fowler, & Sudhalter, 1991).

When conducting an MLU analysis, it is important to decide whether you want to examine the whole file or just a consistent subsegment. For example, many researchers use a section of 50 or 100 utterances to calculate MLU. To do this, you can use the +z switch, which is described in the section on the +Z Option on page 141. Brown recommended using 100 utterances. He also suggested that these should be taken from the second page of the transcript. In effect, this means that roughly the first 25 utterances should be skipped. The switch that would achieve this effect in the MLU program is +z25u-125u.

The computation of MLU requires you to morphemicize words. To save time, you may wish to consider using MLU to compute MLUw (mean length of utterance in words), rather than MLU. Malakoff, Mayes, Schottenfeld, and Howell (1999) found that MLU correlates with MLUw at .97 for English; Aguado (1988) found a correlation of .99 for Spanish; and Hickey (1991) found a correlation of .99 for Irish. If you wish to compute MLUw instead of MLU, you can simply refrain from dividing words into morphemes on the main line. If you wish to divide them, you can use the +b switch to tell MLU to ignore your separators.

5.25.1   MLU Defaults

The CHAT manual explains how to morphemicize words on the main line. The alternative to main line morphemicization is the computation of a full %mor line. If you are just analyzing one or two files at a time, it is probably easier to do main line morphemicization. However, for larger projects, we recommend using the MOR program and the %mor tier instead. By default, MLU operates on the main tier. If you want to compute MLU from the %mor tier, you will need to use the +t%mor switch, as in this example:

```
mlu +t%mor sample2.cha
```

The way in which particular symbols are processed by MLU is described next. These procedures attempt to implement the guidelines laid out by Brown (1973) in his table on page 54. However, these guidelines are a bit incomplete and there are sometimes reasons to modify and Brown's suggestions. Brown wants MLU to be calculated by skipping the first page of a transcript and then counting the next 100 utterances. If we assume that a page contains about 10 child utterances, this would be implemented by the use of the switch +z10u-110u. However, use of a larger number of utterances, if they are available, would certainly make the resultant MLU a better indicator.

1.   MLU excludes from all counts material in angle brackets followed by either [/] or [//]. This can be changed by using the +r6 switch or by adding any of these switches:

```
+s"</>"  +s"<//>"
```

2.   In order to exclude utterances with a specific postcode, such as [+ bch], you can
        use the -s switch:

```
-s"[+ bch]"
```

The use of postcodes needs to be considered carefully. Brown suggested that all sentences with unclear material be excluded. Brown wants exact repetitions to be included and does not exclude imitations. However, other researchers recommend also excluding imitation, self-repetitions, and single-word answers to questions.

3.   The following strings are also excluded:

```
xxx yyy www uh um 0* &* +* -* #* $*
```

where the asterisk indicates any material following the exclusion symbol. If *xxx, yyy,* or *www* occur, the whole utterance is skipped. However, the utterance is not skipped for the other symbols, although they are not counted as morphemes. The symbols xx and yy are counted as morphemes. In fact, the symbols *xx* and *yy* are used as variants of *xxx* and *yyy* specifically to avoid exclusion in the MLU program. If the utterance consists of only excludable material, the whole utterance will be ignored. In addition, suffixes, prefixes, or parts of compounds beginning with a zero are automatically excluded and there is no way to modify this exclusion. Brown recommends excluding *mm* and *oh* by default. However, if you want to exclude these filler words, you will need to list them in a file and use the -s switch, as in:

```
mlu -s@excludewords sample.cha
```

You can use +s to include lines that would otherwise be excluded. For example, you may want to use +s"[+ trn]" to force inclusion of lines marked with [+ trn].

4.   The program considers the following symbols to be word delimiters:

```
. ? ! , ; [ ] < >
```

The space character is also a word delimiter.

5.   The program considers the following three symbols to be morpheme delimiters:

```
- # ^
```

If you want to change this list, you should use the +b option described below. For Brown, compounds and irregular forms were monomorphemic. This means that + and & should not be treated as morpheme delimiters for an analysis that follows his guidelines.

6.   The program considers the following three symbols to be utterance delimiters:

. ! ?

as well as the various complex symbols such as +... which end with one of these three marks.

Brown also explicitly lists a number of forms that he considers monomorphemic in young children. They include: diminutives, auxiliaries, and catentives (*gonna, wanna, hafta*). To follow Brown's guidelines, you should use only the delimiter & or no delimiter at all inside such words. To achieve this systematically, you may need to modify the operation of MOR, since it tends to treat these words as morphologically composed.

5.25.2   Sample Runs

By default, MLU computes MLU counts for each speaker in the file separately on the basis of the main tier. The following example demonstrates a common use of the MLU program:

```
mlu sample.cha
```

Researchers often wish to conduct MLU analyses on particular subsets of their data. As discussed in greater detail in the section on <u>KWAL on page 87</u>, this can be done using commands such as:

```
kwal +t*CHI +t%add +s"mot" sample.cha +d | mlu
```

This command looks at only those utterances spoken by the child to the mother as addressee. KWAL outputs these utterances through a pipe to the MLU program. The pipe symbol | is used to indicate this transfer of data from one program to the next. If you want to send the output of the MLU analysis to a file, you can do this with the redirect symbol, as in this version of the command:

```
kwal +t*CHI +t%add +s"mot" sample.cha +d | mlu > file.mlu
```

5.25.3   Including and Excluding Utterances in MLU and MLT

The inclusion of certain utterance types leasd to an underestimate of MLU. However, there is no clear consensus concerning which sentence forms should be included or excluded in an MLU calculation. The MLU program uses postcodes to accommodate differing approaches to MLU calculations. To exclude sentences with postcodes, the -s exclude switch must be used in conjunction with a file of postcodes to be excluded. The exclude file should be a list of the postcodes that you are interested in excluding from the analysis. For example, the sample.cha file is postcoded for the presence of responses to imitations [+ I], yes/no questions [+ Q], and vocatives [+ V].

For the first MLU pass through the transcript, you can calculate the child's MLU on the entire transcript by typing:

```
mlu +t*CHI sample.cha
```

For the second pass through the transcript you can calculate the child's MLU according to the criteria of Scarborough (1990). These criteria require excluding the following: routines [+ R], book reading [+ "], fillers [+ F], imitations [+ I], self-repetitions [+ SR], isolated onomatopoeic sounds [+ O], vocalizations [+ V], and partially unintelligible utterances [+ PI]. To accomplish this, an exclude file must be made which contains all of these postcodes. Of course, for the little sample file, there are only a few examples of these coding types. Nonetheless, you can test this analysis using the Scarborough criteria by creating a file called "scmlu" with the relevant codes in angle brackets. Although postcodes are contained in square brackets in CHAT files, they are contained in angle brackets in files used by CLAN. The scmlu file would look something like this:

```
<+ R>
<+ ">
<+ V>
<+ I>
```

Once you have created this file, you then use the following command:

```
mlu +t*CHI -s@scmlu sample.cha
```

For the third pass through the transcript you can calculate the child's MLU using a still more restrictive set of criteria, also specified in angle brackets in postcodes and in a separate file. This set also excludes one word answers to yes/no questions [$Q] in the file of words to be excluded. You can calculate the child's MLU using these criteria by typing:

```
mlu +t*CHI -s@resmlu sample.cha
```

In general, exclusion of these various limited types of utterances tends to increase the child's MLU.

5.25.4   Unique Options

+b   You can use this switch to either include or exclude particular morpheme delimiters. By default the morpheme delimiters ~, #, and - are understood to delimit separate morphemes. You can force MLU to ignore all three of these by using the -b#-~ switch. You can use the +b switch to add additional delimiters to the list.

+cS   Look for unit marker S. If you want to count phrases or narrative units instead of sentences, you can add markers such as [c] to make this segmentation of your transcript into additional units. Compare these two commands:

```
mlu sample.cha
mlu +c[c] sample.cha
```

+d   You can use this switch, together with the ID specification described for STATFREQ to produce numbers for a statistical analysis, one per line. The command for the sample file is:

```
mlu +d +t@ID=*CHI sample.cha
```

The output of this command should be:

```
eng samp sample 0110 CHI  5  7 1.400 0.490
```

This output gives nine fields in this order: language, corpus, file, age, participant id, number of utterances, number of morphemes, morphemes/utterances, and the standard deviation of morphemes/utterances. The first five of these fields come from the @ID field. The next four are computed for the particular participant for the particular file. In order to run this type of analysis, you must have an @ID header for each participant you wish to track. Alternatively, you can use the +t switch in the form +t*CHI. In this case, all of the *CHI lines will be examined in the corpus. However, if you have different names for children across different files, you need to use the @ID fields.

+d1   This level of the +d switch outputs data in another systematic format, with data for each speaker on a single line. However, this form is less adapted to input to a statistical program than the output for the basic +d switch. Also this switch works with the +u switch, whereas the basic +d switch does not. Here is an example of this output:

```
*CHI:  5  7 1.400 0.490
*MOT:  8 47 5.875 2.891
```

+g   You can use the +g option to exclude utterances composed entirely of particular words from the MLT analysis. For example, you might wish to exclude utterances composed only of *hi* or *bye*. To do this, you should place the words to be excluded in a file, each word on a separate line. The option should be immediately followed by the file name. That is to say, there should not be a space between the +g option and the name of this file. If the file name is omitted, the program displays an error message: "No file name for the +g option specified!"

+s   This option is used to specify a word to be used from an input file. This option should be immediately followed by the word itself. In order to search for a group of words stored in a file, use the form +s@filename. The -s switch excludes certain words from the analysis. This is a reasonable thing to do. The +s switch bases the analysis only on certain words. It is more difficult to see why anyone would want to conduct such an analysis. However, the +s switch also has another use. One can use the +s switch to remove certain strings from automatic exclusion by MLU. The program automatically excludes xxx, 0, uh, and words beginning with & from the MLU count. This can be changed by using this command:

```
mlu +s+uh +s+xxx +s0* +s&* file.cha
```

MLU also uses several options that are shared with other commands. For a complete list of options for a command, type the name of the command followed by a carriage return in the Commands window. Information regarding the additional options shared across commands can be found in the chapter on Options on page 134.

5.26   MODREP

The MODREP program matches words on one tier with corresponding words on another tier. It works only on tiers where each word on tier A matches one word on tier B. When such a one-to-one correspondence exists, MODREP will output the frequency of all matches. Consider the following sample file distributed with CLAN as modrep.cha:

```
@Begin
@Participants:CHI Child
*CHI:    I want more.
%pho:    aI wan mo
%mod:    aI want mor
*CHI:    want more bananas.
%pho:    wa mo nAnA
%mod:    want mor bAn&nAz
*CHI:    want more bananas.
%pho:    wa mo nAnA
%mod:    want mor bAn&nAz
*MOT:    you excluded [//] excluded [/] xxx yyy www
                 &d do?
%pho:    yu du
%mod:    yu du
@End
```

You can run the following command on this file to create a model-and-replica analysis for the child's speech:

```
modrep +b*chi +c%pho +k modrep.cha
```

The output of MODREP in this case should be as follows:

```
From file <modrep.cha>

 1 I
        1 aI
 2 bananas
        2 nAnA
 3 more
        3 mo
 3 want
        1 wan
        2 wa
```

This output tells us that *want* was replicated in two different ways, and that *more* was replicated in only one way twice. Only the child's speech is included in this analysis and the %mod line is ignored. Note that you must include the +k switch in this command in order to guarantee that the analysis of the %pho line is case-sensitive. By default, all CLAN programs are case-insensitive. However, on the %pho line, UNIBET uses capitalization to distinguish between pairs of different phonemes.

5.26.1   Exclusions and Inclusions

By default, MODREP ignores certain strings on the model tier and the main tier. These include xxx, yyy, www, material preceded by an ampersand, and material preceding the retracing markers [/] and [//]. To illustrate these exclusions, try this command:

```
modrep +b* +c%pho +k modrep.cha
```

The output of this command will look like this:

```
MODREP +b* +c%PHO +k modrep.cha
Thu May 13 13:03:26 1999
MODREP (04-May-99) is conducting analyses on:
  ALL speaker main tiers
       and those speakers' ONLY dependent tiers matching: %PHO;
*****************************************
From file <modrep.cha>
Model line:
you zzz do ?

is longer than Rep line:
yu du

In File "modrep.cha" in tier cluster around line 13.
```

If you want to include some of the excluded strings, you can add the +q option. For example, you could type:

```
modrep +b* +c%pho +k modrep.cha +qwww
```

However, adding the *www* would destroy the one-to-one match between the model line and the replica line. When this happens, CLAN will complain and then die. Give this a try to see how it works. It is also possible to exclude additional strings using the +q switch. For example, you could exclude all words beginning with "z" using this command:

```
modrep +b* +c%pho +k modrep.cha -qz*
```

However, because there are no words beginning with "z" in the file, this will not change the match between the model and the replica.

If the main line has no speech and only a 0, MODREP will effectively copy this zero as many times as in needed to match up with the number of units on the %mod tier that is being used to match up with the main line.

5.26.2   Using a %mod Line

A more precise way of using MODREP is to construct a %mod line to match the %pho line. In modrep.cha, a %mod line has been included. When this is done the following type of command can be used:

```
modrep +b%mod +c%pho +k modrep.cha
```

This command will compare the %mod and %pho lines for both the mother and the child in the sample file. Note that it is also possible to trace pronunciations of individual target words by using the +o switch as in this command for tracing words beginning with /m/:

```
modrep +b%mod +c%pho +k +om* modrep.cha
```

5.26.3   MODREP and COMBO -- Cross-tier COMBO

MODREP can also be used to match codes on the %mor tier to words on the main line. For example, if you want to find all the words on the main line that match words on the %mor line with an accusative suffix in the mother's speech in sample2.cha, you can use this command:

```
modrep +b%mor +c*MOT +o"*ACC" sample2.cha
```

The output of this command is:

```
From file <sample2.cha>
  1 n:a|ball-acc
       1 labda't
  1 n:a|duck-acc
       1 kacsa't
  1 n:i|plane-acc
       1 repu"lo"ge'pet
```

If you want to conduct an even more careful selection of codes on the %mor line, you can make combined use of MODREP and COMBO. For example, if you want to find all the words matching accusatives that follow verbs, you first select these utterances by running COMBO with the +d switch and the correct +s switch and then pipe the output to the MODREP command we used earlier. This combined use of the two programs can be called "cross-tier COMBO."

```
combo +s"v:*^*^n:*-acc" +t%mor sample2.cha +d |
modrep +b%mor +c*MOT +o"*acc"
```

The output of this program is the same as in the previous example. Of course, in a large input file, the addition of the COMBO filter can make the search much more restrictive and powerful.

5.26.4   Unique Options

+b   This switch is used to set the model tier name. There is no default setting. The model tier can also be set to the main line, using +b* or +b*chi.

+c   You can use this switch to change the name of the replica tier. There is no default setting.

+n   This switch limits the shape of the output from the replica tier in MODREP to some particular string or file of strings. For example, you can cut down the replica tier output to only those strings ending in "-ing." If you want to track a series of strings or words, you can put them in a file and use the @filename form for the switch.

+o   This switch limits the shape of the output for the model tier in MODREP to some particular string or file of strings. For example, you can cut down the model tier output to only those strings ending in "-ing" or with accusative suffixes, and so forth. If you want to track a series of strings or words, you can put them in a file and use the @filename form for the switch.

+q   The +q switch allows you to include particular symbols such as xxx or &* that are excluded by default. The -q switch allows you to make further exclusions of particular strings. If you want to include or exclude a series of strings or words, you can put them in a file and use the @filename form for the switch.

MODREP also uses several options that are shared with other commands. For a complete list of options for a command, type the name of the command followed by a carriage return in the Commands window. Information regarding the additional options shared across commands can be found in the chapter on <u>Options on page 134</u>.

5.27   MOR

The MOR program is used to generate a %mor tier for all main tiers in a CHAT file. Successful use of MOR requires a full understanding of the operation of the program, the process of lexicon building, and the use of methods for improving the morphological analysis. MOR is a complex program that is intended for the serious user who is willing to commit a large amount of time and effort in order to achieve a major improvement in analytic capabilities.

The computational design of MOR was guided by Roland Hausser's (1990) MORPH system and was implemented by Mitzi Morris. The system has been designed to maximize portability across languages, extendability of the lexicon and grammar, and compatibility with the CLAN programs. The basic engine of the parser is language independent. Language-specific information is stored in separate data files. The rules of the language are in data files that can be modified by the user. The lexical entries are also kept in ASCII files and there are several techniques for improving the match of the lexicon to a particular corpus. In order to avoid having too large a lexical file, only stems are stored in the lexicon and inflected forms appropriate for each stem are compiled at run time.

MOR automatically generates a %mor tier of the type described in the chapter of the CHAT manual on morphosyntactic coding. Words are labeled by their syntactic category or "scat", followed by the pipe separator |, followed by the word itself, broken down into its constituent morphemes.

```
*CHI:    the people are making cakes .
%mor:    det|the n|people v:aux|be&PRES v|make-ING
                n|cake-PL .
```

The MOR program looks at each word on the main tier, without regard to context, and provides all possible grammatical categories and morphological analyses, as in the following example with the words "to" and "back." The caret ^ denotes the multiple possibilities for each word on the main tier.

```
*CHI:    I want to go back.
%mor:    pro|I v|want inf|to^prep|to
                v|go adv|back^n|back^v|back .
```

In order to select the correct form for each ambiguous case, the user can either edit the file using Disambiguator Mode (as described in the section on <u>Disambiguator Mode on page 22</u>) or use POST, as described in the section on <u>POST on page 121</u>.

One way of restricting the possible categories inserted by MOR is to use the replacement symbol [: text] on the main line for difficult cases. For example, the English form "wanna" could mean either "want to" or "want a". Similarly, "gotta" could be either "got to" or "got a." The transcriber can commit to one of these two readings on the main line by using this method:

```
*CHI:    I wanna [:want to] go back.
%mor:    pro|I v|want inf|to^prep|to v|go adv|back^n|back^v|back .
```
In this example, MOR will only attend to the material in the square brackets and will ignore the form "wanna."

5.27.1   Configuring Your MOR Files

For MOR to run successfully, you need to configure your grammar files and lexicon files into their proper positions in the MOR library directory. You will want to create a specific library directory for MOR that is distinct from the general CLAN **lib** directory. It is often convenient to place this MOR library inside the CLAN **lib** directory. In the MOR library directory, you need these three grammar files on top: engar.cut, engcr.cut, and engsf.cut. Optionally, you may also want to have a file called engdr.cut. Within this directory, you then need to have a subdirectory called englex, which contains all of the various closed and open class lexicon files such as adj.cut, clo.cut, prep.cut, or n.cut. If you have retrieved the MOR grammar from the Internet or the CD-ROM, the materials will already be configured in the correct relative positions.

By default, MOR is looking for grammar files with the form eng*.cut and a lexicon directory called englex. This default is set under the **Edit** menu at the **Set default MOR files** option. If you are working with another language, you will need to change these defaults. For example, for the Spanish MOR, the defaults should be *espanlex* for the lexicon file name and *espan* for the grammar name. For these settings to work correctly, you will need to set your working directory to the place where your *.cha files are located and your library directory to the folder that has your MOR grammar files. For this reason, it is convenient to put your MOR files inside the standard /childes/clan/lib directory or folder. Instead of setting your default MOR file locations through the **Edit** menu, you can use the +g and +l switches described in the options section.

5.27.2   Grammar and Lexicon Files

MOR relies on three files to specify the morphological processes of the language. They are:

1. **The allomorph rules file.** This file lists the ways in which morphemes vary in shape. The rules that describe these variations are called "arules." The name of this file should be *ar.cut. The default name for this file is engar.cut which is the set of allomorphy rules for English.

2. **The concatenation rules file.** This file lists the ways in which morphemes can combine or concatenate. The rules which describe allowable concatenations are called "crules". The name of this file should be *cr.cut. The default name for this file is engcr.cut which is the set of concatenation rules for English.

3. **The special form markers file.** The CHAT manual presents a series of special form markers that help identify lexical types such as neologisms, familial words, onomatopoeia, or second-language forms. MOR can use these markings to directly insert the corresponding codes for these words onto the %mor line. The engsf.cut file includes all of these special form markers. In addition, these types must be listed in the first declaration in the engcr.cut file. For English, all this is already done. If you are creating a grammar for another language, you can model your materials on the English example. The syntax of the lines in the engsf.cut file is fairly simple. Each line has a special form marker, followed by the category information you wish to see inserted in the %mor line. If you wish to pull out capitalization words as being proper nouns, despite the shape of the special form marker, you can place \c to indicate uppercase before the special form marker. You must then add \l on another line to indicate what you want to have done with lowercase examples. See the engsf.cut file for examples.

In addition to these three grammar files, MOR uses a set of lexicon files to specify the shapes of individual words and affixes. These forms are stored in a group of files in the lexicon folder. The affix.cut file includes the prefixes and suffixes for the language. The other files contain the various open and closed class words of the language. At run time, MOR used the grammar rules to "blow up" the content of the lexicon files into a large binary tree that represents all the possible words of the language.

The first action of the parser program is to load the engar.cut file. Next the program reads in englex.cut and uses the rules in engar.cut to build the run-time lexicon. If your englex.cut file is fairly big, you will need to make sure that your machine has enough memory. On Macintosh, you can explicitly assign memory to the program. On Windows, you will have to make sure that your machine has lots of memory. Once the run-time lexicon is loaded, the parser then reads in the engcr.cut file. Additionally, if the +b option is specified, the eng.dr file is also read in. Once the concatenation rules have been loaded the program is ready to analyze input words. As a user, you do not need to concern yourself about the run-time lexicon. Your main concern is about the entries in the lexicon files. The rules in the *ar.cut and *cr.cut files are only of concern if you wish to have a set of analyses and labelings that differs from the one given in the chapter of the CHAT manual on morpho-syntactic coding, or if you are trying to write a new set of grammars for some language.

5.27.3   Unique Options

+b   Use the *dr.cut disambiguation rules.

+c   With this option, clitics such as 'd, n't , and 'll will be treated as separate words. This option must be used when creating the %mor tier for DSS analysis.

+eS   Show the result of the operation of the arules on either a stem S or stems in file @S. This output will go into a file called debug.cdc in your library directory. Another way of achieving this is to use the +d option inside "interactive MOR" which is described in the section on Interactive Mode on page 118.

+g   This switch enables the user to specify an alternative set of grammar files for different languages. The default for this option is "eng" for English. The English files are: engar.cut, engcr.cut, and engdr.cut. (Note: the *dr.cut file is only used it the +b option is given). To specify an alternative set of grammar rules, the +g option must be followed by the stem of the file name. Thus, the switch +gdan for Danish would tell MOR to look at three files: danar.cut, dancr.cut, and dandr.cut. These files must be stored in the **lib** directory or the current working directory. It is best to keep them in a separate library directory that you use only for work with MOR.

+l   This option enables the user to determine a directory in which lexicon files are stored. The default for this option is "englex," which would be a directory inside the library directory. All of the *.cut files in that directory are used as lexicon files. In order to specify an alternative lexicon directory, such as danlex, use the +ldanlex option.

+xi   Run MOR in the interactive test mode. You type in one word at a time to the test prompt and MOR provides the analysis on line. This facility makes the following commands available in the CLAN Output window:

```
word - analyze this word
:q  quit- exit program
:c  print out current set of crules
:d  display application of arules.
:l  re-load rules and lexicon files
:h  help - print this message
```

If you type in a word, such as "dog" or "perro," MOR will try to analyze it and give you its components morphemes. If you change the rules or the lexicon, use :l to reload and retest. The :c and :d switches will send output to a file called debug.cdc in your library directory.

+xl   Run MOR in the lexicon building mode. This mode takes a series of .cha files as input and outputs a small lexical file with the extension .ulx with entries for all words not recognized by MOR. This helps in the building of lexicons.

MOR also uses several options that are shared with other commands. For a complete list of options for a command, type the name of the command followed by a carriage return in the Commands window. Information regarding the additional options shared across commands can be found in the chapter on <u>Options on page 134</u>.

5.27.4   MOR Lexicons

Before running MOR on a set of CHAT files, it is important to make sure that MOR will be able to recognize all the words in these files. This means that either the word itself or the stem of the word must be listed in the lexicon. It is extremely unlikely that every word in any large corpus of child language data would be listed in even the largest MOR lexicon. Therefore, users of MOR need to understand how to supplement the basic lexicons with additional entries. Before we look at the process of adding new words to the lexicon, we first need to examine the way in which entries in the disk lexicon are structured.

The disk lexicon contains truly irregular forms of a word as well as citation forms. For example, the verb "go" is stored in the disk lexicon, along with the past tense "went," since this latter form is suppletive and does not undergo regular rules. The disk lexicon contains any number of lexical entries, stored at most one entry per line. The lexicon may be annotated with comments, which will not be processed. A comment begins with the percent sign and ends with a new line. A lexical entry consists of these parts:

1.   The surface form of the word.

2.   Category information about the word, expressed as a set of feature-value pairs. Each feature-value pair is enclosed in square brackets and the full set of feature-value pairs is enclosed in curly braces. All entries must contain a feature-value pair that identifies the syntactic category to which the word belongs, consisting of the feature "scat" with an appropriate value. Words that belong to several categories will be followed by several sets of feature structures, each separated by a backslash.

3.   If the word has multiple readings, each additional reading is entered by inserting a backslash and then putting the next reading on the next line.

4.   Following the category information is information about the lemmatization of irregular forms. This information is given by having the citation form of the stem followed by the & symbol as the morpheme separator and then the grammatical morphemes it contains.

5.   Finally, if the grammar is for a language other than English, you can enter the

English translation of the word preceded by the = sign.

The following are examples of lexical entries:

```
can      {[scat v:aux]} \
                  {[scat n]}

a                       {[scat det]}

an       {[scat det]} "a"

go       {[scat v] [ir +]}

went     {[scat v] [tense past]} "go&PAST"
```

When adding new entries to the lexicon it is usually sufficient to enter the citation form of the word, along with the syntactic category information, as in the illustration for the word "a" in the preceding examples. When working with languages other than English, you may wish to add English glosses and even special character sets to the lexicon. For example, in Cantonese, you could have this entry:

```
ping4gwo2 {[scat n]} =apple
```

To illustrate this, here is an example of the MOR output for an utterance from Cantonese:

```
*CHI:  sik6 ping4gwo2 caang2 hoeng1ziu1 .
%mor:  |sik6=eat n|ping4gwo2=apple n|caang2=orange n|hoeng1ziu1=banana .
```

In languages that use both Roman and non-Roman scripts, such as Chinese, you may also want to add non-Roman characters after the English gloss. This can be done using this form in which the $ sign separates the English gloss from the representation in characters:

```
pinyin {[scat x]} "lemmatization" =gloss$characters=
```

MOR will take the forms indicated by the lemmatization, the gloss, and the characters and append them after the category representation in the output. The gloss, lemmatization, and characters should not contain spaces or the morpheme delimiters +, -, and #. Instead of spaces or the + sign, you can use the underscore character to represent compounds.

5.27.5   File Preparation

Before starting on the process of lexicon building, you need to verify that your files are in good CHAT format. You do this by running the CHECK program. At this point, it is important that you use the +g3 switch in CHECK, because this will detect many word-internal spelling errors. Cleaning up the various errors noted by CHECK will move you closer to being able to run MOR successfully.

After you have run CHECK, you may wish to scan over the words in your corpus by eye. This can be done by running this FREQ command:

```
freq +r2 -s*@* +d1 +k +f +u *.cha
```

Here is a reminder of the meaning of all the switches:

+r2	show words with their parentheses included as in "(a)bout" to make searching easier
-s*@*	ignore words with special form markers
+d1	makes a list of words, without frequency numbers
+k	case sensitivity to reveal inappropriate capitalization
+f	send to file
+u	all results go to one output file

The output will go into a .frq.cex file with a name derived from the first file in your file set. Capitalized words will appear at the beginning of this file. You should check over the capitalized words to make sure they are proper nouns. Also, you may run into words with apostrophes in them, such as o' which may mean "over" or "of". You can solve this ambiguity inside the file by filling in the missing information in parenthesis, as in o(ver) and o(f).

After you have cleaned up the spellings and typos, you will then need to find the words with @ signs and make decisions about whether or not they are appropriately marked. Typical problems with blurred @ sign assignations occur when unclear distinctions have been made between babbling/word play, neologisms, child forms, word play and familial forms. Forms ending in @n and @f need to be entered in the lexicon. Forms in @c or @wp do not. A true @c word is one that the child made up and used consistently. False @c words may need to be changed to @b, @w, or @o. Whenever possible, mispronunciations or shortening should be noted without special form markers, as in hosie@c => ho(r)sie or faum@c => faum [: farm].

5.27.6   Lexicon Building

Once the file is thoroughly CHECK-ed and its words have been scanned, you are ready to make a first run of MOR. The command is simply:

```
mor +xl *.mor
```

(If you are working with a language other than English, you will need to add the +g and +l switches.) When MOR is run with the +xl flag, the output is a single file with the extension .ulx which contains templates for the lexical entries for all unknown words in a collection of files. Duplicates are removed automatically when MOR creates the .ulx file. A fragment of the output of this command might look something like this:

```
ta              {[scat ?]}
tag             {[scat ?]}
tags            {[scat ?]}
talkative       {[scat ?]}
```

```
tambourine     {[scat ?]}
```

You must then go through this file and determine whether to discard, complete, or modify these entry templates. For example, it may be impossible to decide what category "ta" belongs to without examining where it occurs in the corpus. In this example, a scan of the Sarah files in the Brown corpus (from which these examples were taken), reveals that "ta" is a variant of the infinitive marker "to":

```
*MEL:   yeah # (be)cause if it's gon (t)a be a p@l it's
        got ta go that way.
```

Therefore, the entry for "ta" is amended to:

```
ta              {[scat inf]} "to"
```

The corpus includes both the form "tag" and "tags." However, because the former can be derived from the latter, it is sufficient to have just the entry for "tag" in the lexicon. The forms "talkative" and "tambourine" are low-frequency items that are not included in the standard lexicon file eng.lex. Inasmuch as these are real words, the ? should be replaced by the codes "adj" and "n", respectively. For the example fragment given above, the resulting .ulx file should look like this:

```
ta              {[scat inf]} "to"
tag             {[scat n]}
talkative       {[scat adj]}
tambourine      {[scat n]}
```

Once all words have been coded, you need to insert each new word into one of the lexicon files. If you do not want to edit the main files, you can create new ones such as adj2.cut for all your new adjectives or vir2.cut for additional irregular verbs.

5.27.7   A Formal Description of the Rule Files

Users working with languages for which grammar files have already been built do not need to concern themselves with the remaining sections on MOR. However, users who need to develop grammars for new languages or who find they have to modify grammars for existing ones will need to understand how to create the two basic rule files themselves. You do not need to create a new version of the engsf.cut file for special form markers. You just copy this file and give it a name such as dansf.cut, if the prefix you want to use for your language is something like "dan" for Danish.

In order to build new versions of the arules and crules files for your language, you will need to study the English files or files for a related language. For example, when you are building a grammar for Portuguese, it would be helpful to study the grammar that has already been constructed for Spanish. This section will help you understand the basic principles underlying the construction of the arules and crules.

5.27.7.1   Declarative structure

Both arules and crules are written using a simple declarative notation. The following formatting conventions are used throughout:

1.   Statements are one per line. Statements can be broken across lines by placing the continuation character \ at the end of the line.

2.   Comments begin with a % character and are terminated by the new line. Comments may be placed after a statement on the same line, or they may be placed on a separate line.

3.   Names are composed of alphanumeric symbols, plus these characters:

    ^ & + - _ : \ @ . /

Both arule and crule files contain a series of rules. Rules contain one or more clauses, each of which is composed of a series of **condition** statements, followed by a series of **action** statements. In order for a clause in rule to apply, the input(s) must satisfy all condition statements. The output is derived from the input via the sequential application of all the action statements.

Both condition and action statements take the form of equations. The left hand side of the equation is a keyword, which identifies the part of the input or output being processed. The right hand side of the rule describes either the surface patterns to be matched or generated, or the category information that must be checked or manipulated.

The analyzer manipulates two different kinds of information: information about the surface shape of a word, and information about its category. All statements that match or manipulate category information must make explicit reference to a feature or features. Similarly, it is possible for a rule to contain a literal specification of the shape of a stem or affix. In addition, it is possible to use a pattern matching language in order to give a more general description of the shape of a string.

5.27.7.2   Pattern-matching symbols

The specification of orthographic patterns relies on a set of symbols derived from the regular expression (regexp) system in Unix. The rules of this system are:

1.   The metacharacters are: * [ ] | . ! All other characters are interpreted literally.

2.   A pattern that contains no metacharacters will only match itself, for example the pattern "abc" will match only the string "abc".

3.   The period . matches any character.

4.   The asterisk * allows any number of matches (including 0) on the preceding character. For example, the pattern '.*' will match a string consisting of any number of characters.

5.   The brackets [ ] are used to indicate choice from among a set of characters. The pattern [ab] will match either a or b.

6.   A pattern may consist of a disjunctive choice between two patterns, by use of the

| symbol. For example, the pattern will match all strings which end in x, s, sh, or ch.

7. It is possible to check that some input does not match a pattern by prefacing the entire pattern with the negation operator !.

5.27.7.3   Variable notation

A variable is used to name a regular expression and to record patterns that match it. A variable must first be declared in a special variable declaration statement. Variable declaration statements have the format: "VARNAME = regular-expression" where VARNAME is at most eight characters long. If the variable name is more than one character, this name should be enclosed in parenthesis when the variable is invoked.

Once declared, the variable can be invoked in a rule by using the operator $. If the variable name is longer than a single character, the variable name should be enclosed in parentheses when invoked. For example, the statement X = .* declares and initializes a variable named "X." The name X is entered in a special variable table, along with the regular expression it stands for. Note that variables may not contain other variables.

The variable table also keeps track of the most recent string that matched a named pattern. For example, if the variable X is declared as above, then the pattern $Xle will match all strings that end in "le". In particular, the string "able" will match this pattern; "ab" will match the pattern named by "X", and "le" will match the literal string "le". Because the string "ab" is matched against the named pattern X, it will be stored in the variable table as the most recent instantiation of X, until another string matches X.

5.27.7.4   Category Information Operators

The following operators are used to manipulate category information: ADD [feature value], and DEL [feature value]. These are used in the category action statements. For example, the crule statement "RESULTCAT = ADD [num pl]" adds the feature value pair [num pl] to the result of the concatenation of two morphemes.

5.27.7.5   Arules

The function of the arules is to expand the entries in the disk lexicon into a larger number of entries in the on-line lexicon. Words that undergo regular phonological or orthographic changes when combined with an affix only need to have one disk lexicon entry. The arules are used to create on-line lexicon entries for all inflectional variants. These variants are called **allos**. For example, the final consonant of the verb "stop" is doubled before a vowel-initial suffix, such as "-ing." The disk lexicon contains an entry for "stop," whereas the online lexicon contains two entries: one for the form "stop" and one for the form "stopp".

An arule consists of a header statement, which contains the rulename, followed by one or more condition-action **clauses**. Each clause has a series of zero or more conditions on the input, and one or more sets of actions. Here is an example of a typical condition-action clause from the larger n-allo rule in the engar.cut file:

```
LEX-ENTRY:
LEXSURF = $Yy
LEXCAT = [scat n]
ALLO:
ALLOSURF = $Yie
ALLOCAT = LEXCAT, ADD [allo nYb]
ALLO:
ALLOSURF = LEXSURF
ALLOCAT = LEXCAT, ADD [allo nYa]
```

This is a single condition-action clause, labeled by the header statement "LEX-EN-TRY:" Conditions begin with one of these two keywords:

1. LEXSURF matches the surface form of the word in the lexical entry to an abstract pattern. In this case, the variable declaration is

   Y = .*[^aeiou]

   Given this, the statement "LEXSURF = $Yy" will match all lexical entry surfaces that have a final y preceded by a nonvowel.

2. LEXCAT checks the category information given in the matched lexical item against a given series of feature value pairs, each enclosed in square brackets and separated by commas. In this case, the rule is meant to apply only to nouns, so the category information must be [scat n]. It is possible to check that a feature-value pair is not present by prefacing the feature-value pair with the negation operator !.

Variable declarations should be made at the beginning of the rule, before any of the condition-action clauses. Variables apply to all following condition-action clauses inside a rule, but should be redefined for each rule.

After the condition statements come one or more action statements with the label AL-LO: In most cases, one of the action statements is used to create an allomorph and the other is used to enter the original lexical entry into the run-time lexicon. Action clauses begin with one of these three keywords:

1. ALLOSURF is used to produce an output surface. An output is a form that will be a part of the run-time lexicon used in the analysis. In the first action clause, a lexical entry surface form like "pony" is converted to "ponie" to serve as the stem of the plural. In the second action clause, the original form "pony" is kept because the form "ALLOSURF = LEXSURF" causes the surface form of the lexical entry to be copied over to the surface form of the allo.

2. ALLOCAT determines the category of the output allos. The statement "ALLO-CAT = LEXCAT" causes all category information from the lexical entry to be copied over to the allo entry. In addition, these two actions add the morphological classes such as [allo nYa] or [allo nYb] in order to keep track of the nature of these allomorphs during the application of the crules.

3.   ALLOSTEM is used to produce an output stem. This action is not necessary in this example, because this rule is fully regular and produces a noninflected stem. However, the arule that converts "postman" into "postmen" uses this AL-LOSTEM action:

ALLOSTEM = $Xman&PL

The result of this action is the form postman&PL which is placed into the %mor line without the involvement of any of the concatenation rules.

Every set of action statements leads to the generation of an additional allomorph for the online lexicon. Thus, if an arule clause contains several sets of action statements, each labeled by the header ALLO:, then that arule, when applied to one entry from the disk lexicon, will result in several entries in the online lexicon. To create the online lexicon, the arules are applied to the entries in the disk lexicon. Each entry is matched against the arules in the order in which they occur in the arules file. This ordering of arules is an extremely important feature. It means that you need to order specific cases before general cases to avoid having the general case preempt the specific case.

As soon as the input matches all conditions in the condition section of a clause, the actions are applied to that input to generate one or more allos, which are loaded into the online lexicon. No further rules are applied to that input, and the next entry from the disk lexicon is read in to be processed. The complete set of arules should always end with a default rule to copy over all remaining lexical entries that have not yet been matched by some rule. This default rule must have this shape:

```
% default rule- copy input to output
RULENAME: default
LEX-ENTRY:
ALLO:
```

5.27.7.6   Crules

The purpose of the crules is to allow stems to combine with affixes. In these rules, sets of conditions and actions are grouped together into **if then** clauses. This allows a rule to apply to a disjunctive set of inputs. As soon as all the conditions in a clause are met, the actions are carried out. If these are carried out successfully the rule is considered to have "fired," and no further clauses in that rule will be tried.

There are two inputs to a crule: the part of the word identified thus far, called the "start," and the next morpheme identified, called the "next." The best way to think of this is in terms of a bouncing ball that moves through the word, moving items from the not-yet-processed chunk on the right over to the already processed chunk on the left. The output of a crule is called the "result." The following is the list of the keywords used in the crules:

condition keywords	function
STARTSURF	check surface of start input against some pattern
STARTCAT	check start category information
NEXTSURF	check surface of next input against some pattern

NEXTCAT   check next category information
MATCHCAT   check that start and next have the same value for all the feature-
                         value pairs of the type specified
RESULTCAT   output category information

Here is an example of a piece of a rule that uses most of these keywords:

```
S = .*[sc]h|.*[zxs] % strings that end in affricates
O = .*[^aeiou]o % things that end in o

% clause 1 - special case for "es" suffix
 if
 STARTSURF = $S
 NEXTSURF = es|-es
 NEXTCAT = [scat vsfx]
 MATCHCAT [allo]
 then
 RESULTCAT = STARTCAT, NEXTCAT [tense], DEL [allo]
 RULEPACKAGE = ()
```

This rule is used to analyze verbs that end in -es. There are four conditions that must be matched in this rule:

1.   The STARTSURF is a stem that is specified in the declaration to end in an affricate. The STARTCAT is not defined.

2.   The NEXTSURF is the -es suffix that is attached to that stem.

3.   The NEXTCAT is the category of the suffix, which is "vsfx" or verbal suffix.

4.   The MATCHCAT [allo] statement checks that both the start and next inputs have the same value for the feature allo. If there are multiple [allo] entries, all must match.

The shape of the result surface is simply the concatenation of the start and next surfaces. Hence, it is not necessary to specify this via the crules. The category information of the result is specified via the RESULTCAT statement. The statement "RESULTCAT = START-CAT" causes all category information from the start input to be copied over to the result. The statement "NEXTCAT [tense]" copies the tense value from the NEXT to the RESULT and the statement "DEL [allo]" deletes all the values for the category [allo].

In addition to the condition-action statements, crules include two other statements: the CTYPE statement, and the RULEPACKAGES statement. The CTYPE statement identifies the kind of concatenation expected and the way in which this concatenation is to be marked. This statement follows the RULENAME header. There are two special CTYPE makers: START and END. "CTYPE: START" is used for those rules that execute as soon as one morpheme has been found. "CTYPE: END" is used for those rules that execute when the end of the input has been reached. Otherwise, the CYTPE marker is used to indicate which concatenation symbol is used when concatenating the morphemes together into a parse for a word. According to CLAN conventions, # is used between a prefix and a stem, - is used between a stem and suffix, and ~ is used between a clitic and a stem. In most cases, rules that specify possible suffixes will start with CTYPE: -. These rules are neither start nor end rules and they insert a suffix after the stem.

Rules with CTYPE START are entered into the list of startrules. Startrules are the set of rules applied as soon as a morpheme has been recognized. In this case, the beginning of the word is considered as the start input, and the next input is the morpheme first recognized. As the start input has no surface and no category information associated with it, conditions and actions are stated only on the next input.

Rules with CTYPE END are entered into the list of endrules. These rules are invoked when the end of a word is reached, and they are used to rule out spurious parses. For the endrules, the start input is the entire word that has just been parsed, and there is no next input. Thus conditions and actions are only stated on the start input.

The RULEPACKAGES statement identifies which rules may be applied to the result of a rule, when that result is the input to another rule. The RULEPACKAGES statement follows the action statements in a clause. There is a RULEPACKAGES statement associated with each clause. The rules named in a RULEPACKAGES statement are not tried until after another morpheme has been found. For example, in parsing the input "walking", the parser first finds the morpheme "walk," and at that point applies the startrules. Of these startrules, the rule for verbs will be fired. This rule includes a RULEPACKAGES statement specifying that the rule which handles verb conjugation may later be fired. When the parser has further identified the morpheme "ing," the verb conjugation rule will apply, where "walk" is the start input, and "ing" is the next input.

Note that, unlike the arules which are strictly ordered from top to bottom of the file, the crules have an order of application that is determined by their CTYPE and the way in which the RULEPACKAGES statement channels words from one rule to the next.

5.27.7.7   Drules

In languages like English, French, or Chinese, words often have many alternative readings. For example, the word "back" can be a noun, adjective, verb, or preposition. MOR enters alternative readings into the %mor line using the ^ symbol to join alternative. MOR also provides a method for eliminating some of these ambiguities, even before they are entered into the output file. The use of drules is controlled by the +b option. If you do not add the +b, no disambiguation is attempted. To use this option, you need to build a file of drules or disambiguation rules that are structured much like the arules. Here is an example of a drule from the English engdr.cut file:

```
RULENAME: adj
choose
CURCAT = [scat adj]
when
PREVCAT = [scat OR det det:poss qn]
NEXTCAT = [scat OR n adj pro:indef]
```

This rule selects the adjective reading from a set of alternatives when the previous word is a determiner and the following word is a noun or adjective, as in "the back gate". The application of the drules is strictly ordered, so specific rules should be ordered before general rules. The drule facility should be used with caution. One alternative to use of the drules is hand disambiguation (see the section on the Disambiguator Mode on page 22). The other alternative is to use the POST program (see the section on POST on page 121).

5.27.8   Interactive Mode

When building a grammar for a new language, it is best to begin with a paper-and-pencil analysis of the morphological system in which you lay out the various affixes of the language, the classes of stem allomorphy variations, and the forces that condition the choices between allomorphs. This work should can be guided by a good descriptive grammar of the morphology of the language. Once this work is finished, you should create a small lexicon of the most frequent words. You may want to focus on one part-of-speech at a time. For example, you could begin with the adverbs, since they are often monomorphemic. Then you could move on to the nouns. The verbs should probably come last. You can copy the engsf.cut file from English and rename it.

Once you have a simple lexicon and a set of rule files, you will begin a long process of working with interactive MOR. When using MOR in the +xi or interactive mode, there are several additional options that become available in the CLAN Output window. They are:

```
word - analyze this word
:q   quit- exit program
:c   print out current set of crules
:d   display application of a rules.
:l   re-load rules and lexicon files
:h   help - print this message
```

If you type in a word, such as "dog" or "perro," MOR will try to analyze it and give you its component morphemes. If all is well, you can move on the next word. If it is not, you need to change your rules or the lexicon. You can stay within CLAN and just open these using the Editor. After you save your changes, use :l to reload and retest.

When you begin work with the grammar, you want to focus on the use of the +xi switch, rather than the analysis of large groups of files. As you begin to elaborate your grammar, you will want to start to work with sets of files. These can be real data files or else files full of test words. When you shift to working with files, you will be combining the use of interactive MOR and the +xi switch with use of the lexicon testing facility using +xl. As you move through this work, make copies of your MOR grammar files and lexicon frequently, because you will sometimes find that you have made a change that makes everything break and you will need to go back to an earlier stage to figure out what you need to fix. We also recommend using a fast machine with lots of memory. You will find that you are frequently reloading the grammar using the :l function. Having a fast machine will greatly speed this process.

To begin the process, start working with the sample minimal MOR grammars available from the net. These files should allow you to build up a lexicon of uninflected stems. Try to build up separate files for each of the parts of speech in your language. As you start to feel comfortable with this, you should begin to add affixes. To do this, you need to create a lexicon file, such as aff.cut. Using the technique found in unification grammars, you want to set up categories and allos for these affixes that will allow them to match up with the right stems when the crules fire. For example, you might want to call the plural a [{scat nsfx]} in order to emphasize the fact that it should attach to nouns. And you could give the designation [allo mdim] to the masculine diminutive suffix -ito in Spanish in order to make sure that it only attaches to masculine stems and produces a masculine output.

As you progress with your work, continually check each new rule change by entering :l (colon followed by "l" for load) into the CLAN Output window. If you have changed something in a way that produces a syntactic violation, you will learn this immediately and be able to change it back. If you find that a method fails, you should first rethink your logic. Consider these factors:

1.   Arules are strictly ordered. Maybe you have placed a general case before a specific case.

2.   Crules depend on direction from the RULEPACKAGES statement.

3.   There has to be a START and END rule for each part of speech. If you are getting too many entries for a word, maybe you have started it twice. Alternatively, you may have created too many allomorphs with the arules.

4.   If you have a MATCHCAT allos statement, all allos must match. The operation DEL [allo] deletes all allos and you must add back any you want to keep.

5.   Make sure that you understand the use of variable notation and pattern matching symbols for specifying the surface form in the arules.

However, sometimes it is not clear why a method is not working. In this case, you will want to check the application of the crules using the :c option in the CLAN Output window. You then need to trace through the firing of the rules. The most important information is often at the end of this output.

If the stem itself is not being recognized, you will need to also trace the operation of the arules. To do this, you should either use the +e option in standard MOR or else the :d option in interactive MOR. The latter is probably the most useful. To use this option, you should create a directory called testlex with a single file with the words your are working with. Then run

```
mor +xi +ltestlex
```

Once this runs, type :d and then :l and the output of the arules for this test lexicon will go to debug.cdc. Use your editor to open that file and try to trace what is happening there.

As you progress with the construction of rules and the enlargement of the lexicon, you can tackle whole corpora. At this point you will occasionally run the +xl analysis. Then you take the problems noted by +xl and use them as the basis for repeated testing using the

+xi switch and repeated reloading of the rules as you improve them. As you build up your rule sets, you will want to annotate them fully using comments preceded by the % symbol.

5.28   PHONFREQ

The PHONFREQ program tabulates all of the segments on the %pho line. For example, using PHONFREQ with no further options on modrep.cha will produce this output:

```
2 A     initial =    0, final =    1, other =    1
1 I     initial =    0, final =    1, other =    0
3 a     initial =    1, final =    1, other =    1
2 m     initial =    2, final =    0, other =    0
3 n     initial =    1, final =    1, other =    1
2 o     initial =    0, final =    2, other =    0
2 w     initial =    2, final =    0, other =    0
```

This output tells you that there were two occurrences of the segment /A/, once in final position and once in other or medial position.

If you create a file called alphabet file and place it in your working directory, you can further specify that certain digraphs should be treated as single segments. This is important if you need to look at diphthongs or other digraphs in UNIBET. In the strings in the alphabet file, the asterisk character can be used to indicate any single character. For example, the string *: would indicate any sound followed by a colon. If you have three instances of a:, three of e:, and three of o:, the output will list each of these three separately, rather than summing them together as nine instances of something followed by a colon. Because the asterisk is not used in either UNIBET or PHONASCII, it should never be necessary to specify a search for a literal asterisk in your alphabet file. A sample alphabet file for English is distributed with CLAN. PHONFREQ will warn you that it does not find an alphabet file. You can ignore this warning if you are convinced that you do not need a special alphabet file.

If you want to construct a complete substitution matrix for phonological analysis, you need to add a %mod line in your transcript to indicate the target phonology. Then you can run PHONFREQ twice, first on the %pho line and then on the %mod line. To run on the %mod line, you need to add the +t%mod switch.

If you want to specify a set of digraphs that should be treated as single phonemes or segments, you can put them in a file called alphabet.cut. Each combination should be entered by itself on a single line. PHONFREQ will look for the alphabet file in either the working directory or the library directory. If it finds no alphabet.cut file, each letter will be treated as a single segment. Within the alphabet file, you can also specify trigraphs that should override particular digraphs. In that case, the longer string that should override the shorter string should occur earlier in the alphabet file.

5.28.1   Unique Options

+b   By default, PHONFREQ analyzes the %pho tier. If you want to analyze another tier, you can use the +b switch to specify the desired tier. Remember that you might still need to use the +t switch along with the +b switch as in this command:

```
phonfreq +b* +t*CHI modrep.cha
```

+d   If you use this switch, the actual words that were matched will be written to the output. Each occurrence is written out.

+t   You should use the +b switch to change the identity of the tier analyzed by PHONFREQ. The +t switch is used to change the identity of the speaker being analyzed. For example, if you want to analyze the main lines for speaker CHI, you would use this command:

```
phonfreq +b* +t*CHI modrep.cha
```

PHONFREQ also uses several options that are shared with other commands. For a complete list of options for a command, type the name of the command followed by a carriage return in the Commands window. Information regarding the additional options shared across commands can be found in the chapter on Options on page 134.

The lexicon could be much smaller if more rules were written to handle derivational morphology. These would handle prefixes such as "non#" and derivational suffixes such as "-al." The grammar still needs to be fine-tuned in order to catch common over-regularizations, although it will never be able to capture all possible morphological errors. Furthermore, attempts to capture over regularizations may introduce bogus analyses of good forms, such as "seed" = "*see-PAST." Other areas for which more rules need to be written include diminutives, and words like "oh+my+goodness," which should automatically be treated as communicators.

5.29   POST

POST was written by Christophe Parisse of INSERM, Paris for the purpose of automatically disambiguating the output of MOR. The POST package is composed of three CLAN commands: POST, POSTTRAIN, and POSTLIST. POST is the command that runs the disambiguator. POST needs a database which contains information about syntactic word order. Databases are created and maintained by POSTTRAIN and can be dumped in a text file by POSTLIST. In this section, we describe the use of the POST command.

In order to use POST, you must first have a database of disambiguation rules appropriate for your language. For English, this file is called eng.db. As our work with POST progresses, we will make these available for additional languages. To run POST, you can use this command format :

```
post *.cha
```

This command assumes the default values of the +f, +d, and +s switches described below. The accuracy of disambiguation by POST will be above 95 percent. However, there will be some errors. To make the most conservative use of POST, you may wish to use the +s2 switch. The options for POST are:

+dF   use POST database file F (default is "eng.db"). This file must have been created by POSTTRAIN. If you do not use this switch, POST will try to locate the eng.db file.

+e[1,2]c this option is a complement to the option +s2 and +s3 only. It allows you to change the separator used (+e1c) between the different solutions, (+e2c) before the information about the parsing process. (c can be any character). By default, the separator for +e1 is # and for +e2, the separator is /.

+f   send output to file derived from input file name. If you do not use this switch, POST will create a series of output files named *.pst.

+fF   send output to file F. This switch will change the extension to the output files.

-f   send output to the screen

+sN   N=0 (default) replace ambiguous %mor lines with disambiguated ones
             N=1 keep ambiguous %mor lines and add disambiguated %pos lines,
             N=2 output as in N=1, but with slashes marking undecidable cases
             N=3 keep ambiguous %mor lines and add %pos lines with debugging info
             N=4 for develop use only

With the options +s0 and +s1, only the best candidate is outputted. With option +s2, second and following candidates may be outputted, when the disambiguation process is not able to choose between different solutions with the most probable solution displayed first. With option +s3, information about the parsing process is given in three situations: processing of unknown words (useful for checking these words quickly after the parsing process), processing of unknown rules and no correct syntactic path obtained (usually corresponds to new grammatical situations or typographic errors).

+tF   use the stem tags in file F along with the other syntactic categories. The tags created by MOR have the shape:

```
category | stem & fusional
```

By default, the POST grammar only uses the category information to the left of the bar symbol. However, in some cases, disambiguation can be improved by including information to the right of the bar. To do this, simply list the names of the stems or fusional categories in a file and use the +t switch.

5.30   POSTLIST

POSTLIST provides a list of tags used by POST. It is run on the *.db database file. The options for POSTLIST are as follows:

+dF   this gives the name of the database to be listed (default value: 'eng.db').
+t   outputs the list of all tags present in the database.
+r   outputs all the rules present in the database.
+w   outputs all the word frequencies gathered in the database.
+m   outputs all the matrix entries present in the database.

If none of the options is selected, then general information about the size of the database is outputted.

5.31   POSTTRAIN

POSTTRAIN was written by Christophe Parisse of INSERM, Paris. In order to run POST, you need to create a database file for your language. For several languages, this have already been done. If there is no POST database file for your language or your subject group, you can use the POSTTRAIN program to create this file. The default name for this file is eng.db. Before running POSTTRAIN, you must make sure that all of your files have a %mor line as described in the section on <u>MOR on page 104.</u> In addition, your files must have a fully disambiguated %trn line. The %trn line has the same form as the %mor line, but has no ambiguous entries. One way of creating files with the %mor and %trn lines is to run MOR on your data, do a full hand disambiguation using Disambiguator Mode (as described in the section on <u>Disambiguator Mode on page 22</u>), rename %mor to %trn using CHSTRING, and then run MOR again to create a %mor line. If a POST database file already exists for your language, then you do not need to worry about using POSTTRAIN at all. However, the more you train a POST database with good disambiguated input data, the more accurate it will become.

The options for POSTTRAIN are:

+a   train word frequencies even on utterances longer than length 3.
+c   create new POST database file with the name eng.db
+cF   create new POST database file with the name F
-c   add to an existing version of eng.db
-cF   add to an existing POST database file with the name F
+mN   load the disambiguation matrices into memory (about 700K)
           N=0 no matrix training
           N=2 training with matrix of size 2 (best for child corpora)
           N=3 training with matrix of size 3
           N=4 training with matrix of size 4
+sN   N=0 error log listing mismatches between the %trn and %mor line.
           Lines that begin with @ indicate that the %trn and %mor had different num-

bers of elements. Lines that do not begin with @ represent simple disagreement between the %trn and the %mor line in some category assignment. For example, if %mor has "pro:dem^pro:exist" and %trn has "co" three times. Then +s0 would yield:

```
3 there co (3 {1} pro:dem (2) pro:exist)
```

               N=1 similar output in a format designed more for developers.
               N=2 complete output of all date, including both matches and mismatches
+tF   use the stem tags in file F along with the other syntactic categories

5.32   RELY

This program has two functions. The first is to check reliability. When you are entering a series of codes into files using the coder's editor, you will often want to compute the reliability of your coding system by having two or more people code a single file or group of files. To do this, you can give each coder the original file, get them to enter a %cod line and then use the RELY program to spot matches and mismatches. For example, you could copy the sample.cha file to the samplea.cha file and change one code in the samplea.cha file. In this example, change the word "in" to "gone" in the code on line 15. Then enter the command

```
rely sample.cha samplea.cha +t%spa
```

The output in the sample.rly file will look like the basic sample.cha file, but with this additional information for line 15:

```
%spa:    $RDE:sel:non $RFI:xxx:gone:?"samplea.cha"
         $RFI:xxx:in:?"sample.cha"
```

If you want the program to ignore any differences in the main line, header line, or other dependent tiers that may have been introduced by the second coder, you can add the +c switch. If you do this, the program will ignore differences and always copy information from the first file. If the command is:

```
rely +c sample.cha samplea.cha +t%spa
```

then the program will use sample.cha as the master file for everything except the information on the %spa tier.

The second function of the RELY program is to allow multiple coders to add a series of dependent tiers to a master file. The main lines of master file should remain unchanged as the coders add additional information on dependent tiers. This function is accessed through the +a switch, which tells the program the name of the code from the secondary file that is to be added to the master file, as in

```
rely +a orig.cha codedfile.cha +t%spa
```

5.32.1 Unique Options

+a   Add tiers from second file to first, master, file.

+c   Do not check data on nonselected tier.

RELY also uses several options that are shared with other commands. For a complete list of options for a command, type the name of the command followed by a carriage return in the Commands window. Information regarding the additional options shared across commands can be found in the chapter on Options on page 134.

5.33 SALTIN

This program takes SALT formatted files and converts them to the CHAT format. SALT is a transcript format developed by Jon Miller and Robin Chapman at the University of Wisconsin. By default, SALTIN sends its output to a file. Here is the most common use of this program:

```
saltin file.cut
```

It may be useful to note a few details of the ways in which SALTIN operates on SALT files:

1. When SALTIN encounters material in parentheses, it translates this material as an unspecified retracing type, using the [/?] code.

2. Multiple comments are placed on separate lines on a single comment tier.

3. SALT codes in square brackets are converted to CHAT comments in square brackets and left in the original place they occurred, unless the + symbol is added to the SALT code. If it is present, the code is treated as a postcode and moved to the end of the utterance when SALTIN runs. The CHSTRING program can be used to insert + in the desired codes or in all codes, if required.

3. Times in minutes and seconds are converted to times in hours:minutes:seconds.

4. A %def tier is created for coding definitions.

5.33.1 Unique Options

+h   Some researchers have used angle brackets in SALT to enter comments. When the original contains text found between the < and the > characters this option instructs SALTIN to place it between [% and]. Otherwise, material in angle brackets would be coded as a text overlap.

+l   Put all codes on a separate %cod line. If you do not select this option, codes will be placed on the main line in the [$text] format.

SALTIN also uses several options that are shared with other commands. For a complete list of options for a command, type the name of the command followed by a carriage return in the Commands window. Information regarding the additional options shared across commands can be found in the chapter on Options on page 134.

5.34   STATFREQ

The STATFREQ program provides a way of producing a summary of word or code frequencies across a set of files. However, within each of the files, you can only look at one speaker at a time. This summary can be sent on as the input to statistical analysis by programs such as SAS or BMDP. Here is the output from a STATFREQ run on sample.cha:

```
a cat chalk+chalk fine here just minute mommy neat no not
that the uhhuh what's white yeah
1.25.8.2  0   0   1   0   0   0   0   1   1   0   0   1   0   0   1   0   2
1.26.8.2  1   1   0   1   1   1   1   0   0   1   1   0   1   1   0   1   0
```

In order to get this type of output, you need to go through three steps. The actual running of STATFREQ is the last of these three steps.

1.   First, you must assign appropriate @ID header lines to the files to be analyzed. You can use the ID program described on page 85 to do this. There can be only one @ID header per speaker. These lines take the following shape:

```
@ID:    eng.samp.sample.0110=CHI
```

There is a tab after the colon and there are no spaces around the = sign. The material before the = sign is the speaker ID and the material after the = sign is the participant's three-letter code as given in the @Participants line.

2.   Next, use FREQ with the +t option followed by the appropriate speaker code. You must also use the +d2 option in the FREQ command line. This will produce a temporary file called stat.out. Here is an example of a FREQ command that outputs data for a STATFREQ analysis:

```
freq +d2 +t@ID=eng.samp.*.0110*CHI sample.cha
```

This command selects out all the utterances in the sample data for 2-year-olds. Because you will probably issue this command using NE20 as your working directory, the command could also have the form:

```
freq +d2 +t@ID=*.02* *.cha
```

STATFREQ will produce one line for each file. If your @ID code matches more than one speaker, frequency information from the various speakers that it matches will be merged together. Therefore, you want to make sure that you use the various pieces of information in the @ID field to select out exactly the material you want to match.

3.   FREQ will tell you to run STATFREQ by typing

```
statfreq stat.out.cex
```

You should enter that command. If you want the output to go to a file, use the +f option:

```
statfreq +f stat.out.cex
```

If the @ID header is not found in a given file, the message NO ID GIVEN will be produced by the program.

You may wish to do some additional processing on the final output of STATFREQ. The best way to do this is to merge rows and columns within either a database management system or the data structure programs of statistical packages such as Minitab and SAS.

The only option unique to STATFREQ is+d which removes the file headers so that the data can be sent directly into a program for statistical analysis. It also replaces missing values with a period, which is usually a symbol representing missing data for statistical analysis. STATFREQ uses several options that are shared with other commands. For a complete list of options for a command, type the name of the command followed by a carriage return in the Commands window. Information regarding the additional options shared across commands can be found in the chapter on <u>Options on page 134</u>.

5.35   TEXTIN

The TEXTIN program is quite simple. It takes a set of sentences in paragraph form and converts them to a CHAT file. Blank lines are considered to be possible paragraph breaks and are noted with @Blank headers. To illustrate the operation of TEXTIN, here are the results of running TEXTIN on the previous three sentences:

```
@Begin
@Participants: T Text
*T:    the textin program is quite simple.
*T:    it takes a set of sentences in paragraph form and converts
       them to a chat file.
*T:    blank lines are considered to be possible paragraph breaks and
       are noted with @blank headers.
@End
```

There are no options that are unique to TEXTIN. However, it uses several options that are shared with other commands. For a complete list of options for a command, type the name of the command followed by a carriage return in the Commands window. Information regarding the additional options shared across commands can be found in the chapter on <u>Options on page 134</u>.

5.36   TIMEDUR

The TIMEDUR program computes the duration of the pauses between speakers and the duration of overlaps. This program requires a %snd tier created through sonic CHAT. The data is output in a form that is intended for export to a spreadsheet program. Columns labeled with the speaker's ID indicate the length of the utterance. Columns labeled with two speaker ID's, such as FAT-ROS, indicate the length of the pause between the end of the utterance of the first speaker and the beginning of the utterance of the next speaker. Negative values in these columns indicate overlaps.

The only unique option in TIMEDUR is +a, which you can use to specify that the time markers should be taken from the %mov tier instead of the default %snd tier. TIMEDUR also uses several options that are shared with other commands. For a complete list of options for a command, type the name of the command followed by a carriage return in the Commands window. Information regarding the additional options shared across commands can be found in the chapter on <u>Options on page 134</u>.

5.37   VOCD

The VOCD command was written by Gerard McKee of the Department of Computer Science, The University of Reading. The research project supporting this work was funded by grants from the Research Endowment Trust Fund of The University of Reading and the Economic and Social Research Council (Grant no R000221995) to D. D. Malvern and B. J. Richards, School of Education, The University of Reading, Bulmershe Court, Reading, England RG6 1HY.

Measurements of vocabulary diversity are frequently needed in child language research and other clinical and linguistic fields. In the past, measures were based on the ratio of different words (Types) to the total number of words (Tokens), known as the type–token Ratio (TTR). Unfortunately, such measures, including mathematical transformations of the TTR such as Root TTR, are functions of the number of tokens in the transcript or language sample — samples containing larger numbers of tokens give lower values for TTR and vice versa (Richards & Malvern, 1997a). This problem has distorted research findings (Richards & Malvern, 1997b). Previous attempts to overcome the problem, for example by standardizing the number of tokens to be analyzed from each child, have failed to ensure that measures are comparable across researchers who use different baselines of tokens, and inevitably waste data in reducing analyses to the size of the smallest sample.

The approach taken in the VOCD program is based on an analysis of the probability of new vocabulary being introduced into longer and longer samples of speech or writing. This probability yields a mathematical model of how TTR varies with token size. By comparing the mathematical model with empirical data in a transcript, VOCD provides a new measure of vocabulary diversity called D. The measure has three advantages: it is not a function of the number of words in the sample; it uses all the data available; and it is more informative, because it represents how the TTR varies over a range of token size. The measure is based on the TTR versus token curve calculated from data for the transcript as a whole, rather than a particular TTR value on it.

D has been shown to be superior to previous measures in both avoiding the inherent flaw in raw TTR with varying sample sizes and in discriminating across a wide range of language learners and users (Malvern & Richards, in press; Richards & Malvern, 1998).

5.37.1 ORIGIN OF THE MEASURE, D

TTRs inevitably decline with increasing sample size. Consequently, any single value of TTR lacks reliability as it will depend on the length in words of the language sample used. A graph of TTR against tokens (N) for a transcript will lie in a curve beginning at the point (1,1) and falling with a negative gradient that becomes progressively less steep (see Malvern & Richards, 1997a). All language samples will follow this trend, but transcripts from speakers or writers with high vocabulary diversity will produce curves that lie above those with low diversity. The fact that TTR falls in a predictable way as the token size increases provides the basis for our approach to finding a valid and reliable measure. The method builds on previous theoretical analyses, notably by Brainerd (1982) and in particular Sichel (1986), which model the TTR versus token curve mathematically so that the characteristics of the curve for a transcript yields a valid measure of vocabulary diversity.

Various probabilistic models were developed and investigated in order to arrive at a model containing only one parameter which increases with increasing diversity and falls into a range suitable for discriminating among the range of transcripts found in various language studies. The model chosen is derived from a simplification of Sichel's (1986) type–token characteristic curve and is in the form an equation containing the parameter D. This equation yields a family of curves all of the same general and appropriate shape, with different values for the parameter D distinguishing different members of this family (see Malvern & Richards, 1997). In the model, D itself is used directly as an index of lexical diversity.

In order to calculate D from a transcript, the VOCD program first plots the empirical TTR versus tokens curve for the speaker. It derives each point on the curve from an average of 100 trials on subsamples of words of the token size for that point. The subsamples are made up of words randomly chosen (without replacement) from throughout the transcript. The program then finds the best fit between the theoretical model and the empirical data by a curve-fitting procedure which adjusts the value of the parameter (D) in the equation until a match is obtained between the actual curve for the transcript and the closest member of the family of curves represented by the mathematical model. This value of the parameter for best fit is the index of lexical diversity. High values of D reflect a high level of lexical diversity and lower diversity produces lower values of D.

The validity of D has been the subject of extensive investigation (Malvern & Richards, 1997; Richards & Malvern, 1997a; Richards & Malvern, 1998; Malvern & Richards, in press) on samples of child language, children with SLI, children learning French as a foreign language, adult learners of English as a second language, and academic writing. In these validation trials, the empirical TTR versus token curves for a total of 162 transcripts from five corpora covering ages from 24 months to adult, two languages and a variety of settings, all fitted the model. The model produced consistent values for D which, unlike TTR and even Mean Segmental TTR (MSTTR) (see Richards & Malvern, 1997a: pp. 35-38), correlated well with other well validated measures of language. These five corpora also provide useful indications of the scale for D.

5.37.2   CALCULATION OF D

In calculating D, VOCD uses random sampling of tokens in plotting the curve of TTR against increasing token size for the transcript under investigation. Random sampling has two advantages over sequential sampling. Firstly, it matches the assumptions underlying the probabilistic model. Secondly, it avoids the problem of the curve being distorted by the clustering of the same vocabulary items at particular points in the transcript.

In practice each empirical point on the curve is calculated from averaging the TTRs of 100 trials on subsamples consisting of the number of tokens for that point, drawn at random from throughout the transcripts. This default number was found by experimentation and balanced the wish to have as many trials as possible with the desire for the program to run reasonably quickly. The run time has not been reduced at the expense of reliability, however, as it was found that taking 100 trials for each point on the curve produced consistency in the values output for D without unacceptable delays.

Which part of the curve is used to calculate D is crucial. First, in order to have subsamples to average for the final point on the curve, the final value of N (the number of tokens in a subsample) cannot be as large as the transcript itself. Moreover, transcripts vary hugely in total token count. Second, the equation is an approximation to Sichel's (1986) model and applies with greater accuracy at lower numbers of tokens. In an extensive set of trials, D has been calculated over different parts of the curve to find a portion for which the approximation held good and averaging worked well. As a result of these trials the default is for the curve to be drawn and fitted for N=35 to N=50 tokens in steps of 1 token. Each of these points is calculated from averaging 100 subsamples, each drawn from the whole of the transcript. Although only a relatively small part of the curve is fitted, it uses all the information available in the transcript. This also has the advantage of calculating D from a standard part of the curve for all transcripts regardless of their total size, further providing for reliable comparisons between subjects and between the work of different researchers.

The procedure depends on finding the best fit between the empirical and theoretically derived curves by the least square difference method. Extensive testing confirmed that the best fit procedure was valid and was reliably finding a unique minimum at the least square difference.

As the points on the curve are averages of random samples, a slightly different value of D is to be expected each time the program is run. Tests showed that with the defaults chosen these differences are relatively small, but consistency was improved by VOCD calculating D three times by default and giving the average value as output.

5.37.3   Sample Size

By default, the software plots the TTR versus token curve from 35 tokens to 50 tokens. Each point on the curve is produced by random sampling without replacement. VOCD therefore requires a minimum of 50 tokens to operate. However, the fact that the software will satisfactorily output a value of D from a sample as small as 50 tokens does not guarantee that values obtained from such small samples will be reliable. It should also be noted that random sampling without replacement causes the software to run noticeably more slowly when samples approach this minimum level.

5.37.4 Preparation of Files

Files should be prepared in correct CHAT format and should pass through CHECK, using the +g3 switch to track down spelling and typographical errors. The FREQ program should then be used to create a complete wordlist that can be scanned for further errors. The output from FREQ also allows the researcher to see exactly what FREQ (and therefore VOCD) will treat as a word type. From this information, an exclude file of non-words can be compiled (e.g. hesitations, laughter, etc). These can then be filtered out of the analysis using the -s switch.

5.37.5 The Output from VOCD

To illustrate the functioning of VOCD, let us use a command that examines the child's output in the file 68.cha in the NE32 sample directory in the lib folder in the CLAN distribution. The +r6 switch here excludes repetitions, the +s@exclude lists a file of words to be excluded, and the +s"*-%%" instructs CLAN to merge across variations of a base word.

```
VOCD +t"*CHI" +r6 -s@exclude +s"*-%%" 68.cha
```

The output of this analysis has four parts:

1. A sequential list of utterances by the speaker selected shows the tokens that will be retained for analysis.

2. A table shows the number of tokens for each point on the curve, average TTR and the standard deviation for each point, and the value of D obtained from the equation for each point. Three such tables appear, one for each time the program takes random samples and carries out the curve-fitting.

3. At the foot of each of the three tables is the average of the Ds obtained from the equation and their standard deviation, the value for D that provided the best fit, and the residuals.

4. Finally, a results summary repeats the command line and file name and the type and token information for the lexical items retained for analysis, as well as giving the three optimum values of D and their average.

For the command given above, the last of the three tables and the results summary are:

tokens	samples	ttr	st.dev	D
35	100	0.7963	0.067	54.470
36	100	0.8067	0.054	60.583
37	100	0.8008	0.059	59.562
38	100	0.7947	0.056	58.464
39	100	0.7831	0.065	55.124
40	100	0.7772	0.054	54.242
41	100	0.7720	0.064	53.568

42	100	0.7767	0.057	56.720
43	100	0.7695	0.051	55.245
44	100	0.7650	0.057	54.787
45	100	0.7636	0.053	55.480
46	100	0.7626	0.057	56.346
47	100	0.7543	0.052	54.403
48	100	0.7608	0.050	58.088
49	100	0.7433	0.058	52.719
50	100	0.7396	0.049	52.516

```
D: average = 55.770; std dev. = 2.289
D_optimum      <55.63; min least sq val = 0.001>

VOCD RESULTS SUMMARY
====================
        Command line:  vocd +t*CHI +r6 -s@exclude +s*-%% 68.cha
           File name:  68.cha
    Types,Tokens,TTR:  <129,376,0.343085>
    D_optimum  values:  <55.36, 55.46, 55.63>
    D_optimum average:  55.48
```

5.37.6   Unique Options

+a0   Calculate D_optimum using the split half with evens.

+a1   Calculate D_optimum using the split half with odds.

+c   Include capitalized words only.

+d   Outputs a list of utterances processed and number of types, tokens and TTR, but does not calculate D.

+d4   Outputs number of types, tokens and TTR only.

+dsN   The +ds switch allows separate analysis of odd and even numbered words in the transcript. The results of this can then be fed into a split-half reliability analysis. This switch can have one of two values: +ds0 (for even numbered words) or +ds1 (for odd numbered words).

VOCD also uses several options that are shared with other commands. For a complete list of options for a command, type the name of the command followed by a carriage return in the Commands window. Information regarding the additional options shared across commands can be found in the chapter on <u>Options on page 134</u>.

5.38   WDLEN

The WDLEN program tabulates word lengths and prints a histogram. The program reads through data files, tabulating the frequencies of various word and utterance lengths.

The output consists of word lengths (in characters) and utterance lengths (in words), the frequencies of these lengths, and a histogram of these frequencies. The "Wdlen" in the output represents the word length. The "Utt len" in the output represents the utterance length. The basic use of the WDLEN program is as follows:

```
wdlen sample.cha
```

The only option unique to WDLEN is +hwhich allows you to extend the length of the longest line on the histogram. WDLEN also uses several options that are shared with other commands. For a complete list of options for a command, type the name of the command followed by a carriage return in the Commands window. Information regarding the additional options shared across commands can be found in the chapter on Options on page 134.

6:   Options

This chapter describes the various options or switches that are shared across CLAN commands. To see a list of options for a given program such as KWAL, type *kwal* followed by a carriage return in the Commands window. You will see a list of available options in the CLAN Output window.

Each option begins with a + or a -. There is always a space before the + or -. Multiple options can be used and they can occur in any order. For example, the command:

```
kwal +f +t*MOT sample.cha
```

runs a KWAL analysis on sample.cha. The selection of the +f option sends the output from this analysis into a new file called sample.kwa.cex. The +t*MOT option confines the analysis to only the lines spoken by the mother. The +f and +t switches can be placed in either order.

6.1   +F Option

This option allows you to send output to a file rather than to the screen. By default, nearly all of the programs send the results of the analyses directly to the screen. You can, however, request that your results be inserted into a file. This is accomplished by inserting the +f option into the command line. The advantage of sending the program's results to a file is that you can go over the analysis more carefully, because you have a file to which you can later refer.

The -f switch is used for sending output to the screen. For most programs, -f is the default and you do not need to enter it. You only need to use the -f switch when you want the output to go to the screen for CHSTRING, FLO, and SALTIN. The advantage of sending the analysis to the screen (also called standard output) is that the results are immediate and your directory is less cluttered with nonessential files. This is ideal for quick temporary analysis.

The string specified with the +f option is used to replace the default file name extension assigned to the output file name by each program. For example, the command

```
freq +f sample.cha
```

would create an output file sample.frq.cex. If you want to control the shape of the extension name on the file, you can place up to three letters after the +f switch, as in the command

```
freq +fmot sample.cha
```

which would create an output file sample.mot.cex. If the string argument is longer than three characters, it will be truncated. For example, the command

```
freq +fmother sample.cha
```

would also create an output file sample.mot.cex.

On the Macintosh, you can use the third option under the File menu to set the directory for your output files. On Windows you can achieve the same effect by using the +f switch with an argument, as in:

+fc: This will send the output files to your working directory on c:.
+f".res"   This sets the extension for your output files.
+f"c:.res"   This sends the output files to c: and assigns the extension .res.

When you are running a command on several files and use the +f switch, the output will go into several files – one for each of the input files. If what you want is a combined analysis that treats all the input files as one large file, then you should use the +u switch. If you want all of the output to go into a single file for which you provide the name, then use the > character at the end of the command along with an additional file name. The > option can not be combined with +f.

6.2   +K Option

This option controls case-sensitivity. A case-sensitive program is one that makes a distinction between uppercase and lowercase letters. The CLAN programs are not case-sensitive by default. The exception to this is CHSTRING. Use of the +k option overrides the default state and allows the other programs to become case-sensitive as well. For instance, suppose you are searching for the auxiliary verb "may" in a text. If you searched for the word "may" in a case-sensitive program, you would obtain all the occurrences of the word "may" in lower case only. You would not obtain any occurrences of "MAY" or "May." Searches performed for the word "may" using the +k option produce the words "may," "MAY," and "May" as output.

6.3   +P Option

This option allows you to define a custom punctuation set. Because most of the programs in the CLAN system are word-oriented, the beginning and ending boundaries of words must be defined. This is done by defining a punctuation set. The default punctuation set for CLAN includes the space and these characters:

$$, \quad . \quad ; \quad ? \quad ! \quad [\quad] \quad < \quad >$$

This punctuation set applies to the main lines and all coding lines with the exception of the %pho and %mod lines which use the UNIBET and PHONASCII systems. Because those systems make use of punctuation markers for special characters, only the space can be used as a delimiter on the %pho and %mod lines.

All of the word-oriented programs have the +p option. This option allows the user to redefine the default punctuation set. This is useful because the CHAT coding conventions use special characters that at times are used as delimiters and other times as parts of words. For example, sometimes the - character is used as a morpheme boundary marker and, therefore, should not be considered part of the word. This is also quite useful when you are working on a language that uses diacritics. To change the punctuation set, you must create a small file that lists all the punctuation marks present in the file. You do this by simply typing out all the punctuation marks on a single line with no spaces between them. This line will change the punctuation set of the main speaker tiers and the code tiers. The name of your new punctuation file should immediately follow the +p in the command line. Here is an example situation. Suppose you wish to change both the main speaker tier and the code tier punctuation sets from the default to the set in newpunct.cut. The contents of the newpunct.cut file are as follows:

```
$*&^!
```

This line indicates the desired punctuation set for the main line and coding tier. You can now issue commands such as the following:

```
freq +pnewpunct.cut sample.cha
```

If you use the +p switch with no file name, the programs look for a file called punct.cut in the current working directory. If you do not use the +p switch at all, the programs look for a punctuation file called punct.cut. If the punct.cut file is not found, the program will then use the default built-in punctuation set. It is advisable to create a punct.cut file when the punctuation characters of the language being analyzed are different from the default punctuation characters. The punct.cut file should contain the new punctuation set and should be located in the current working directory. Because the punct.cut file is referred to automatically, this feature allows you to change the punctuation set once for use with all the CLAN programs. If you do not want CLAN to ever change the default punctuation set, make sure you do not have a punct.cut file in your current working directory and make sure you do not use the +p switch.

6.4   +R Option

This option deals with the treatment of material in parentheses.

+r1   **Removing Parentheses.** Omitted parts of words can be marked by parentheses, as in "(be)cause" with the first syllable omitted. The +r1 option removes the parentheses and leaves the rest of the word as is.

+r2   **Leaving Parentheses.** This option leaves the word with parentheses.

+r3   **Removing Material in Parentheses.** This option removes all of the omitted part.

Here is an example of the use of the first three +r options and their resulting outputs, if the input word is "get(s)":

Option	Output
"no option"	gets
"+r1"	gets
"+r2"	get(s)
"+r3"	get

+r4   **Removing Prosodic Symbols in Words.** By default, symbols such as #, /, and : are ignored when they occur inside words. Use this switch if you want to include them in your searches. If you do not use this switch, the strings cat and ca:t will be seen as the same. If you use this switch, they will be seen as different. The use of these prosodic marker symbols is discussed in the CHAT manual.

+r5   **Text Replacement.** By default, material in the form [: text] replaces the material preceding it in the string search programs. If you do not want this replacement, use this switch.

+r6   **Retraced Material.** By default, material in retracings is included in searches and counts. However, this material can be excluded by using the +r6 switch. In the MLU and MODREP programs, retracings are excluded by default. For these programs, the +r6 switch can be used to include material in retracings.

6.5   +S Option

This option allows you to search for a particular string. The +s option allows you to specify the keyword you desire to find. You do this by putting the word in quotes directly after the +s switch, as in +s"dog" to search for the word "dog." You can also use the +s switch to specify a file containing words to be searched. You do this by putting the file name after the +s preceded by the @ sign, as in +s@adverbs, which will search for the words in a file called adverbs.cut. If you want to look for the literal character @, you need to precede it with a backslash as in +s"\@".

By default, the programs will only search for this string on the main line. Also by default, this switch treats material in square brackets as if it were a single "opaque" form. In effect, unless you include the square brackets in your search string, the search will ignore any material that is enclosed in square brackets. The COMBO program is the only one that allows you to specify regular expressions with this option. The only programs that allow you to include delimiters in the search string are COMBO, FREQ, and KWAL.

It is possible to specify as many +s options on the command line as you like. Use of the +s option will override the default list. For example, the command

```
freq +s"word" data.cut
```

will search through the file data.cut looking for "word."

The +s/-s switch is usually used to include or exclude certain words. However, it can actually be used with five types of material: (1) words, (2) codes or postcodes in square brackets, (3) text in angle brackets associated with particular codes within square brackets, (4) whole utterances associated with particular postcodes, and (5) particular postcodes themselves. The effect of the switch for the five different types is as follows.

Table 5: Search Strings for Five Types of Material

Level	+s	-s	+s+
Word	+s"dog"	-s"dog"	+s+xxx
	only the word "dog"	all words except "dog"	all words plus "dog"
[code]	+s"[//]"	by default, all codes are excluded	+s+"[//]"
	only this code		all text plus this code
<text>[x]	+s"<//>"	-s"<//>"	+s+"<//>"
	only text marked by this code	all text except material marked by this code	all text plus material marked by this code
Utterance	+s"<+imi>"	-s"<+imi>"	by default, all utterances are included
	utterances marked with this postcode	utterances not marked with this postcode	
Postcode	+s"[+imi]"	by default, all postcodes are excluded	+s+"[+imi]"
	only this postcode		all text plus postcode

Multiple +s strings are matched as exclusive or's. If a string matches one +s string, it cannot match the other. The most specific matches are processed first. For example, if your command is

```
freq +s$gf% +s$gf:a
```

and your text has these codes

```
$gf $gf:a $gf:b $gf:c
```

your output will be

```
$gf%              3
$gf               1
```

Because $gf:a matches specifically to the +s$gf:a, it is excluded from matching +s$gf%.

One can also use the +s switch to remove certain strings from automatic exclusion. For example, the MLU program automatically excludes xxx, 0, uh, and words beginning with

& from the MLU count. This can be changed by using this command:

```
mlu +s+uh +s+xxx +s+0* +s+&* file.cha
```

6.6 +T Option

This option allows you to include or exclude particular tiers. In CHAT formatted files, there exist three tier code types: main speaker tiers (denoted by *), speaker-dependent tiers (denoted by %), and header tiers (denoted by @). The speaker-dependent tiers are attached to speaker tiers. If, for example, you request to analyze the speaker *MOT and all the %cod dependent tiers, the programs will analyze all of the *MOT main tiers and only the %cod dependent tiers associated with that speaker.

The +t option allows you to specify which main speaker tiers, their dependent tiers, and header tiers should be included in the analysis. All other tiers, found in the given file, will be ignored by the program. For example, the command

```
freq +t*CHI +t%spa +t%mor +t"@Group of Mot" sample.cha
```

tells FREQ to look at only the *CHI main speaker tiers, their %spa and %mor dependent tiers, and @Situation header tiers. When tiers are included, the analysis will be done on only those specified tiers.

The -t option allows you to specify which main speaker tiers, their dependent tiers, and header tiers should be excluded from the analysis. All other tiers found in the given file should be included in the analysis, unless specified otherwise by default. The command

```
freq -t*CHI -t%spa -t%mor -t@"Group of Mot" sample.cha
```

tells FREQ to exclude all the *CHI main speaker tiers together with all their dependent tiers, the %spa and %mor dependent tiers on all other speakers, and all @Situation header tiers from the analysis. All remaining tiers will be included in the analysis.

When the transcriber has decided to use complex combinations of codes for speaker IDs such as *CHI-MOT for "child addressing mother," it is possible to use the +t switch with the # symbol as a wildcard, as in these commands:

```
freq +t*CHI-MOT sample.cha
freq +t*#-MOT sample.cha
freq +t*CHI-# sample.cha
```

When tiers are included, the analysis will be done on only those specified tiers. When tiers are excluded, however, the analysis is done on tiers other than those specified. Failure to exclude all unnecessary tiers will cause the programs to produce distorted results. Therefore, it is safer to include tiers in analyses than to exclude them, because it is often difficult to be aware of all the tiers present in any given data file.

If only a tier-type symbol (*, %, @) is specified following the +t/-t options, the programs will include all tiers of that particular symbol type in the analysis. Using the option +t@ is important when using KWAL for limiting (see the description of the KWAL program), because it makes sure that the header information is not lost.

The programs search sequentially, starting from the left of the tier code descriptor, for exactly what the user has specified. This means that a match can occur wherever what has been specified has been found. If you specify *M on the command line after the option, the program will successfully match all speaker tiers that start with *M, such as *MAR, *MIK, *MOT, and so forth. For full clarity, it is best to specify the full tier name after the +t/-t options, including the : character. For example, to ensure that only the *MOT speaker tiers are included in the analysis, use the +t*MOT: notation.

As an alternative to specifying speaker names through letter codes, you can use the form:

`+t@id=idcode`

In this form, the "idcode" is any character string that matches the type of string that has been declared at the top of each file using the @ID header tier. The basic form of this code is language.corpus.file.age=XXX where XXX is the participant code.

All of the programs include the main speaker tiers by default and exclude all of the dependent tiers, unless a +t% switch is used.

6.7   +U Option

This option merges specified files together. By default, when the user has specified a series of files on the command line, the analysis is performed on each individual file. The program then provides separate output for each data file. If the command line uses the +u option, the program combines the data found in all the specified files into one set and outputs the result for that set as a whole. If too many files are selected, CLAN may eventually be unable to complete this merger.

6.8   +V Option

This switch gives you the date when the current version of CLAN was compiled.

6.9   +W Option

This option controls the printing of additional sentences before and after a matched sentence. This option can be used with either KWAL or COMBO. These programs are used to display tiers that contain keywords or regular expressions as chosen by the user. By default, KWAL and COMBO combine the user-chosen main and dependent tiers into "clusters."

Each cluster includes the main tier and its dependent tiers. (See the +u option for further information on clusters.)

The -w option followed by a positive integer causes the program to display that number of clusters before each cluster of interest. The +w option followed by a positive integer causes the program to display that number of clusters after each cluster of interest. For example, if you wanted the KWAL program to produce a context larger than a single cluster, you could include the -w3 and +w2 options in the command line. The program would then output three clusters above and two clusters below each cluster of interest.

6.10   +Y Option

This option allows you to work on non-CHAT files. Most of the programs are designed to work best on CHAT formatted data files. However, the +y option allows the user to use these programs on non-CHAT files. The program considers each line of a non-CHAT file to be one tier. There are two values of the +y switch. The +y value works on lines and the +y1 value works on utterances as delimited by periods, question marks, and exclamation marks. Some programs do not allow the use of the +y option at all. Workers interested in using CLAN with nonconversational data may wish to first convert there files to CHAT format using the TEXTIN program described on page 127 in order to avoid having to avoid the problematic use of the +y option.

6.11   +Z Option

This option allows the user to select any range of words, utterances, or speaker turns to be analyzed. The range specifications should immediately follow the option. For example:

+z10w	analyze the first ten words only.
+z10u	analyze the first ten utterances only.
+z10t	analyze the first ten speaker turns only.
+z10w-20w	analyze 11 words starting with the 10th word.
+z10u-20u	analyze 11 utterances starting with the 10th utterance.
+z10t-20t	analyze 11 speaker turns starting with the 10th turn.
+z10w-	analyze from the tenth word to the end of file.
+z10u-	analyze from the tenth utterance to the end of file.
+z10t-	analyze from the tenth speaker turn to the end of file.

If the +z option is used together with the +t option to select utterances from a particular speaker, then the counting will be based only on the utterances of that speaker. For example, this command

```
mlu +z50u +t*CHI 0611.cha
```

will compute the MLU for the first 50 utterances produced by the child.

If the user has specified more items than exist in the file, the program will analyze only the existing items. If the turn or utterance happens to be empty, because it consists of special symbols or words that have been selected to be excluded, then this utterance or turn is not counted.

The usual reason for selecting a fixed number of utterances is to derive samples that are comparable across sessions or across children. Often researchers have found that samples of 50 utterances provide almost as much information as samples of 100 utterances. Reducing the number of utterances being transcribed is important for clinicians who have been assigned a heavy case load.

You can use the +z switch with KWAL and pipe the results to a second program, rather than using it directly with FREQ or MLU. For example, in order to specifically exclude unintelligible utterances in an MLU analysis of the first 150 utterances from the Target Child, you could use this form:

```
kwal +z150u  +d +t*CHI 0042.cha -syyy -sxxx | mlu
```

You can also use postcodes to further control the process of inclusion or exclusion.

6.12   Metacharacters for Searching

Metacharacters are special characters used to describe other characters or groups of characters. Certain metacharacters may be used to modify search strings used by the +s/-s switch. However, in order to use metacharacters in the CHSTRING program a special switch must be set. The CLAN metacharacters are:

*	Any number of characters matched
%	Any number of characters matched and removed
%%	As above plus remove previous character
_	Any single character matched
\	Quote character

Suppose you would like to be able to find all occurrences of the word "cat" in a file. This includes the plural form "cats," the possessives "cat-'s," "cat-s'" and the contractions "cat-'is" and "cat-'has." Using a metacharacter (in this case, the asterisk) would help you to find all of these without having to go through and individually specify each one. By inserting the string cat* into the include file or specifying it with +s option, all these forms would be found. Metacharacters can be placed anywhere in the word.

The * character is a wildcard character; it will find any character or group of continuous characters that correspond to its placement in the word. For example, if b*s were specified, the program would match words like "beads," "bats," "bat-'s," "balls," "beds," "bed-s," "breaks," and so forth.

The % character allows the program to match characters in the same way that the * symbol does. Unlike the * symbol, however, all the characters matched by the % will be ignored in terms of the way of which the output is generated. In other words, the output will treat "beat" and "bat" as two occurrences of the same string, if the search string is b%t. Unless the % symbol is used with programs that produce a list of words matched by given keywords, the effect of the % symbol will be the same as the effect of the * symbol.

When the percentage symbol is immediately followed by a second percentage symbol, the effect of the metacharacter changes slightly. The result of such a search would be that the % symbol will be removed along with any one character preceding the matched string. Without adding the additional % character, a punctuation symbol preceding the wildcard string will not be matched ane will be ignored. Adding the second % sign can be particularly useful when searching for roots of words only. For example, to produce a word frequency count of the stem "cat," specify this command:

```
freq +s"cat-%%" file.cha.
```

The first % sign matches the suffixes and the second one matches the dash mark. Thus, the search string specified by the +s option will match words like: "cat," "cat-s," "cat-'s," and "cat-s" and FREQ will count all of these words as one word "cat." If the data file file.cha had consisted of only those four words, the output of the FREQ program would have been: 4 cat. The limitation of this search is that it will not match words like "cats" or "cat's," because the second percentage symbol is used to match the punctuation mark. The second percentage symbol is also useful for matching hierarchical codes such as $NIA:RP:IN.

The underline character _ is similar to the * character except that it is used to specify any single character in a word. For example, the string b_d will match words like "bad," "bed," "bud," "bid," and so forth. For detailed examples of the use of the percentage, underline, and asterisk symbols, see the section on <u>FREQ on page 72</u>.

The quote character (\) is used to indicate the quotation of one of the characters being used as metacharacters. Suppose that you wanted to search for the actual symbol (*) in a text. Because the (*) symbol is used to represent any character, it must be quoted by inserting the (\) symbol before the (*) symbol in the search string to represent the actual (*) character, as in "string*string." To search for the actual character (\), it must be quoted also. For example, "string\\string" will match "string" followed by "\" and then followed by a second "string."

7: Exercises

This chapter presents exercises designed to help you think about the application of CLAN for specific aspects of language analysis. The illustrations in the section below are based on materials developed by Barbara Pan originally published in Chapter 2 of Sokolov and Snow (1994). The original text has been edited to reflect subsequent changes in the programs and the database. Many thanks to Barbara Pan for devising the initial form of this extremely useful set of exercises.

7.1   Contrasting Four Measures

One approach to transcript analysis focuses on the computation of particular measures or scores that characterize the stage of language development in the children or adults in the sample.

1.   One popular measure (Brown, 1973) is the MLU or mean length of utterance, which can be computed by the MLU program.

2.   A second measure is the MLU of the five longest utterances in a sample, or MLU5. Wells (1981) found that increases in MLU of the five longest utterances tend to parallel those in MLU, with both levelling off after about 42 months of age. Brown suggested that MLU of the longest utterance tends, in children developing normally, to be approximately three times greater than MLU.

3.   A third measure is MLT or Mean Length of Turn which can be computed the the MLT program.

4.   A fourth popular measure of lexical diversity is the type–token ratio of Templin (1957).

In these exercises, we will use CLAN to generate these four measures of spontaneous language production for a group of normally developing children at 20 months. The goals are to use data from a sizeable sample of normally developing children to inform us as to the average (mean) performance and degree of variation (standard deviation) among children at this age on each measure; and to explore whether individual children's performance relative to their peers was constant across domains. That is, were children whose MLU was low relative to their peers also low in terms of lexical diversity and conversational participation? Conversely, were children with relatively advanced syntactic skills as measured by MLU also relatively advanced in terms of lexical diversity and the share of the conversational load they assumed?

The speech samples analyzed here are taken from the New England corpus of the CHILDES database, which includes longitudinal data on 52 normally-developing children. Spontaneous speech of the children interacting with their mothers was collected in a play setting when the children were 14, 20, and 32 months of age. Transcripts were prepared according to the CHAT conventions of the Child Language Data Exchange System, including conventions for morphemicizing speech, such that MLU could be computed in terms of morphemes rather than words. Data were available for 48 of the 52 children at 20 months. The means and standard deviations for MLU5, TTR, and MLT reported below are based on these 48 children. Because only 33 of the 48 children produced 50 or more utterances during the observation session at 20 months, the mean and standard deviation for MLU50 is based on 33 subjects.

For illustrative purposes, we will discuss five children: the child whose MLU was the highest for the group (68.cha), the child whose MLU was the lowest (98.cha), and one child each at the first (66.cha), second (55.cha), and third (14.cha) quartiles. Transcripts for these five children at 20 months can be found in the /ne20 directory in the /lib directory distributed with CLAN.

Our goal is to compile the following basic measures for each of the five target children: MLU on 50 utterances, MLU of the five longest utterances, TTR, and MLT. We then compare these five children to their peers by generating *z*-scores based on the means and standard deviations for the available sample for each measure at 20 months. In this way, we were will generate language profiles for each of our five target children.

7.2   MLU50 Analysis

The first CLAN analysis we will perform calculates MLU for each child on a sample of 50 utterances. By default, the MLU program excludes the strings xxx, yyy, www, as well as any string immediately preceded by one of the following symbols: 0, &, +, -, #, $, or : (see the CHAT manual for a description of transcription conventions). The MLU program also excludes from all counts material in angle brackets followed by [/], [//], or [% bch] (see the CLAN manual for list of symbols CLAN considers to be word, morpheme, or utterance delimiters). Remember that to perform any CLAN analysis, you need to be in the directory where your data is when you issue the appropriate CLAN command. In this case, we want to be in /childes/clan/lib/ne20. The command string we used to compute MLU for all five children is:

```
mlu +t*CHI +z50u +f *.cha
```

+t*CHI	Analyze the child speaker tier only
+z50u	Analyze the first 50 utterances only
+f	Save the results in a file
*.cha	Analyze all files ending with the extension .cha

The only constraint on the order of elements in a CLAN command is that the name of the program (here, MLU) must come first. Many users find it good practice to put the name of the file on which the analysis is to be performed last, so that they can tell at a glance both what program was used and what file(s) were analyzed. Other elements may come in any order.

The option +t*CHI tells CLAN that we want only CHI speaker tiers considered in the analysis. Were we to omit this string, a composite MLU would be computed for all speakers in the file.

The option + z50u tells CLAN to compute MLU on only the first 50 utterances. We could, of course, have specified the child's first 100 utterances (+z100u) or utterances from the 51st through the 100th (+z51u-100u). With no +z option specified, MLU is computed on the entire file.

The option +f tells CLAN that we want the output recorded in output files, rather than simply displayed onscreen. CLAN will create a separate output file for each file on which it computes MLU. If we wish, we may specify a three-letter file extension for the output files immediately following the +f option in the command line. If a specific file extension is not specified, CLAN will assign one automatically. In the case of MLU, the default extension is .mlu.cex. The .cex at the end is mostly important for Windows, since it allows the Windows operating system to know that this is a CLAN output file.

Finally, the string *.cha tells CLAN to perform the analysis specified on each file ending in the extension .cha found in the current directory. To perform the analysis on a single file, we would specify the entire file name (e.g., 68.cha). It was possible to use the wildcard * in this and following analyses, rather than specifying each file separately, because:

1.   All the files to be analyzed ended with the same file extensions and were in the same directory; and

2.   in each file, the target child was identified by the same speaker code (i.e., CHI), thus allowing us to specify the child's tier by means of +t*CHI.

Utilization of wildcards whenever possible is not only more efficient than repeatedly typing in similar commands, but also cuts down on typing errors.

By default, CLAN computes MLU in morphemes, rather than words, if the transcript is morphemicized on the main line. The user may override this default and have CLAN ignore morphemicization symbols by using the option, followed by those symbols to be ignored. For example, -c# would instruct CLAN to ignore the prefix symbol in words such as un#tie; -c#-would result in both the # and - symbols in un#tie-ed being disregarded. Thus, researchers can choose not to count morphemes they believe the child is not yet using productively. To have all morphemicization symbols ignored, one would use -c#&- .

For illustrative purposes, let us suppose that we ran the above analysis on only a single child (68.cha), rather than for all five children at once (by specifying *.cha). We would use the following command:

```
mlu +t*CHI +z50u 68.cha
```

The output for this command would be as follows:

```
> mlu +t*CHI +z50u 68.cha
mlu +t*CHI +z50U 68.cha
Wed Oct 20 11:46:51 1999
mlu (18-OCT-99) is conducting analyses on:
```

```
ONLY speaker main tiers matching: *CHI;
*****************************************
From file <68.cha>
MLU for Speaker: *CHI:
  MLU (xxx and yyy are EXCLUDED from the utterance and morpheme counts):
          Number of: utterances = 50, morphemes = 133
          Ratio of morphemes over utterances = 2.660
          Standard deviation = 1.570
```

MLU reports the number of utterances (in this case, the 50 utterances we specified), the number of morphemes that occurred in those 50 utterances, the ratio of morphemes over utterances (MLU in morphemes), and the standard deviation of utterance length in morphemes. The standard deviation statistic gives some indication of how variable the child's utterance length is. This child's average utterance is 2.660 morphemes long, with a standard deviation of 1.570 morphemes.

Check line 1 of the output for typing errors in entering the command string. Check lines 3 and possibly 4 of the output to be sure the proper speaker tier and input file(s) were specified. Also check to be sure that the number of utterances or words reported is what was specified in the command line. If CLAN finds that the transcript contains fewer utterances or words than the number specified with the +z option, it will still run the analysis but will report the actual number of utterances or words analyzed.

7.3   MLU5 Analysis

The second CLAN analysis we will perform computes the mean length in morphemes of each child's five longest utterances. To do this, we direct the output of one program to a second program for further analysis. This process is called piping. Although we could accomplish the same goal by running the first program on each file, sending the output to files and then performing the second analysis on the output files, piping is more efficient. The trade-off is that the analysis must be done on one file at a time (by specifying the full file name), rather than by using the * wildcard. The CLAN command string we use is:

```
maxwd +t*CHI +g1 +c5 +d1 68.cha | mlu > 68.ml5.cex
```

+t*CHI	Analyze the child speaker tier only
+gl	Identify the longest utterances in terms of morphemes
+c5	Identify the five longest utterances
+dl	Output the data in CHAT format
68.cha	The child language transcript to be analyzed
| mlu	Pipe the output to the MLU program
>	Send the output of MLU to a file
68.ml5.cex	Create a file for the output, called ml5.cex

If we run simply the first part of this command up to the pipe symbol, the output would look like this:

```
*CHI:    <I want to see the other box> [?] .
*CHI:    that-'is [= book] the <morning # noon and night> ["] .
*CHI:    there-'is a dolly in there [= box] .
*CHI:    it-'is [= contents of box] crayon-s and paper .
*CHI:    pop go-es the weasel .
```

By adding the MLU command after the pipe, we are telling CLAN to take this initial output from MAXWD and send it on for further processing by MLU.

The string +g1 tells MAXWD to identify longest utterances in terms of morphemes per utterance. If length is to be determined instead by the number of words per utterance, the string +g2 would be used; if by number of characters per utterance, +g3 would be used. For the +g1 switch to work well, we need to either break words into morphemes on the main line (as described in the CHAT manual) or else run this command on the %mor line.

The string +c5 tells MAXWD to identify the five longest utterances.

The string +d1 tells MAXWD to send output to the output file in CHAT form, that is, in a form that can be analyzed by other CLAN programs.

The piping symbol | (upright bar or vertical hyphens) separates the first CLAN command from the second, and indicates that the output of the first command is to be used as the input to the second.

Finally, the redirect symbol > followed by the output file name and extension specifies where the final output file is to be directed (i.e., saved). Omission of the redirect symbol and file name will result in output being displayed on-screen rather than recorded in a file. Here we are specifying that the output from MLU should be recorded in an output file called 68.ml5.cex. The contents of this file are as follows:

```
MLU for Speaker: *CHI:
  MLU (xxx and yyy are EXCLUDED from the utterance and morpheme counts):
        Number of: utterances = 5, morphemes = 31
        Ratio of morphemes over utterances = 6.200
        Standard deviation = 0.748
```

The procedure for obtaining output files in CHAT format differs from program to program but it is always the +d option that performs this operation. You must check the +d options for each program to determine the exact level of the +d option that is required. We can create a single file to run this type of analysis. This is called a batch file. The batch file for this particular analysis would be:

```
maxwd +t*CHI +g1 +c5 +d1 14.cha | mlu > 14.ml5.cex
maxwd +t*CHI +g1 +c5 +d1 55.cha | mlu > 55.ml5.cex
maxwd +t*CHI +g1 +c5 +d1 66.cha | mlu > 66.ml5.cex
maxwd +t*CHI +g1 +c5 +d1 68.cha | mlu > 68.ml5.cex
maxwd +t*CHI +g1 +c5 +d1 98.cha | mlu > 98.ml5.cex
```

To run all five commands in sequence automatically, we put the batch file in our working directory with a name such as batchml5.cex and then enter the command

```
batch batchml5
```

This command will produce five output files.

7.4   MLT Analysis

The third analysis we will perform is to compute MLT (Mean Length of Turn) for both child and mother. Note that, unlike the MLU program, the CLAN program MLT includes the symbols xxx and yyy in all counts. Thus, utterances that consist of only unintelligible vocal material still constitute turns, as do nonverbal turns indicated by the postcode [+ trn] as illustrated in the following example:

```
*CHI:   0.[+ trn]
%gpx:   CHI points to picture in book
```

We can use a single command to run our complete analysis and put all the results into a single file.

```
mlt *.cha > allmlt.cex
```

In this output file, the results for the mother in 68.cha are:

```
MLT for Speaker: *MOT:
  MLT (xxx and yyy are INCLUDED in the utterance and morpheme counts):
 Number of: utterances = 331, turns = 227, words = 1398
          Ratio of words over turns = 6.159
          Ratio of utterances over turns = 1.458
          Ratio of words over utterances = 4.224
```

There is similar output data for the child. This output allows us to consider Mean Length of Turn either in terms of words per turn or utterances per turn. We chose to use words per turn in calculating the ratio of child MLT to mother MLT, reasoning that words per turn is likely to be sensitive for a somewhat longer developmental period. MLT ratio, then, was calculated as the ratio of child MLT over mother MLT. As the child begins to assume a more equal share of the conversational load, the MLT ratio should approach 1.00. For this example, the MLT ratio would be: $2.241 \div 6.159 = 0.3638$.

7.5   TTR Analysis

The fourth CLAN analysis we will perform for each child is to compute the TTR or-type–token ratio. For this we will use the FREQ command. By default, FREQ ignores the strings xxx (unintelligible speech) and www (irrelevant speech researcher chose not to transcribe). It also ignores words beginning with the symbols 0, &, +, -, or #. Here we were interested not in whether the child uses plurals or past tenses, but how many different vocabulary items she uses. Therefore, we wanted to count "cats" and "cat" as two tokens (i.e., instances) of the word-type "ca". Similarly, we wanted to count "play" and "played" as two tokens under the word-type "play". When computation is done by hand, the researcher can exercise judgment online to decide whether a particular string of letters should be counted as a word type. Automatic computation, however, is much more literal: Any unique string will be counted as a separate word type. In order to have inflected forms counted as tokens of the uninflected stem (rather than as different word types), we morphemicized inflected forms in transcribing. That is, we transcribed "cats" as "cat-s" and "played" as "play-ed". Using our morphemicized transcripts, we then instructed FREQ to ignore anything that followed a hyphen (-) within a word. The command string used was:

```
freq +t*CHI +s"*-%%" +f *.cha
```

+t*CHI	Analyze the child speaker only
+s"*-% %"	Ignore the hyphen and subsequent characters
+f	Save output in a file
*.cha	Analyze all files ending with the extension .cha

The only new element in this command is +s"*-%%". The +s option tells FREQ to search for and count certain strings. Here we ask that, in its search, FREQ ignore any hyphen that occurs within a word, as well as whatever follows the hyphen. In this way, FREQ produces output in which inflected forms of nouns and verbs are not counted as separate word types, but rather as tokens of the uninflected form. The output generated from this analysis goes into five files. For the 68.cha input file, the output is 68.frq.cex. At the end of this file, we find this summary analysis:

```
85      Total number of different word types used
233     Total number of words (tokens)
0.365   Type/Token ratio
```

We can look at each of the five output files to get this summary TTR information for each child.

7.6   Generating Language Profiles

Once we have computed these basic measures of utterance length, lexical diversity, and conversational participation for our five target children, we need to see how each child compares to his or her peers in each of these domains. To do this, we use the means and standard deviations for each measure for the whole New England sample at 20 months, as given in the following table.

Table 6: New England 20 Means

Measure	Mean	SD	Range
MLU50	1.400	0.400	1.02-2.64
MLU5 longest	2.848	1.310	1.00-6.20
TTR	0.433	0.102	0.266-0.621
MLT Ratio	0.246	0.075	0.126-0.453

The distribution of MLU50 scores was quite skewed, with the majority of children who produced at least 50 utterances falling in the MLU range of 1.00-1.20. As noted earlier, 15 of the 48 children failed to produce even 50 utterances. At this age the majority of children in the sample are essentially still at the one-word stage, producing few utterances of more than one word or morpheme. Like MLU50, the shape of the distributions for MLUS and for MLT ratio were also somewhat skewed toward the lower end, though not as severely as was MLU50.

Z-scores, or standard scores, are computed by subtracting each child's score on a particular measure from the group mean and then dividing the result by the overall standard deviation:

`(child's score - group mean) ÷ standard deviation`

The results of this computation are given in the following table.

Table 7: Z-scores for Five Children

Child	MLU50	MLU5	TTR	MLT Ratio
14	0.10	0.12	1.84	-0.90
55	-0.70	-0.65	-0.15	-0.94
66	-0.25	-0.19	-0.68	-1.14
68	3.10	2.56	-0.67	1.60
98	-0.95	-1.11	-0.55	0.31

We would not expect to see radical departures from the group means on any of the measures. For the most part, this expectation is borne out: we do not see departures greater than 2 standard deviations from the mean on any measure for any of the five children, except for the particularly high MLU50 and MLU5 observed for Subject 068.

It is not the case, however, that all five of our target children have flat profiles. Some children show marked strengths or weaknesses relative to their peers in particular domains. For example, Subject 14, although very close to the mean in terms of utterance length (MLU5O and MLU5), shows marked strength in lexical diversity (TTR), even though she shoulders relatively little of the conversational burden (as measured by MLT ratio). The strengths of Subject 68, on the other hand, appear to be primarily in the area of syntax (at least as measured by MLU50 and MLU5); her performance on both the lexical and conversational measures (i.e., TTR and MLT ratio) is only mediocre. The subjects at the second and third quartile in terms of MLU (Subject 055 and Subject 066) do have profiles that are relatively flat: Their z-scores on each measure fall between -1 and 0. However, the child with the lowest MLU50 (Subject 098) again shows an uneven profile. Despite her limited production, she manages to bear her portion of the conversational load. You will recall that unintelligible vocalizations transcribed as xxx or yyy, as well as nonverbal turns indicated by the postcode [+ trn], are all counted in computing MLT. Therefore, it is possible that many of this child's turns consisted of unintelligible vocalizations or nonverbal gestures.

What we have seen in examining the profiles for these five children is that, even among normally developing children, different children may have strengths in different domains, relative to their age mates. For illustrative purposes here I have considered only three domains, as measured by four indices. In order to get a more detailed picture of a child's language production, we might choose to include other indices, or to further refine the measures we use. For example, we might compute TTR based on a particular number of words, or we might time-sample by examining the number of word types and word tokens the child produced in a given number of minutes of mother–child interaction. We might also consider other measures of conversational competence, such as number of child initiations and responses; fluency measures, such as number of retraces or hesitations; or pragmatic measures, such as variety of speech acts produced. Computation of some of these measures would require that codes be entered into the transcript prior to analysis; however, the CLAN analyses themselves would, for the most part, simply be variations on the techniques I have discussed in this chapter. In the exercises that follow, you will have an opportunity to use these techniques to perform analyses on these five children at both 20 months and 32 months.

7.7   Further Exercises

The files needed for the following exercises are in two directories in the /lib folder: NE20 and NE32. No data are available for Subject 14 at 32 months.

1.   Compute the length in morphemes of each target child's single longest utterance at 20 months. Compare with the MLU of the five longest utterances. Consider why a researcher might want to use MLU of the five longest rather than MLU of the single longest utterance.

2.   Use the +z option to compute TTR on each child's first 50 words at 32 months. Then do the same for each successive 50-word band up to 300. Check the output each time to be sure that 50 words were in fact found. If you specify a range of 50 words where there are fewer than 50 words available in the file, FREQ still

performs the analysis, but the output will show the actual number of tokens found. What do you observe about the stability of TTR across different samples of 50 words?

3. Use the MLU and FREQ programs to examine the mother's (*MOT) language to her child at 20 months and at 32 months.What do you observe about the length/complexity and lexical diversity of the mother's speech to her child? Do they remain generally the same across time or change as the child's language develops? If you observe change, how can it be characterized?

4. Perform the same analyses for the four target children for whom data are available at age 32 months. Use the data given earlier to compute z-scores for each target child on each measure (MLU 50 utterances, MLU of five longest utterances, TTR, MLT ratio). Then plot profiles for each of the target children at 32 months. What consistencies and inconsistencies do you see from 20 to 32 months? Which children, if any, have similar profiles at both ages? Which children's profiles change markedly from 20 to 32 months?

5. Conduct a case study of a child you know to explore whether type of activity and/or interlocutor affect mean length of turn (MLT). Videotape the child and mother engaged in two different activities (e.g., bookreading, having a snack together, playing with a favorite toy). On another occasion, videotape the child engaged in the same activities with an unfamiliar adult. If it is not possible to videotape, you may audiotape and supplement with contextual notes. Transcribe the interactions in CHAT format. You may wish to put each activity in a separate file (or see CLAN manual for how to use the program GEM). Compare the MLT ratio for each activity and adult–child pair. Describe any differences you observe.

8: References

Aguado, G. (1988). Appraisal of the morpho-syntactic competence in a 2.5 month old child. *Infancia y Aprendizaje, 43,* 73-95.

Blake, J., Quartaro, G., & Onorati, S. (1970). Evaluating quantitative measures of grammatical complexity in spontaneous speech samples. *Journal of Child Language, 20,* 139-152.

Bohannon, N., & Stanowicz, L. (1988). The issue of negative evidence: Adult responses to children's language errors. *Developmental Psychology, 24,* 684-689.

Brainerd, B. (1982). The type–token relation in the works of S. Kierkegaard. In: R. W. Bailey (ed.) Computing in the humanities (pp. 97-109). Amsterdam: North-Holland.

Brown, R. (1973). *A first language: The early stages.* Cambridge, MA: Harvard.

Demetras, M., Post, K., & Snow, C. (1986). Feedback to first-language learners. *Journal of Child Language, 13,* 275-292.

Hausser, R. (1990). Principles of computational morphology. *Computational Linguistics,* 47.

Hickey, T. (1991). Mean length of utterance and the acquisition of Irish. *Journal of Child Language, 18,* 553-569.

Hirsh-Pasek, K., Trieman, R., & Schneiderman, M. (1984). Brown and Hanlon revisited: Mother sensitivity to grammatical form. *Journal of Child Language, 11,* 81-88.

Hoff-Ginsberg, E. (1985). Some contributions of mothers' speech to their children's syntactic growth. *Journal of Child Language, 12,* 367-385.

Klee, T., Schaffer, M., May, S., Membrino, S., & Mougey, K. (1989). A comparison of the age-MLU relation in normal and specifically language-impaired preschool children. *Journal of Speech and Hearing Research, 54,* 226-233.

Lee, L. (1974). *Developmental Sentence Analysis.* Evanston, IL: Northwestern University Press.

Malakoff, M.E., Mayes, L. C., Schottenfeld, R., & Howell, S. (1999) Language production in 24-month-old inner-city children of cocaine-and-other-drug-using mothers. *Journal of Applied Developmental Psychology, 20,* 159-180..

Malvern, D. D., & Richards, B. J., (1997). A new measure of lexical diversity. In: A. Ryan and A. Wray (Eds.) Evolving models of language. Clevedon: Multilingual Matters.

Malvern, D. D., & Richards, B. J. (in press). Validation of a new measure of lexical diversity. In B. v. d. Bogaerde & C. Rooijmans (Eds.), Proceedings of the 1997 Child Language Seminar, Garderen, Netherlands. Amsterdam: University of Amsterdam.

Moerk, E. (1983). *The mother of Eve as a first language teacher.* Norwood, NJ: Ablex.

Nelson, K. E., Denninger, M. S., Bonvilian, J. D., Kaplan, B. J., & Baker, N. D. (1984). Maternal input adjustments and non-adjustments as related to children's linguistic advances and to language acquisition theories. In A. D. Pellegrini & T. D. Yawkey (Eds.), *The development of oral and written language in social contexts.* Norwood, NJ: Ablex.

Nice, M. (1925). Length of sentences as a criterion of a child's progress in speech. *Journal of Educational Psychology, 16,* 370-379.

Pan, B. (1994). Basic measures of child language. In J. Sokolov & C. Snow (Eds.), *Handbook of research in language acquisition using CHILDES* (pp. 26-49). Hillsdale NJ: Lawerence Erlbaum Associates.

Richards, B. J., & Malvern, D. D, (1997a). Quantifying lexical diversity in the study of language development. Reading: University of Reading, The New Bulmershc Papers.

Richards, B. J., & Malvern, D. D. (1997b). type–token and Type-Type measures of vocabulary diversity and lexical style: an annotated bibliography. Reading: Faculty of Education and Community Studies, The University of Reading. (Also available on the World Wide Web at: http://www.rdg.ac.uk/~ehsrichb/home1.html)

Richards, B. J., & Malvern, D. D, (1998). A new research tool: mathematical modelling in the measurement of vocabulary diversity (Award reference no. R000221995). Final Report to the Economic and Social Research Council, Swindon, UK.

Rivero, M., Gràcia, M., & Fernández-Viader, P. (1998). Including non-verbal communicative acts in the mean length of turn analysis using CHILDES. In A. Aksu Koç, E. Taylan, A. Özsoy, & A. Küntay (Eds.), *Perspectives on language acquisition* (pp. 355-367). Istanbul: Bogaziçi University Press.

Rondal, J., Ghiotto, M., Bredart, S., & Bachelet, J. (1987). Age-relation, reliability and grammatical validity of measures of utterance length. *Journal of Child Language, 14*, 433-446.

Scarborough, H. S. (1990). Index of productive syntax. *Applied Psycholinguistics, 11*, 1-22.

Scarborough, H. S., Rescorla, L., Tager-Flusberg, H., Fowler, A., & Sudhalter, V. (1991). The relation of utterance length to grammatical complexity in normal and language-disordered groups. *Applied Psycholinguistics, 12*, 23-45.

Sichel, H. S. (1986). Word frequency distributions and type–token characteristics. *Mathematical Scientist, 11*, 45-72.

Snow, C. E. (1989). Imitativeness: a trait or a skill? In G. Speidel & K. Nelson (Eds.), *The many faces of imitation.* New York: Reidel.

Sokolov, J. L., & MacWhinney, B. (1990). The CHIP framework: Automatic coding and analysis of parent-child conversational interaction. *Behavior Research Methods, Instruments, and Computers, 22*, 151-161.

Templin, M. (1957). *Certain language skills in children.* Minneapolis, MN: University of Minnesota Press.

Wells, G. (1981). *Learning through interaction: The study of language development.* Cambridge, Cambridge University Press.

9:   Index

GAYLORD S